This edition published in 1995 by Parrallel Books
Unit 13–17 Avonbridge Trading Estate
Atlantic Road
Avonmouth
Bristol BS11 9QD

Produced by Marshall Cavendish Books, London
(a division of Marshall Cavendish Partworks Ltd)

First published 1979
Reprinted 1983, 1984, 1986, 1987, 1988, 1989, 1990, 1991, 1992
Revised and updated 1995

ISBN 0 75251 299 4

Printed and bound in Italy

THE COMPLETE GUIDE TO
FISHING

FISH, TACKLE AND TECHNIQUES

||| ·PARRALLEL· |||

Contents

Game Fishing

Introduction

During the past few years the sport of fishing has become more popular than ever before. Modern technology has helped to make equipment more reliable and easier to handle as stainless steel and glass and carbon fibres have replaced wood, split cane and greenheart. The modern angler can now find the correct tool to cater for his own specialised needs. Related to this, the sport has expanded so that, whatever you may require of a hobby, fishing should be able to provide an area to suit you. If you require to escape from the pressures imposed by modern society you can relax on a grassy river bank miles away from the ringing telephone. On the other hand, if it is excitement that you seek, wreck fishing for conger or fighting a threshing shark will provide this.

A Complete Guide to Fishing: Fish, Tackle and Techniques approaches the subject in three sections dealing with coarse fishing, game fishing and sea angling. Within each area, the book describes the main species likely to be encountered, relating their life styles, characteristics and food preferences and the baits which are most likely to attract them. Bait itself is dealt with individually — each bait having a chapter of its own describing the bait and outlining its method of collection and preparation. Each item of equipment is considered with reference to its use and the other tackle which will be required for the intended style of fishing. Finally, the various techniques required for fishing a certain type of water or seeking a particular species of fish are discussed. Where relevant, more specialised issues such as fly tying for the game fishermen and small boats and cruisers for the sea angler are included.

Whatever branch of the sport draws you, whether you are a beginner needing information before you start or an experienced enthusiast, you will find something of interest in these pages.

Coarse Fishing

Roach

You will rarely hear an angler speak of the roach in terms of fishy 'battles' or 'rod-benders'. He cannot stretch his arms apart to describe this fish. The average mature roach is between 8in and 10in long, and the vast majority of fish are considerably smaller.

It is very difficult for the non-angler to appreciate what impels anglers to rise at four in the morning in search of this humble and extremely common fish. Yet any Saturday or Sunday morning will find thousands of them deserting their beds in a passion of anticipation for a 10in fish which is quite inedible.

Fish that casts a spell

Few anglers could explain such enthusiasm. It is an act of faith, almost a religion. Those who tried would probably describe the spell the roach casts in terms of variety—variety of shape, colour and size, variety of waters to fish, variety of baits and methods, and the ever-changing and endless variety of landscapes and environments to which the angler is led in his quest for excellent roach fishing. More than any other species, the roach shows that fishing is not just about catching fish.

Roach are not much to look at, but their variety does begin with colour and shape. There are two extreme forms of coloration in mature fish. Most anglers are familiar with the bronze-flanked roach found in the Kennet or Hampshire Avon, as well as with the more common silver-flanked fish found in most waters. Both varieties are nevertheless found side by side in many waters. The body shape of mature fish varies in that most roach are slim and streamlined, reminiscent of the dace, while, also found, but less common, is the full-bodied, deep-bellied fish that is often found among the angler's specimens.

General factors

It is tempting to suppose that the slimmer fish are found in swift streamy waters such as Thames, Avon or Stour, where their streamlining would be advantageous. You might also fairly expect that the fuller-bodied variety would inhabit the sluggish rivers, lakes and other stillwaters. Nothing could be further from the truth for both shapes are found not only in the same rivers or lakes, but also in the same shoals. Clearly,

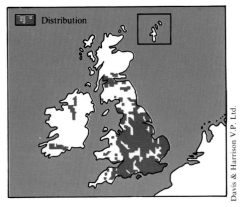

Distribution

Davis & Harrison V.P. Ltd.

Habitat

The roach, Rutilus rutilus, *is common in all English freshwaters which support weeds, insects, snails and algae that form its natural diet.*

Bait

All freshwater baits, float-fished or on ledger rig, catch the roach.
(Below) The slow-flowing rivers of East Anglia are ideal for the roach fisherman.

Rod Sutterby

England Scene

Roach

these variations of colour and shape are due to genetic and not environmental factors, the characteristics being transmitted from parents to offspring.

The roach (*Rutilus rutilus*) is found commonly in southern, central, and northern England as well as in southern Scotland and eastern Wales. It is less common in the North and West, and not found in the extreme West of England and Wales, nor north of Loch Lomond.

Where 'roach' are rudd

Roach are not indigenous to Ireland, but coinciding with the coarse angling boom in Southern Ireland over the past two decades they appeared and are now established in the Foyle river system, and in Fairey Water and other places. No doubt further introductions will occur. The rudd, which is common there, has always traditionally been called 'roach' by the Irish. Anglers fishing in Southern Ireland would therefore be wise to bear this in mind, and treat the local use of the term 'roach' with some reserve.

A roach of a pound is a good fish in any water. Over this it is excellent. Two pounders are not common, and specimens above this size are, for most anglers, the fish of a lifetime.

Anyone examining a roach for the first time would probably notice the lack of teeth, which would at least establish that the species is non-predatory. A closer examination, by dissection, reveals that like all fishes of the carp family (to which roach belong) the roach has pharyngeal teeth set at the back of the throat. These, bearing on the upper hard palate, enable the fish to grind up food before swallowing it.

Dissection also reveals that the roach has no stomach, the gullet extending from the throat, thickening, and then folding upon itself to pass directly to the vent where wastes are expelled. The digestive processes are carried out by enzymes and bacteria lining this gullet. As with most non-predators, the diet is mixed and, while over half the roach's

Peter Stone

Snails

Caddis larvae

4

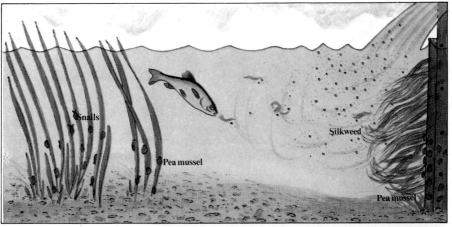

Snails

Silkweed

Pea mussel

Pea mussel

Rod Sutterby

(Above and right) Roach and other mid-water fishes are attracted to the well-aerated water in the vicinity of weirs, feeding on snails, silkweed and the pea-mussel. Punts make ideal fishing platforms at weirs. (Left and below) In slower stretches, such as the Dorset Stour in our photograph, the roach feed on snails on the waterplants, the freshwater shrimp, and bottom-living creatures such as the caddis larva.

Bill Howes

food consists of plants and such algae as silkweed, it also eats insects, crustaceans, molluscs and diatoms.

The haunts of roach are as variable as their shape and colour. However, they prefer gravel, rock or hard bottoms and will settle over hard clay or mixed sand rather than silt or soft mud. Often they have little choice as the waters in which they are found vary from the swiftest chalk streams to the most sluggish and coloured lowland streams and small ponds. To survive, shoals must locate good feeding. For this they turn to the weed beds, not only for their plant food but for insects and other creatures. Roach, there-fore, often shoal within easy reach of such

natural larders, which also offer them protection from predators.

In rivers the current forms an endless conveyor belt bringing food along to waiting shoals. Roach will sample almost any suitably sized morsel brought down by the stream. They can sample and reject in-credibly swiftly any item which arouses their suspicions, as anglers well know.

Testing Food

In this kind of habitat the shoals lie below the overhanging weed beds reaching up to the surface, often on the edge of a run between the weed. From this vantage point they regularly sally into the clear runs to take other foods.

5

(Above) Roach eggs are left attached to water-weed stems and small stones.
(Left) Male roach develop 'nuptial tubercles' in the spawning season.

Eric Birch

As the need arises, fish will cruise from one weed-bed to another. From time to time they must cross open water, cruising on to the bottom, hugging the deeps, probing the mud or gravel for molluscs and larvae. Adventurous fish on the fringes of such shoals patrol the outer cruising area, occasionally rising to a surface morsel.

In stillwaters the absence of a stream means fish will be found in or hovering over weeds, or cruising. They cover the marginal waters at depths between 5ft and 15ft, foraging into marginal reed fringes and weed. Here, the angler hopes his groundbait will allay their natural suspicions, hold them in the vicinity, and get them to take his hookbait.

Reproduction

During the closed season roach move into the gravelly shallows, seeking a compromise between the gravel they love and the silt and mud inevitable in weedy fringes and shallow margins. Between March and June—later or earlier according to the severity or mildness of the season—the concentrations of fish build up until spawning occurs. Individual fish dart in and out of the dense mass, jostling and splashing. Prior to spawning, the male fish develop temporary warty growths or 'tubercles' on the scales of the head and shoulder. These enable fish to distinguish the sex of their neighbours and

no doubt play a part in courtship preliminaries. Spawning is communal, often as if at a given signal. Then the quivering mass of fish discharges eggs and milt into the water in large clouds. The eggs are fertilized in the water, sinking slowly to adhere to reed and weed stems until hatching later in the season.

Such indiscriminate spawning gives rise to hybridism with other species. There is always considerable competition for suitable spawning places on the shallows, and it is not unusual for shoals of bream, rudd, dace or chub or even bleak, to be spawning in close proximity to the roach shoals. Fish on the edges of the shoals sometimes intermingle, and eggs from one species are then fertilized by milt from another. The result is hybrids, usually with characteristics intermediate between parents. These give rise to occasional problems of identification for the angler.

Recognizing a hybrid

Every year the current roach record is assailed by claims for fish which, upon examination, prove to be hybrids. The bream/roach hybrid is usually the culprit. Such fish should be recognised immediately by any angler of experience but, regrettably, they are not. The angler should be suspicious when he takes a good fish which seems to be slimier than usual. Its identity can be established by counting the number of

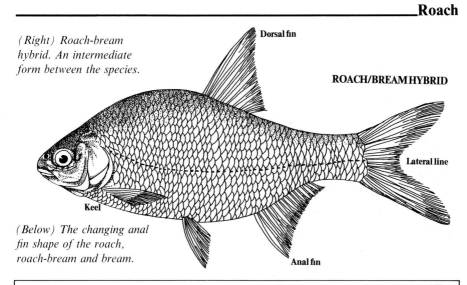

(Right) Roach-bream hybrid. An intermediate form between the species.

ROACH/BREAM HYBRID

Dorsal fin

Lateral line

Keel

(Below) The changing anal fin shape of the roach, roach-bream and bream.

Anal fin

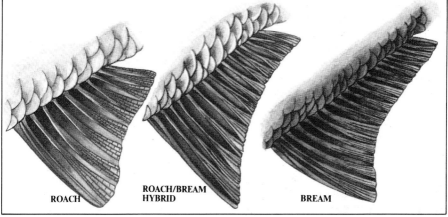

ROACH

ROACH/BREAM HYBRID

BREAM

Lyn Cawley

branched rays in the anal fin. Roach have 9-12, bream 23-29, while the hybrid is intermediate with 14-19..If the specimen has more than 12 such rays it cannot be a roach.

By mid-June, when the fishing season opens, the roach shoals have forsaken the shallows for the streamy runs, weirpools and swifter reaches, where the well-oxygenated water restores their lost condition within a week or a month according to locality and the kind of year. By July or August they have moved into deeper waters, lying in the swift current between and under weed beds. In lakes, they will be farther from the margins. Now they must make the most of high summer and plentiful food.

By October, the onset of colder weather and shorter days cause roach to settle in the depths. In shallow lakes their choice is restricted, and in very deep ones they seldom penetrate below 20ft or so as food supplies below this depth are limited. A lessening of activity coincides with the fall of leaves into the water.

In winter stillwater roach only become active during mild spells, when they temporarily resume feeding. By now the best of lake fishing is over. In rivers, there is a resumption of activity after autumn when rain arrives and the river is flushed. When flooding occurs the shoals will often follow the levels over the banks to flooded meadows

7

Roach

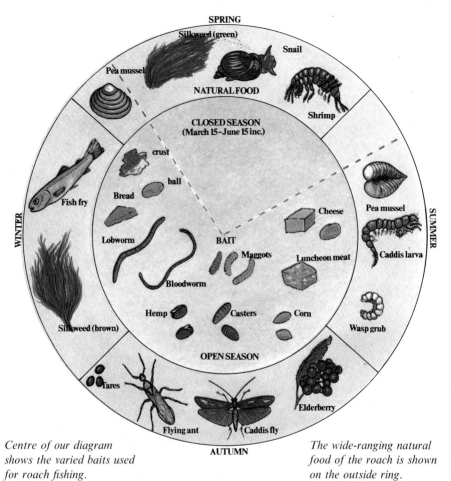

SPRING

Silkweed (green)

Snail

Pea mussel

NATURAL FOOD

CLOSED SEASON
(March 15 – June 15 inc.)

Shrimp

crust

ball

Bread

Fish fry

Cheese

Pea mussel

SUMMER

Lobworm

BAIT

Maggots

Luncheon meat

Caddis larva

Bloodworm

Hemp

Casters

Corn

Wasp grub

WINTER

Silkweed (brown)

OPEN SEASON

Tares

Elderberry

Flying ant

Caddis fly

AUTUMN

Rod Sutterby

Centre of our diagram shows the varied baits used for roach fishing.

The wide-ranging natural food of the roach is shown on the outside ring.

where food is replenished by the new pastures, and where lay-bys are favourite places to take refuge, or rest from the force of the river in spate. When levels fall again, the fish instinctively seek deeper water to avoid being left stranded. Throughout winter they cruise in the deep and feed as they can to attain a superb condition. In spring the cycle starts again.

This varying pattern of feeding and movement dictates the range of methods that the skilled roach angler must be able to command. In the early season he must often use fine tackle to tempt fish from their weedy strongholds in gin-clear water. Silkweed is a good bait then, and he must wield this light

tackle with precision and finesse to present the bait in a natural manner, and so produce a take. He needs swift reflexes to hook this flighty fish, and angling skill to keep it from the weed in order to land it.

By the end of the year, with vastly different conditions, he must use heavily-shotted tackle to cope with the river in spate. He will cast accurately and surely to the shoals, or perhaps fish lay-bys or eddies with ledgered tackle. Between the extremes he must practise a wide variety of methods at different times of year and in differing waters.

The angler must also relate his baits to his knowledge of the natural feeding habits of

8

the fish. Fortunately, the maggot is similar to many underwater larval forms, and the worm, which resembles other water creatures, is also found by roach grubbing on the bottom. Wheat, barley, hemp, tares, corn and other cereal baits are familiar to fish in their natural form at harvest time, during high winds, and in flood conditions. The enterprising angler will always find suitable baits. Caddis fly, bloodworm, freshwater snail and shrimp, mussel and woodlice are all effective alternatives to the more usual baits. Silkweed too can usually be had at the fishing place. Bread baits such as paste, flake and crust, are all proven and easily obtained. The prime consideration is that all baits must be presented in the right place at the right time.

Where roach are found

You can confidently expect good roach from any major river system within the areas where roach are found. Specimens of 3lb are recorded from Hampshire's Test and Avon, and the Dorset Stour. In the Home Counties they come from the Thames, Medway, Kennet and Essex Stour. In the Midlands and North, the Trent, Colne and Great Ouse produce big fish, while the Norfolk Bure, Waveney and Broadland lakes offer excellent prospects. Many reservoirs and gravel pits, to be found all over the country, also produce good fish.

The angler may fish in silent reed-fringed fenland dykes with a very fine line and a matchstick float to take a good bag. He may stret-peg the Thames, Kennet, Ouse or Trent, or shot-ledger in gravel pits and ponds. Long-trotting in quiet streams bordered by the Dales or rolling a ledger on the northern border rivers will take roach too. He can take his pick of silent shallow marshy meres or inland lakes; southern chalk streams or lowland canals. All provide good roach, and each favours its own local styles of fishing.

A superb catch of well-conditioned roach up to 2lb from the River Kennet at Newbury. There is one small perch among them.

P. H. Ward, Natural Science Photos

Chub

Predominantly a river fish, the chub (*Leuciscus cephalus*) is found where currents flow fast over gravel or stony beds. It is a fish of clean, unpolluted water where both oxygen and food exist in plenty. The species provides fishing of quality for the angler prepared to stalk this cautious and stealthy prey with great care and skill. The chub is shy in habit—a thick-bodied ghost that fades into the depths at sight or sound of man or beast. Yet the chub is renowned for the dogged resistance it displays to the efforts of angler and rod.

Chub in Ireland?

While the chub is found throughout most of England, it is absent from West Wales and from Scotland above the Forth-Clyde valley. Until recently the species was not thought to exist in Ireland but reports indicate the possibility that the fish has been introduced into the Blackwater river system, possibly as livebait by pike fishermen.

We think of the chub as a pure river fish but it has been successfully introduced to stillwaters, where it thrives and can grow larger than its river counterpart. Where rivers are diverted, notably by the construction of motorways, stillwaters are formed which are populated by chub, barbel and dace.

The chub is one of Britain's bigger coarse fish but even so it rarely reaches 6lb (although specimens of nearly 10lb have been taken from salmon rivers in the Scottish Borders). The present record fish weighed 7lb 6oz and fell to Bill Warren while fishing the Royalty in 1957.

The chub belongs to the carp family, though it does not resemble the carp in appearance. The mature fish is solidly built, with a blunt head, large mouth, and thick, pale lips. The back is greenish brown and the belly a yellowy white. The fins, which are well-defined and powerful, can range from colourless to a rich red. It is easy to identify by its large scales, which have a slight black edging, and can only be confused with other fish when young, when it is often mistaken

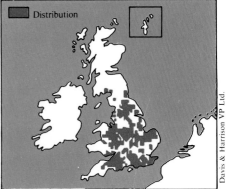

Distribution

Rod Sutterby

Davis & Harrison VP Ltd.

Baits

The chub can be caught on all the freshwater angler's baits, including plugs and spinners.

Habitat

Although a river fish, it is also found in small streams and rivers. (Below) The Avon at Ibsley is a beautiful example of a typical chub river, with weed-channels and plenty of bankside cover where trees overhang the water.

Robin Fletcher

11

for a dace. The distinction between the two should be clear, however, for the chub has large fins with rounded, convex rear edges, especially noticeable on the anal fin, and has 44-46 scales along the lateral line, while the dace's fins have concave rear edges and its lateral line averages 47-54 scales. The dace is a much slighter fish and is about 12oz when fully grown.

Spawning

Like other coarse fish, the chub spawns in the spring. Different water and weather conditions affect breeding times but this usually occurs between April and early June. The eggs are small—the female will release over 100,000 which stick to plants and river debris. After about 8-10 days hatching takes place in the shallow water of the gravelly runs favoured by the species. After cleaning itself in the fast water of the shallows, the fish will slowly head for deeper waters, where it has both security and space.

The chub is more solitary than other river species and tends to establish a definite territory. Old fish, particularly, will seek out a hole and lie up for long periods. All rivers have known chub holes, which the seasoned angler can point out to the newcomer, but it is unlikely that more than one or two chub can be caught from the swim. Younger chub do shoal and form mixed shoals with dace and roach in areas that can provide the necessary abundance of food.

Hybridization occurs as a result of this mixed shoaling and cross-breeding between the chub and the bream, roach, rudd or dace is quite common. This can lead to identification problems, especially for the claimant to a record for a species.

Trespassing chub

Chub often inhabit stretches of river set aside for trout fishing. Anglers are sometimes encouraged to fish for them during the trout close season and to remove their catch to conserve the game fishing.

Chub are famed for their wide-ranging

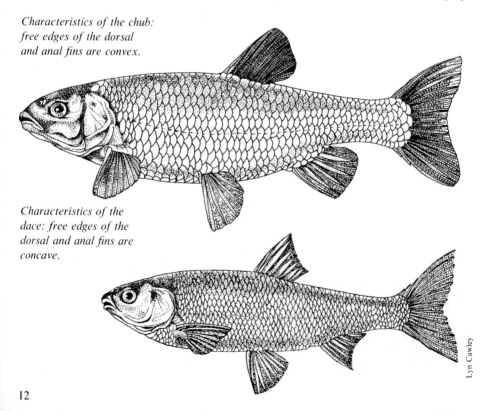

Characteristics of the chub: free edges of the dorsal and anal fins are convex.

Characteristics of the dace: free edges of the dorsal and anal fins are concave.

Lyn Cawley

P. H. Ward. Natural Science Photos

The merest flicker of an eyelid will be enough to send these wary chub back into the depths.

Peter Ward demonstrates the correct way to 'hold fish for photographing. The chub is being supported properly, with wet hands, and there is little pressure on its body or gills.

The kingdom of the chub. This tiny pool on the River Itchen at Ovington, Hampshire, has all the signs of chub territory—even though the Itchen is a chalkstream carefully maintained and preserved as an exclusive trout fishery and coarse fish are not encouraged. Learn to read the water: that dark hole beneath the gnarled willow, a tangle of vegetation on the left, the stand of reeds in mid-stream. All these must hold fish. Why? Insects, berries and food particles will drop from the tree's over-hanging branches and the bushes, and in these calcium-rich waters the reeds always harbour aquatic life of many sorts—nymphs, larvae, snails, shrimps, crayfish, so fish will feed there.

appetites and can be taken on a variety of baits. Try float-fishing with cheese, ripe-fruits, especially berries, bread, worms, silkweed, dried blood, slugs, or maggots. Natural and artificial flies can also be used, as can other insects and grubs. The smaller members of a shoal will feed on aquatic insects and bottom-dwelling invertebrates, while the older fish will add a substantial amount of vegetable matter to their diet and will chase and eat the fry of many species, including their own. Livebaiting with minnows and small fish gives good results.

Anything edible ...

The chub rises, trout-like, from deep water to take a small fish, fly or anything edible that disturbs the surface. A rapid rise in air or water temperature will encourage the fish to lie, head to current, just beneath the surface, watching for anything the current brings along above it.

Remember that fruits fall constantly into rivers and that the chub expects to feed on them. Baits such as elderberries may not be an obvious choice, but they produce results, especially after high winds or other disturbances have swept a lot of fruit or berries into the water.

Other baits available at the water's edge

Robin Fletcher

15

include crayfish, which can be gathered by scraping the undercut banks below the water level, and swan mussels, which are used as a bait for other large species as well.

The chub's carnivorous inclinations mean that it can occasionally be taken on a small blade spinner intended for trout. This often happens when the fish is in shallow water after spawning,—when its large appetite will overcome its usual caution.

The all-rounder

The chub's taste for many types of bait and the fact that it can be caught at any time of year, if the right technique is used, make it something of an all-rounder for the angler. It can be relied on to give good sport and to repay the concentration and patience with which it must be hunted. The chub can also provide a fine bonus to a day spent fishing for other species for it sometimes quite un-expectedly and impulsively takes a bait such as a lobworm float-fished along the far bank, which it may have been ignoring for hour after hour.

Such a fish will probably not shatter any records. Nevertheless we can confidently expect the capture of a fish to at least match the 10lb 8oz chub taken from the Annan by Dr J. A. Cameron in 1955. This specimen has since had its record status withdrawn but the once-awesome 10lb barrier has proved breakable.

(Above) Peter Ward playing a 4lb chub to the net from a classic fishing position on the River Kennet in Berkshire. This stretch holds many fine specimen chub, but being narrow it demands a very cautious approach by the angler. (Left) The bait that tempted the chub being played by Peter Ward in our photograph above. It is luncheon meat and one of the favoured and successful chub baits.

P. H. Ward. Natural Science Photos

P. H. Ward. Natural Science Photos

In 1653, Izaak Walton recommended the large black slug as a bait for the chub, this 'fearfullest of fishes'. The fish has not changed since then—it still falls to a fat slug impaled through its body on a No. 4 or 6 hook (right) offered to it.

Lyn Cawley

17

Common bream

The freshwater bream, *Abramis brama,* has a dark green or brown back, but in older fish it may take on a slate grey hue. The flanks of the bream are olive-bronze and their white or creamy underside is often marked with scarlet streaks. The body is heavily covered with a thick layer of slime, which sometimes gives the fish a blue appearance. The bream is deep-bellied and full-backed. The tail is unsymmetrical, the lower lobe being rounded and the upper lobe pointed. A long anal fin extends almost from the middle of the belly to the tail.

Habitat
The body-shape of the bream gives some clue to its habits. Not only is the shape suited to bottom living, but also enables the fish to swim easily through the closely-spaced stems of reeds and sedges common in sluggish and stillwaters. This increases the potential feeding grounds for the fish as well as providing ready shelter from predators.

Normally bream are bottom feeders, and as shoals may contain as many as 50 fish they

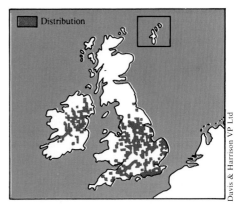

Distribution

Davis & Harrison VP Ltd

Rod Sutterby

Habitat
The Common Bream, Abramis abrama, *naturally occurs in the rivers of Eastern England, but is also found in many enclosed waters. The Silver Bream is localized.*
Bait
Bream can be taken on bread, maggots, sweet corn and worms.
(Below) Farnborough Lakes, Hants, where bream and other species may be caught.

Bill Howes

Bream

Irish Tourist Board

(Above) Some of the best fishing in the British Isles is found in Ireland. This angler is about to net a bream from Grove Lake, Tulla, County Clare.
(Right) With its wide-ranging feeding habits the bream falls to many baits.
(Below) This Fenland dyke, or drain, is typical of many waters in the Eastern Counties. They hold bream shoals.

Bob Church

SNAILS

LEECHES

20

must cruise continuously to find food. They feed extensively on algae, plankton, insect larvae, crustaceans and molluscs, also grubbing among the bottom debris for the many micro-organisms which live there.

Once feeding the shoals move slowly along the bottom, rather like a flock of sheep working its way across the meadow when grazing. The comparison is apt because the fish soon denude the bottom of food, like sheep cropping grass. Fortunately, when the bream have passed, other small bottom-living creatures will soon take up residence.

When feeding in earnest a large shoal will stir up a great deal of mud. Gases are released which carry the colour of the mud quickly to the surface, even in quite deep waters. Anglers seeking bream should be aware of this, and keep an eye open for both the bubbles and the muddy colouring. In stillwaters this is invaluable in locating feeding fish. In rivers some judgement is required to decide how far the current has washed the colour from the feeding place,

and whether or not to fish up or downstream. Fortunately bream also like to roll about, playing on or near the surface prior to feeding.

Twilight and dusk are good times to seek bream, which take advantage of the failing light to enter the shallower marginal waters in search of food. Sometimes they give themselves away by gently moving the marginal reeds, and a bait on the edge of the margins will often take fish.

Spawning occurs in May or June. After a severe winter anglers will sometimes take bream spawning as late as the end of June and even after the season has opened. The males can be recognised by the tubercles on the head and shoulder, typical of cyprinoids during spawning. The fish usually seek wide reedy bays and margins, and sometimes enter the tangles of waterside tree roots which extend below undercut banks. Once spawned they move into deeper water, remaining there throughout the summer, cruising when feeding, or lying motionless.

MINNOWS

BLEAK

LARVAE

MARSHWORMS

PEA MUSSELS

SWAN MUSSELS

Rod Sutterby

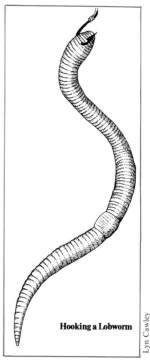

Hooking a Lobworm

Lyn Cawley

*(Above) Peter Stone's own preferred method of hooking worms for bream fishing.
(Left) Unhooking this good bream over the keepnet is a wise safety measure in case the fish jumps loose.*

Bill Howes

When frost sets in they seek out the deeper gullies and holes in the bottom, moving out at intervals to feed, and remaining quite active, especially at night when the water is warmer than the air, or by day during bright sunny spells. In stillwaters bream tend to become comatose during winter, moving only when tempted out of their sleepiness by warmer weather.

Bream growth

The freshwater bream generally attains a length of 3-4in during the first year. During the second year it will probably double its length, and weigh up to 20oz. This is the angler's typical 'tinplate bream'. In the third year the body fills out and the fish attains 9in

by the time it is 12in long it is four to five years old. A specimen of 7lb is probably 10 years old, and fish in the record class of approximately 12lb may be between 12 and 15 years old. In Britain this is probably close to the maximum life span.

The search for big bream has continued for many years. Before the war the British Record Fish lists noted many fish over 12lb, and during the war a 13lb 8oz record was set by Mr E. Costin fishing at Chiddington Castle lake. These older records were abandoned when the new British Record (rod-caught) Committee was set up. The current record is a 12lb 14oz common bream taken from the Suffolk Stour, in 1972. Ten pounders are listed from both the Thames and the Lea.

The freshwater bream is common in most parts of England except the western extremities. It is also plentiful in Ireland, where the average run of fish is larger than elsewhere. It is less common in Southern Scotland, and absent north of Loch Lomond; is found throughout Europe north of the Alps and the Pyrenees, except in the west and north of Scandinavia, and in the south and west of the Balkans. Anglers on holiday in Europe have a chance of good bream fishing.

Throughout their range, bream are as much at home in lakes as in rivers. They prefer sluggish waters and in swift large rivers tend to be found in the slower reaches. They attain the best sizes in stillwaters, but fight better when taken in such faster waters as the Thames, Trent, or Great Ouse, where they turn their broad flanks to the current when hooked. Some of the best bream waters are in the Norfolk Broads waterways, and in the Lincolnshire and Fenland drain systems. Traditionally, too, the Arun, Nene, Welland and Witham are noted for bream. Some of the best specimens in the last few decades, however, have been taken from the reservoirs of Walthamstow, Tring, Staines and Marsworth.

Confusion with rudd

Bream are not easily confused with roach, but may be mistaken for large rudd. The short anal fin of the rudd should separate them. Unfortunately, bream spawn in similar places to those sought by roach and rudd, and the species occasionally interbreed accidentally when fish on the edge of shoals intermingle. Eggs from one shoal are sometimes fertilized by milt from the other, and the resulting hybrids are fairly common. In England the common roach x bream hybrid was once believed to be a separate species, and called 'Pomeranian bream'. It even warranted its own specific title, *Abramis buggenhagii*, which is still found in older text books on fish. Now it is known to be a hybrid

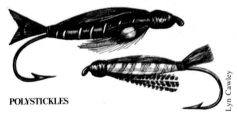

POLYSTICKLES

(Left) Polystickle, imitations of the tiny stickleback. Bream are known to eat them. (Below) While bream can be caught on all the usual roach baits—bread, maggots, worms, and so on. Their habit of taking small fish suggests bleak, which bream have been seen to attack.

Lyn Cawley

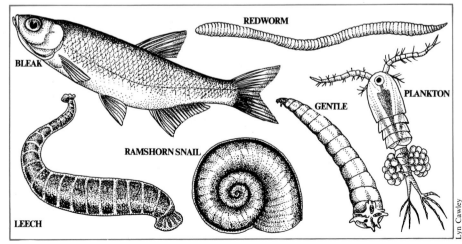

REDWORM

BLEAK

PLANKTON

GENTLE

RAMSHORN SNAIL

LEECH

Lyn Cawley

Bream

P. H. Ward/Natural Science Photos

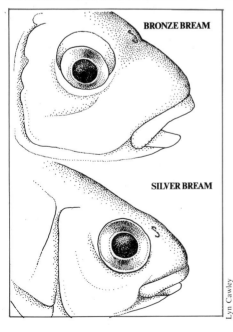

BRONZE BREAM

SILVER BREAM

Lyn Cawley

(Above) Top is the silver bream and beneath it the common.
(Left) Eye position is an identification point between the two species.

which is nevertheless popular with anglers. Sharing the characteristics of its parents it sometimes attains good weights. When it exceeds three or four pounds there is a danger of wishful thinking, and the fish is put up as a record roach, or at least as a specimen. No angler should make such a mistake because the anal fin of each fish is distinctive, bearing a specific number of branched rays. True roach have 9-12, true bream 23-29, and the hybrid 15-19. This is a very simple count to make and if the branched rays are counted at the outside edge of the fin they cannot easily be confused with the unbranched rays at the fore-edge.

The rudd x bream hybrid is not often

found in England, but is common in Ireland, where, to complicate matters further, the native true rudd has traditionally been called 'roach'. Such hybrids are fortunately easy to recognise if the anal fin ray count is carried out. True rudd have 10-13 branched rays and the hybrid has 15-18. If your specimen has more than 13 branched rays in its anal fin it cannot be a rudd. If more than 12, it cannot be a roach.

Almost all roach baits will take bream, but usually bream like a good mouthful. The bait must therefore be bigger and presented on hooks up to size No. 8 or No. 6. Good baits are bread derivatives, sweet corn, worms, swan mussels and gentles. A bunch of gentles will often work, and a large lobworm will often take the better fish. When fish are coy a maggot or a brandling may tempt them.

White bream

The white or silver bream, *Blicca bjoerkna*, is only found in a few slow-flowing rivers and stillwaters in the East of England. It is similar in shape and colour to the common freshwater bream but the pale flanks have a silvery sheen. Other distinguishing features are the two rows of pharyngeal teeth and a 'V'-shape under the abdomen where the scales lie back to back along the ridge.

White bream are similar to the common bream in habitat and diet, but tend to be more selective in their feeding and are less confirmed bottom-feeders. Bream caught in midwater are always worthy of a close scrutiny. White bream are small reaching a maximum length of 9½in and the current British Record (rod-caught) is open at 1lb 8oz, and will perhaps be surpassed by the first angler who can correctly recognize the species.

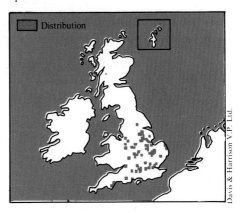

Davis & Harrison V.P. Ltd.

(Above) Distribution map of the silver bream shows it is not as wide-spread as the common species.
(Below) Smaller of the two freshwater bream the silver record is open at 1lb 8oz.

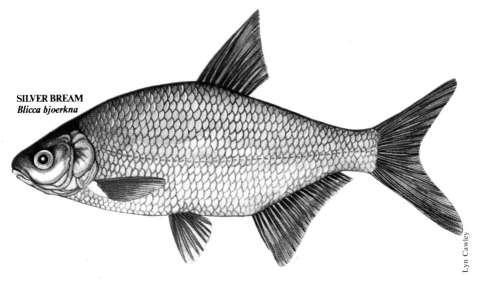

SILVER BREAM
Blicca bjoerkna

Lyn Cawley

Wild carp

In evolutionary terms a relatively young freshwater fish, unlike the pike, for instance, the carp originated in Central Asia, around the area of the watershed of the Black Sea and the Caspian Sea, during the last post-glacial period. There followed a natural spread east into China and the surrounding regions, and west, as far as the Danube.

The carp, *Cyprinus carpio,* has always been one of the most important to mankind of freshwater fish. Carp breeding is the oldest form of fish culture, and has been practised for at least 2,400 years in China and 1,900 years in Japan, while in Europe the Romans transferred wild carp from the Danube to Italy during the first to fourth centuries AD. After the collapse of the Roman Empire, and with the advent of Christianity, further western introductions took place, the carp gradually spreading throughout Europe. The earliest reference to carp in England dates from 1462, and so it appears that the species was introduced at least some little time before.

The wild carp is among the most majestic and beautiful of our freshwater fish, and for no little reason was it referred to by Izaak Walton as 'the queen of rivers'. Furthermore, its natural attributes make it almost certainly the most difficult to catch. It grows to a large size where there is an ample food supply, to become an extremely strong and tenacious fighter, and a fish with a cunning second to none.

Introduction of King carp

Unfortunately, the wild carp is slowly becoming less widespread, not only in Britain, but throughout the world. One reason suggested for this is that the introduction of the 'King' carp strain into many habitats has caused interbreeding, thus losing forever the purity of the wild carp stock. However, there is evidence to suggest that with adequate spawning facilities, the true wild carp and the selectively bred 'King' carp will not spawn together.

Probably, the most significant reasons for the drop in numbers have been, with the

26

Carp

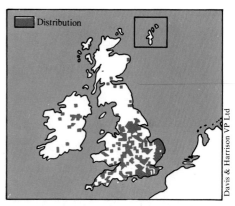

Distribution

Davis & Harrison VP Ltd

Rod Sutterby

Habitat
The wild carp, Cyprinus carpio, *introduced into Britain hundreds of years ago, is found now in slow-moving rivers, ponds and shallow lakes. Typical is Brooklands Lake, Dartford (below), a popular carp fishery.*

Baits
Although naturally a herbivore, the carp is caught on maggot and worm, as well as bread, meat, potato and cereal baits.

N. J. Fickling

enormous increase in popularity of carp fishing since the 1950s, the detrimental changes which have taken place in their particular habitats, and because the species has been overshadowed to some extent by the faster-growing 'King' carp.

The wild carp has a much more slender body, similar in some respects to that of the chub, than the cultivated species, which is often hump-backed and much deeper. In Britain the wild carp seldom exceeds 10lb in weight, although a few over 15lb have been captured, and the maximum, under favourable conditions, is probably about 25lb.

Carp coloration

Coloration is variable, depending mainly on the environment. Usually, the top of the head and body are dark brownish-blue, the sides bright golden, and the underside off-white near the head, changing to a yellowish near the tail. The dorsal fin has the same colour as the top of the body, as does the upper portion of the tail, while the lower part of the tail often has a reddish-orange tinge. The pectoral, ventral and anal fins vary between slate-grey and pale reddish-orange. Variations in colour in individual fish can take place throughout the year, and are especially noticeable during spawning.

Carp variety identification

There exist discrepancies in the literature regarding identification of the carp. A notable example is that for the number of scales along the lateral line, Wheeler (1969) quotes a figure of 35-40, while Sigler (1958) gives 32-38, Muus and Dahlstrom (1967) quote 33-40, and Dick Walker, in a letter to an angling magazine, states that all carp he had examined had 37 such scales. The present author found that in several carp there were between 37 and 39 scales in the lateral line.

Wild carp usually mature at about 2-4 years, the male often reaching maturity earlier than the female. The time taken appears to depend to a large extent upon temperature, for under artificially controlled conditions carp have reached maturity after only 4-8 months.

The wild carp is an adaptable fish, surviving and flourishing in a wide variety of habitats in Britain. Generally, however, it favours shallow lakes and ponds, rich in aquatic vegetation, and still, sluggish, or

Bill Howes

(Above) The lean lines of this carp caught by Bill Rushmer make it plain that the fish is a wildie.
(Left) Thicker in the body, a 19lb 8oz common carp taken by Peter Ward.
(Right) The sun goes down over Bill Chillingworth's Woolpack Fishery. Time for the carp to begin their nightly patrols.

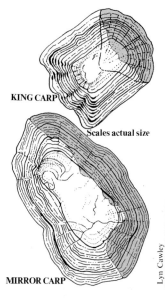

KING CARP

Scales actual size

MIRROR CARP

Lyn Cawley

P. H. Ward/Natural Science Photos

29

Carp

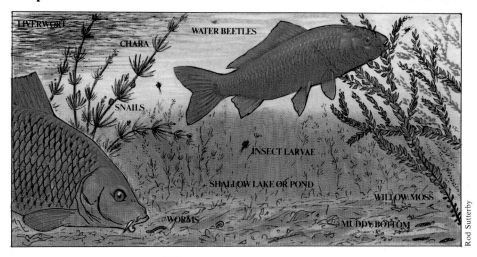

Rod Sutterby

Hooking Kit-e-Kat Paste and Sweetcorn

Lyn Cawley

(Above) The carp's habitat: shallow lakes, slow rivers, with plenty of weed and cover. (Left) Among the many carp baits are sweet corn and certain branded cat-foods. (Below) A sunny summer's day at Essex Carp Fisheries, South Ockendon. (Below right) The carp's natural food.

slow-moving rivers and canals. Since Britain is at the northernmost limit of the area in which carp reproduce, it follows that, in general, the distribution and occurrence of the species are greater in the south of these islands than in the north. The most northerly wild carp fisheries the author knows of are Bayton pond, near Aspatria in Cumbria, and Danskine Loch, in Scotland.

Spawning generally takes place between early May and late July, and is primarily dependent upon water temperature. Usually, this needs to be in excess of 17°C (62.6°F) to stimulate the wild carp into spawning. There is strong evidence to suggest that spawning is often prolonged over a period of several days, or even weeks, although whether different fish are involved, or the same fish makes repeated efforts, is not apparent.

The eggs are usually shed in shallow water, on soft aquatic vegetation. In deep ponds and lakes, with no shallows, the carp have been known to come close to the margins to spawn on overhanging vegetation, and even on fibrous roots and branches. The female is generally accompanied by two or more males, and the actual spawning is carried out very energetically so that the splashing and slapping of the fish near the surface may be audible over considerable distances.

Carp eggs

The small, translucent-grey eggs, 1mm in diameter, swell and are sticky on contact with water, and then become attached singly to whatever medium the carp are spawning over. The amount of eggs carried by the female is directly related to her size, but may also vary according to environmental fac-

tors. The proportion by weight of eggs in a female wild carp, just prior to spawning, is less than in the cultivated 'King' carp variety, amounting to approximately 10-20% of body weight, while the roe of a female 'King' carp can represent up to one third.

Development

The eggs hatch in 4-8 days, depending on the temperature, the newly hatched larvae having a yolk-sac on which to feed initially. The larvae are able to attach themselves to plants, or will lie on the bottom, before floating to the surface after two or three days to fill their swimbladders with air. They then become free-swimming, and feed on microscopic algae, rotifers and water fleas. Growth is variable and depends mainly on the amount of food available and water temperature, but other factors, such as the oxygen content, also have an effect.

Adult wild carp typically inhabit warmer environments, such as shallow areas of ponds and lakes, or slack eddies in rivers, usually where there is aquatic vegetation. On

Bill Howes

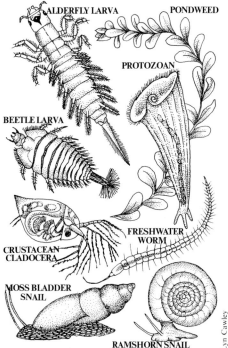

ALDERFLY LARVA   PONDWEED

PROTOZOAN

BEETLE LARVA

FRESHWATER WORM

CRUSTACEAN CLADOCERA

MOSS BLADDER SNAIL

RAMSHORN SNAIL

Lyn Cawley

LEATHER CARP
Cyprinus carpio

MIRROR CARP
Cyprinus carpio

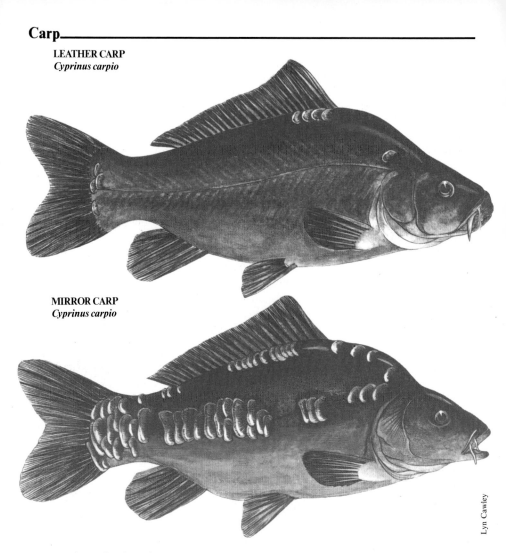

Lyn Cawley

rare occasions, they have been noted in swift, mountainous trout streams, and netted to depths of nearly 100ft.

Browsing carp

The adult fish slowly browse on food from the bottom of ponds and lakes, using their well-developed senses of sight, smell and taste. Sometimes, they feed at mid-water and on the surface, especially when the water temperature is very high. Their natural food consists mainly of crustaceans, worms, insect larvae, protozoans, small molluscs, and vegetable matter such as the various algae and the seeds of water plants.

It has been suggested that water fleas such as daphnia and cyclops also form a substantial part of the adult wild carp's diet, but the author has found that when other, larger items of food are available, water fleas are eaten only by carp of up to about 2-3lb. There are also reports of small fish found in the stomachs of carp, but it is generally assumed that these were dead at the time of the carp's swallowing them.

Wild carp grow, according to the environment, for about 12-18 years, but can live considerably longer, and certainly, under favourable conditions, can attain 40 years.

A myth perpetuated among carp anglers in the past, and indeed which was recently put to the author in no uncertain terms by the Secretary of a well-known carp angling organization, is that there is no biological difference between the wild carp and the domesticated 'King' carp. In fact there are many differences. For example, the wild carp has 18-19% more red blood corpuscles and haemoglobin than the 'King' carp. Its blood sugar and serum are 16-26% higher, and it has much less water in the liver and muscles. Furthermore, the wild carp has a higher concentration of fat in individual organs, glycogen in the liver, and Vitamin A in the eyes, liver and entrails.

Although often scorned by many of today's 'ultra-cult' carp anglers because it does not grow to the same massive size as the domesticated variety, the wild carp, because of these differences, is not only a much stronger fighter, but is also equipped to battle for longer periods. Moreover, as has been demonstrated in recent experiments by Beukema, in Holland, the wild carp, not having the 'King' carp's 'in-built' desire to feed intensively, is a more difficult fish to catch under similar conditions.

Wildie is supreme

There can be little doubt among those who have given this beautiful freshwater fish a fair chance to show its qualities, that the capture of a large 'wildie' is a supreme achievement.

(Left) Both Cyprinus carpio, *but the leather is almost scaleless, while the mirror has groups or rows of very large scales.*
(Right) Smiling John Wilson with a 16½lb leather carp he is about to return to a syndicate water in Norfolk.
(Below) A fine specimen of a young mirror carp. The large scales along the lateral line show up well on the photograph.

John Wilson

Bill Howes

Pike

Ask any freshwater angler which fish he fears most and with certainty he will say, 'The pike', Why the pike (*Esox lucius*) should be feared is debatable. The fish is by no means the only fresh-water predator—the perch and the brown trout also eat other species. Indeed, the trout kills more immature shoal fish than either the pike or the perch.

The solitary pike
Streamlined, powerful but graceful, the pike is the supreme predator in our rivers and streams because of the enormous size it can grow to. It leads a solitary life, lying in ambush to dart out and feed on smaller shoal fish—species such as roach, rudd and bream. The pike is built for speed, but only over short distances. It prefers to wait until an unwary fish comes within striking distance, then, in a burst of energy launches its body forward to grasp its prey.

As the pike gets older and slower it becomes a scavenger, seeking out ailing fish and searching the bottom of the lake or river for dead fish. In this way the pike contributes

to the balance of Nature, regulating the numbers of fish that any water is able to support. At the same time, by removing sickly or stunted fish, the feeding habits of the pike ensure the long-term health of other species.

The pike is widely distributed throughout the British Isles. It is found in both flowing and stillwaters. Lakes, especially those containing vast shoals of fodder fish, will hold the larger pike. An absence of current is a further attraction to the pike as energy, otherwise spent on battling currents, can be diverted to the kill.

Maturity and spawning
The female pike will always grow larger than the male, which rarely exceeds 10 lb in body weight. During spawning, which can occur at various times, depending on geographical location and temperature, a number of male fish will accompany each egg-laden female. Often these male fish are only a pound or so in weight. They become sexually mature after the third year of life, whereas female

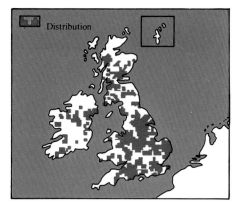

Distribution

Habitat
The natural habitat of the pike (Esox lucius)
is river, lake, reservoir or pond.
Bait
It is caught by livebaiting with most coarse
fish, including its own species; by deadbaiting
with these or with herring, sprats or mackerel;
and on all types of spinners and plugs.

Rod Sutterby.

*Silvergrove Lough in County Clare, Ireland
– an example of the pike's ideal habitat.*

Mike Prichard

Pike

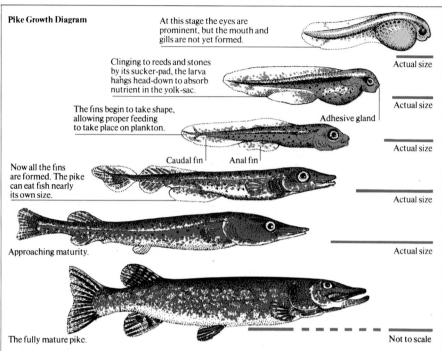

Pike Growth Diagram

At this stage the eyes are prominent, but the mouth and gills are not yet formed.

Actual size

Clinging to reeds and stones by its sucker-pad, the larva hangs head-down to absorb nutrient in the yolk-sac.

Actual size

The fins begin to take shape, allowing proper feeding to take place on plankton.

Adhesive gland

Actual size

Now all the fins are formed. The pike can eat fish nearly its own size.

Caudal fin   Anal fin

Actual size

Approaching maturity.

Actual size

The fully mature pike.

Not to scale

Lyn Cawley

fish mature slightly later—between the third and fifth year. Spawning begins in March but may extend to June in northerly areas. Pike seek out shallow parts of a lake or stream and have a liking for flooded grassland around the perimeters of stillwater and for the water meadows that border some of our rivers. The slightly sticky eggs are released haphazardly to adhere to grass stems and waterweed.

If the temperature is right—about 11°C— the eggs will hatch in 10-15 days. The tiny pike will remain attached to the plant stems for a few days until they absorb the yolk sac. An adhesive pad on the head prevents their being swept away by currents. When the sac has been absorbed and the mouth fully formed, the larvae become free-swimming, moving to the surface to feed on minute water life. If the water is warm enough, the larvae grows fast over the first few months, attaining 3-7 in in a year, but many of them will be eaten by other predatory fish. Over a period of two or three weeks a female pike of

(Above) During its life, the pike grows from half an inch to possible lengths of 4 or 5ft.
(Below) Even at a few weeks, the pike is an active predator, even on its own species. Here a hungry hunter swallows a fish of its own size.

Lyn Cawley

36

14 lb probably spawns around 100,000 eggs, of which only a few will make a year's growth, with even fewer growing to the size of the female parent.

Record pike

The present record pike weighed 40 lb when taken from Horsey Mere, Norfolk, by Peter Hancock in February 1967, but numerous specimens of over 40 lb, and one of 53 lb have been taken from Irish and Scottish water. A 43 lb pike was caught in this country in 1974 but following a spurious claim the fish was never credited to its true captor whose name did not enter the record fish lists. There is some evidence for the existence of pike of up to 70 lb in British waters. Certainly, if you wish to join the record-breakers, it is advisable to fish in the early part of the season when female fish are heavy with spawn. But conservation-minded anglers may object to this.

To locate the pike, inspect the likely lying-up places for signs of activity. A sudden wild splashing from a rudd as it leaps clear of the water is a possible indication of a pike's presence. The movement of fish on the surface may also indicate an urgent desire to escape the attentions of a predator.

Learning to 'read' the water is something all anglers should do. It involves studying the area and deciding where fish are likely to be found. And to do this an understanding of the pike's habits and needs is invaluable. Pike often lie in holes in the undercut banks of rivers and streams. Where a tree has fallen into the water it diverts the flow and sets up an eddy, which produces a drastic slowdown in the current. This creates a natural lie for a predator. On stillwaters the pike will pounce from the edge of beds of reedmace and rushes, coming out from gaps between the stalks, where it has cover.

But finding pike on large lakes and reservoirs can be more difficult. Stillwater lacks the identifying features which aid the angler's search. Underwater contours assume importance in this situation. Natural fall-offs in the slope of the lake bed, ledges and underwater obstructions are the places

MONA'S LENGTH WEIGHT PIKE SCALE			
in	lb	in	lb
20	2·500	41	21·537
21	2·894	42	23·152
22	2·327	43	24·845
23	3·802	44	26·602
24	4·300	45	28·476
25	4·882	46	30·457
26	5·492	47	32·444
27	6·150	48	34·585
28	6·860	49	36·774
29	7·621	50	39·062
30	8·437	51	41·453
31	9·309	52	43·940
32	10·240	53	46·524
33	11·230	54	49·207
34	12·282	55	51·992
35	13·398	56	54·880
36	14·580	57	57·872
37	15·829	58	60·972
38	17·147	59	64·180
39	18·537	60	67·500
40	20·000		

to find pike. But as these places are invisible to the angler he must locate them by plumbing.

Pike can be made to come to the angler in just the same way as smaller fish are lured. Groundbait, though not of the cereal type, can attract pike. Mashed fish offal with pilchard oil added and mixed into a stiff paste may be dropped into likely spots. The pike's acute senses allow it to detect food at some distance.

Pike can be caught by a variety of methods. Because of the fish's voracious appetite, it will attack both live and deadbaits. Fish, for example, can be presented either live, swimming in mid-water, or as deadbait, lying on the bottom. Practically any species can be used as a live-bait—even small pike are an attractive lure for the larger ones. The most important thing is to use a lively bait that will work well, swimming strongly in order to arouse the attention of a pike. However many anglers consider the use of one fish to catch another as being cruel. Indeed, the use of livebaits has been banned recently in Ireland, although the Irish authorities were not concerned with cruelty so much as with the transfer of shoal fish species from one water to another.

Artificial lures play an important part in pike fishing. Spinning is both a pleasurable and successful method. Almost any material can be employed in the manufacture of lures but metal is most often used. Essentially, this is because metal can be worked and bent to the required shape to provide the spinner or spoon with an attractive action when pulled through the water. Obviously metal has its own weight so there is little need to add lead

to the end tackle in order to cast it. There is much controversy about the type of action that a spinner should have to make it attractive to the pike and other fish. Trout and perch will dash after a minute blade spinner that represents a small, lively fish. On the other hand, pike, especially the big ones, are only prepared to surge after a lure over short distances.

It pays to experiment
The spoon should be larger for pike and incorporate good-quality treble hooks. Bright colours seem to attract pike. A copper spoon with one side painted red will give alternating flashes that simulate the appearance of an escaping rudd, while a silver

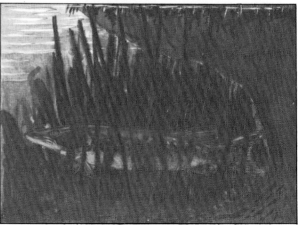

(Above) Pike tend to keep to constant depths when patrolling for food. They also hang around protruding ledges and the spot marked 'X' on our diagram would be a good place from which to fish. (Right) The mottled green and brown flanks of the pike, speckled with lighter spots, help the fish to blend into the bed of similarly coloured reeds.

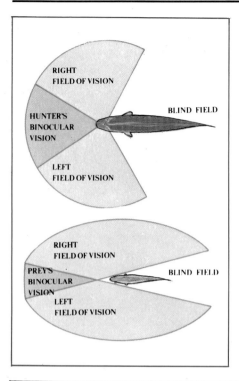

spoon with red stripes resembles a roach. The colour combinations are never-ending and should be exerimented with. Quite often a black-painted spinner is the only type that induces pike to attack. It could be that the pike see the lure as a moving silhouette, which annoys it. An attack (that cannot be called a 'feeding response') is often made on an artificial lure. Is the pike responding to an invasion of its territory when it strikes to kill or drive away?

Plugs came to us from America, where they are used successfully to catch a wide variety of species. Made of wood or plastic, they do not really resemble anything found in Nature. Anglers rely on the action built

(Left) A predator needs a good field of binocular vision to attack and grasp its food. But its prey only needs monocular vision. (Below) After attacking and grasping its prey the pike turns away and moves off for a few yards before swallowing the fish head first.

Rod Sutterby.

(Right) Distinctive pores on the gills and head of a young pike act as sensors for the predator. (Below) The pike's skull showing the complex bone structure. Age can be assessed by the circular growth markings on the gill covers. Evidence of the pike's predatory nature are the huge teeth.

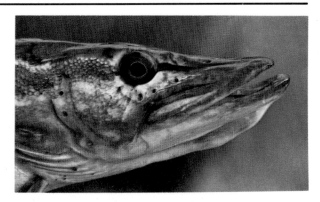

Lyn Cawley

Bill Howes

into the plug to attract fish. The shape of the plug, position of the diving-vane and treble hooks all serve to give the plug a motion that urges pike to attack. There are plugs, and the colour patterns range from the sensible to quite outrageous combinations—but they all catch fish.

One can vary pike-fishing methods by setting out to accurately simulate what pike might eat in the course of a feeding session. Lures simulating mice and voles can be made from fur and leather strips. Plastic frogs and fish are already available but their value to the pike fisherman is doubtful. This type of artificial lure rarely has the natural appearance and movement necessary to

Unhooking a pike taken on deadbait. The fish is held behind the gills to stop the head turning, while forceps are used to extract the hook. The mouth is kept open by a gag, used sparingly to avoid tearing. (Right) Using a large net to boat a pike. Note the unusual use of a fly rod.

simulate the living creature's movement.

Where the pike fisherman can score is in extending the sport of fly fishing to the species. All that is needed is to tie large flies from materials that will look like a small fish. These have been used with encouraging results on the Irish pike loughs.

With its beautiful marbling of green and brown, the pike is superbly camouflaged. The supreme hunter in our rivers and lakes, this species needs to be stalked with care by the angler, and when caught deserves to be treated with respect. Put the fish back into its environment for it is as important to preserve the species as it is to safeguard the future of our pike fishing.

Bill Howes

Here a young angler carefully returns a fine 28lb pike to the water. Note the way in which the fish is firmly supported and held close to the body so that it is not dropped and cannot turn its head to bite.

Mike Prichard

Float rods

(Left) Terry Houseago of Dereham in Norfolk lands a prime grayling from a Hampshire chalkstream using a superlight carbon-fibre 13ft float rod, in conjunction with a 2lb reel line and size 14 hook tied direct. Hence the landing net. Pound plus grayling cannot be swung in. (Right) A selection of modern, slim-profile, 3-piece, carbon-fibre float rods and a selection of free-running centrepin reels used for the enjoyment of long trotting with these lightweight rods. Note that each rod has lined rings and a slim 1in diameter handle entirely of cork or a cork/duplon mix with lightweight sliding reel fittings.

John Wilson

Float rods are also called 'bottom' or 'match' rods and are available in lengths from 11-15ft, generally in three sections of equal length. When fixed-float fishing in depths from 10-14ft or at great distances, the longest float rod available is imperative. Conversely for close-in fishing along the margins of a shallow, overgrown stream, a model of 11 or 12½ft will suffice. For all-round use a 13-footer is best.

Action

Modern float or 'match' rods are based upon two distinct actions. Most have what is called a 'waggler' action. That is to say a forgiving, yet 'snappy' to 'medium-fast' action for use in both still and running water, particularly with waggler-style floats which are fished 'bottom end' only.

Such a rod enables small registrations of

the float to be hit, but should a tench or even a modest-sized carp or barbel be hooked whilst roach fishing with just a 2-3lb reel line, it will also hoop over into an even curve, thus cushioning sudden runs or lunges and alleviate any unnecessary breaks even if used with reel lines of up to 4 and 5lb test.

The 'stick float' or tip-actioned rod applies to models of between 12 and 13ft long with a spliced, incredibly fine and sensitive tip section. Designed to hit the tiniest of bites from species like dace and roach when using reel lines of between 1½ and 2lb test and still-lighter hook lengths presenting tiny baits on tiny hooks, this rod is indeed a tool for a specific job. Namely, short-range control and super-fast striking of shy biting fish whilst trotting with a stick

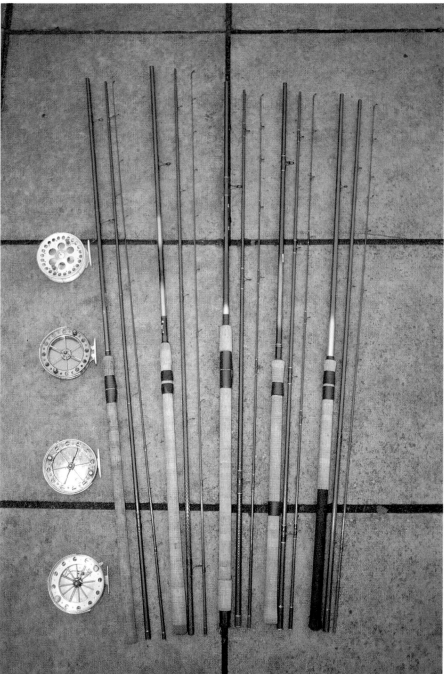

Float rods

S.L. Ward/Tackle Carrier, Watford

John Wilson

(Above) Here, Peter Ward demonstrates two types of float rod. In his right hand he holds a 13ft tip-action match rod, and in the left a 13ft soft-action float rod.
(Left) This is the correct way to attach a reel to a match rod.
(Right, top) Swing or quiver tips are attached to rod tips by being screwed into specially designed tip rings.
(Right, bottom) Roach-pole tip showing the method of attaching the alloy crook and the elastic shock-absorber.

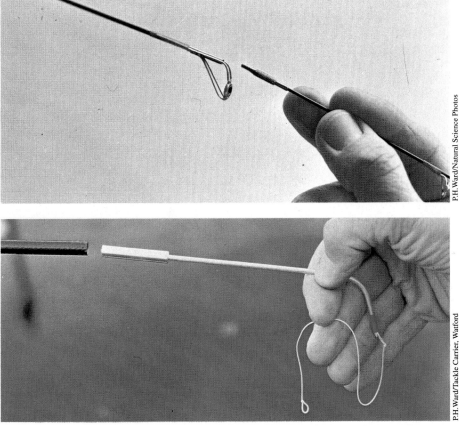

P.H. Ward/Natural Science Photos

P.H. Ward/Tackle Carrier, Watford

float attached 'top and bottom.'

Many budget-priced hollow glass rods are still manufactured for the youngster or novice market, in lengths from 10 to 12ft and these invariably come fitted with a screw-in tip ring (which accepts both swing and quiver-tip indicators) so they double up as a ledger rod. The vast majority of float rods however are now built on super lightweight, hollow carbon blanks with either spigot or overfit integral joints and have extremely sensitive tips down to just 1½mm in diameter, which are not designed for use with an indicator. Replacing the standard tip ring therefore, for one fitted with a screw thread, is simply asking for a broken top joint.

Float rods with super narrow profiles and minimal wall thickness are sometimes reinforced with a fine carbon thread weave or the more popular wrap of 'Kevlar' which increases the rod's resistance to sudden shock.

Accessories

Slimline 1in diameter cork, or cork and duplon, handles of between 22 and 25in long fitted with lightweight sliding reel fittings are most practical.

Rod rings are of paramount importance and the main cause (when grooved) of excessive and rapid line wear. The best and most expensive float rods are usually fitted with silicon carbide 'stand off' rings. Next in terms of hard-wearing ability come those with aluminium-oxide centres.

Poles

Poles are available in numerous formats from telescopic hollow glass or carbon

45

'whips' in lengths of between three and six metres, to monstrously long (and expensive) carbon-fibre, super-rigid models of over 14 metres long which may have up to a dozen or more sections. In such poles the lower sections have integral put-over joints, meaning that the bottom of each higher section fits over the top of the lower joint.

All joints or sections fit inside each other for convenient storage and transportation. In both cases the float rig, which can be considerably more sensitive than running float tackle, is fished extremely close to the pole tip, resulting in accurate presentation of the bait over loose feed and instant striking of the tiniest bites through direct line contact.

'Whips' have the line tied direct to a tiny ring at the very tip of the pole, while many

Roach-pole fishing is now coming back into fashion with a vengeance. It is a very sensitive method of taking small coarse fish and demands a particular expertise. Here, Peter Ward is attaching a section of a Shakespeare roach-pole before fishing.

long poles are used with shock-absorber elastic. A short length may be tied to the very tip and then joined to the float rig, but far more elasticity is achieved by cutting the first or second tip section back, which makes it more rigid, and fitting either an alloy 'crook', or internal elastic. The latter then slides effortlessly backwards and forwards through the now 'wider' pole end, through a specially designed PTFE collar, permitting the very largest fish to be beaten on the very lightest of terminal rigs.

Ledger rods

Ray Forsberg

Just as float rods are purposefully designed for controlling and subsequently striking sensitive movements of the float, ledger rods have been developed for accurate casting of the terminal rig, whether incorporating bomb or feeder and hitting bites resulting from the bait lying static on the bottom, be it a canal roach sucking in two maggots or a pike engulfing half a mackerel presented 80 yards out on the bottom of a deep gravel pit.

Although budget-priced ledger rods are still manufactured from hollow fibre-glass, the majority are made from super light hollow carbon-fibre (often reinforced with 'Kevlar') for a rapid-response to tiny bites. Lengths vary from 9 to 13ft, covering both close-range and distance ledgering and most

(Above) Two-rod ledgering for barbel on the Swale at Thornton Bridge.

are of two-piece construction, although three-section models are offered by some manufacturers with either spigot or overfit integral ferrules.

Quiver-tip rods

The most sensitive of all ledger rods, also referred to as 'feeder rods', have a built-in 18-24in finely tapered quiver tip (of solid fibre-glass or carbon) which registers the most delicate bites when using reel lines of between 2½-5lb test and hook lengths down to as low as 1½ lb. Economy models simply come fitted with a threaded end ring into which a quiver-tip, spring-tip or swing-tip bite indicator is then screwed. 'Multi-tip'

47

Ledger rods

rods are equipped with a choice of between two and four push-in quiver tips of varying tapers, usually stored in the rod handle. Quiver-tip or feeder rods are used by both match and specialist anglers alike for a variety of species from dace to barbel. Even stillwater tench and carp anglers use quiver tip rods on occasion, such is their popularity and versatility.

The Avon quiver-tip rod for instance, considered the most powerful of all quiver tip rods, has two top sections; one with a built-in quiver tip, the other with a threaded end ring, enabling it to be used with a 'tip' indicator or without, such as ledgering whilst using a 'bobbin' or 'monkey-climber' type indicator, sometimes in conjunction with an electronic alarm like the 'Optonic' as the front rod rest, and when float fishing for barbel, tench or specimen bream, even carp.

All these match Avon-style ledger rods usually have a slim 1in diameter cork or half-cork, half-duplon 'mixture handle' of between 20-24in, with sliding reel fittings.

An angler deep in concentration and water while ledgering for bream. He is using a swing-tip.

Specialist rods

Handle construction contrasts noticeably with ledger rods possessing greater power and these come fitted with abbreviated handles comprising a 'Fuji-style FPS' screw-reel fitting sandwiched between two short sections of preformed duplon, plus a hand grip of the same at the butt.

There is an enormous range of specialist ledger rods available from 11ft all-through action 'Avon style' models to veritable 'meat sticks' of 12 and 13ft long designed for the purpose of casting and picking up line at distances in excess of 100 yards.

Test curves

It is very much a horses for courses situation, so specialist rods are rated in test curves of between 1-3lb, which provides an excellent guide to their credentials. Simply multiply the rod's test-curve rating (usually printed on the handle just above the reel fitting) by 5 to arrive at its ideal line strengths. A 1¼ lb test-curve Avon rod, for instance, is best used with lines of around 6lb test (give or take a pound either way) while a 2¼ lb test-curve carp rod is nicely matched to lines of 11-12lb test, and so on.

You then select a rod capable of dealing with the particular type and style of

Bill Howes

ledgering involved. In addition, many specialist ledger rods are available in either an all-through action for close-range work, or medium-to-fast tip actions designed to handle big fish such as pike and carp in the middle-to-long distance range, between 50 and over 100 yards.

It may now seem rather contradictory to suggest these same ledger rods can also be used for float fishing, but the truth is many double up as excellent float rods where big fish and heavy lines are concerned. It just happens that all come under the overall classification of ledger or specialist rods.

The 9ft hollow-glass Hardy Touch Ledger, designed by Fred Taylor. A long pike rod lies next to the Touch Ledger.

Rod rings

The best-quality ledger rods are fitted with rings of either aluminium oxide or silicon-carbide. Quiver tip or feeder rods usually have stand-off rings reducing along the top joint down to tiny single leg rings which do not impair the sensitivity of the finely tapered tip.

Specialist ledger rods are equipped with rugged, low-set Fuji-type rings with either aluminium-oxide or silicon-carbide centres. Distance rods which only bend noticeably in the tip section are fitted with just five or six large diameter rings to help reduce line friction during casting. Rods which progress into a full bend when under pressure are fitted with sufficient rings to support the line along the entire curvature.

Spinning rods

Spinning rods may usually be classified by the weights they can cast and the line strengths the rod can handle, their basic function being to cast a lure and control a hooked fish.

As a general rule, the lighter the lure or spinner to be cast, the lighter and shorter the rod. In general also, the lighter the lure, the finer will be the line used with it. This is because the heavier and thicker the line the more weight is required in the lure to overcome the drag of the line, which is to be avoided when long casts are needed.

Most rods designed for use with the lighter spinning lures (up to $\frac{1}{2}$oz) are 6–8ft long and are teamed with fixed-spool reels and relatively light lines of 4–8lb b.s. Rods for heavier lures are more often 8–10$\frac{1}{2}$ft long and may be used with fixed-spool or multiplier reels loaded with lines up to 20lb b.s. These heavier spinning rods are very often used with two hands when casting and so are

naturally referred to as 'double-handed'.

In addition to the standard patterns of spinning rods, there is a special type which originated in the US and is known as a 'bait casting' rod. This rod, designed to be used in conjunction with a multiplier, features a pistol-grip, cranked handle to allow the fisherman to cast and control the reel using one hand. It is made with a one-piece top 5–6ft long, and the reel is mounted on top of the rod. This arrangement enables accurate casting but has the disadvantage that long-distance casts are not possible.

Baitcasting rods
These outfits are used extensively in America for freshwater black bass fishing, but are not popular in Britain as they are best used with plug baits which, by contrast with spinners, spoons, Devon minnows and similar lures, have not yet gained wide acceptance here. Baitcasting rods also require a fairly heavy plug or lure to cast well

(Left) Spinning and baitcasting rods from 6 to 9ft and the reels to use with them. Note the American-style pistol-grip, for one-handed casting.

(Below) Heavy-duty spinning rods are long and may need two hands for casting. Such rods, some of which are up to 10ft 6in long, are designed to cast weights up to 2$\frac{1}{4}$oz.

CASTING DOUBLE HANDED SPINNING ROD

Face target squarely both hands at eye level.

Bring rod to vertical position with accelerating force.

Line released from index finger as rod nears vertical position.

Rod Sutterby

Spinning rods

and it is still more usual in Britain to use longer rods in this situation.

For light spinning for trout, sea trout, perch and pike, a rod of 7–8ft long, capable of casting up to $\frac{3}{4}$oz, makes a good all-round tool when coupled with a small-to-medium fixed-spool reel carrying line of 4–8lb b.s. depending on the type of fishing. This pattern of rod is usually made of hollow glass-fibre, with cheaper rods in solid glass.

A cork handle about 18in long, fitted with a screw winch-fitting to hold the reel securely is the basis of all spinning rods. The size of rod rings should be graduated to aid casting

strong, with a test curve of $1\frac{1}{2}$–$2\frac{1}{4}$lb. This type of rod is very often used with a multiplier, for heavy spinning. The handles are usually 24–28in long.

Greenheart rods

The design of spinning rods has altered considerably over the past 50 years. The original rods were heavy and long, and made for salmon spinning. They were usually of greenheart (a special type of hardwood), or built cane. The centrepin reel used with these rods required them to be slow in action to assist the revolving drum to accelerate evenly and allow line to flow off without jamming.

With the introduction of the fixed-spool reel, rod action could be improved. They could be faster in action, as well as lighter. The fixed-spool reel could cast lighter baits

(Above) Heavy-duty spinning rod with a multiplier mounted on top.
(Right) Spinning rod with fixed-spool reel.

S. L. Ward/Natural Science Photos

by ensuring smooth line flow from the spool.

A rod suitable for heavier types of lures in the $\frac{1}{2}$–1oz range should be $8\frac{1}{2}$–$9\frac{1}{2}$ft long. The handle should be about 24in long, with a screw winch-fitting about 14in from the bottom of the handle when used with a fixed-spool reel, and 2–3in higher with a multiplier. This subsitution of lines of 9–15lb b.s. makes the outfit suitable for the heavier types of freshwater spinning—salmon and pike—and for lighter saltwater spinning for bass, pollack, mackerel and other species.

Heavy-duty spinning rods

The heaviest patterns of rod are required for spinning with deadbaits for salmon and large pike in very unfavourable water conditions. The deadbaits can weigh up to 2oz, and lines up to 20lb b.s. are needed.

A rod capable of handling heavy lures and leads should be $9\frac{1}{2}$–10ft long and fairly

and, because the spool of the reel did not revolve, the line did not jam or overrun, making casting much easier.

The multiplier became popular at about the same time, and was an improvement over the centrepin so far as casting was concerned. However, it is only in the last 10 years or so that the multiplier's braking systems for casting have been developed enough to allow rod-makers to match them with the lighter, faster-actioned rods now favoured. The latest material to be used in spinning rods is carbon-fibre. These rods are expensive, but perform well.

Prices for the various types of spinning rod vary considerably, depending on the quality of the materials and workmanship. A good tubular glass rod by a reputable maker costs from £20–£50, while imported rods may be bought for as little as £10.

Centrepin reels

John Wilson

The centrepin reel

A centrepin is a reel acting as a line resevoir with its axis at right angles to the rod. Good centrepins consist of a flanged drum, machined to very fine tolerances, which revolves freely on a precision-engineered steel axle. The centrepin is simple in construction, and—by virtue of this—reliable, as well as being easy to operate and to maintain. It is important as a beginner's reel because it helps to develop basic casting skills. Once the use of the centrepin is mastered many anglers prefer it to the fixed spool to be discussed in a later feature.

The centrepin is used, preferably in conjunction with an Avon-type rod, which has an all-through action, mainly for 'trotting'—allowing the river's current to

This ultra-modern 'Purist' centrepin made by Youngs of Redditch is produced from high-grade aluminium bar stock and runs on two ball races with spindle adjustment for fine tuning.

carry float-tackle smoothly down-stream, allowing the bait to cover long stretches of water at one cast. It is with this method that the free-running centrepin drum is put to best advantage. To recover line quickly, the experienced user will give the drum a series of taps with all four fingers in a practice called 'batting'.

The diameter of the reel can vary, but most are between 3½in and 41½in. The drum's diameter will be almost as large, and the larger the drum the more rapid will be the

Bill Howes

line recovery. Most centrepins have a line-guard and optional ratchet, while some also have a drag mechanism. An exposed smooth rim, which allows finger-pressure to be applied to control the line when casting or playing a fish, is a valuable feature of some varieties. Many of the older centrepin reels are now very much in demand for their fine, free action.

Centrepin's comeback

Although the centrepin is still widely used—and indeed has made a come-back in recent years—its popularity suffered greatly when the fixed-spool reel was introduced 40 years ago. This reel permits almost effortless long casting, because the drum is at right-angles to the rod. To achieve similar distances with a centre-pin is a satisfying accomplishment.

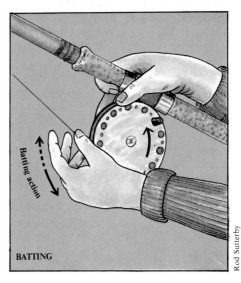

Batting action

BATTING

Rod Sutterby

54

Multiplier reels

Even taking into account the smaller diameter spool of the multiplier compared with the centrepin, because its retrieval rate is at least trebled through internal gearing (most multipliers have a 1-3½ or 4½ line retrieval ratio) considerably more line is recovered by a single turn of the handle. It is instantly thrown out of gear for casting by a spool-release lever and many models automatically engage again when the handle is turned. Larger format reels are engaged manually.

To the beginner the multiplier may appear complicated and it may seem strange that the reel is used on top of the rod as opposed to underneath. But for casting artificial lures when pike or salmon fishing, when beachcasting and especially for the rigours of boat fishing, the reel is invaluable and the

best tool for the job. This is because line is wound directly on to the spool and not around a bale-arm as with fixed-spool reels. Small models are fitted with a level-wind mechanism to ensure line is evenly and neatly distributed across the spool's width, ensuring smooth, trouble-free casts.

To reduce the possibility of overruns when long casting, or lowering the bait through deep water down to the sea bed, the spool must be controlled by gentle thumb-pressure against the line.

Many distance-casting models are equipped with tiny break blocks which are thrown out of centrifugal motion at one end of the spool, retarding its speed as the lead or lure starts to plummet downwards towards the surface. Top-quality models are fitted with a series of internal magnets for a

Multiplier reels

MULTIPLIER (Freshwater)

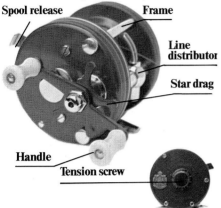

Spool release

Frame

Line distributor

Star drag

Handle

Tension screw

This precision-made freshwater reel is a multiplier, the Ambassadur 5000. It is ideal for baitcasting and spinning with weights between ¹/₂oz and 1 oz. A level-wind line distributor ensures the line is rewound evenly. This reel, with a gear-ratio of 1:3¹/₂, has a line retrieve of 15¹/₂in per single turn of the handle on a full spool.

substantially more-effective result.

Spool revolution is also controlled by a tension knob in the middle of the end plate which puts pressure to bear against the spindle, so prior to casting it should be adjusted to ensure the spool does not over-spin. Some reels have tension knobs at both ends.

The spools of most small top-quality multipliers are made from lightweight adonised aluminium or duralium so they do not act like a fly wheel and cause overruns. Many of the larger saltwater models also have spools of adonised aluminium or chrome-plated brass. To eradicate distortion whilst under pressure one-piece frames are used in large-capacity multipliers, which also have a low-gear ratio, enabling maximum torque to be used when pumping up heavy fish from great depths.

Most multipliers are right-handed and cannot be adapted for reeling in with the left-hand. Small specialist models however are available in left-hand wind and are an

absolute delight to use for single-handed casting when artificial lure fishing in freshwater.

For the purpose of playing fish via the clutch, multipliers are fitted with a unique drag system of discs and pads. The star drag is simply what its name implies – a star-shaped collar which if rotated clockwise increases drag upon the spool and if wound anti-clockwise releases drag, enabling large fish to run and to be played out to a standstill without fear of breakage.

Far easier and much quicker to use is the modern lever drag which applies drag through simple use of forward or backward thumb-pressure against a lever. It is especially beneficial when boat fishing off-shore for the largest of sea species.

When saltwater fishing it is essential after each trip to rinse the multiplier thoroughly under a freshwater tap and after leaving to dry out lubricate generously as recommended by the manufacturer. Failure to remove all traces of saltwater from the multiplier is only asking for corrosion to take place, resulting in a very short life for the reel.

Line retrieve. The centrepin (1:1) compared with the multiplier (1:3¹/₂). Amount of line on the spool is an added factor.

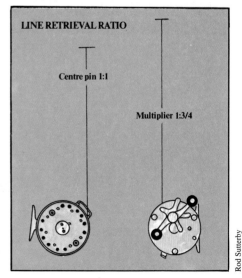

LINE RETRIEVAL RATIO

Centre pin 1:1

Multiplier 1:3/4

Fixed spool reels

The original fixed-spool reel was patented by Alfred Illingworth in 1905. It incorporated the basic principle of today's reels in that although the spool moved up and down to ensure even line lay, it stayed fixed (hence the name fixed-spool reel) whilst the line spilled effortlessly over the rim upon casting.

Nowadays fixed-spool reels, also referred to as spinning reels, are available in a wide variety of retrieve ratios from 5:1 down to 3:1 to suit every situation from the speed of match fishing and working artificial lures, to the rigours of extreme range shore casting.

Body shells are constructed from cast alloys to hi-tech, lightweight carbon and other corrosion-resistant materials with either stainless steel or graphite bearings for smooth, trouble-free operation.

Spools are skirted so the line cannot slide down and tangle around the rotor and the manufacturers of most top-quality fixed-spool reels now boast bale-arms with springs that should last a lifetime.

One touch 'finger dab' bale-arms are an important feature on match models, permitting speedy one-hand operation. The bale-arm does not have to be opened with the other hand, simply touched with the index-finger tip of the casting hand and release is immediate. A similar action exists on the 'autocast' fixed-spool reel, except

This modern stern drag fixed-spool reel has a lightweight graphite body and runs smoothly on ball bearings.

John Wilson

that the forefinger crooks around a lever next to the bale-arm roller and gathers the line simultaneously. Gentle pressure then opens the bale-arm, leaving the line already around the forefinger for instant casting.

By far the most useful step forward in recent years is the 'baitrunner' or 'bite-and-run' facility built into specialist reels designed for carp and pike fishing, which through a free-spool lever allows the spool to become completely disengaged from the winding mechanism. This permits larger species to run with the bait and take line without feeling resistance, although there is spool tension adjustment to prevent overruns.

Winding the handle immediately puts the reel back into gear and to the preset clutch drag, whereupon the strike can be made.

The slipping clutch

All modern fixed-spool reels, even budget-priced models, have the most sensitive of

(Above) When the bale-arm is closed, the line can be held back by a finger.

Bill Howes

slipping clutch mechanisms operated either via a drag knob on the top of the spool, or via a calibrated, multi-disc 'stern drag' knob which applies pressure progressively in click adjustments to hard-fighting species.

Whilst a proportion of specialist anglers prefers to ignore the drag system by flicking the anti-reverse lever off and simply backwinding to give line as a large fish runs off, learning to use the reel's slipping clutch mechanism provides greater control.

With the anti-reverse lever on, simply adjust the tension knob (whether on top of the spool or at the rear) so that under a firm prolonged pull the spool will rotate smoothly and give line. If it is set too loosely the spool will turn whilst trying to pump a fish in and cause line twist. If it is set too firmly under severe pressure from a fast-running fish the line will break. So remember never to attempt winding whilst the spool is turning and the line is being pulled over the bale-arm roller.

To recover line once the fish starts to slow down, lower the rod tip and whilst holding the spool firmly with the ball of your index finger ease the rod up to the vertical. If the fish pulls back allow line to be taken. If not, wind to recover line whilst lowering the rod and keep repeating the process, winding only as the rod is being lowered, never on the upwards movement.

'Pumping', as this technique is commonly known, is the most effective way of subduing large fish on any reel but most especially using the fixed-spool, due to the excessive friction which arises from the line passing at right angles around the bale-arm roller.

For long effortless casting it is imperative that the spool be filled with fresh monofilament to the very rim of the spool. Allow the manufacturer's plastic spool of line to turn around a pencil or 6in nail whilst winding the line on firmly. Under-filled spools drastically inhibit accurate casting, to say nothing about the lack of distance.

Spools

Many shore-casting and specialist reels used

in carp and pike fishing have long-coned spools for extra-long trouble-free casts. The spools of most front-drag reels can be changed by undoing the top drag knob whilst others are released by push-button, as are all stem-drag models.

Top-quality reels generally come with an extra spool or even two, enabling you to make an instant changeover from one strength of line to another. For those which do not, it is wise to purchase extra spools and have them preloaded with a variation in line strengths.

Match-type fine-line spools which are available for many reels simply require just 100 yards of line before they are filled to the rim. With deeper spools filling them up can

Two modern hi-tech closed-face reels, manufactured (left to right) by Ryobi and ABU. The latter has a sensitive drag knob built into the handle.

prove rather expensive. So, either purchase a quality line in bulk and wind on until the spool is filled, or use old line or thread as backing to half-fill the spool before winding on 100 yards of new line. Only when beachcasting to extreme-range, carp and pike fishing, is there a necessity for using more than 100 yards.

Long trotting

Long trotting is a method for which many anglers prefer a centre-pin reel, but this does not mean that the float cannot be properly controlled with a fixed-spool reel. The technique is to take up slack after casting and with the bale-arm left open allow the float to drift or trot down through the swim, pulling line freely from the spool. If the line runs out too quickly the extended forefinger is used to slow it down. When the float disappears the same finger clamps down hard on the spool rim as the rod is swept back quickly. Then the bale-arm is clicked

John Wilson

over to gather the line from the finger and wind it around the spool. It is imperative that slack does not occur at this moment or the fish could be lost.

One of the minor problems of the fixed-spool reel is that line occasionally springs off the spool without warning, causing unwanted slack between float and rod tip. Sometimes this is due to overloading, sometimes to wind.

Closed-face reel

The closed-face reel was designed to overcome these problems and provide easier line control. This kind of reel is closely related to the fixed-spool and actually works on the same principle in that the spool stays fixed yet as line spirals off and out through the circular vent, friction is slightly greater. Match anglers especially like the closed-face reel for its simple design. Instead of a bale-arm, a rotating aluminium cap fits over the spool. This carries a retractable stainless

(Above) This is the correct grip to be used when fishing with a closed-face reel. Pressure on the reel face releases the line; a turn of the handle engages the spool for retrieval.

steel, highly polished stud against which the line is trapped. A second cap or outer casing fits over the aluminium cap preventing line slipping off the stud, which revolves when the reel handle is turned, thus acting rather like an internal bale-arm, laying the line evenly on the reciprocating inner spool. The stud is linked to a release catch which operates when finger pressure is applied to the top of the spool-housing, allowing line to run freely out on the cast.

The casting action is similar to that of the fixed-spool except that instead of having to support the line across a crooked finger once the bale-arm is pulled open, line is free to peel out once the forefinger lifts.

Also like the fixed-spool reel the closed-face model has an adjustable clutch mechanism which operates via a knob on the winding handle instead of the spool, although some models come fitted with a sophisticated rear drag and are ambi-dextrous. There are also models available which offer 'back winding' as the only method of playing fish. And with these reels great care must be taken when using light lines.

It is interesting to note that heavy lines do not marry with closed-face reels, due to the limited capacity of their shallow spools and excess friction within the reel's inner working parts. Therefore only fine lines of between 2-5lb test are recommended, the only exception being closed-face spinning reels of American design which fit on top of the rod like a multiplier and happily handle lines to 10lb test. These models have a small-diameter vent through which the line flows from the spool, with a thumb-press casting button situated at the rear of the reel. There is a stardrag lever on the handle for slipping clutch adjustment, enabling single-handed casting and retrieving.

Unfortunately most are right-handed and not ambidextrous so that a right-handed person must switch hands after casting to wind in, which becomes rather laborious considering the amount of casts that will be made in a day working artificial lures.

Bill Howes

Nylon line

Fishing line is one of the most sophisticated and important items of tackle. For many years anglers had to use lines of such materials as braided flax or silk, with a hook link of gut made from the stretched silk-glands of the silkworm. No other material suitable for a hook line could be made in sufficient lengths for use as a continuous line, and no material which was made in lengths of over about 15 yards was fine or strong enough. The invention of nylon in the 1930s and its subsequent development mean that anglers now have a tool suited to the job.

Artificial silk

An angler writing in 1949, having tried the 'new' line for the first time, said that the monofilament he had bought had increased his casting distances amazingly. It had enabled him to catch 34 perch up to 2lb using spinners tied to $5\frac{1}{2}$lb b.s. nylon.

Nylon was first developed as an artificial silk, copying its molecular structure, but capable of manufacture in much greater quantities than could be produced by the silkworm. This was achieved by joining simple molecules into long 'chains'. The addition of other elements can be used to change the structure of the nylon, so producing different physical properties.

Monofilament line

Nylon monofilament line, the kind used by most anglers, is manufactured by first drawing the nylon into a thread while in a semi-molten state and then straightening out the molecular chains by drawing it out a second time. Its value to the angler lies in its great strength, fineness, and resistance to kinking. All these qualities are supplemented by nylon's natural elasticity.

Nylon line has the property of absorbing between 3 and 13 per cent of its own weight of water. This has the effect of reducing the breaking strain, in some cases by 10 per cent.

Figures issued by one nylon manufacturer showed that a line of 3.2lb b.s. out of water would absorb sufficient liquid to reduce its breaking strain to 2.2lb.

Another advantage is that it deteriorates, very slowly, if at all, even with frequent use. There used to be a suspicion that if not stored in the dark nylon tended to weaken quickly because of the ultra-violet rays in daylight. Certainly the lower breaking strains of line, up to about 3lb, were likely to snap very easily after a season's fishing. But it is debatable whether this was due to continued strain or to ultra-violet light. Another boon to anglers is that nylon line does not need stripping off the reel and drying after use, a chore users of silk had to reckon with.

It should be mentioned that the elasticity which aids strength also has a definite disadvantage in that a strike is softened by the line stretching, especially if it is of low breaking strain. This must be borne in mind and a strike over long distance made correspondingly more forceful if the fish is not to be missed. Braided nylon, which stretches less, is sometimes used in sea fishing to overcome this difficulty.

Camouflage

Manufacturers claim that their clear nylon lines are virtually invisible in water, but even so camouflaged varieties in blue, green or brown can be bought. Some enthusiasts even dye their lines themselves to match water conditions.

Spools of nylon monofilament come in lengths of up to 100 yards, but when they are received from the suppliers the spools are not separated. This enables the angler to buy total lengths in multiples of 100 yards.

When nylon is retrieved onto the spool under pressure, as when playing a large fish the drag created by the weight on the line can cause it to wind back on the reel tightly, this is especially the case with a multiplier reel. After fishing, the line should be wound at normal speed onto another reel, for if left on the first it can distort the spool and ruin the reel. It is also worthwhile to wind off your line occasionally and then wind it back onto the spool, making sure that it is distributed evenly. When tying hooks

Nylon line

(Right) A sight too often seen. This bird died when an unthinking angler left some unwanted nylon about. Always take it home and burn it.

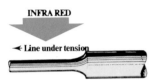

INFRA RED

◄ **Line under tension**

(Above) Nylon receives its strength when it is extruded and, under tension and heat, its molecules bond together. (Below) The transparent nylon monofilament and its strong braided form.

Monofilament

Braided nylon

Peter Burt

A. J. Deane Bruce Coleman Ltd.

directly to your nylon, be careful to remember that one of the properties of nylon is that the old-fashioned 'granny-knot' will not hold. The best knot for tying hooks to nylon is the half-blood.

Discarded line

As with nylon line's elasticity, its resistance to decay has a serious drawback. Hook lengths, 'bird's nests' and odd lengths of unwanted line are frequently thrown away or left at the waterside after fishing. These coils and loops can easily become entagled in birds' feet, especially as they will often investigate the remnants of bait that anglers also leave nearby. Birds are even hooked occasionally on discarded tackle. The consequences of careless jettisoning of line are all too often fatal for birds and so it should be taken home and disposed of, or burnt at the waterside.

It is always advisable to fill your spool with line, especially if the reel is of the fixed-spool variety, for this will mean that line flows off more easily when casting and will be more rapidly retrieved on account of the increased diameter of the loaded spool. While freshwater fish tend to make shorter runs than saltwater types, it is advisable to have a good reserve of line on the spool in case a fish should make a long run, taking a good proportion of your line. A fish can easily be lost through lack of line on which the angler can play it. Backing lines are available from tackle dealers and are used to pad out the spool, which, on a fixed-spool reel, should be filled to within $\frac{1}{8}$in of the rim.

Freshwater hooks

Hooks are the most important items of an angler's tackle and yet, all too often, they are not chosen with enough care. Admittedly the range of hooks available is bewildering to the beginner, but in order to enjoy consistent success a reliable hook is indispensable.

Categories of hooks

Freshwater hooks fall into three categories: eyed, spade-end and ready tied to nylon. The first are tied to the line by the angler, who can use a variety of knots. The important thing is to be sure the knot holds, as this can easily be the weak point in your tackle which will fail when most needed. Spade-end hooks, as the name suggests, are flattened at the top end and are whipped to nylon or gut using the method illustrated or some other reliable method. Ready tied hooks are bought already whipped to a short length of line, nowadays usually nylon.

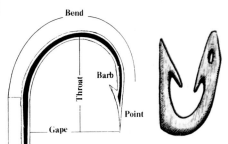

(Left) The main dimensions of a hook—length of shank and throat, width of gape, and angle of bend— determine its gauge.
(Above, right) A Stone Age bone hook with the essential features plus a second barb. Its length is nearly 3in.
(Below) The main knots, whipping and kinds of hook used in freshwater fishing.

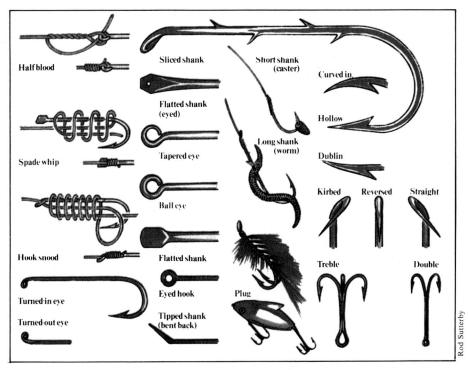

Freshwater hooks

There are many variations as to bend, length of shank and so on, but these are mainly variations on the three main kinds of hook. Double and treble hooks are mounted on lures and spinners for pike, perch, chub and trout. Stewart hooks comprise two single hooks set a couple of inches apart.

The basic requirements

The essential requirements of a hook are the same for all kinds. It should be well-tempered and thin in the body (or 'wire'); the point and barb should be sharp; the barb should be set close to the point and not stand out at too great an angle from the body.

The thickness of the 'wire' is very important. The weight of a thick hook can cause a bait, especially a light one such as maggot or caster, to sink too quickly when 'freelining'—using no float but allowing the bait to sink naturally down to the fish. An additional disadvantage of a hook that is too thick is that it can puncture a bait instead of entering it cleanly.

Before using a hook, test the temper of the wire. Under pressure it should bend but not remain bent, and it certainly should not snap. To test it, hold the hook by the shank and pull just above the point with pliers.

The barb is most often the trouble-spot in a hook. Most are cut too deep (stand out too far from the body), which causes weakness at that point. This, coupled with the common

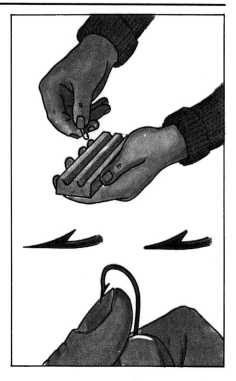

(Above) Test a hook's temper by pulling it against a thumb-nail. This also tests its sharpness. It should resemble the point seen above, left. A blunt point (above, right) can be sharpened on a carborundum stone (top), which every angler should carry. (Below) A selection of freshwater hooks.

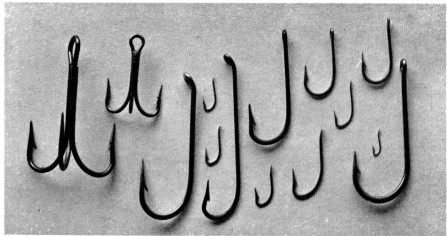

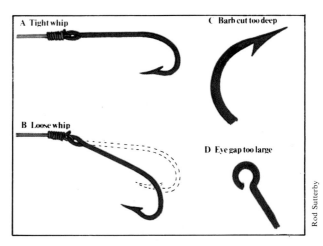

(A) A correctly whipped hook lies straight. (B) Faulty whipping causes it to dangle. (C) A deeply cut barb weakens the hook. (D) Line will slip through an overlarge eye-gap (Below) Anglers sometimes remove the barb.

Rod Sutterby

fault of the barb being set too far from the point, means that undue force is required to drive home both point and barb, sometimes causing the line to break. If the strike is less forceful, a hook of this sort will not fully penetrate the fish's skin, particularly if it is a hard-boned and tough-skinned species like the pike, perch or barbel. A big, deeply-cut barb may look effective but is not.

The eyes on eyed hooks should be examined. The size of the eye will depend on the gauge of the hook but always try to pick one which will just take the thickness of the line you intend to use—there is no point in having a gaping, obtrusive eye which causes the hook to hang at an odd angle.

The length of the shank is important where some baits are concerned. For crust, paste, lobworms and sweetcorn a long shank is best; for maggots a short one. For casters, the variety with a long shank, known as a 'caster hook', is essential. It should be remembered, however, that the longer the shank relative to the eye, the smaller will be the angle of penetration. This means that the hook will penetrate more easily but to a lesser depth. With short-shanked hooks it takes a stronger strike but the hook will drive home deeper.

Hooks to nylon should always be treated with caution. First, see whether the whipping reaches the top of the shank. On some hooks it is too short, thus causing the hook to turn over when making contact with a fish and preventing proper penetration. Make sure that there is sufficient varnish on the whipping, for there are many with too little, which fall apart after taking a few fish, especially if a disgorger has been used. Examine the loop at the end of the nylon trace. If the loop is not straight it has been tied badly and may be unreliable.

Sizes and patterns

The size of hooks is indicated by even numbers on a scale from 2 to 24; the lower the number the larger the hook. A number 2 is about ¾in long, a 12 is ⅜in and a 20 is ⅛in. Hook sizes, unfortunately, are not yet standardized. The 'Goldstrike', to illustrate this, is one size bigger than most other brands.

The angler will sometimes use a different pattern of hook to suit particular circumstances. The 'Crystal' is a combination of curved and angular, which requires little force to drive home but which, because of its sharp bend, is weakened and not recommended for strong, fighting fish such as carp or tench. The 'Round Bend' has a curve with plenty of 'gape', and is preferred for use with lobworms by many anglers.

The 'Model Perfect' is an old-established hook patented by Allcocks. The point, which is off-set, has wonderful holding power and has accounted for a great number of big carp.

Shot and shotting

Following escalating numbers of mute swan deaths during the 1960s, 70s and 80s, which were directly attributed to anglers' split-shot lying discarded on the bank and amongst the bottom silt of the marginal shallows, the use of lead split-shot finally became illegal in 1987.

Unfortunately swans ingested small hard particles such as split-shot in mistake for the gravel needed to grind their food into swallowing pulp. They ground the lead down and developed lead poisoning from which a huge percentage weakened and eventually died. The poisoning could even be passed on from a mother through her eggs down to the cygnets. Anglers all over the country became committed to putting their sport into acceptable order by switching over from lead to non-toxic split-shots and ledger weights.

Non-toxic

Nowadays all split-shots from tiny size 8 (called dust shot) upwards to ledger weights of up to 1oz are manufactured entirely from non-toxic metals. Tiny micro dust shots from size 9 upwards to sizes 12 and 13 are still made from lead and perfectly legal to use, as are lead ledger weights heavier than 1oz.

The hardened shot put into shotgun cartridges however is still made from lead. Indeed the sport of shooting is actually responsible for numbering the sizes of fishing split-shot. The only difference is that in shotgun cartridges the shots are not split. They might contain for instance various amounts of No. 4 or No. 6 shots or (and here is an irony if ever there was one) so many SSG or swan-shots. Once upon a time, like many large edible birds, swans were of course shot for the table and a cartridge containing a few large shots did the job.

Although micro shots are available in sizes 9, 10, 11, 12, 13 and even smaller, being particularly popular on the continent of Europe with pole fishermen, the standard sizes in the UK are (starting with the smallest) No. 8, 6, 4, 3, 1, BB, AB, AAA, AS, SGG (swan) 2 x SSG, 3 x SSG. All these are manufactured in non-toxic metals and whilst size-for-size they are slightly larger compared with the old lead split-shots, modern shots are wildlife-friendly and just as easy to use.

The main difference is that while lead shot was soft and actually moulded itself firmly around the line, modern shots do not. Non-toxics are quite hard but because most are now double-cut with a small expansion slit directly opposite the main deep-cut slit, they can be fixed on to the line quite firmly using thumb and forefinger pressure or with the teeth. Shot pliers are also used for the job but over-squeezing will damage the line.

Care must also be taken when repositioning non-toxic shot and the split eased open with a thumbnail before sliding it along the line. Never move non-toxic shot without loosening it first or the line could weaken and snap when least expected, if it does not fracture instantly.

For attaching waggler floats to the line with SSG 'locking shots' some anglers protect the line by threading on short sections of narrow-gauge silicon rubber tubing both immediately above and below the float.

Continental-type shots

Popularized by continental pole fisherman and now very much part of the British freshwater match-fishing scene are the oblong 'style' type non-toxic split-shots, sometimes called mouse droppings because that's exactly what they look like. Due to

(Right) Shot-pliers are better than teeth, and more healthy. (Far right) Tiny shot for matchmen, called 'mouse-droppings', need special flat-sided pliers to squeeze them onto a fine line.

their unique shape these shots do not attract false bites when using stewed hempseed on the hook which to the fish is not too dissimilar from round split-shots. Style shots are grooved and the groove is shaped so that even the finest lines are not damaged. Purposefully designed 'style' flat-sided shot pliers are used to squeeze these shots on to the line and they are now available in as many sizes as round split-shots.

Favoured by pole fishermen who wish to get the bait down quickly either through a dense shoal of small fish to bream on the bottom, or straight down to the river bed in deep, flowing water, are the tubed 'Olivetti' style shots. These simply sleeve on to the line and can be positioned anywhere as the bulk weight required for a particular float, by pinching a tiny split-shot on the line immediately above and below. Olivetties are rated in grams like all pole floats and are available in an enormous selection of sizes from the giant 10 grams, down to 0.20 of a gram. These are also made from non-toxic metals, usually alloy, brass or even from tungsten.

Shots may be purchased in plastic tubs of an individual size or in small, medium and large dispensers containing anything from just four to a dozen different sizes.

Shotting patterns

Now on to the actual shotting of float rigs, which of course varies considerably with each type of method. Fishing in deep still waters for instance (unless fishing on the drop in the upper water layers) demands a reasonable amount of shot on the line in bulk form to get the bait down quickly, so group most of the float's capacity some 2-3ft feet above the hook with just one or two tell-tale shots between.

When float ledgering, presenting a perfectly static bait, all the weight is concentrated in a swan shot link ledger or small bomb stopped by a single BB or AA shot several inches from the hook.

To fish the famous lift method, so deadly for species like tench which characteristically stand on their noses to suck the bait in, it is essential not to have any shots bulked around the float. So attach the float bottom-end only with silicon tubing (peacock waggler floats are best due to their inherent buoyancy) and pinch on to the line just a single AA or swan-shot (depending upon the float's capacity) 3-4in above the hook. Set the float slightly overdepth and wind down so that only ¼in of the tip remains visible. The float will then rise when a tench sucks up the bait and dislodges the single shot, or glide confidently under should the fish run along the bottom directly away from the rod.

To offer a bait falling gently through the lower layers close to the bottom in shallow-to-mid depth swims, lock most of the shotting capacity evenly each side of the float with a couple of small shots down the line spaced at 18in intervals above the hook.

To fish 'on the drop' requires a string of tiny shots spread evenly 'shirt-button style' in 12-18in intervals between float and hook. Baits such as casters work best, especially those darker casters which are buoyant and you must watch the float tip carefully for any strange or inconsistent movement during the time you know it will take for the string of shots to hang vertically and subsequently cock it. The secret in fishing 'on the drop' is to copy perfectly if possible the natural falling rate of loose-fed casters

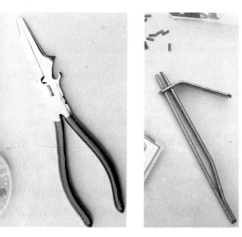

Ken Whitehead

Shot and shotting

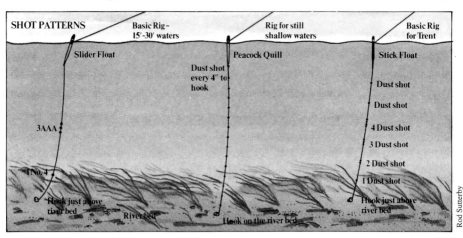

SHOT PATTERNS | Basic Rig – 15'-30' waters | Rig for still shallow waters | Basic Rig for Trent

Slider Float

Peacock Quill

Stick Float

Dust shot every 4" to hook

Dust shot

Dust shot

3AAA

4 Dust shot

3 Dust shot

2 Dust shot

No. 4

1 Dust shot

Hook just above river bed

River bed

Hook just above river bed

Hook on the river bed

(Above) Shot patterns–the way shot is grouped on the line below the float–can bring success or failure whether they are used in specimen hunting or matches. (Below) When it is correctly shotted, the float in the lift-method should sit well down in the water. As the fish bites the weight is lifted off the float, which shoots upwards and lays flat on the surface.

(the sinkers) and the way they behave. Even a medium-wire hook will make the caster sink faster than those around it, so fish as light and fine as possible in both hooks and line.

Shotting the float in running water is not quite as critical as in still water because fish generally have less time to inspect the bait. They have two choices; either to suck it in quickly before the current whisks it away downstream or loose out. This is why complicated shotting patterns are not required for long trotting in fast water for species such as chub or grayling. Using a wide-topped, easy-to-see chubber or Avon-style float, simply bulk all the shot 10-12in above the hook.

Juggling around with shots on the line between float and this bulk grouping is pointless if the fish are holding just above bottom. The bait must be taken straight down to their level and trotted along where they all have a chance of accepting it.

To present small baits such as casters or maggots in rivers of medium pace such as the Trent or the Thames, use a stick or balsa stick float for close-in runs and spread the shotting capacity evenly between float and hook to drift the bait steadily along just above bottom. For holding back so the bait wavers enticingly upwards set the float slightly over depth, with a dust shot 12-15in above the hook.

Freshwater leads

As mentioned in Shot and Shotting, since 1987 the use of lead weights of 1oz or less has been illegal. So all ledger weights of below 1oz are now manufactured from wildlife-friendly non-toxic metals such as zinc or brass, while weights of 1¼oz and above are still made from lead and come in varying shapes and sizes to suit different fishing techniques.

The sheer choice is mind-blowing as a glance at the display counters in modern tackle shops will prove. Small wonder so many anglers are confused as to exactly which shape to use.

Forty years ago the range was limited with the most popular ledger weights being the coffin, drilled bullet and barley corn or barrel as it is now better known, which have centre holes through which the line passes. To make a simple running ledger rig you pinch a single split-shot on the line to stop the weight, somewhere between 6-20in above the hook. Today these drilled weights (particularly bullets) are used mainly as bulk weight for cocking pike floats and threaded on to the line just above the trace swivel, as opposed to pinching several swan-shots on the line to accomplish the same.

During the 1950s the late Richard Walker designed the famous swivel-topped 'Arlesey Bomb' (for reaching perch lying in deep water at great distances in Arlesey Lake in Bedfordshire) and most of today's ledger weights are based upon this proven design where the line passes freely through a swivel instead of through the weight itself.

These bombs are available in ⅛, ¼, ⅓, ½, ¾, 1oz and ¼ or ½ oz divisions up to 4oz. The bomb is stopped on the line with a single shot or plastic-ledger stop, the desired distance above the hook as with drilled ledger weights. Alternatively, it may be tied to a separate link made from thicker monofilament than the reel line to minimise

This selection of freshwater weights includes both lead and lead-free, non-toxic products from the 2-4oz bombs, balls and risers used in bolt rig carp fishing to double cut split shot which replaces the old lead split shot of yesteryear.

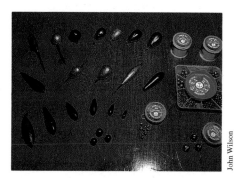

John Wilson

tangles. The link can be joined to the reel line via a four-turn water knot, or small junction swivel to create a fixed paternoster ledger rig. Or a swivel or small ring may be added to the top of the link enabling it to slide freely up the line, stopped the desired distance from the hook by a split-shot, plastic-ledger stop or swivel and cushioning bead, thus creating a sliding or running link ledger which is particularly useful when fishing over bottom weed. Any type of ledger weight can be used on the sliding or running link, not just bombs. An inexpensive, yet versatile rig is made simply by pinching sufficient swan-shots on to the link to hold bottom (if river fishing) or achieve effective casting distance.

Making link ledgers

Large non-toxic shots are perfect for making up paternoster or running link ledger rigs

Freshwater leads

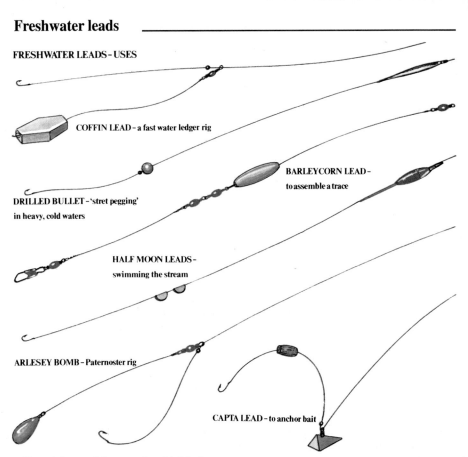

COFFIN LEAD - a fast water ledger rig

BARLEYCORN LEAD -
to assemble a trace

DRILLED BULLET - 'stret pegging'
in heavy, cold waters

HALF MOON LEADS -
swimming the stream

ARLESEY BOMB - Paternoster rig

CAPTA LEAD - to anchor bait

(Above) Some of the ways in which ledger weights are used in freshwater.
(Right) The plummet is an important item for checking the depth of water.

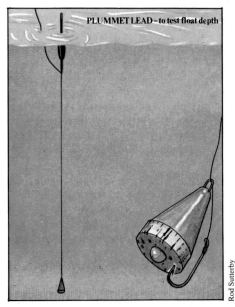

PLUMMET LEAD - to test float depth

Rod Sutterby

simply by pinching sufficient on to a 10in length of monofilament of the same breaking strain or slightly heavier (to avoid tangles) than the reel line. Conversely, if fishing in really weedy or snaggy situations where the ledger link might become caught up, use a lighter (weaker) mono link which will break and jettison the non-toxic shots before the reel line itself snaps, permitting the fish to be played out and landed.

In running water, where the ledger link is sometimes required to gently ease round in the current, making the link from large split-shots is much preferred to a single large ledger weight. Shots can be added or taken off in a jiffy, thus presenting the bait naturally in varying flows without having to undo knots or dismantle part of the rig.

By using this rig and adding or removing shots, the angler is able to adjust his tackle to fine limits, the bait either rolling along the bottom or remaining stationary to suit his purpose. There is a further advantage in that because the shots are positioned away from the reel line, less resistance is felt by a biting fish. In addition, when the line becomes snagged the shots will either pull off or the link itself will break if constructed from lighter test than the reel line, thus avoiding the loss of the hook and perhaps yards of line and even a large fish.

Following the design of the Arlesey Bomb the pyramid-shaped Capta lead appeared on the market and while this shape was outstandingly successful for anchoring the bait on the bottom of deep, fast-flowing rivers, its general use was rather limited. In recent years it has fallen from popularity, giving way to an entirely new breed of ledger weights such as bombs, balls, pears and risers, all designed specifically for the intricacies of bolt-rig fishing for carp.

To ensure the carp 'bolts off' having sucked up a boilie or particle bait either side hooked or presented on a hair rig (hence the terminology) use of a heavy lead of somewhere between 2-4oz incorporated into the rig is imperative. And there are several designs of shock, or bolt-rig leads from which to choose. Some are simply swivelled, chunky, pear-shaped leads, while others are balls with a swivel in the top, the idea being to concentrate the weight into a small mass (for greater effect upon the carp so it instantly bolts off) as opposed to an elongated shape. In-line leads are bomb or pear-shaped and revert to the line passing through the leads centre via a sleeve of protective plastic tubing. As there is no call for sensitivity (indeed the carp is encouraged to feel resistance from the lead so that it bolts off) in-line leads are extremely popular for this technique. For general use they would be considered insensitive, just as the old coffin and barrel ledgers were considered restrictive upon the

invention of the swivelled Arlesey Bomb.

Tadpole leads in either bomb or ball formats are equipped with detachable rubber connections through which the trace passes so that should the reel line snap and a carp swim away towing a heavy ledger rig, the lead will come free. 'Riser leads' which are more or less an elongated swivelled bomb with one flat side and the other fluted, are used for bolt-rig fishing in areas of dense weed or snags. Upon reeling in fast the lead quickly rises (hence its name) to the surface on the retrieve, thereby minimizing the chances of snagging up. Many of these designer 'bolt-rig' leads are painted in black or camouflage colours for use in clear water and various kits are available for disguising the shiny surface of new leads as part of the bottom, by applying a glue to which sand-like particles are added.

As shock or bolt-rig fishing necessitates the use of leads heavy enough to make the carp panic off, do not try to fish more sensitively by using a lighter ledger than 2oz.

Other weights include the 'fold over' or 'half moon' which is used for spinning, adding casting weight to light artificial lures and to act as an anti-kink agent when folded over the wire trace just below the junction swivel of the reel line end.

The famous Wye lead now of course is also available in non-toxic metal, is spiral shaped and has a wire spiral top and bottom. This allows the weight to be attached and detached without disconnecting the trace line and when slightly bent it has a useful anti-kink effect. Employed mainly by salmon anglers this particular weight is not used by coarse fishermen.

Plummets were also once made of lead but now from various wildlife-friendly metals. The basic bell-shaped plummet has a loop in the top and a wedge of cork in its flat bottom into which the hook is pricked once it is passed through the loop.

The plummet's weight carries the terminal rig down to the bottom whereby the float can subsequently be adjusted so that the bait will either rest on or just above the bottom.

Float making-quills

Peacock quills are the 'Jack of all trades' of float-making and are used in pieces. An average peacock quill can be used to make two, three or even four floats, all for a few pence. To make a very versatile float from a length of peacock quill, all you need is a length of peacock as straight as possible and around 7 or 8in in length, a piece of welding rod or thin cane— depending upon whether you want the float partially self-cocking or not—a used ballpoint refill, a razor blade, pliers, waterproof glue and emery paper.

First, clean the quill

The first job is to clean up the quill, rubbing down with emery paper or fine 'wet and dry'. You will see the quill is thicker at one end; after cleaning, carefully insert the piece of cane or welding rod into this thick end—use welding rod if you want the float loaded or partially self-cocking—so that the quill and cane are as straight as possible. Then separate the cane and quill again, add glue and then place them back into position. The piece of cane or rod should protrude from the quill about ¾in.

The next job is to cut the ball-point refill into small pieces about an inch long. Slide a suitable piece onto the cane or rod and again glue it in position, leaving a quarter inch of the tubing protruding beyond the cane at the bottom. When the glue has set, heat this bottom 'overhang' and then tightly squeeze it with either pliers or a pair of forceps to flatten it, so making a tab. When the plastic has cooled and hardened, all that remains to do is to make a hole in the centre of the tab with a fine piece of wire or a needle and then to trim the tab with the razor blade.

A simple and useful float

Finished off with a lick of paint, this simple float is very useful on stillwaters such as ponds or canals. An added refinement, favoured by some anglers to increase sensitivity, is to insert a second, finer peacock quill or cane into the quill at the top end. But

SIMPLE PEACOCK QUILL FLOAT

Cane or Welding Rod glued into bottom

Rub down quill with emery or wet–and–dry paper

unless the original peacock used is very thick, this is not usually worthwhile. The dimensions of the float as described can be varied, to give you a range of very useful floats.

The cane or welding rod at the bottom is essential in making the float as it gives at least one part which can be handled without damage. The ball-pen tubing, too, makes a very tough base, not liable to corrode as wire does. Simply pass the line through it and it can either be locked on with shot or used as a simple slider. The base can also be loaded with lead wire if required—again without damage to the peacock.

The versatility of these floats can be increased by using a set of float corks. Ream out the holes in the corks carefully—a round file is suitable for this—so that they just fit over the peacock and can be pushed down to the base of the quill. When this is done, the simple float is transformed into a waggler or a small zoomer for occasions when extra distance is required.

A little extra effort, to mark the bodies of your homemade floats with the amount of

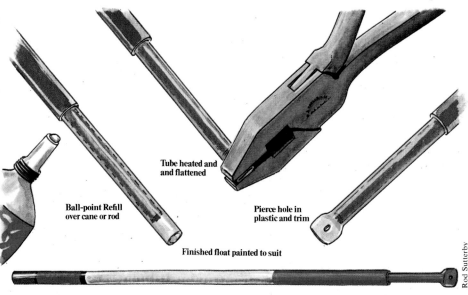

Rod Sutterby

Ball-point Refill
over cane or rod

Tube heated and
and flattened

Pierce hole in
plastic and trim

Finished float painted to suit

(Above) The basic peacock quill float can be made with a few simple tools and will help the angler cut tackle costs.

(Below) Painting home-made quill floats is easy. They can be coloured to suit the angler's preference.

shotting they will take, is well worth the trouble. It saves a lot of time on the bank. Once more the tough base is useful here in avoiding damage to the quill when pushing on the weights.

A goose-quill float

The peacock quill float just described is fine for stillwaters, such as canals, but for fishing big rivers with delicate baits such as wasp grub or bread flake, a better float can be made from a combination of goose quill and balsa wood. To make it, first cut off the top inch or so of a goose quill—this is not quite so simple as it sounds for it is surprisingly tough and care is needed to make sure it is cut straight. Then obtain a 4in length of $\frac{3}{8}$in balsa wood, and taper it from one end to the other with the thick end just rubbed gently with rough sandpaper to give it a round 'shoulder' instead of a rough edge. When it is roughly shaped, give it a smooth finish with 'wet and dry', and finally, glue the goose quill to the top of the 'shoulder'.

Before tapering the balsa, however, drill a small hole into the future base—the thin

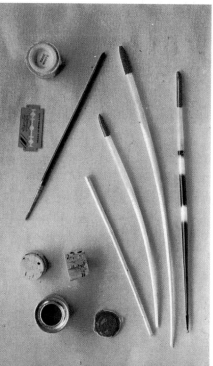

P. H. Ward/Natural Science Photos

two-thirds up the line—bearing in mind this is a float to be fished in water not much deeper than, say, 7ft—and perhaps an AAA halfway between hook and bulk shot.

Finally, a few general hints on float making. First of all finishing. Colour is entirely up to the angler's personal taste, as is the choice of a matt or a shiny paint, but to get a good finish, care is essential. Primer, undercoat and top coat must be applied and allowed to dry properly. And they must also be rubbed down well between coats. Fluorescent paints *must* be applied over the correct white-undercoat if they are to work properly, while to get a straight edge when

(Above) Float-making at home can be done using the minimum of tools and without creating a mess. A board should always be used for cutting and glueing.
(Right) The steps in making an antenna and quill/balsa float. The shotting for the quill/balsa float is illustrated.

end— insert a small piece of cane, about ½in long, and glue it in place. For strength the cane should be inserted as far into the balsa as it protrudes outside—like this it provides a strong place to which the line can be attached without damage. Balsa is so soft it can easily be drilled using any sharp pointed object carefully worked round and round; but if you want to save yourself trouble you can buy balsa which has been already drilled.

Better than balsa
Fished double rubber—that is, attached to the line at top and bottom with elastic bands— this goose quill is a superb float for such fish as chub and barbel. It gives better buoyancy at the tip than a straight balsa because, as the goose quill head is hollow, you are virtually fishing with an air bubble. One point which must be emphasized when using it, however, is that it should only be cast underhand or sidearm. Cast a float like this overarm and you are inviting tangles.

The float should take between two and three swan shot: basically a No. 4 right under the float to stop it sliding down, the bulk

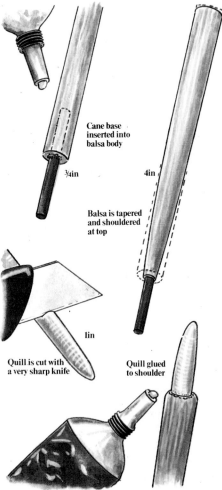

Cane base inserted into balsa body

¾in

4in

Balsa is tapered and shouldered at top

1in

Quill is cut with a very sharp knife

Quill glued to shoulder

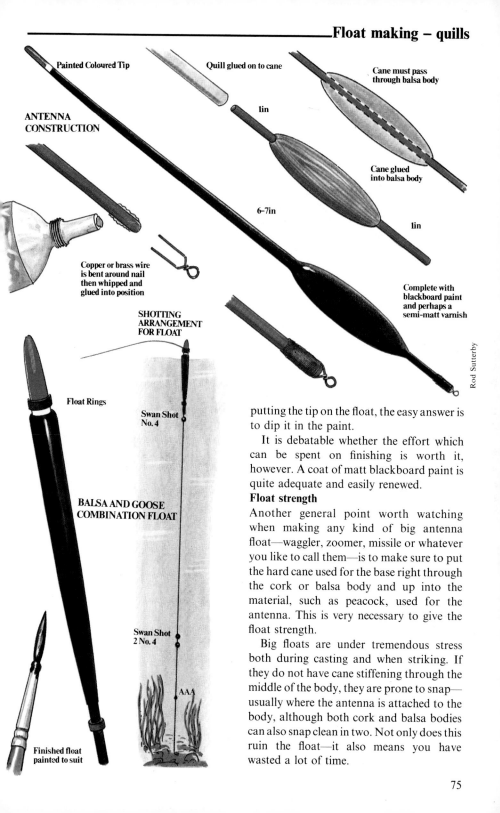

ANTENNA
CONSTRUCTION

Painted Coloured Tip

Quill glued on to cane

Cane must pass
through balsa body

1in

Cane glued
into balsa body

6–7in

1in

Copper or brass wire
is bent around nail
then whipped and
glued into position

Complete with
blackboard paint
and perhaps a
semi-matt varnish

Rod Sutterby

SHOTTING
ARRANGEMENT
FOR FLOAT

Float Rings

Swan Shot
No. 4

BALSA AND GOOSE
COMBINATION FLOAT

Swan Shot
2 No. 4

AAA

Finished float
painted to suit

putting the tip on the float, the easy answer is
to dip it in the paint.

It is debatable whether the effort which
can be spent on finishing is worth it,
however. A coat of matt blackboard paint is
quite adequate and easily renewed.

Float strength

Another general point worth watching
when making any kind of big antenna
float—waggler, zoomer, missile or whatever
you like to call them—is to make sure to put
the hard cane used for the base right through
the cork or balsa body and up into the
material, such as peacock, used for the
antenna. This is very necessary to give the
float strength.

Big floats are under tremendous stress
both during casting and when striking. If
they do not have cane stiffening through the
middle of the body, they are prone to snap—
usually where the antenna is attached to the
body, although both cork and balsa bodies
can also snap clean in two. Not only does this
ruin the float—it also means you have
wasted a lot of time.

75

Slider floats

Peacock Quill

Cane

Balsa Body

The Ian Heaps slider float, developed by Ian Heaps and his father, who say it is an improvement on old designs.

Balsa Body

10lb Line
Whipped onto
Cane

Lead Wire

No. 12 Swivel

Rod Sutterby

Slider floats are enjoyable and effective in use, but curiously neglected. It is difficult to understand why anglers will sit all day watching a motionless swingtip without trying a slider which, by giving a greater variety of presentation and often a little movement, provides a better chance of fish, particularly bream.

Length of float

Many sliders have no loading and, although they are effective, the floats developed by my father and myself are better. With these, it is important that the cane goes into the peacock quill, producing a strong joint. The length of the float is not particularly important, although it must be long enough to keep line below the surface drift. The peacock quill should be anything from 6in to a maximum of 10in long.

The amount of lead wire required is just enough to sink the balsa barrel, leaving the full length of the peacock quill standing above the surface.

The swivel is important, for it allows the float to turn in the air without the line tangling. A size 12 swivel is ideal in that it is small enough to stop at the knot tied for that purpose. If you cannot get so small a swivel, however, a larger one with a small bead positioned between the stop-knot and float may help.

As to tackling-up, it must be stressed that this float is intended to slide up and down the line and to stop at a certain depth. The required depth is obtained by using a stop-knot to halt the float. A simple way to tie a

stop-knot is to take a few inches of 4–6lb line, form a coil with two tails alongside the reel line and pass either tail through the loop, and around the reel line and the other tail four times before pulling both ends tight. Not too tight, however, because although the knot has to stay in place, it is important that it can be moved without having to break the reel line. If the stop-knot does move when you are casting and reeling in, do not tighten it more, but tie on another stop-knot an inch above it. This will act in the same way as a locking nut.

Another important point to remember is to trim the tails to a length of ¾in after tying the knot. There are two reasons for this. If the tails are too short they will be bristly rather than flexible and will not pass through the rod-rings easily enough. Second, when fishing extreme depths, the knot, or knots, will be lying on the reel and short tails will impede line flowing off the spool. The longer ones will lie flat as line is wound over them.

Shots

Each kind of shot used with this tackle has a specific function. The job of the stop-shot is to keep the float off the bulk shot and so minimize tangles on the cast—but do not confuse it with the stop-knot. This stop-shot should be as small as possible, say a No. 6, to

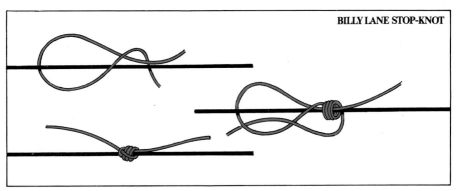

BILLY LANE STOP-KNOT

keep bending of the line or 'waggling' to a minimum during casting.

The bulk-shot is used to get the bait down to the fish and also to pull down most of the peacock quill. The weight needed will be found by trial and error.

The tell-tale shot's function is to show bites, and remember, you get a lot of 'lift' bites with this method. This tell-tale must be heavy enough to alter the setting of the float noticeably. In deep water I seldom use smaller than a No. 4 and often a BB shot.

Lift bites

Incidentally, why so many 'lift' bites— when the fish actually lifts the tell-tale shot and so causes the float to rise in the water—when using this method? It seems to result from the way a bream feeds. A bream's body is distinctly oval in shape and so has to tilt forward to pick up a bait from the bottom and when it comes back to an even keel it inevitably lifts the shot.

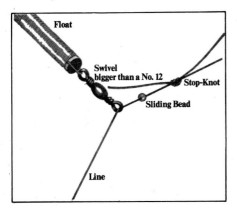

The tell-tale shot also helps get the depth without using a plummet. Keep moving the knot to a deeper setting until the shot does not act on the float; the tell-tale must then be on the bottom. Once this is done, measure the position of the stop-knot by holding the hook at the rod-butt and seeing where the knot lies—fishing 20ft deep with a 13ft rod, for instance, will put the knot around halfway. Make a careful note of this because if tackling up again no time need be lost in resetting the right depth.

Shotting is very important and experiments over the years seem to show that the following distances are correct for use in water over some 14ft deep: from hook to tell-tale shot 17in; from tell-tale shot to bulk shot 43in; from bulk shot to stop-shot 66in. The last two distances can be scaled down proportionally in shallower water.

Great accuracy and distance

The loaded slider float really scores when casting, giving greater accuracy and distance. This is because the weight of the float has it pushing against the stop-shot and consequently helping it out while the weight in the nose gives the float a 'flight' as in a dart. An unloaded slider float is far more likely to waggle in the wind and, in the case of a facing wind, actually 'climb back' towards the angler. Both of these situations take the force out of a cast and so limit casting distance.

For large swivels a sliding bead can be used between it and the stop-knot.

Slider floats

Many anglers cast a slider underhand, but it might be better to put the float well up in the air with a smooth action, avoiding snatching. Then, when it is starting to drop from the highest point of its flight, draw back the rod and 'feather' the line off the reel with the forefinger. This holds back the rig and straightens it so that it enters the water with the minimum of fuss and also reduces tangles. This last point is important, because the risk of tangling puts many anglers off the slider, which need not be.

When the float hits the water, get the rod tip well under the surface to sink the line, after winding three or four times to take up the slack, then start the 'countdown' as the bait sinks. It is possible to establish a standard time between tightening the line and the tell-tale shot pulling the float to the fishing position. If subsequent counts go more than five seconds past the standard time, strike for there is every chance that a fish has the bait in its mouth, holding up the tell-tale—known as a bite 'on the drop'.

Remember if you tighten up the line to the float that the bait will drop much more slowly than if allowed to run freely off the reel. Make sure you fish to the same pattern each cast, although when fish are taking 'on the drop', slowing down the bait gives the bait more time in the catching zone.

Following these points provides a good basis to practise slider float techniques. These can provide interest—and fish—when other methods fail.

(Previous page) The Billy Lane stop knot. It holds firmly but can be slid up or down. (Below) Details of the lift-bite method using the specially designed Ian Heaps slider float.

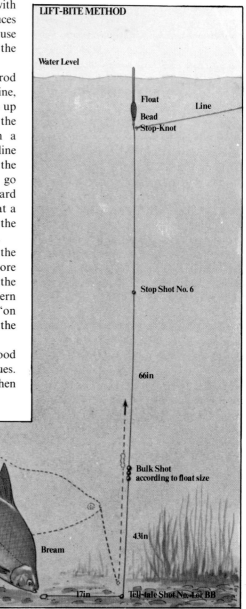

LIFT-BITE METHOD

Water Level

Float

Line

Bead

Stop-Knot

Stop Shot No. 6

66in

Bulk Shot according to float size

43in

Bream

River Bed

17in

Tell-tale Shot No. 4 or BB

Rod Sutterby

78

Keepnets

Most modern coarse-species anglers use keepnets whether for specimen hunting, pleasure angling, or competition fishing. The match-man obviously needs to weigh in his catch at the end of the match to establish who wins the prize. The keepnet enables him to do so without killing the fish. Pleasure anglers once used to return fish as soon as they were unhooked. Nowadays we often carry a camera and record the catch in photographs. The keepnet enables us to do this with no damage to the fish. Specimen hunters often keep a very detailed log of their catches, recording weight, girth and length and other details. They too find the keepnet a valuable accessory.

The important thing about these differing groups of anglers is that they all return their catch alive as soon as possible. All are strongly conservation minded, not only carrying out the law with regard to immature fish, but returning also the big ones which, a couple of decades ago, would probably have finished up in glass cases.

Introduction of the keepnet

The match fisherman was responsible for the introduction of the keepnet. Before its arrival, every fish caught during a contest was thrown on the bank to be collected and weighed when fishing ceased. The drain on the fish population, even in the best-stocked waters, eventually led to the use of a net to keep fish alive for the duration of the match. Although those early nets were small and manufactured from heavy twine, they were of vital importance.

Today's nets are available in a vast choice of sizes. Naturally, the bigger the net, the less risk of damage to fish through overcrowding. Although most anglers favour a round net, there is a distinct advantage in using a rectangular one when shallow waters are fished. These models will allow a greater area to remain submerged, providing more water space for their inhabitants.

Many Water Authorities now specify the minimum size of keepnets to be used in their waters. Where the Water Authorities fail to do so, most of the larger and forward-thinking clubs themselves specify minimum keepnet sizes to be used by their members. Some clubs go even further and specify how many fish of each species may be kept in the net. A dozen roach in a net 6ft long with 18in hoops would seem to be in no danger, but a dozen bream, or even carp or pike, would suffer. Bream are especially vulnerable to overcrowding as their narrow body cross-section causes those at the bottom of the net to be forced on their sides and crushed if they are overcrowded. They are also the most sought-after quarry of the competition fisherman.

Vulnerable species

Barbel and carp are also vulnerable to keepnets because both species bear large serrated-edged spines on the dorsal and anal fins, and these often tend to tangle in the mesh during movement, suffering considerable damage if the fish struggle to free themselves.

The organized match-angling world is also very concerned with this problem. To prevent overcrowding in well-organized

Ray Forsberg

A small perch about to be put—not dropped—into a square-shaped keepnet.

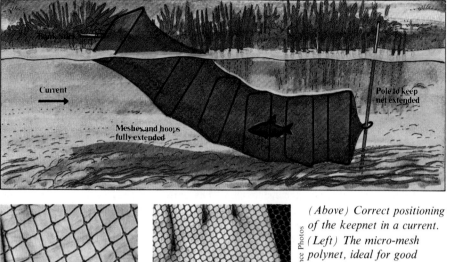

Rod Sutterby

Current

Meshes and hoops
fully extended

Pole to keep
net extended

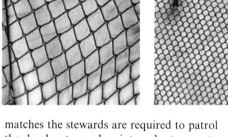

(*Above*) *Correct positioning of the keepnet in a current.*
(*Left*) *The micro-mesh polynet, ideal for good keepnet construction.*
(*Far left*) *This knotted nylon keepnet mesh is known as the 'fish mincer' due to the way it can rip away the scales of fish.*

P H Ward Natural Science Photos

matches the stewards are required to patrol the bank at regular intervals to empty competitors' nets and weigh and record the contents. When you consider that a match champion may take several hundred pounds of fish in the course of the match, it requires little imagination to appreciate the suffering to fish which could arise in a single match.

Keepnets vary a great deal according to their specific function. The match angler's net is likely to be about 8 or 10ft long, with hoops of at least 15 or 18in. His specimen-hunting counterpart will probably use a far larger net which may be up to 12ft long with hoops up to 3ft in diameter.

Spacing rings

Spacing rings, to provide support and strengthen the net, are manufactured either from galvanised wire or plastic. Wire rings are joined by brass ferrules that have an annoying habit of pulling apart. They can be glued with Araldite or soldered, but will always be suspect. Plastic rings rarely break and being soft reduce the chance of

damage to fish. But being pliable they tend to become oval-shaped and thus crowd fish together. They are also lighter than wire, which may cause smaller nets to roll in a strong current, but stone in the base of the net will hold it down.

But however big the net, it cannot do its job if it is badly placed in the water. If the net is not properly extended, 10ft of netting is of little value, and hoops of 2ft diameter are useless in 18in of water. They are usually attached by a screw fitting to a bank stick conveniently placed to allow the angler easy access to the open end. They can also be prevented from collapsing with the aid of mesh-spreaders which attach to the rings and hold them apart.

The ring at the neck, into which the bankstick is mounted, is important. Many models have a very small ring, which makes it more difficult to slide a fish into the bag of the net. Choose the net with the biggest ring possible, and plastic-coated, so that if a fish is dropped against it there will be less risk of injury. Some rings have a dent or curve so that a rod can be rested across the net while the angler unhooks a fish—an advantage, if the net is firmly fixed to the bank.

Nylon netting is available in several mesh sizes, from 'minnow' upwards, and if machined in a tubular run will be free of knots. This means that the only stitching should be at the base and neck ring—both weak areas that must be examined even in a new net. A recent introduction and improvement on the nylon mesh is micromesh, a soft nylon material with extremely small holes that is reported to cause little or no damage to fish. A few clubs and authorities are already insisting on its use in an effort to reduce the incidence of disease. Micromesh is expensive, but weighs little and dries quickly.

Need for maintenance

Regular maintenance is needed if a keepnet is to remain efficient. Although mesh may be advertised as 'rot-proof' it is still liable to strain, especially if a large weight of fish is lifted awkwardly. Check the base of the net at the join for signs of fraying, and replace it at once if need be.

Fish slime, allowed to accumulate with repeated use, can work its way into the mesh, stiffening the net to such an extent that it will have the effect of glass paper on fish scales. Washing the keepnet in clean cold water and thoroughly drying it after each outing will prevent this and leave the net more wholesome to handle.

Remember that fish naturally face the current, and so the net should lie parallel to the bank, the mouth facing upstream. Provided the net is long enough, there should be no difficulty in arranging this. The mouth of the net should lie close to the angler at a height convenient for handling.

Most damage to keepnets occurs when they are lifted with their contents at the end of the day. Grabbing the neck ring and pulling will eventually split open the bottom. The correct method is to retrieve the net hand over hand by the spacing rings, and then lift it, holding the bottom and the gathered rings in separate hands. Better quality nets have a small ring attached at the base with which to hold and lift.

Once onto the bank, avoid tipping the net on its side and shaking the fish free. This will dash them against the mesh, removing scales and ripping fins. Instead, collapse the net so that hands can be inserted, and lift out fish individually. After weighing or photographing, they should be returned to the water immediately, not re-netted—a practice that can cause further abrasions if the fish are tipped back using the net as a shute.

Peter Ward uses a long landing-net handle to extend a keepnet to its full length.

Bite indicators

Bite indicators are in effect the ledger fisherman's 'float' providing him with a visual or audible (or both) indication of the bait being taken. When freelining or ledgering by day or by night the angler will require an indicator light enough to allow a fish to run unchecked with the bait, but heavy enough to withstand disturbance from wind, current (if river fishing) and debris hitting the line, all of which so often registers false bites.

Simple indicators

As can be seen from the diagram of sensitive yet easy-to-make indicators, something must be attached, slipped on to or over the line to register bites. Watching the line itself for hour upon hour is totally impractical. Though rarely used nowadays the simple dough bobbin moulded around the reel line between the reel and first ring or between first and second rings and allowed to hang down instantly registers a bite as the line is pulled forward by a biting fish. If the fish swims towards the rod thus creating slack and a 'drop-back bite' the dough bobbin will fall backwards towards the ground.

Various cork bottle top clip-on bobbins can be made with the aid of map pins (glued in) and hair grips as the diagram shows. And even an old plastic line spool around which the reel line has been wound once, has its uses when still-water pike fishing as an indicator lying motionless on the ground, but which suddenly turns turtle as the line is pulled forwards. It will not of course register drop-back bites and so the occasional run where the pike swims directly towards the rod having sucked up a static deadbait could well result in a deeply hooked fish.

A coil or cylinder of aluminium cooking foil makes a handy indicator for freelining or close-range ledgering in still water. To protect it from wind, either hang in a small plastic flower pot or slide on to a twig, float or knitting needle pushed into the ground

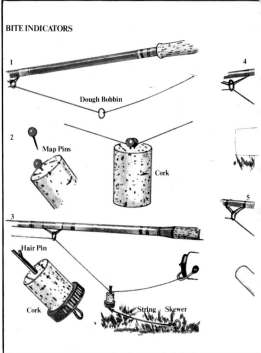

BITE INDICATORS

Dough Bobbin

Map Pins

Cork

Hair Pin

Cork

String   Skewer

and facing towards the first ring.

Before any of these indicators can be used the two rod rests should be firmly set and the immediate area cleared of leaves and other vegetation. After the cast is made and the line sunk, pointing directly at the bait, the rod should be laid upon the rests and the line wound gently tight so the ledger weight can almost be felt.

A loop of line can then be pulled gently from the reel by flicking the anti-reverse lever off (don't forget to flick it on again) and the indicator fixed on. For a front rod rest top always use the keyhole type which permits the line to be pulled or to drop back without resistance and not trapped by the rod resting upon it. The back rest can be a simple V or U type.

Bobbin-type indicators

Commercially manufactured ledger bobbins

(Below) Sensitive bite indicators, from 1 to 5, can easily be made.

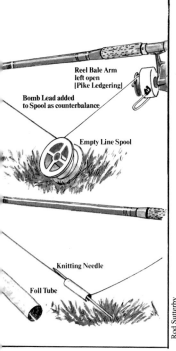

Reel Bale Arm left open [Pike Ledgering]

Bomb Lead added to Spool as counterbalance

Empty Line Spool

Knitting Needle

Foil Tube

Rod Sutterby

Ken Whitehead

A tube of silver foil is a sensitive bite indicator. Placed in a small plastic flowerpot, wind will not affect it.

The same silver foil, but here with a knitting needle pushed into the ground to prevent wind action giving false signs.

with sprung wire clips for line retention and a bottom loop through which a retaining cord can be connected to the front rod rest, are the next step up from simple indicators. Some are brightly coloured while others have clear plastic bodies to accept a betalight, luminous element for night fishing. An element rated at around 300 microlamberts is quite sufficient and should provide good service for several years. The luminosity of betalights does in fact reduce yearly by roughly 10 per cent.

Specialist, heavyweight 'drop-back bobbins' in a variety of colours are used by carp anglers fishing the deadly 'bolt-rig method' where all the line instantly falls back 'slack' should a carp tow the heavy ledger weight towards the rod. Some have additional clip-on weighted collars so that the bobbin's weight may be adjusted to suit

extreme wind and water conditions.

For a bobbin 'retention cord' use heavy-gauge dacron or a length of old fly line, both of which hang limply and because they are without stretch do not twang and wrap around the front rod rest on a fast strike like even heavy-gauge monofilament.

If going up-market in ledger bobbins to models protected completely by wind but as sensitive as clip-on bobbins connected to a retaining cord, the answer has to be the 'monkey climber'. These are in effect bobbins on a needle. The best have super-smooth bodies with a clip at the top which hangs over the line, and run up or down effortlessly on PTFE covered 24-36in stainless-steel needles, creating the very minimal resistance to a biting fish. When a fish pulls the bobbin (or monkey) to the top of the needle the line flies completely clear on the hardest of strikes while the bobbin slides back down the needle. So ridiculously simple yet so effective, which is why the majority of carp and tench fishermen use these particular indicators usually in conjunction with an electronic bite alarm unit as the front rod rest.

Electronic bite alarms

The most basic electronic bite alarm works on the 'contact breaker' principle, whereby the line hangs around an antenna which moves sideways and completes the circuit when the line is pulled forwards, resulting in a buzzing sound (hence the nickname of 'buzzers' for bite alarms) and warning light from an LED (light emitting diode).

In recent years these bite indicator alarms (they perform both functions) have moved forward in leaps and bounds. The most popular models work either through a photo-electric cell or a magnetic reed switch. Quite simply after casting the rod is laid upon the rests where the line falls down into a slot and lays across a super sensitive roller of the alarm unit screwed into the front rod rest.

Once the bobbin or monkey climber indicator has been attached the alarm is switched on and should the line move either backwards or forwards more than ½in a high-pitched bleep (various tones are available with top of the range models) is emitted plus a light from an LED for every ¾in of line moving across the roller.

In audible terms alone it is instantly possible to determine whether a fish has picked up the bait, in which direction it is moving (drop-back bites are registered with equal accuracy) and whether the fish is moving away slowly or at speed. Some units have both volume control and tone control and even an extra LED (usually green

(Below) Bite indicators which depend upon visual signals transfer the horizontal movement of the line to a vertical one supplemented by eye-catching objects. The Harlow model does this with a red indicator on a clipped-on wire.

(Right) Modern bite indicator/alarms such as the 'Optonic' shown here, operate via a photo-electric cell which produces a high-pitched bleep tone for every ¾in of line that passes forwards or backwards over the sensitive roller.

P.H. Ward/Natural Science Photos

John Wilson

N.J.Fickling

coloured) that stays on for several seconds to indicate on which rod (for those fishing with two or three rods) the bite happened. Short 'twitch' bites occur when carp are moving somewhere between the bait and rods, brushing across the line and causing the bite alarm to bleep momentarily. The angler then has the option of repositioning his bait to cover those fish or not. At least he is aware of fish movement within his casting range and so raises his level of attack accordingly.

Anglers who use their electronic bite indicators simply as alarm clocks often miss out when waking up suddenly in the early hours in pitch darkness from a deep sleep to the piercing squeal of an electronic bleep tone alarm sounding off at full volume. But it is a common sound at carp fisheries all over the British Isles.

Drop arm indicators

In electronic wizardry the pike fisherman is well catered for by the 'back biter' range of electronic drop-arm indicators. These extremely visual predator indicators are also available in basic form and consist of a 10in needle-like arm with a terry clip at one end (which clamps around the rear rod rest) and a 1½in diameter fluorescent orange poly ball and bobbin-type line clip at the other. After setting the rod in two rests with the bait placed in the desired spot the line is tightened and the bale-arm opened. A loop of line is then pulled backwards and clipped into the drop arm's retaining clip.

Should a predator move off with the bait and pull the line from the clip, the arm instantly drops down. And should the fish move towards the rod it will also drop down. The electronic versions of the above with audible warning are available in both single and double units.

(Left) A triple battery of rods set with visual bite indicators. This is a neat and efficient-looking set-up, with the angler seated well back from the water's edge. But what happens if all indicators twitch at once?

Forceps and disgorgers

A selection of three different-sized plastic or alloy barrel-type disgorgers and two pairs of long-nosed locking artery forceps, one 5-7in in length and a longer second pair of 10-12in, are all that the freshwater angler requires in the way of tools for unhooking his catch and returning it safely to the water in order for it to fight another day.

Barrel disgorgers are the easiest type to use and far kinder to the fish than other designs. They are available in ultra-fine barrel heads to accommodate miniscule spade-end match hooks up to size 26 and in medium-to-large formats which cover eyed hooks as large as size 10 or 8. Beyond this, long-nosed locking forceps are of course the answer.

Simply sliding the disgorger down the line and blindly stabbing away not only inflames the fish's throat tissue it may even push the barb of the hook in further. The easiest method and by far the kindest to the fish, is to hold it firmly but gently with a wet hand, just behind the gills, or cradle it on your lap upon a wet towel, or lay it on the landing net over grassy banking with the head raised.

Hold taut the line leading into the mouth and ease the slit in the disgorger's barrel head over the line. Now gently twist the disgorger clockwise around the line a couple of times so all is held tight and slowly slide the barrel down towards the hook. Once it has locked over the hook shank (spade-end hooks are the easiest to remove due to their neat shape) push forward gently and east out all in one motion. This is where micro and especially barbless hooks are so beneficial. They literally fall out to the most gentle pressure from the disgorger. Barrel-type disgorgers are best kept ready for immediate use connected to a 24in loop of old fly line and hung around the neck.

Long-nosed locking artery forceps are without question the finest tool for removing both spade-end and eyed hooks larger than size 12 from all freshwater species. As one would expect, the medical profession demands exact requirements from these stainless-steel locking forceps and all 'seconds' not quite up to standard are usually jobbed out to the fishing tackle industry to the benefit of anglers and their catch. The pointers to look out for are

(Above) Heavy-duty gardening gloves are a good substitute for the spring gag, and artery forceps, for pike and zander fishing. (Right) V-end and tubular disgorgers for all other fish species.

P.H. Ward/Natural Science Photos

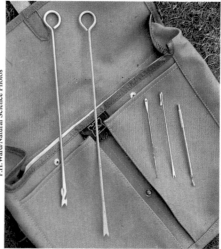

Ken Whitehead

strong, long handles (especially if using them for unhooking predatory species) and a fine nose with interlocking teeth that can easily get to grips with even modest-sized hooks.

But beware, using locking forceps to remove fine-wire hooks can easily distort them and in most cases a barrel-type disgorger is in fact more efficient.

One way of unhooking pike is to gently release a spring gag (with the V prongs removed and taped up to protect the fish's jaws) to hold its mouth open while the hooks are removed and many pike anglers are happy using them.

The gag is a simple, safety pin-style piece of sprung steel that, when opened, will hold the jaws of a pike apart. This enables the angler to use two hands to remove the hook without fear of the jaws snapping shut and damaging a finger or thumb. Small gags are useless, and the very largest heavily pronged models, decidedly brutal. Modern patterns such as the 'Humane Pike gag' are 7in ling with rubber-topped chrome-plated T-bar ends to ensure minimum harm to the pike. In addition to this improved design, other models with ball-ends are also available.

There is however a far easier and certainly more positive method of keeping a pike's mouth open during hook removal which is

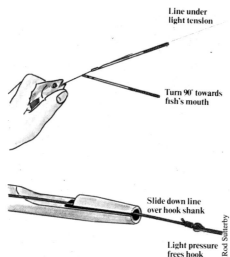

Line under light tension

Turn 90° towards fish's mouth

Slide down line over hook shank

Light pressure frees hook

Rod Sutterby

less hassle and far less dangerous for both pike and the angler. First of all, invest in either a left-handed (assuming you are right-handed) industrial-type latex rubber glove or a fine chainmail 'fish n fillet'-style glove made by Normark Sports. As a last resort, use an old leather gardening glove. This is unquestionably the only tool to ensure pike are handled easily and sympathetically and whatever it costs a good unhooking glove is worth its weight in gold.

Simply insert all four fingers of the gloved (left) hand gently into the pike's 'left' gill opening and clamp down against them on the outside with your thumb. Providing you hold on tightly the pike can now be lifted vertically from the landing net and laid carefully upon an unhooking mat or wet grassy bank on its back. For extra support a wet towel can be laid across its upturned belly and the ends pinned to the ground with your knees. Now simply curl your left hand upwards almost into a fist, whereupon the pike's lower jaw has no option but to fall open. Its upper jaw cannot move being part of the skull and so it is the lower jaw which opens against its weight lying on the ground.

To remove the treble hooks of an artificial lure or snap tackle, carefully ease out with long-nosed forceps. Where the hooks are deeply embedded in the throat tissue, carefully insert the long-nosed forceps through the fish's right gill opening and once detached from the flesh, remove via the jaws. This is why long-nosed locking artery forceps of 10-12in long are so valuable. It is pointless risking injury to your hands by using shorter models.

In the event that clean unhooking

(Left) The tubular disgorger is run down the line to the eyed or spade-end shank. Held by the disgorger the hook is pushed down to dislodge the barb, then drawn out.
(Overleaf, left) It is wrong to put your hand behind the gill cover.
(Overleaf, right) A spring clamp can exert too much force and damage the pike's jaw.

becomes impossible due to the hooks being embedded too far down the pike's throat, cutting the trace wire as far down as possible is the best option. So keep a pair of scissors or wire cutters handy. Stomach acids quickly corrode the metal of hooks (don't use stainless-steel trebles) and they will disintegrate within a short space of time. This is always a last option however and provided care is taken in the unhooking process only very rarely is this action necessary. Far too many pike anglers give up too quickly because they are unsure and scared of handling large predatory fish like the pike. So practice the art of holding and unhooking them using the gloved-hand technique until you feel totally confident.

Were pike fishermen to use semi-barbless hooks when live or deadbaiting (techniques where gorging of the bait is most likely to happen – as opposed to lure fishing) then hook removal would be far, easier. Simply crunch down two of the barbs on each treble leaving one for holding the bait and unhooking becomes a quick and simple task, not a surgical operation. Of course there are times when a fish bolts the bait down with such speed that throat hooking is inevitable but many such cases could be avoided if proper attention were paid to the rod with the angler close at hand ready for

action (as he should be) and not several yards along the bank chatting with friends.

A large soft rubberized unhooking mat (those used for unhooking carp will easily double up) should be in every pike fisherman's kit, especially those who regularly fish gravel pits. A pike flapping around on any hard uneven surface, particularly loose gravel, can injure itself all too easily. And once its protective slime has been removed together with masses of scales, infection will set in. When boat fishing use an old piece of carpet or carpet underlay over the floorboards to protect the pike whilst the hooks are being removed. It will also cushion the general noise and vibrations which occur when out boat fishing.

When a pike comes to the boat with trailing 'trebles' where at least one of the hooks is clearly visible on the outside of the jaws, do not on any account attempt to net the fish. 'Flying trebles' all too easily become jammed into the mesh of the net, and should the pike then decide to 'twist' before unhooking commences, extracting the hooks is guaranteed to take a long time.

Simply play the pike to a complete standstill, and bring alongside, where with long-handled forceps the hooks can be eased out without removing it from the water.

Ken Whitehead

Ken Whitehead

Spinners

A spinner can be defined as an artificial lure that usually comprises of a blade or body which rotates quickly about a straight line axis consisting often of a wire bar. Spoons, in contrast, have a wobbly retrieve and do not usually spin. Plugs are artificial fish-like objects, made of various materials, which wobble on retrieve. These distinctions are not clear cut, and it is possible to buy, or make, spinners that are headed by a sizeable body and are therefore halfway between spinners and plugs (such as the famous Voblex), and spinners with so much hair or feather that they approach flies in construction, but with the added flash of a small rotating blade. There is great scope for inventiveness among anglers and many new combinations are possible, if not many new basic designs.

Five basic spinners

There are five basic kinds of spinners—artificial minnows, wagtails, mackerel spinners, fly spoons, and barspoons. It is unfortunate that the last two incorporate the word 'spoon' in their names, for they are in fact spinners with a straight axis around which the blade spins.

Of all the kinds of spinners, artificial minnows most closely represent fish,

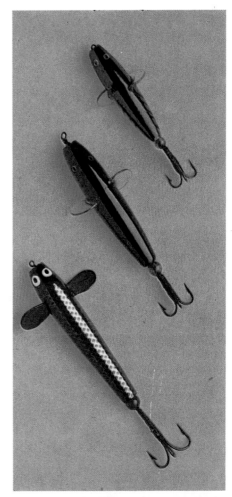

(*Right*) *Devon minnows, the most fish-like spinners. The vanes cause rotation.*
(*Below*) *The Voblex, another favourite.*

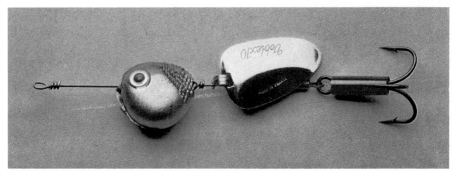

Steve Bicknell

Spinners

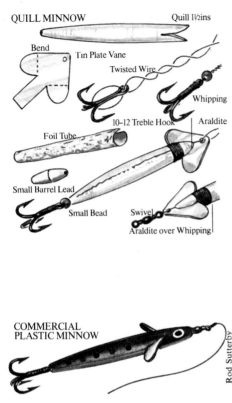

QUILL MINNOW — Quill 1½ins

Bend
Tin Plate Vane
Twisted Wire
Whipping
10-12 Treble Hook
Araldite
Foil Tube
Small Barrel Lead
Small Bead
Swivel
Araldite over Whipping

A home-made quill minnow, identical in action to the Devon minnow. The barrel lead is slid down the wire inside.

occasionally incorporated in such other lures as plugs.

The head of the minnow has a pair of vanes which cause it to rotate. Some makes have adjustable vanes so that the spin can be reversed, and lure twist reduced.

Minnow variation

A variation on the minnow theme is the quill minnow, a superb lure for fishing for trout in hill streams. The whole body of the quill minnow rotates, often including the bar wire through its middle, so that the swivel has to work well to avoid line twist, and an anti-kink vane is usually necessary. These lures usually have up to three sets of treble hooks and since many hill trout take the spinner crossways, this is an advantage despite the tendency of the lure to become hooked up in rocks and other snags.

Wagtail movement

Wagtails look more creature-like when still than when moving. They usually have a head complete with eyes, spinning vanes, a swivel and tube-like body hidden inside two long rubber flaps which are pointed at the tail end, close to the treble hook. The name comes from this loose, flapping rubber. All this detail disappears, however, when the whole body rotates quickly and, other than in body softness, the wagtail probably differs little from the various minnows. Wagtails can be made to quite large sizes and with a slow spin. This can occasionally be an advantage over the commercial minnows. Like minnows, wagtails are mostly used when fishing for salmon, sea trout and trout, but can be very effective for pike.

COMMERCIAL PLASTIC MINNOW

Rod Sutterby

both still and on the move. The body, made of either wood, plastic or metal, is round in cross section, minnow-like in profile, and has a hole along its length through which a metal bar or wire trace passes. At the tail is a treble hook and at the head a swivel which can be attached to the reel line or, if fishing for pike, to a wire trace link swivel. Generally, the swivel at the head has a smaller overall diameter than the hole through the middle of the lure so that on the take the fish tends to blow the lure up the line, giving itself nothing to lever against as it tries to throw the hook. This is an excellent feature of the design which is

Wagtails look unnatural when still, but in action they work in a life-like manner. One side piece is shown removed to illustrate the wagtail's structure.

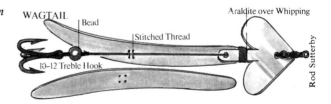

WAGTAIL
Bead
Stitched Thread
Araldite over Whipping
10-12 Treble Hook
Rod Sutterby

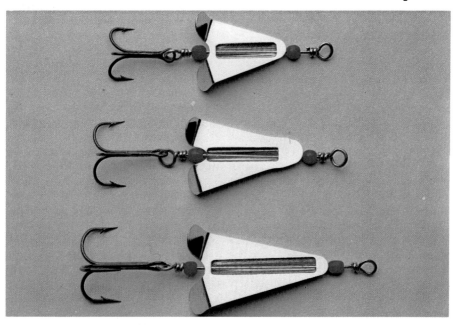

Mackerel spinners are superb lures for any predatory fish. They do not work well if more than 2½in long, but most commercial ones are 2in or less. They have a tube around the axial wire, and this tube is, brazed to a triangular-shaped plate that has the spinning vanes at the rear, near the treble hook. Mackerel spinners can be retrieved in very shallow water and with extreme slowness at any depth. For catching large numbers of perch and pike they are perhaps the best lures ever designed, and should be fished on lines of 6-8lb b.s. to obtain the best casting results out of their aerodynamic shape. Mackerel spinners have advantages over other spinners, as they are very cheap and nearly indestructible but they are the only spinner that is not easy to make unless you dispense with the tube and make do with a couple of bent eyes at the front and back of the blade.

Fly spoons, as their name implies, have traditionally been used for game fish, but are very effective for chub and perch on small streams. They are small, twinkling lures, most of which spin rather than wobble, and are essentially spinners for

(*Above*) *Both simple and superb, mackerel spinners work at low retrieve rates.*
(*Below*) *Fly spoons, for light spinning.*

Spinners

short casts on light tackle of 2-6lb b.s. monofilament lines. This can even be fished on fly tackle with fly lines. This is probably how they originated but today it is unusual to see them fished in this way. Many fly spoons are constructed with a spinner blade attached at only one end to a split ring connecting two swivels. A treble hook is attached to the other end of one swivel and the reel line to the opposite end of the other swivel.

Barspoons are more correctly classified as spinners since they have a straight axis of wire around which the blade, attached at one end, rotates with a strong vibration. Weight is added to the bar, just behind the spinning blade, and this weight can be made to look like a body and can be painted different colours. Bar spoons are among the most versatile of lures and all except the very heavy ones are retrievable

even in very shallow-water conditions.

Heavy barspoons, however, can be cast a long way, and many can be fished very deep and slow. Making your own is easy provided you attach the blade to the bar with a separate link, rather than passing the bar through a hole in the blade. Popular commercially made barspoons are Ondex, Veltic and Mepps.

A change in the blade shape has given rise to some classic lures: the Vibro has the end away from the bar quite sharply pointed, and the result is a spinner which vibrates very strongly. The kidney spoon has a kidney-shaped blade which gives a pulsating spinning action.

Perhaps in a category of its own is the Colorado which has a spoon-shaped blade attached at both ends. It spins about a bar axis by means of spinning vanes at the head end. It is one of the oldest lures

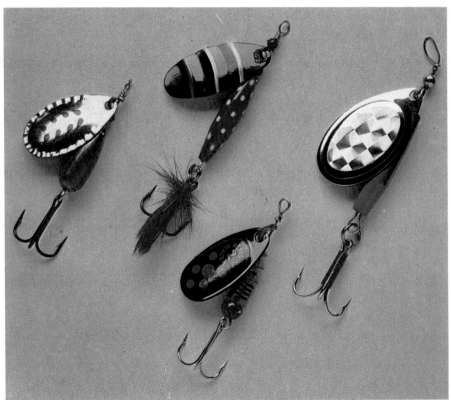

Steve Bicknell

available, and in its smaller sizes can be extremely effective for perch.

Do-it-yourself enthusiasts can have a field day with spinners. Spinner blades are lighter than most spoon blades and they can be easily cut with tin snips. Even plastic blades can be used successfully. All you need are lengths of wire, round-headed long-nosed pliers to bend the wire into terminal loops, and the ability to cut various weights of metal sheet into blades that can be beaten to the required curve.

Antikink vanes

There is one more thing the spinning angler needs—antikink vanes to prevent line twist. Half moon leads which can be clamped to the reel line or trace are one of the best. They range in size from minute to very large and for really heavy spinning they can always be used in multiples. Many more antikink devices are available, and it is wise to try them all, but make sure they are firmly fixed to the line or trace, otherwise they are totally ineffective.

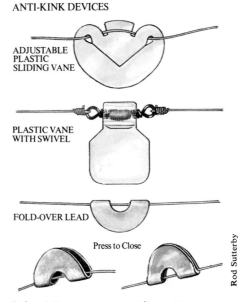

ANTI-KINK DEVICES

ADJUSTABLE PLASTIC SLIDING VANE

PLASTIC VANE WITH SWIVEL

FOLD-OVER LEAD

Press to Close

Rod Sutterby

(*Above*) *Devices to prevent line twist.*
(*Below Colorado (top) and kidney spoons.*
(*Left) Colourful bar spoons for deep fishing.*

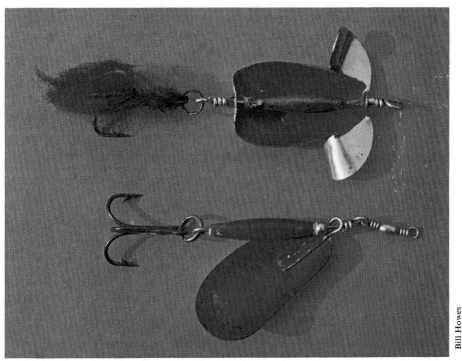

Bill Howes

John Wilson

Plugs

The best description of a plug is a cross between a spinner and a deadbait. In shape it resembles a dead fish with hooks ready-set. In use it is retrieved in much the same way as a spinner. But a plug possesses advantages that neither spinner nor deadbait has – it can be made to work with innumerable variations on a straight retrieve at any of many chosen depths.

Plugs fall into four general categories that coincide with the depth at which they should work. There are surface lures, floating divers, sinkers, and deep divers. Their shape, especially at the nose, often gives a clue to their working use. But it is left to the angler to actually get the best action from them when he is fishing.

Kinds of plug

Floating plugs are light, usually made from wood, and have a 'V'-shaped wedge inserted in the nose. There are models made to represent mice, and one has broad arms, or sweeps, that vibrate backwards and

A chub, with a selection of plugs with varying actions. The placing of the vanes dictates whether the plug dives or rises.

forwards during the retrieve; they are intended to represent a surface-swimming fish in distress – rather in the fashion of one with swimbladder trouble.

They should be cast close to the bank, under overhanging trees and bushes and retrieved alternately fast and slow, causing them to dive a few inches under the surface, then pop up to the top. The bow wave caused by this sudden dive is the lure's main attraction.

Most versatile plugs

Floating divers are the most versatile of all plugs. They have lightweight bodies with a medium-sized diving nose (or lip) set into the head. After being cast, they will lie on the surface, only diving when the angler commences the retrieve. The faster the motion, the deeper they will dive – short, hard turns on the reel and then a few seconds with the handle stationary, produce a series of swoops and rises that few fish can resist. They have an added advantage in snaggy waters. By stopping the retrieve when an underwater obstruction is reached, the plug is allowed to float up, and can be coaxed gently past the danger area before continuing with the normal dive and rise action.

Sinking plugs

Sinking plugs are for very deep gravel pits and reservoirs where the lure has to sink some way before it can be fished usefully. In order to find and keep the 'taking' depth, the count-down method should be used. After the lure has hit the water, the angler counts from, say, one to six, then starts his retrieve. On the next cast, he may count to seven, then eight on the following casts – and so on until a fish is taken. This will probably be the taking depth, and future casts should be allowed the same length of time before retrieve begins.

Few plugs in this category have a diving vane, all are heavy, and some models have a metal ball sealed into a cavity in the body.

Ken Whitehead

Plugs

FLOATING PLUG

FLOATING DIVER

SINKING PLUG

DEEP DIVER

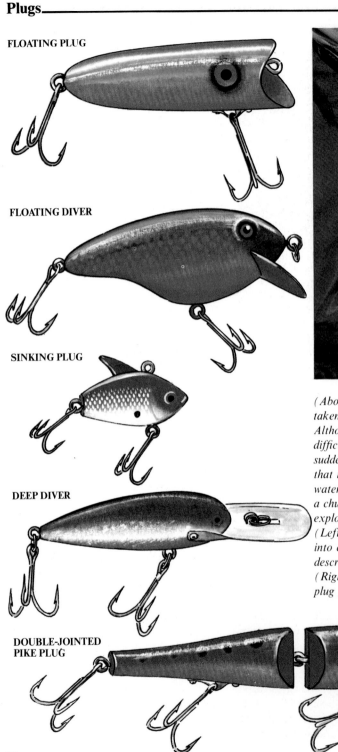

DOUBLE-JOINTED PIKE PLUG

(Above) A small chub taken on a medium plug. Although a wary fish and difficult to tempt, the sudden appearance of a plug that is plopped into the water near it often triggers a chub into a sudden, explosive take.
(Left) Plugs can be put into categories which describe their action.
(Right) The vanes on a plug give it action.

Ken Whitehead

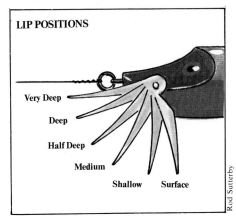

LIP POSITIONS

Very Deep

Deep

Half Deep

Medium

Shallow   Surface

Rod Sutterby

a sharp angle. As with sinkers, the count-down method is the best when exploring with this type of lure.

The colour range of plugs displayed in a tackle shop can be quite staggering. But action is more important than colour in a plug, and generally those with green, yellow and a little red coincide with the natural colours of fish and appear the most acceptable.

Most important of all is the construction of the plug. Hooks should be neither so large that they dwarf the body, nor so small that they will fail to set into the jaws of a fish on striking. The best hooks are made from fine wire, with well-defined barbs. Most of them are mounted into the body by screw eyes or metal bands secured with screws. These should be most carefully checked, and, if they appear loose, should be removed and re-set with a little Araldite glue to hold them firm. The eye-loop at the head, to which the trace will be mounted, should also be carefully looked at to ensure that it is firmly closed, otherwise the trace will slip free from it during a cast.

Size not important

One naturally thinks of pike fishing in connection with plugs, and most of the sinking and deep-diving models will take good fish. Size does not seem important where pike are concerned – 4 and 5in double-bodied plugs that simulate the flowing movements of a swimming fish, down to tiny $1\frac{1}{2}$in minnow imitations, will all produce results. Perch take a running plug, too, especially in reservoirs and gravel pits. Their large, 'telescopic' mouths are perfectly capable of tackling the large lure intended for a pike. Chub are appreciative of surface plugs that can be persuaded to make a large disturbance on top of the water – especially the more gaudy, tassle-embellished models. Shallow divers of the minnow size are worth a trial during the winter months.

But there are few fish that have not, at some time or other, fallen for a plug – particularly in the early season when many of the old adult stock have turned cannibal.

When the retrieve begins, the action of the plug under the water causes this ball to rattle, making vibrations that attract predators.

Deep divers

The last selection of plugs, the deep divers, are easily recognized by the extra large metal vane set into the head. This broad lip sets up drag against the water when the retrieve starts and causes the plug to dive quickly, at

Maggots

Maggots are bred as bait from flies, most often the bluebottle (above).

The maggot is the most popular coarse fishing bait used in Britain. Almost all our freshwater species may be taken on it, major competitions have been won on it, and it has also accounted for some record fish.

Maggots are small, easy to buy, transport and use. Not so long ago they were cheap, but prices have risen steeply. Maggots now cost about £1 a pint. They are sold this way because pint beer glasses were once used to scoop them up for sale.

The maggot is the larva, or grub, of the fly. The maggots of the bluebottle, greenbottle, and common housefly are the ones used by the angler.

There are four stages in the life-cycle of a fly: egg–grub–pupa–fly. The female of the common housefly lays between 120 and 150 eggs at a time and deposits several batches in a lifetime.

Maggot breeding

Breeding maggots is big business. Millions are sold every week by tackle dealers all over the country. Professional breeders use bluebottles for mass production of the ordinary maggot. The common housefly's maggots are known as 'squatts', and being smaller than the bluebottle larvae they are used as 'feeders' thrown in to attract fish. Maggots from the greenbottle are called 'pinkies'. These are also small and used as 'feeders', but may be used on the hooks when circumstances require very fine tackle.

Special fly-houses holding the breeding stocks are maintained at constant temperatures 21.1 C-23.9 C (70-75 F). This enables maggot production to meet the year round demand.

Maggot breeding starts when meat or fish is placed in the fly-house so that the breeder flies can lay their eggs. When this is done the meat is said to be 'blown'. The meat is then removed from the fly-house and placed on trays in long sheds. When the maggots hatch they begin to feed and grow. On reaching bait size they are transferred to another tray filled with bran or sawdust. As they wriggle

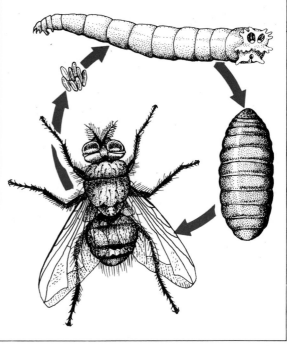

The greenbottle (top) produces the maggots known as 'pinkies'; the housefly (lower) those called 'squatts'. (Right) The life-cycle of a fly: egg-grub-pupa-fly.

Lyn Cawley

through this they are cleaned and then ready for despatch, usually in large biscuit tins, to tackle shops. There they are kept in fridges to prevent them reaching the pupa (or chrysalis) stage too soon.

Maggots are usually sold in the sawdust or bran. To improve their taste remove them from the sawdust or bran and transfer them to a clean bait box containing custard or blancmange powder, flour, or a similar substance. As they crawl through this they become well-coated and tiny specks flake off to add an extra attraction for the fish.

Breeding your own maggots

Many anglers are now breeding their own maggots, and producing very high quality hook-bait. This must be done in garden sheds or somewhere away from the house. (Even professional breeders are often asked by local authorities to move on because of the smell associated with their business.) Quality maggots may be obtained from chicken carcasses. Put these in a container—a large biscuit tin is ideal—and make sure the

lid fits perfectly. Make a 2-3in diameter hole in the top and leave the tin outdoors. After a couple of days the chicken flesh will be blown, with clusters of eggs visible.

Wrap the blown chicken carcass in old newspaper and replace it in the tin. The eggs will hatch a few days later and the grubs will begin to feed on the nutritious meat. To help the maggots grow fat, add soft brown sugar or even the cream off the top of the milk.

Keep the chicken wrapped in the paper, watching at intervals to see how the maggots are growing. When they stop feeding, place the maggots in bran for 24 hours. Next, tip onto a sieve and allow the bran and maggots to separate. Now add clean bran, plus more sugar, which will ensure that the maggots remain soft until needed.

The 'gozzer' is a very soft, white maggot, the larval form of a type of bluebottle, reared mainly on pigeon carcass, pig's or sheep's heart. After five or six days of feeding, these should be given a final bran 'bath' and left until required.

Maggots

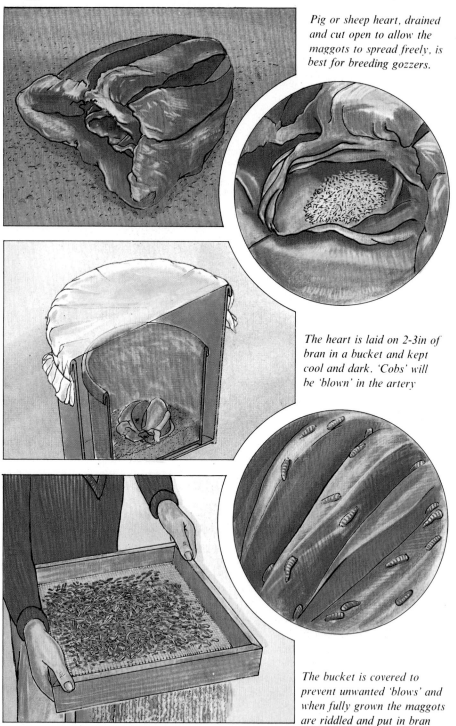

Pig or sheep heart, drained and cut open to allow the maggots to spread freely, is best for breeding gozzers.

The heart is laid on 2-3in of bran in a bucket and kept cool and dark. 'Cobs' will be 'blown' in the artery

The bucket is covered to prevent unwanted 'blows' and when fully grown the maggots are riddled and put in bran

100

Hook the maggot through the vent at the blunt end. This will allow it to wriggle attractively to tempt the fish. Be careful not to pierce your thumb

A very succulent maggot, the 'gozzer's' powers of attraction are highly valued, especially by match fishermen.

Coloured maggots

To increase the attractiveness of maggots to fish, they may be dyed a variety of colours, and indeed can be bought coloured orange, red or yellow. Tackle dealers can supply non-toxic dyes in small amounts such as Auramine O for yellow, and Rhodamine B for red but today most maggots are sold uncoloured. The maggots can be coloured by raising them on foodstuffs treated with a small amount of the dye. The second method is best for maggots that have already been cleaned, as they are when bought. For this, sprinkle dye on them and stir well, then leave for three or four hours according to the depth of colour desired. Next, add bran or sawdust on which they will deposit excess dye. Lastly, sieve them to remove the bran, and they are ready for use.

The 'annatto' is a special colour-fed maggot whose yellow colour comes from the dye used to colour butter. Gozzers and other extra-soft maggots produce the best results with this dye. Annatto is bought in roll form and must be cut into slices and mixed into a thin paste with water before use. The best time to introduce annatto is when the maggots are about half-grown. Spread the paste on the meat and replace in the bran. When the maggots stop feeding they are ready for use.

To prevent your maggots from turning into chrysalids, or casters, before you want them to, when the weather is warm, place them securely in a plastic bag and store them in your domestic fridge where they will become cold and still. No harm will come to food there if they are secure. Remember, too, that maggots need air, so ensure your bait containers are ventilated with pin-holes.

Lastly, if buying maggots from a shop, be sure they are fresh and do not include remnants of last week's stock. They should be shiny and wriggle vigorously.

Casters

The chrysalis, or pupa, of the fly is known to anglers as a caster. At this point in its life-cycle (from egg to grub, or maggot, to pupa, to fly) it is an excellent bait. First made popular by match anglers in roach waters, some experts consider casters to be the most important new bait adopted in recent years. Although the maggot remains the most popular general bait, the time may be near when the caster will have replaced it. As well as roach, chub and dace are partial to it and it has accounted for bream, gudgeon and tench. When first introduced to a stretch of water the fish may be uninterested but, once sampled, every caster is likely to be taken. The fish probably gets its food more easily from the insect at this time in its life-cycle than when it was a mere maggot.

Home production

Casters can be purchased from a tackle-shop or bait dealer and kept in a refrigerator for about a week. Home production can work out to be more expensive than buying them ready-bred, but the angler needs chrysalids (or casters) as sinkers: too fast a metamorphosis and the caster becomes a floater, of no practical use except as a means to check on the presence of fish in unknown water. The keen angler who needs a constant supply, therefore, will want to produce his own, in order to control the speed of change. After a little trial and error the angler can have casters in perfect condition and colour in the quantities he needs as and when he wants them for a day's fishing.

Test for freshness

Whether you buy casters from the dealer or raise maggots, and casters as well, yourself you will need about five pints of maggots to produce three pints of good quality casters — enough for a match or a day's fishing.

For large casters, choose large maggots. To test for freshness if you are buying the maggots, look for the food pouch—the small black speck under the skin. This pouch

(Above) Five pints of maggots give a day's supply of casters. (Below) In five or six days most of the maggots turn to casters.

(Below) The casters are separated at regular intervals from the maggots. (Right) Casters and maggots laid out at the swim.

Bill Howes

102

carries all the food the insect needs to complete the stages of its development to a fly, and should still be visible.

It takes a fresh maggot, one that has just been taken from its feed medium, five to six days to turn into a chrysalis with the temperature at between 65° and 70°F (18° to 21°C). To slow development, put the maggots, in a plastic bag, into the refrigerator for three days—more in very hot weather, less in cold.

Tip the maggots on to a sieve to be riddled and cleaned, then into tins of dry sawdust, so that maggots and sawdust cover the bottoms of the tins to a depth of not more than a couple of inches. The tins of maggots should now be kept in a cool place: a garage or cool outhouse is ideal.

After about 24 hours the first of the casters will be seen. Once this stage is reached put

the contents of the tins on to a riddle over a larger container and the maggots will wriggle through, leaving the already-turned casters on the mesh, with any dead maggots which should be thrown away.

Return the live maggots to their tins. Repeat this inspection and selection process every 7 or 8 hours. Each batch of casters can be rinsed in water to remove bits of sawdust, drained on the riddle and then placed, in sealed plastic bags, in the refrigerator, at not less than 34°F (1°C).

By rinsing the casters, any floaters can be removed at this stage. Damp casters, however, can sour in the refrigerator and some anglers prefer to omit rinsing at this stage, as a final check should may be made before setting off, or at the water-side.

If you do not want to use the refrigerator for collecting the bags of casters, you can put

Don Bridgewood

them direct from the riddling into a bucket, just covering them with water and adding to their number as they develop. Floaters can thus be eliminated as they appear and the bucket kept in the same cool outhouse as the tins of maggots.

Uniform colour

Whichever method you use, you will find that the casters vary in colour. Casters of a uniform dark red colour—the favourite—can be achieved quite simply. On the evening before use, put all the casters into a wet towel, fold it over them and leave in a bucket overnight. Next morning all the casters will be the same colour.

The size of hook will be governed by the size of the caster. The biggest you can use will probably be a 14, but generally a 16 or 18 will be necessary. The hook must be buried in the caster. Hold the caster between thumb and forefinger and, with the hook in the other hand, pierce the head of the caster with the point. Turn the hook very gently into the caster and, with some of the shank still showing, lightly tap the top of the shank until the hook sinks into the caster.

Casters as groundbait

In deepish, fast flowing water, casters are best introduced as groundbait. Where there are plenty of fish and once they are taking them, you can put as many as two dozen casters in every cast. A 'cocktail' mixture of worm tipped with a caster is particularly deadly with bream.

(Right) To hook a caster, hold it gently between thumb and forefinger, pierce the head with the point and sink the bend and most of the shank in the bait. Tap the shank lightly so that all of the hook is now concealed.

(Below) A catapult is used by match anglers to hurl casters with accuracy into a distant swim.

Hooking a caster

Lyn Cawley.

Don Bridgewood

Caterpillars and mealworms

P. H. Ward/Natural Science Photos

The idea that any caterpillar accidentally found along the river bank should be mounted onto a hook and dapped through the bushes, is one of angling's popular misconceptions. There are better techniques, and although it is true that many fish, including dace, chub and roach, will feed on the surface during very warm weather, not every caterpillar is attractive to fish, or useful as a bait.

Natural protection

Many species of grubs and caterpillars are naturally protected either by their startling colour or shape, or by a repulsive taste or smell made when danger is sensed, usually effected by means of a discharge through the skin. So the angler using a bait which has either of these protections is likely to find that, although a fish may show an interest, his offering could well be rejected almost immediately, and long before there has been a chance to strike.

Caterpillars are best gathered before the angler goes fishing and not left to a chance finding on the day. Despite the number of modern sprays and insecticides in use, the larvae of the Large White (better known as the Cabbage White) butterfly are still plentiful: few gardeners or allotment holders will resent anglers searching the leaves of the cabbages, mustard, turnips or radish plants for full-grown grubs.

Storing and carrying

These grubs should be stored in a large plastic box with ample ventilation and with a few leaves of the host plant. If there is a handle by which the box can be tied onto a waist-belt, so much the better—it will allow the angler complete mobility as he fishes and save constant trips to where the box has been left. Keep the box in a cool, dark place before going to fish, and try to protect it from the sun as far as possible when actually fishing.

Dapping is one way in which the caterpillar can be fished. Usually a long general-purpose trotting rod is best, and this is rigged without a float but with just one large swan or BB shot pinched above the hook. The caterpillar is mounted by its tail end—an easy task providing that the hook is of very fine wire and has recently been sharpened. Loose line below the rod tip is wound round the rod, which can then be poked through gaps in overhanging bushes and the bait released to dap on the surface of the water.

In theory this method is sound and will generally produce a few fish. But in practice, the disturbance through vibrations made by the angler, either on the bank or by the rod tapping against branches prohibit the better fish from being attracted. Even if a fish is hooked, the angler is often unable to play or land it because of obstructions surrounding his rod.

A far better approach can be made when the angler is in the water, either wading where this is possible, or from a boat. A short, light rod—a fly rod is ideal—and a free-running centrepin or light fixed-spool reel with a light line in the region of 3lb b.s. will enable accurate casting to be achieved with the minimum exertion. Accuracy is all-important, but you should nevertheless aim to use as little lead on the line as possible, and cast the caterpillar under bushes and between reeds or weedbeds from the midstream position.

fact, where brickwork lines or crosses water. Many insects live or hibernate in masonry, and naturally fall onto the surface from time to time in these areas.

Mealworms

Mealworms make an excellent bait. The long, straw-coloured grubs, segmented and rather similar to a centipede in appearance, are the larvae of a large beetle found in granaries and flour mills. They can occasionally be purchased at pet stores, where they are sold as food for insectivorous birds and mammals. Although they are expensive, they can be stored for a very long period in a ventilated tin of fine bran or oatmeal. If an even temperature is maintained, they will often go through the chrysalis stage, adult insect, and breed, allowing a succession of baits from the one purchase.

(Left) Probably the most commonly seen caterpillar, the Large White. Fish take but may also reject like lightning, so be prepared to miss some bites.
(Right) Mealworms are not worms, but the larvae of beetles found in granaries and flour mills. They make good baits right through their larval, chrysalis and adult stages.

D. B. Lewis/Natural Science Photos

Time is well spent in watching the surface for movements from a fish before casting to it. The angler can wade slowly upstream and position himself below the fish he has located. Two tail-hooked caterpillars will create sufficient disturbance as they land to ensure that immediate interest is shown, and no attempt should be made to strike until the fish has turned away with the bait—an action that can be judged by movement of the line across the water's surface.

Dapping

Dapping in one form or another can also be successfully undertaken in the region of locks, bridges, canal wharfs—anywhere, in

The two rigs described for using caterpillar baits are equally successful when fishing mealworms, although they should be mounted through a middle segment rather than one near the tail end, which is rather delicate and likely to break away during the cast.

Even if there is no acceptance of a mealworm bait on or just below the surface, it should be allowed to sink and lie on the bottom for a short time before being retrieved gently. The larva is not strong enough to withstand constant casting, and its light colouring makes it a distinctive mouthful appreciated by any bottom-feeding fish.

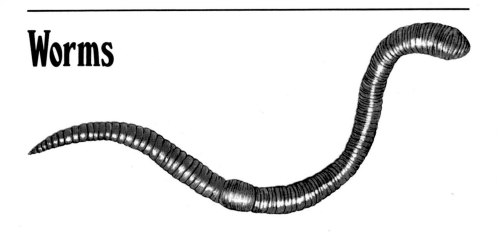

Worms

Earthworms have been used as a bait for fish for a thousand years and more, and today they are just as effective. All species of freshwater fish can be caught on worms, and indeed several record fish have fallen to this bait. And to the horror of game fishermen, even the salmon or trout may be taken in this way, sometimes deliberately, sometimes by chance.

There are some 25 kinds of earthworm found in Britain, but only three species are of real interest to the coarse fisherman—the lobworm, the redworm and the brandling. The lobworm, sometimes called the dew-worm, is the largest, the most used as bait and probably the easiest to find. It is fished whole for the bigger fish, but just the head or tail, commonly offered to roach, will often take larger species.

Best places and times

Lobworms may be gathered from a lawn, but if the grass is long it may be difficult. Cricket pitches and close-cut sports fields will also yield lobworms in plenty if access, at the right time, is available to the angler. The best periods are after dark and following a heavy dew or shower or, when conditions are dry, after a lawn has been watered. Early morning can also prove fruitful for worm collecting. It is important to move stealthily, for worms are very sensitive to vibrations and will soon dig themselves in if disturbed. At night it is necessary to use a dim torch or a

The three kinds of earthworm used commonly by the coarse fisherman.

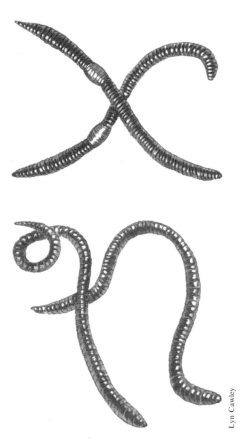

Lyn Cawley

Peter Burt

beachcaster's lamp that straps on to the head and leaves both hands free.

A worm must be seized quickly and firmly when it has come partly out of its hole on to the wet grass. Carry a tin of fine sand in which to dip your fingers to give them a grip on the slippery creature. The lobworm has tiny clusters of erectile bristles at intervals along its length, and these enable it to grip the sides of its burrow. So having got hold of the worm, maintain a steady pressure until it relaxes and comes out with its fish-attracting tail intact.

The redworm

The redworm is a smaller species, not usually over 4in long, and is a very useful roach, dace and rudd bait, although any species of worm may appeal to all freshwater fish. This worm is found in compost heaps, under large stones or rotting logs, in fact any sizeable object in the garden could conceal enough worms for a good day's fishing.

The brandling is of similar size to the redworm but is distinguishable by a series of

Earthworms can be obtained from most garden lawns, especially after rain.

The worm is hooked at least twice or, if preferred, two hooks can be used.

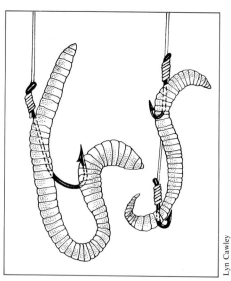

Lyn Cawley

 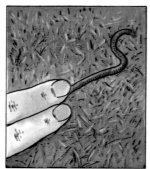 

Rod Sutterby

The best time to gather worms is after rain. In dry weather water the lawn to bring the worms to the top.

The worm's body can grip the sides of its hole. Stop it from going back down by using light finger pressure.

Grip the worm firmly, using fine sand to improve your hold. Gentle pressure will coax the worm from its hole.

yellowish rings around its red, often shiny, body. It can be collected from manure piles or compost heaps. The presence of a compost heap will, of course, mean a regular supply of worms. If the wormery is tended by adding vegetable matter, tea leaves and vegetable waste the worms will grow much bigger and probably breed there, thus supplying a constant store of bait. Where grassy conditions are suitable, worms can be dug at the river bank. Be careful to fill all the holes in and not leave places which other anglers can stumble over.

Keep them alive

Although very effective on the hook, most worms become soft and lifeless very quickly in water and often drop off the hook during casting out. Their quality can be improved to overcome this by allowing the worms to work through a good soil for a few days prior to use. Sink a box in the earth, providing small holes in the bottom for drainage. Place the worms on a bed of soil (a dark, loamy kind is best) and cover with sacking. In wriggling through the soil they will scour themselves to emerge brighter and so more attractive to the fish. They will also be tougher, and will stay on the hook longer and wriggle more enticingly. 'Faddist' used to recommend that worms be kept in fine red sand or brickdust, suggesting that this gave them an added colouring as well as

making the texture of their skins tougher.

Alternatively, a bucket containing sphagnum moss (obtainable cheaply from a florist) provides a medium for cleaning and toughening your worm bait. They will burrow through the moss, which should be damp but not wet. To keep worms fresh immediately before and during use, put them in clean moss and place in a linen bag. Tins and jars should be avoided, for they do not allow the worms to breathe properly. Remember also to weed out dead and dying worms, for one dead worm in a bait tin triggers off an extremely fast mass mortality among the rest.

Hooking the worm

It is important to hook a worm correctly, for this ensures that it stays on the hook and that it will wriggle naturally to attract the fish. A whole worm can be hooked anywhere along its length, but make sure that pieces cannot be bitten off by the fish without it also taking the hook. If necessary, pierce a long worm several times and feed it along the hook. Tails or pieces of worms should present no problem and stay on the hook. In general do not try to cover the hook, for a worm is a very tempting bait and, if lively, will probably wriggle enough to expose part of the hook anyway.

Look after worms, they are an all-purpose all-weather angling bait

Bread

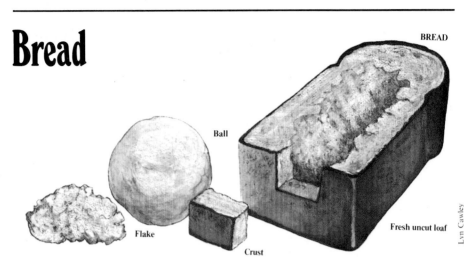

BREAD

Ball

Flake

Crust

Fresh uncut loaf

Lyn Cawley

Bread is not only an old-fashioned bait but also a very successful one. In recent years, and on many waters, it has been neglected, perhaps because its uses are not fully understood. Four different baits can be made from a white loaf—flake, crust, balanced crust and paste. The first two of these come from a new loaf, the third from an old loaf, the fourth from either.

Flake

Flake is the name given to the crumb of new bread. The crumb of two-day-old loaf is difficult, if not impossible, to place on the hook. When removing the crumb from the loaf a light touch is essential. Take hold of the required amount of crumb and lightly pull it from the loaf: it should be like a sponge with one edge sealed between thumb and forefinger. With the other hand take the hook, push the shank into the 'sponge' and gently pinch the crumb over it. Both the bend—or part of it—and the point of the hook will be exposed. The two sides of the crumb must be joined together with the minimum of pressure. If the sponge falls apart, the bread is too old: one light edge-pinch should be sufficient to keep it together. If the flake is pinched too tightly the bait will be hard and unattractive.

The size of flake, and therefore the size of hook, depends upon the fish you expect to catch, the water you are fishing and the time of year. Chub, barbel, carp and tench during

(Above) The different forms of bread bait: flake, crust, ball taken from an uncut loaf. (Below) Flake pressed onto the hook. Be careful not to pinch too hard.

P. H. Ward/Natural Science Photos.

the early part of the season, big roach in waters not too heavily fished, can all be taken on a No. 6 hook. For bream, chub in winter, roach in some waters, tench, grayling and crucian carp, use a No. 10. For dace in heavily fished waters, or in winter, use a No. 12; in exceptional circumstances, when, for example, the fish are shy or in very cold water, a No. 14.

How to cast flake

Many anglers dislike flake because it is difficult to cast. The cast must always be a soft one, smooth and unhurried. Generally a sideways cast is best or, when fishing close in, an underhand one. When proficient, overhead casts can be made without bait and hook parting company in mid-air. An advantage of flake is that, whether trotted or ledgered, small particles constantly break off, thus attracting fish from downstream. into ones swim, especially in fast water.

Crust is self-explanatory. It must come from a newish loaf, not more than two or three days old, The loaf should be kept in the shade because, once hardened, the crust is useless. Depending upon the species being sought, sliced and unsliced loaves can be used. For such small fish as roach, dace and grayling, a cut loaf is best: where larger pieces are required for such species as chub and carp, an uncut loaf is necessary, especially when using floating crust. Floating crust is not only popular among carp and chub fishermen, but is also highly successful. The crust must be soft, so the baking of the loaf and its freshness are very important. Hard, brittle crust is useless. Some fastidious anglers order specially-baked loaves but this should not be necessary if you choose a loaf baked to a light brown colour.

(Below) One of the standard bread baits used by carp fishermen is the floating crust. It can be fished close to lily pads, with the line running across them. This method shows no tell-tale line in the water. It also indicates the smallest twitch bite.

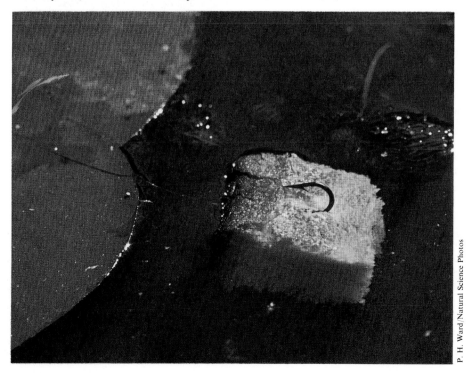

P. H. Ward/Natural Science Photos

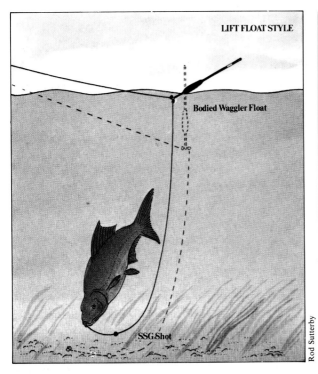

LIFT FLOAT STYLE

Bodied Waggler Float

SSG Shot

Rod Sutterby

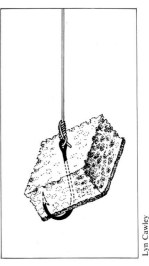

Lyn Cawley

(Above) Crust for hooking must not be stale.
(Left) The lift method relies on the float popping to the surface as the fish takes, thus lifting the shot.

Crumbly or too-hard crust from stale loaves is also useless, breaking up as the hook is pushed through it. A fairly large piece of crust, say 1½in square, is often used with a cast of 20 yards or more. For distance-casting the corners and edges of the loaf are, for a given size, heavier than the flat areas and therefore cast better. As no floats or weights are used, however, some weight might be given to the bait, so just before casting the crust is dipped into the water for a moment. This is called 'dunking'.

Hooking the crust

Opinions differ as to which side up the crust should lie. To make the bait hang crust side down take the crust and the hook, push the hook into the crumb side, out of the crust, then back through the crumb until both bend and part of the shank of the hook protrude. The opposite actions will make the bait hang with the crust up. About half the shank with the point and barb should always protrude from the crust. A hook slightly larger than the crust must be used. If the

hook is completely buried, the wet crust is liable to fall or cast off.

Crust will catch fish at all seasons but it is especially useful in winter, fished stationary, close to the bottom. The distance it is presented off the bottom is determined by how far the weight is stopped from it: 6in from the crust and the crust will be fishing about 6in off the bottom.

In June and July crust is especially good for tench, fished either under a float, 'lift' style, or simple ledgered. It can be fished in rivers, trotted and ledgered, floating on a weightless line. In stillwaters, ledgered and floating crust has probably accounted for more carp than any other bait.

Although a soft bait, crust will withstand quite a hard, forceful cast. An overhead cast is best, especially when fishing big pieces of crust on the surface for chub and carp. With this style of fishing, remember, the cast must be made immediately the crust has been dunked, otherwise it will become waterlogged and tend to fall off the hook during the cast.

Meats

Corned Beef

Pet Food

Sausage Meat

Luncheon Meat

Pork Rind

Liver Sausage

Lyn Cawley

At the turn of the century the angling press was astonished by the report of a man who had caught a fish on a sausage out of his luncheon pack. It was, the experts said, an exceptional happening. No one should consider catching a fish on a meat bait. There was only one form of bait used at that time with any association to meat, and that was greaves, a waste product of tallow obtained from candle manufacturers and used both as hook and groundbait at Thames weirpools to catch barbel.

Today, meat baits—pure meat and not merely by-products—are commonplace, and barbel, roach, bream, chub, tench and carp are regularly caught on them throughout the year. Much of the present day angler's success is the result of modern meat preparation of meat products which are packed with a consistency that not only allows easy mounting on the hook, but also a slow break-down in the water allowing flavour and smell to remain around the lure.

Luncheon meat

The best known and most used of the meat baits is undoubtedly luncheon meat. The tinned types are easily carried and provide a hefty chunk of meat from which substantial sized cubes can be cut. Blind buying of the first tin on the shelf is not advised. There are many cheap varieties of luncheon meat which have a very high fat content, and this means a soft cube of hookbait that will either

(Above) *A selection of meat baits used in freshwater. Barbel and chub are the prey usually associated with these.*

break away from the hook during the cast, or fall apart within a few minutes of lying in the water, especially if the swim lies in fast water.

A few extra pence will purchase a good meat mix that should be kept refrigerated until required, and thereafter kept as cool as possible while the angler is fishing. Once the tin is opened, keep the contents out of the sun and packed away in an airtight box. Drop any unopened tins held in reserve into the shallows at your feet—probably the best refrigerator on a warm day.

Mounting the bait

Mounting cubes of bait onto the hook requires care. Choose a hook too big rather than too small—sizes 8-4 are usual—and push the point of the hook slowly into the centre of the cube before threading it round onto the bend, making sure that the barb shows. To help the bait from jerking free on the cast use a small portion of green leaf or fine clear polythene bag folded double. This should be pushed over both point and barb to act as a platform behind the cube, and into which it will press during the thrust of the cast. It will not effect the hooking properties, and will save endless re-baiting.

There are variations on the luncheon meat theme—Prem and Spam are excellent baits,

Meat

as is liver sausage. But strangely enough, the majority of Continental processed meats that are highly seasoned, usually with garlic, seem to be inferior to the straight tinned varieties. Corned beef is excellent, but used straight from the tin tends to shred very quickly. A better method is to cut the cubes beforehand and then fry them for a few minutes to seal the fibres.

Sausage meat

Sausage meat, purchased in bulk and not made into sausages is another excellent meat bait. Again, it is too soft in its natural form to stand hard casting or long immersion in water, and it is better stiffened with breadcrumbs or, better still, sausage rusk, until it assumes the properties of putty. Another deadly bait is sausage meat mixed together with rusk and soft cheese with a little plain flour to harden the balls once they have been shaped into bait-sized pieces.

Tinned pet food, especially the cat types with a high proportion of fish in their ingredients, hit the headlines a few years ago as a deadly carp bait. Preparation of the bait for the hook is messy, and requires a little trouble, but results are usually worth the effort. Ideally the tin should be opened at the bank, hook-sized lumps moulded, and these dipped into boiling water to form a hard glaze over the surface which helps hold them in place during a cast. Obviously some soap and a towel are essential items using this method, otherwise the whole of one's tackle smells very strongly by the end of the day.

One variety of meat that is used in

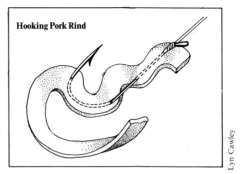

Hooking Pork Rind

Lyn Cawley

(*Above*) *Pork rind firmly mounted on a single hook.* (*Below*) *A cube of Spam set on a leaf to cushion the cast.*

freshwater fishing, although not in the way discussed so far, is pork rind, or strip. The use of this bait has been in vogue for some years now in America, where it can be purchased uncooked, vacuum-packed and ready for the hook. Usually the strips are hooked into the treble of a spinning lure, and it is claimed that baits treated with this addition of two or three worm-like strands towed astern really tempt the big fish.

The other way of using bacon strips is to hook-mount it as one would a worm, on a single large hook, and slowly reel this without a float and with the minimum of lead through areas where predators are found. As yet the method is practically untried in this country, but well worth some experiment, especially during the winter months.

Where to fish

Where one should fish with meat is an important decision. Naturally, it has a better chance of success in waters where it has been accepted for a number of years, and some species take it more willingly than others. Probably the natural place for its use is when fishing for barbel and chub in a weirpool, where luncheon meat is best.

A solitary piece flung just anywhere into the pool and left is hardly likely to be effective. To reap the maximum from meat, back up its use with groundbait. Fast water that washes away free offerings or hook bait from the hook, is a dead loss.

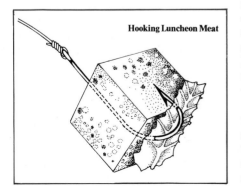

Hooking Luncheon Meat

Choose an edge of the pool, preferably as close to the sill as possible and at one side of the main flow of water. Depth is decidedly useful, and if there is an undercut to the structure so much the better—an eddy will probably be created holding the bait in one place. Make several trial casts and search for the slack water that always lies at the head of a pool before deciding to bait the area.

Other places

Other places where meat will often do well are above the weir—where the river and navigation channel divide providing deep water under the rod—and where erosion has taken a bank away, leaving a deep cut and slow stream. Lock cuttings are worth a try, but there is always a risk of too much attention from eels, especially during the autumn months.

Other natural places that suggest themselves as places to try meat baiting are where human food is readily available. This means boatyards and houseboats moored along the banks of a canal.

Tinned meats are an excellent bait for barbel, chub and large coarse fish. For groundbaiting, add a cereal.

To use meat on its own as a groundbait would obviously cost a fortune. The solution is to use a little, and to eke it out with cereal bait to give bulk, then to add, where it is possible to obtain it, some blood to spread scent over the area. An alternative, especially with sausage meat, is to roll a large supply of very small balls that can, if necessary, be catapulted into a distant swim.

Fish that accept meat baits generally do so with a bang, and the angler should always be prepared for the bite. Rods left in rests are in danger of being pulled onto the bank, and floats left unwatched can lose the angler fish after fish. By far the best way of using meat in all of its forms is with the ledger, and the rod should be hand held, with one rest only giving support along the upper third of the rod itself. Once the tip bounces, then the strike should be immediate.

John Wilson

Wasp grubs

G. E. Hyde

For float fishing in clear, fairly fast-flowing river water, there are few deadlier hookbaits than wasp grub. From late August onwards sport is often hectic and bites so positive they are hard to miss.

So effective has the bait proved to be that its use is banned in many contests. It is even barred completely on some controlled waters, so always check before using it.

Fishing the bait is simple, finding it a bit more difficult. A lot of anglers are just too lazy to take time to go out and collect this quite remarkable bait, and you will need at least three nests for a good day's fishing. Even so, wasp nests are more prevalent than most people think.

Where there's muck there's wasps
Wasps are not the most clinically particular creatures. Where there is muck, there you will find wasps. Strange as it may seem, there are more wasp colonies per acre in towns than in country. The author has collected, in one evening, as many as ten nests from city parks, commons and gardens.

Evening is usually the best time for wasp spotting. To find a nest, pick a likely area of waste land, banks or hedges, then watch. If you see a wasp idly meandering, stopping here and there, ignore it. If you see one flying straight and with purpose, mark mentally the direction of its flight path; the nest is rarely more than 100 yards away.

Another wasp will soon come along the flight line. Follow it fast, and as far as you can. It may beat you, but the next will probably lead you to the nest entrance. This is usually underground but rarely deep down. Found in soft earth, often under a hedge or bush, nests are round or oval in shape and made up of layers closely resembling papier mâché.

The next problem is in removing the nest while avoiding painful stings. Reassuringly, a wasp sting is not as dangerous as that of the honey bee which carries a venom akin to that of a cobra. The danger in a wasp sting comes usually from the bacteria injected at the same time–so take care!

117

Wasp Grubs

Although cyanide-based insecticide compounds are on the market (Cymag is the most efficient), their general use cannot be recommended. Unless stored and used correctly, they can be dangerous (you will have to sign a poison register to obtain them) and safer proprietary insecticides are preferable, although not so effective as Cymag.

Beware—Cyanide Fumes

Whether you use a cyanide-based mixture or another type, it should be applied using a large tablespoon tied firmly to a 3ft stick. Put one spoonful as far into the nest entrance as possible and make quite sure that you are upwind of the nest so that noxious fumes blow *away* from you. Another spoonful is sprinkled around the entrance. All this is best done in the early evening when the wasps have returned home. Next, block the entrance with a clod of earth and wait for at least two hours, preferably overnight.

The nest should be removed as carefully as possible, since every bit of it can be used by the angler. Dig round the nest, scraping away all loose earth and lift it whole.

In comparison to the maggot, wasp grubs are big, creamy and soft. The biggest and plumpest were destined to be queen wasps; they also make the best hookbaits. Remove and lay aside all you want for this purpose

(Above) Plenty of big-fish bait in this wood-wasp nest, Stamford Spinney, Devon. (Below) Ray Forsberg extracting grubs from a piece of wasp-nest 'cake'. The cake helps make a useful attractor groundbait.

Ray Forsberg

118

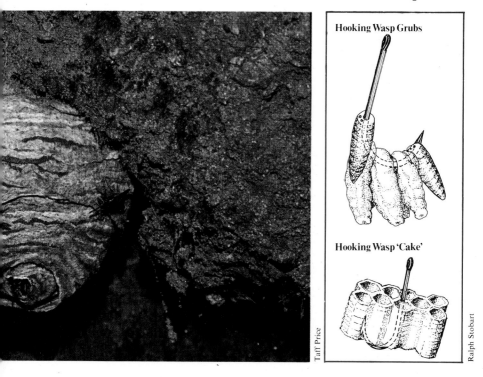

Hooking Wasp Grubs

Hooking Wasp 'Cake'

Taff Price

Ralph Stobart

from their tube-like homes in the nest centre.

The smaller grubs and any damaged ones are then scalded, along with the nest of 'cake', for use as the attractor groundbait. This can be used mixed with breadcrumbs or on its own. It is also worth trying as hookbait once in a while.

Champion wins on wasp grub

Wasp grubs are best used with float tackle of the kind suited to fishing bread flake. Bob Morris became Severn Champion using wasp grub bait to take a record 55lb of chub from the breamy lower end of that river. His tip was to put a piece of bread flake on the hook every half dozen casts or so. This often tempts the bigger chub which tend to lie at the rear of the shoal.

Now and then it is necessary to fish wasp grubs hard on the river bed. Most fish take 'on the drop'. There is no mistaking the bite, particularly with chub. With a size 10 or 12 barbless hook, all that is needed is to tighten line quickly–and your fish is on.

Apart from the Severn Championship

win, wasp grub has accounted for a record-breaking Trent Championship victory. It will tempt most species. Single grubs on the hook will lure roach, and at least one carp of over 20lb has fallen to a ledgered grub.

As soon as a tinge of colour creeps in to cloud the water, sport comes to a halt. The reason for this is not yet fully understood. Possibly the suspended sediment causing the coloration dulls either the fishes' senses or that peculiar flavour that makes wasp grub so irresistible to them.

There are other successful grub baits, too. Dock, or docken, grubs, which grow large and live long, are excellent baits for roach, chub, dace and grayling. Barbel have been caught from the Severn with these, as they have with caddis, the larvae of the sedge fly, and with meal worms.

Most caterpillars make great grayling baits, and if you are not squeamish, wood-lice, earwigs and most bankside beetles will catch fish. It pays to try, and the unusual often gets results.

Silkweed

Ken Whitehead

(*Above*) *The ideal silkweed fishing gear.*
(*Left*) *Always keep silkweed moist. Once
dry it is useless as a bait.*
(*Right*) *Shrimp and (far right) diatoms
live in the silkweed and are eaten by
fish and fish fry.*

From June to October weir structures,
bridge supports, lock gates, posts and piles
which support the river banks are covered
below the water line with thick green bands
of silkweed. Hidden within the weed is a
mass of minute animal life that provides an
abundance of food for fish and can provide
the angler with one of the best natural baits
available. From August onwards, roach,
dace and chub graze or feed on the weed,
browsing like cattle when the water is quiet,
or lying in the weirpools to take small
particles of weed as it is dislodged and
worked downstream by the current.

Origins of silkweed fishing

Silkweed fishing has a style and method
that originated in the Thames weirpools.
Acceptance of silkweed as a bait, at least
on the part of the fish, is not, however,
confined to the Thames, and any weirpool
throughout the country is worth trying in the
warmer months.

Collecting silkweed to use as a hookbait requires care. Pulling tufts by hand

from the weir surrounds will crush all
animal life that it contains. It is better to
rub a patch free with the handle of a landing
net or bankstick, then scoop it into a large
plastic bait box that is half-filled with water.
Do not place a lid on the box—on a warm
day it will cook and spoil the weed.

How to use silkweed

Baiting is accomplished by pulling the
hook through the ball of weed within the
bait box, then folding the weed round the
hook several times to form a sizeable clump
before pushing the hook through again. It
has been suggested that the hook can be
baited by pulling it through growing weed
on the lasher of the weir. Certainly it is a
quick method, but also one guaranteed to
take the edge off the hook within seconds.

The ideal tackle for silkweeding is a
long 11-12ft rod with a free running
centrepin reel loaded with line of 3lb b.s.
Selecting a suitable float needs thought.
Anything with a fine stem cannot be seen in
the swirl of water and froth of a weir pool

and a float needing very few shot is unlikely to get the bait down below the surface. Suitable floats are big-topped celluloid ones, or round corks coloured bright red that are usually associated with minnow fishing. Clumsy though these floats seem, they are not required to register a bite in the accepted sense of the term but merely to allow the angler to see where his bait is.

Find your fish

The depth at which fish are feeding on weed is usually 2-3ft below the surface, but bright sunlight or water temperatures that are lower than normal will send the fish down to the 5 or 6ft mark. When fish appear not to be feeding or suddenly go off the silkweed, experiment by trial and error

over a range of depths until the fish are located again.

A spin-off from silkweed is often over-looked. It is a natural hiding and feeding place for small fish fry, a fact known to every predatory fish in the river. It is well worth spinning any area alongside weed-covered marks, either with a small leaf-type spinner or a shallow diving plug—a trick that any Thames trout fishing enthusiast will confirm.

Standing on the weir

Where the angler should stand when fishing depends largely on the construction of the weir. Traditionally the Thames angler stands on the apron or sill (the concrete stretch which the water hits after

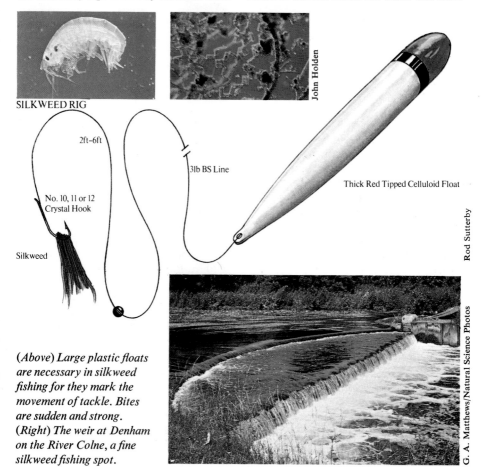

SILKWEED RIG

2ft–6ft

3lb BS Line

No. 10, 11 or 12 Crystal Hook

Silkweed

Thick Red Tipped Celluloid Float

John Holden

Rod Sutterby

G. A. Matthews/Natural Science Photos

(*Above*) *Large plastic floats are necessary in silkweed fishing for they mark the movement of tackle. Bites are sudden and strong.*
(*Right*) *The weir at Denham on the River Colne, a fine silkweed fishing spot.*

spilling over the gates) and drops his float at his feet, allowing it to run downstream. This method is simple, but it does have some disadvantages.

Importance of waders

First, water flows over the apron, making wellingtons or waders a necessity. The apron will be covered in weed, making it as slippery as an ice-rink. One false step and the angler goes into the pool below, with little chance of recovery once his wellingtons are full of water. They act as anchors. So thigh-length waders are preferable, for they tend to hold pockets of air. It does not support the body of the angler, but does show where he is.

Another disadvantage for the angler standing on the sill is that he is visible to the fish below and silhouetted against the sky. A better position, and a safer one, is at the side of the weir, where the current is still within easy casting distance, and also where there is usually a dry patch to stand on.

Keep a tight line

Following the cast, all line between the rod tip and float should be kept as tight as possible, with the rod kept at an angle of 45 degrees. Feed line out slowly, keeping the float in check, and be prepared for bites which will be felt, not seen, against the rod tip. The thumb can be clamped against the reel in a split second and the hook driven home.

Landing fish in a weirpool can present difficulties, more so when the angler is sited well above the water level. Use a net with a very long handle, and fix a stone or ledger weight into the mesh at the bottom. This prevents it being turned inside out when dipped into the running water below.

An angler silkweed fishing on the River Lea at Kingsweir, near Broxbourne, Herts. His position is just right for casting into the swirls and eddies under the sill. The large red tip of the plastic float can be seen bobbing in the foam. He is standing firmly on dry rock without fear of a sudden slip into the water.

Float fishing

The waggler

The large antenna float—the waggler—seems to be the float most abused by lazy .anglers. Certainly, in the past two or three years, it has been responsible for winning a lot of matches. Yet is this because it is the most effective float, or because it is being used when it shouldn't be?

This is not so contradictory as it sounds. People are winning matches with the waggler, but with other floats, such as a stick, they would have won with even more fish. And while a waggler is comparatively easy to fish, it will not enable the angler to get the best out of every swim.

The reason for this is simple. The waggler does not allow the same degree of control over the presentation of the bait as a double-rubbered float. When it is being properly used it is fished attached by its bottom end only and has a lot of tip showing above the water. This is because it is fished with a shot dragging the bottom and the float must not be sensitive enough to be dragged under.

(Above) Peter Burton using an extending landing net to bring in a fish caught on the very popular waggler float.
(Right) Shot pattern for the waggler.

Float fishing is probably the most popular form of coarse fishing. There are a great number of different types of float and methods of float fishing, but all too many anglers, having found that one tactic and one float work reasonably well, stick to this without considering other methods. Rather than just settling for the most convenient method, the angler should try to achieve the best possible presentation of the bait in each situation. He should go for the most effective method. This might not be the easiest, but it is the angler with the techniques and ability to do this who will more often than not catch the most fish.

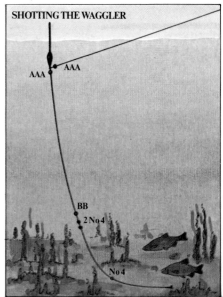

SHOTTING THE WAGGLER

AAA AAA

BB
2 No 4

No 4

Shotting the balsa is important and must be carefully balanced. The tell-tale's weight depends on strength of current.

Even so, despite its size, try to hold it back against the water flow, so that the bait is presented in a slow, attractive manner, and what happens? It just drags under because of the effect of the line between rod tip and float—unless you have achieved a degree of expertise and control of the float possessed by very few anglers. By contrast, a stick or balsa, fished double-rubber, can be held in the stream so that the bait just trickles along.

All this is not to say that the waggler cannot be a very useful float in certain circumstances. In difficult conditions, rough water and a fierce downstream wind, for example, or when the fish are biting freely three or four rod-lengths out—when it has the edge in speed—it can be ideal. In other circumstances, on rivers such as the Ribble, which has an uneven flow, other floats are more successful. Here, use an Avon, or balsa fished double-rubber.

The Avon balsa

The size of the balsa is important. It must be big enough to carry sufficient weight to allow you to pull back on the rod without it dragging into the bank too quickly—a float which can carry about two or three swan shot serves the purpose. Shotting is simple: all you need is a small shot, say a No.4 (directly under the float to stop it sliding down the line under the pressure of striking), the bulk shot roughly halfway between the float and the hook, and the tell-tale which goes 1ft to 18in from the hook. The purpose of the tell-tale shot here is to regulate the presentation of the bait. The size of the tell-tale will depend on the strength of the flow.

The method with this rig is to cast out to the area you wish to fish—with this rig the under-arm cast is a must if tangles are to be avoided—and then to mend the line—that is to lift the line and swing it upstream if it threatens to put drag on the float and bait—until the float settles. Then lift the rod-tip high in the air so that the line goes directly to

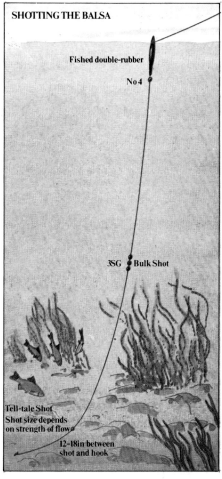

SHOTTING THE BALSA

Fished double-rubber

No 4

3SG — Bulk Shot

Tell-tale Shot
Shot size depends on strength of flow

12-18in between shot and hook

Rod Sutterby

the float tip without touching the water.

If you choose a float with plenty of bulk and weight-carrying capacity, it will strip line from the reel at the pace you dictate and carry on the current far more smoothly than a waggler. Furthermore, if you check the line on the rim of the spool with your fingertip, you can slow the float right down or even momentarily stop it—something you can't do with a waggler.

There's no doubt that this pays off. If you have studied the swim properly, you should know what part of it is most likely to produce a fish; you can then slow up the float when it is approaching the area, relaxing again when it has passed on downstream.

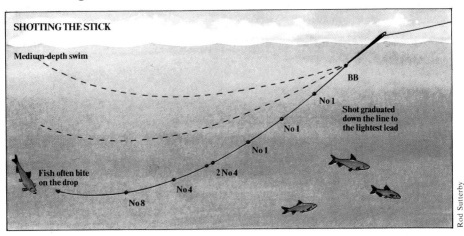

SHOTTING THE STICK

Medium-depth swim

BB

No 1

Shot graduated
down the line to
the lightest lead

No 1

No 1

Fish often bite
on the drop

2 No 4

No 4

No 8

Rod Sutterby

Big stick floats

Big stick floats are another useful tool
ignored by many anglers nowadays. With
wind blowing upstream and out from the
bank, the big stick is probably easier to
handle than a waggler. This is because the
effect of the wind on the line when the float is
being fished double-rubber slows down the
bait without any effort from the angler.
Again, underarm casting is essential.

Another 'old-fashioned' method of fishing
which receives too little attention nowadays
is stret-pegging. It has largely been aban-

*The shotting pattern for big stick floats is a
steady graduation from the top down. A BB
stops the float running down the line on the
strike. No. 8 is the lightest.*

doned in favour of swingtip rods and there is
little doubt that when the bait is wanted hard
on the bottom in the middle of a river it is by
far the best solution. Nevertheless, if the fish
are closer in, then stret-pegging is deadly,
particularly if the river is carrying a lot of
water. In fact, in flood conditions, it is as
likely a method as any to pick up a fish.

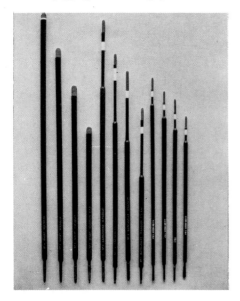

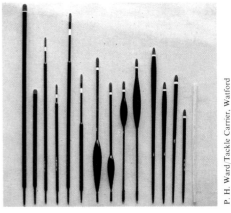

P. H. Ward/Tackle Carrier, Watford

*(Above) Wagglers, Avons and reversed
Avons with some stick floats. On the right
is a 6in peacock quill, which should be
fished double-rubber for stret-pegging.*

S. L. Ward/Natural Science Photos

Stret-pegging

When stret-pegging, the float—a peacock is ideal—is fished double-rubber, over-depth and over-shotted. Basically, this means that the line between float and hook should be about twice as long as the water is deep and should carry roughly double the amount of shot the float can support. For example, if you have a 6in length of peacock quill capable of carrying half a dozen BB shot, load it up with 12 BB, concentrated around 6in from the hook and if the water is 4ft deep, set the float at 8ft. The bait then bobs around in the current just off the bottom, while the line stretches at an angle of 45° from the float to the weight at the bottom.

The technique is basically simple. Just cast out and allow the tip to pull round. But although this sounds simple, it is not that

(Top) One method of slowing the tackle is to use the thumb on the reel drum.
(Above) Another way of controlling the line is by running it over the forefinger.

easy. The line must be held tight between float and rod tip and the float literally held up—otherwise, being heavily over-shotted, it just dives to the bottom. However, if used properly, you'll be surprised at just how positive the bites are.

If the fish are not biting, try varying the presentation of the bait by slightly lifting the rod and 'inching' the business end of the rig across the bottom. This diversion will often take a 'bonus' fish.

A stillwater alternative to ledgering is the lift method of float fishing for which, conveniently, you can use the same piece of

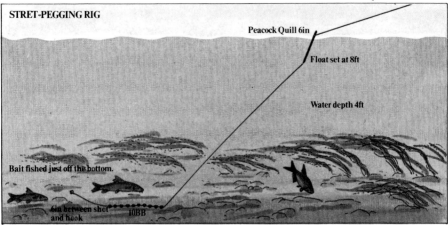

STRET-PEGGING RIG

Peacock Quill 6in

Float set at 8ft

Water depth 4ft

Bait fished just off the bottom.

6in between shot and hook   10BB

Rod Sutterby

peacock as for stret-pegging. But instead of a bunch of small shot, use one big one, say a swan, although once again the rig is fished over-shotted, and over-depth as with stret-pegging. The difference is that the float is fished peg-leg—that is attached by its bottom end only. Furthermore, unlike stret-pegging, the hook should be very near to the shot, say, only two or three inches away.

With the lift method, cast out to your swim, and allow the shot to hit bottom. The float will, of course, lie flat. Then gently tighten the line until the float cocks and is dotted down—that is, it has only the smallest amount possible showing. When a fish picks the bait off the bottom—this method is particularly effective for tench—the result is the most dramatic bite in fishing. To swallow the bait, the fish must also pick up the shot and the float pops up like a Jack-in-the-box!

Stret-pegging, sometimes the only way to fish fast-flowing rivers successfully. A typical river is the fast, weedy Avon.

Curiously enough, the big shot does not seem to put off the fish—although obviously the method can be scaled down using, say, a reversed crowquill or an even more sensitive pheasant-tail quill.

S. L. Ward/Natural Science Photos

(Above) Be careful not to miss out any rod rings when tackling up. This can lead to difficult casting when the line becomes wet.
(Left) When putting the rod sections together, starting with the top, make sure that the rod rings are ranged in a straight line. If not, the line is slowed during the cast.

John Wilson

129

Ledgering

Once, ledgering was considered a crude and clumsy way of fishing, only resorted to when float fishing had failed to catch fish. Now, ledgering has a separate and valued status as a means of fishing, and the varied styles and techniques have led to the capture of many large fish.

Basically the method presents the bait on the bottom of a lake, reservoir, stream or river where coarse species such as bream, barbel, carp and tench normally feed.

The short, stiff and insensitive rod once used for ledgering was poor for detecting bites. Now, needlessly heavy tackle has been replaced gradually by more suitable and effective equipment. Today purpose-built ledgering rods are available which incorporate a fine tip to greatly improve bite detection. Heavy leads, often of the 'coffin' variety, have given way to lighter weights

which are designed to lessen resistance of the tackle felt by biting fish. A nylon monofilament line of 5-6lb b.s. is suitable for most freshwater ledgering.

Ledgering has some distinct advantages over float fishing techniques. First, waters deeper than the rod-length can be bottom-fished. Second, there is the advantage that the weight of a ledger rig allows long casts so that a greater area, or swims inaccessible to float tackle, can be fished.

Anchored bait

Also important is the fact that the bait is anchored (unless intentionally allowed to drift slowly) in the spot the angler wishes to fish. This is not possible with float tackle in a current. The bait stays on the bottom, where it will be most effective and appears more natural than one suspended in mid-water beneath a float. Ledger tackle, furthermore,

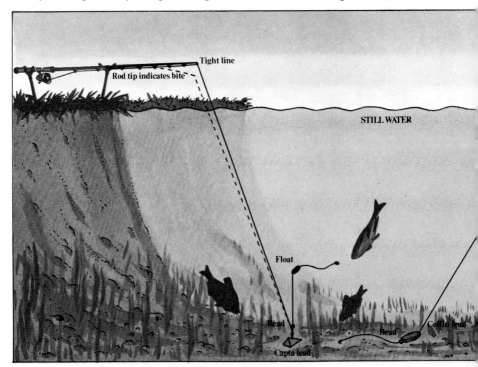

Tight line

Rod tip indicates bite

STILL WATER

Float

Bead

Bead

Coffin lead

Capta lead

(*Above*) *Two methods of ledgering, one with a swing-tip, the other keeping the rod-tip under the surface. (Left) Stillwater ledgering. Two methods of anchored bait.*

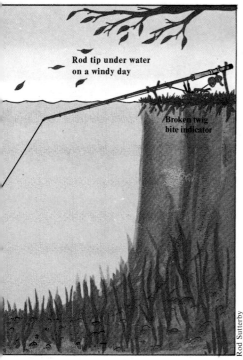

Rod tip under water on a windy day

Broken twig bite indicator

Rod Sutterby

Bill Howes

is not so obtrusive as the float silhouetted on the surface, which can easily frighten off fish. Lastly, ledgering allows night fishing, which is impractical with a float.

Leads

Rigs for ledgering vary, usually according to water conditions. A fast river will require a heavy lead if the bait is to be anchored and the same weight will be useful where a long cast, on river or lake, is required. A lighter lead will provide sufficient weight to take the bait to the bottom and keep it there in stillwater or in a slow current. For many years the most commonly used leads were the 'coffin' and the 'bullet'—a lead sphere with a hole through which the line passes. The weight lies on the bottom and the line can be pulled through it by a fish taking the bait. In this way, the fish does not feel the

131

resistance from the tackle—in contrast to float fishing—but only from the rod tip. A compromise is a lead of the 'Arlesey Bomb' kind devised by Richard Walker. The line passes through a swivel at the top of this pear-shaped lead and less resistance is transmitted to the fish. The 'Capta' lead performs similarly but is preferable for use when the bait is to be anchored rather than rolled by the current or slope of the bed.

Link-ledgering

The technique known as link-ledgering has become increasingly popular in recent years. For this, a short, lead-shotted trace is attached at right-angles to the reel line by a free-running swivel. This rig combines the advantage of reduced resistance with that of allowing the bait to 'roll' with the current or by flexing the rod tip. In link-ledgering, as with all ledgering styles, a stop must be attached to the line—usually 2-3ft above the hook—to prevent the ledger from running down on to it, thus producing a bait that is unnaturally heavy and, of course, appears strange to the fish. A split shot is commonly used, but care must be taken to pinch it immovably on to the reel line. This can weaken the line, and some anglers prefer, especially with a link-ledger rig, to insert a split ring or a swivel to keep the weight the required distance from the baited hook.

To ledger in stillwater, cast out the tackle and give it time to sink. The line is then tightened, without dragging the ledger off the bottom, and the rod laid horizontally on twin rod rests. Bites will be indicated by the movement of the rod tip or line or by the action of one of a number of kinds of bite indicator.

In river fishing, where the pull of the current can make it difficult to detect a bite, it is advisable to hold the rod and so be prepared to strike quickly. The rod can be supported on one knee and the line held between thumb and forefinger so that a bite can be felt. The tip of the rod must be sensitive, so that it trembles to indicate a bite. With practice, a take by a fish will be distinguished from the natural movement of the tackle with the current. The tackle can be cast into one spot and anchored there, but it usually pays to cover a larger area,

(Right) Simplest of all ledger rigs: two swan-shot on a short nylon leader.
(Below) Moving-water ledgering and two methods which are successful. The rolling ledger (bottom left) shows the effect of current.

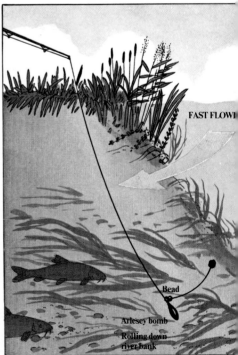

FAST FLOW

Bead

Arlesey bomb

Rolling down river bank

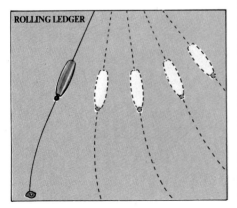

ROLLING LEDGER

particularly if the water if unfamiliar, by allowing a light rig such as a link-ledger to drift across the bed. Cast down and across stream and cover a stretch of river with repeated arcs, progressively moving downstream.

Upstream ledgering is less often practised, but seems to have good results with barbel. Striking is more difficult as the fish, having taken the bait, will run downstream, towards the angler. This means that a slackening in the line will indicate a take. In order to connect, the strike must be calculated to take up the slack as well as driving the hook home.

The question of bite detection is of prime importance in ledgering. There are various methods of detecting a fish. First, the rod tip acts as an indicator. Alternatively, greater sensitivity can be gained by the use of the swing-tip or the quiver-tip, both of which are available in various patterns.

Bite indicators

For ledgering in stillwater these tips may be used, but other indicators are equally useful. The simplest consists of a ball of bread paste hung on a 'v' of the line between reel and butt ring. This will twitch noticeably with a bite. A metal bite indicator can be purchased (or improvised). This consists of a straight length of metal strip attached to 2in of rubber, or sometimes a spring, and clipped to the rod butt. The line runs through some models; others are attached to the line after casting. After tightening the line the indicator is allowed to hang down, as with the swing-tip. A bite will cause this very sensitive mechanism to move. Electric bite indicators can be bought. These are used for night fishing but their use is regarded by some as unsporting.

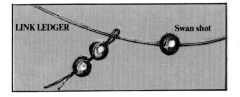

LINK LEDGER   Swan shot

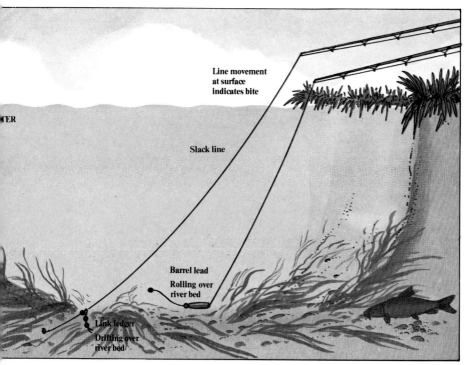

Line movement at surface indicates bite

Slack line

TER

Barrel lead
Rolling over river bed

Link ledger
Drifting over river bed

Pole fishing

Up until the 1960s, the finest in bamboo, brass-ended poles were produced by Sowerbutts and had been since as far back as 1815. These superbly crafted poles were made to order in the traditional way. Selected white tonkin cane was carefully cleaned and cut. Small distortions were straightened by heating the cane gently over a soft flame and mending against the bench side. When the whole rod, which was usually 18-22ft in length was aligned, heavy brass ferrules and butt caps were added and hundreds of yards of best silk whipped around the nodes before several coats of copal varnish were applied and the pole was ready.

After World War II other companies began to import low-quality poles superficially resembling the Sowerbutts original in the form of cheap Japanese and Brazilian ready-shaped canes which were whipped at the ends, as opposed to fitted brass ferrules. Usually available in lengths up to 18ft these bamboo cheapies were poor substitutes compared to Sowerbutts beauties, but their price at least allowed youngsters to become equipped and get interested in the delights of pole fishing.

From cane to glass fibre

The transition from cane to fibre-glass poles took place through the growing demands of match fishermen. For several years the sport had been growing in popularity and by the 1970s many matchmen were looking to the continental angler whose techniques with the pole were far in advance of those in this country. With its fixed line providing superior float control at close range and instant strike 'fish whipping' could take the prize money time after time.

The name roach pole suggests that a pole can be used only for catching small fish. This is a misconception. Used properly a pole can also handle big fish such as tench, bream, chub and barbel – even modest-sized carp,

Mansell Collection

once the top sections have been converted with an elastic kit.

Which pole?
Poles generally fit into three categories. Hollow glass telescopic cheapies; telescopic carbon whips (some have put-over joints) and long 8-16 metre high-performance carbon-fibre poles which consist of several put-over joints plus two or three telescopic top joints.

Hollow glass, telescopic poles are available in lengths from 3-7 metres and are ideal for youngsters and anyone starting out pole fishing on a tight budget. Most come complete with a tiny ring glued on to the top joint to which the line of the pole rig is then attached.

(Left) A 10-metre carbon pole supported on the angler's knee. (Below) The original bamboo pole by Sowerbutts. (Right) A fibreglass pole.

Telescopic carbon-fibre whips are also available in 3-7 metres (top-quality whips have put-over joints in the lower sections) and for their length they are incredibly light and sensitive. Whips are generally used for 'speed fishing' 'to hand' and due to their lightness supported along the forearm and held just like a rod with the terminal rig line, identical in length to the number of joints being used.

Fish can then be swung in straight to the unhooking hand. Thus the term 'to hand'. Though whips are generally no longer than 6 metres, due to the nature of the way they are held (the forearm can only support so much length of pole) certain manufacturers nevertheless offer one or even two extension

John Wilson

Bill Howes

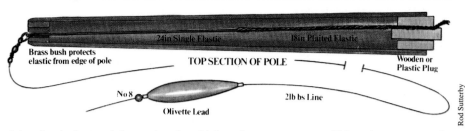

Brass bush protects
elastic from edge of pole

24in Single Elastic

18in Plaited Elastic

TOP SECTION OF POLE

Wooden or
Plastic Plug

No 8

Olivette Lead

2lb bs Line

Rod Sutterby

joints for the butt end, increasing the whip's length to 7 or even 8 metres.

It will be noticed that pole terminology is in metres rather than feet, due to the dominating continental influence upon this style of fishing. Because whips have super-fine, often spliced in carbon tips (referred to as a flick tip) an elastic shock absorber is unnecessary, whether short lining using just 3 or 4m rigs with punched bread or squats etc for tiny fish or fishing the full size of up to say 7metres and swinging in 4oz roach or skimmer bream to hand.

High-performance poles consist of 10 or more sections and can measure 14 metres in length (increasing to 16 metres with extra butt and extra-long top kit) and are manufactured from the highest grade of reinforced carbon for strength and rigidity. Top-of-the-range, state-of-the-art models, can actually cost more than the price of a reliable secondhand car, so great care must be taken in selecting a suitable pole. In fact the newcomer would be wise to start at the shorter end of the scale and choose an affordable pole of around 9 metres. Such a pole should comprise mostly of easy-to-slide, put-over joints and a telescopic 2 or 3-joint top section. In addition to the standard flick-tip some manufacturers include a second complete 2 or 3-joint elasticated top section within the price of their long poles, enabling the angler to have an elasticated 'second rig' ready and waiting with an 'alternative float rig' set up.

Attaching elastic

At one time the shepherd's crook made from tubular alloy was an extremely popular way of attaching elastic to the pole tip. The top or second (depending upon their diameter) joint was simply cut back with a fine-tooth hacksaw to the same diameter as that of the crook. The crook was then glued or pushed firmly on and the elastic formed into a loop which fitted into the crook's end slot and secured with a plastic sleeve sliding over the end.

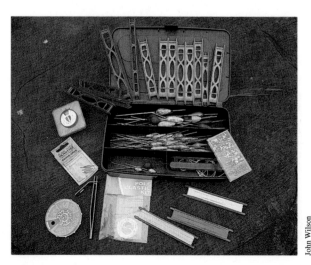

(Above) The action end of a modern pole. From primitive beginnings it has developed into an effective, sensitive angling unit.
(Left) A selection of pole winders, floats, rubbers, weights and elastic.
(Above right) A selection of pole floats and ready made rigs on winders.
(Right) A float rig for pole fishing.
(Far right) The cross-over hand method of unshipping pole sections.

John Wilson

John Wilson

Fitting internal elastic is now considered superior and is easy to achieve. Using a fine-tooth hacksaw the tip or second joint is cut back to accept a PTFE bush through which the elastic will run. It is possible to buy bushes which fit 'internally' or 'fit over' the cut-back pole joint. Into the bush fits a rig connector to which the elastic is tied. The elastic is in fact threaded down through the reduced tip and joined to a coned uni-bung (elastic kits to fit any pole are available at all tackle shops), the wide-end of which can be reduced in diameter to fit neatly several inches up inside the second top section, leaving a tail of fine plastic protruding. To pull the bung out again for a change of elastic you simply pull on the end of the tail.

Applying a few drops of elastic lubricant ensures the elastic will run effortlessly back and forwards through the PTFE bush, permitting even large fish eventually to be played to a standstill on super-light tackle and tiny hooks. And it is all due to that 'buffer' provided by the elastic, which is available in several thicknesses and strengths to suit the task at hand.

Fishing the pole

Holding a long pole of say 8 metres and over is most comfortable when the butt is saddled across your right knee (if right-handed) and cupped steadily in front with your left hand. The butt end should be held tightly in your right hand. To strike, don't attempt to heave the pole upwards, simply turn the right-hand clockwise and the pole will lift sufficiently across your knee for the hook to be set. There should always be a tight line from float tip to pole tip.

Alternatively, stick the butt end into and against your crotch and seat top (a seat box rather than a soft-topped chair) and support the pole at arm's length with your right (or strongest) hand or both hands. The latter method is a rather tiring technique but maximizes on the pole's effective length (as opposed to losing 2ft when held by the former method) and is particularly useful for presentation in extremely deep water.

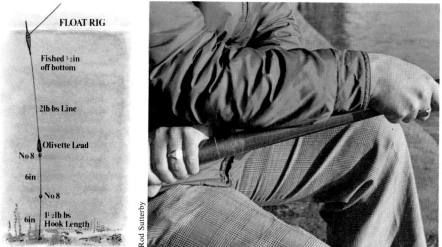

FLOAT RIG

Fished ¹⁄₂in off bottom

2lb bs Line

Olivette Lead

No 8

6in

No 8

6in — 1¹⁄₂lb bs Hook Length

Rod Sutterby

Derrick Jones

137

Pole fishing

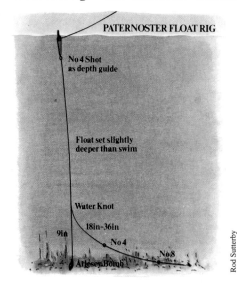

PATERNOSTER FLOAT RIG

No 4 Shot
as depth guide

Float set slightly
deeper than swim

Water Knot

18in-36in
9in
No 4
No 8
Arlesey Bomb

Rod Sutterby

(Above) A pole-fishing ledger rig.
(Right) Fitting the elastic loop into the slot
of the crook-tip. When in position, the
plastic sleeve is pulled over it.

Many pole experts manage to hold the pole (light models only) with both hands close together, resting the butt over their right (if right-handed) thigh and can fish for many hours in this way, particularly in calm conditions. But at the end of the day it is all down to personal preference and unless standing to fish when the pole butt is steadied in the crotch, one of the most important factors is fishing from a steady and level seat box. This is why platforms with adjustable legs are so popular with pole exponents.

When bites are few and far between a simple pole-rest system of a shepherd's crook and front U screwed on to the right-hand side of your seat box will prove invaluable. End tackles or rigs as they are more commonly called are carried ready made up on plastic winders to save time and troublesome fiddle on the bankside, something that would be a considerable problem when one appreciates that hook lengths down to just 8oz may be used along with hooks down to a minute size 26.

In order to avoid confusion with various hook and line sizes, tackle winders can be purchased in varying colours so that a code may be devised by the individual, allowing him to select or replace end tackle of equal balance immediately.

The rod tip is the vital part of the pole and it should follow the float and remain directly above it, otherwise the strike will be delayed fractionally by slack line just as it is when using a float rod, and this could mean the difference between a hooked or missed fish. Once a fish is hooked the rod point should

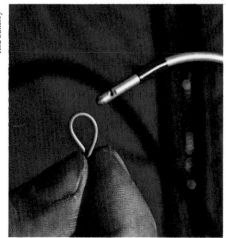

Derrick Jones

follow and be kept immediately above it. You will quickly get used to the fact that there is no reel and learn to use the stretch of the elastic instead of the slipping clutch of a reel.

Unless fishing 'to hand' with the same amount of line out as the pole's length it is imperative to shorten the pole so it is roughly the same length as your rig length. This is known as shipping and is easily done by pushing the pole back behind you (a roller rest is invaluable here) until it is a length commensurate with that of the rig. Then you need only to ship it (take it apart) at one junction instead of several. After unhooking the fish or rebaiting the pole is reconnected, pushed out, and the rig swung out into the swim.

Groundbaiting

Bill Howes

(*Above*) *In match-fishing groundbaiting is essential if the fish are to be held in the swim.*
(*Right*) *Groundbait is cast upstream, to break up and settle near the hookbait.*

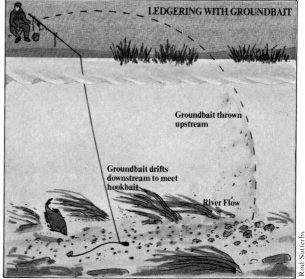

LEDGERING WITH GROUNDBAIT

Groundbait thrown upstream

Groundbait drifts downstream to meet hookbait

River Flow

Rod Sutterby

Groundbaiting is carried out to attract fish into a swim and set them feeding. There are various methods of groundbaiting, depending mainly upon the type of water, the rate of flow, and the species of fish sought.

Groundbaiting in fresh water

Groundbaiting with a heavy mixture which drops to the bottom fast is needed at times, but once there it should break up quickly. In fast-flowing water, when barbel or bream are the quarry, a ball of groundbait which sinks quickly is thrown in slightly upstream so that when it hits the bottom and breaks up, the particles drift along the bottom and through the swim. Bream usually swim in large shoals, feeding on the bottom, and large amounts of groundbait are often needed to concentrate the shoal in the swim. A large bucketful of groundbait is generally the minimum required for a day's fishing.

Baiting up a swim several days in advance can pay dividends, particularly when bream, tench or carp are sought. This can draw a big shoal of bream into the swim and hold them there until fishing starts, even though their usual tendency is to be on the move.

A ball of groundbait can be used to land a quantity of loose maggots on the bed of a deep swim. In strong-flowing water, such as a weir stream, bank clay can be worked into the mixture for this purpose. It is then moulded in the shape of a cup, the cavity filled with maggots, worms or another bait, and the top closed over. A strong flow, coupled with the action of the wriggling bait, will soon break up the balls, sending the hookbait samples trickling along the bottom to bring fish close.

Groundbaiting from a boat

When fishing from a boat, groundbait can be dropped over the side or lowered to the bottom in a meshed bag weighted with stones. An occasional tug on a cord attached to the bag will release and circulate particles of the groundbait into the swim.

When ledgering, it is essential to get the groundbait in the right place, and then to fish the baited hook in the middle of it or as close as possible—on the downstream side.

Groundbaiting is frequently done with the

Groundbaiting

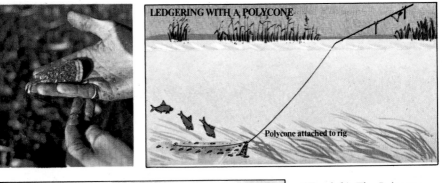

(Top left) The Polycone swimfeeder allows maggots to be placed near the hook.
(Above) The Polycone swimfeeder used as a weight in ledgering.
(Left) Feeding a swim from a boat by the use of a mesh bag or bucket. It can be placed directly upstream.

use of mechanical devices, such as bait-droppers, swim-feeders and catapults. One sure way of landing loose maggots, or other hookbait samples, on the bottom, is to put them there by means of a bait-dropper, of which there are various kinds on the market. The loaded bait-dropper is lowered to the bottom of the swim, when a trip wire opens the lid and releases the contents. The match angler usually starts by putting down several droppers full of hookbait samples. Once the fish move into the swim, the bait-dropper should be used with caution, for it may scare the fish.

Scattering by hand

Bait-droppers are obviously not so useful when fishing on the drop, or if taking fish from under the surface when small fish are relied on to make up the match weight. Scattering bait loosely by hand or by catapult is more effective in that case.

Good catches of fish are often made by using choice maggots as hookbait and groundbaiting with inferior maggots, or feeders as they are known. Feeders are generally used in conjunction with a cloudbait. As one becomes expert in casting with one hand and tossing the feed or attractor in with the other, both hookbait and groundbait will enter the water together. The choice maggots on the hook will sink slowly and enticingly amidst the dissolving cloudbait and the feeders.

Use of the swimfeeder

When ledgering in midstream an effective way of getting maggots down to the bed of the river is to use a gadget known as a swim-feeder. These come in various designs and sizes, but the basic model is a celluloid tube that is attached to the ledger tackle. The open-ended type is packed with maggots, with breadcrumbs as plugs at both ends.

With groundbait plugs the feeder can also be used to concentrate hempseed or casters in the vicinity of the baited hook. The closed or blockend type is filled with maggots only.

After the tackle is cast out it reaches the bottom and the flow of water swings the baited hook to a position downstream of the swim-feeder. From this the maggots will

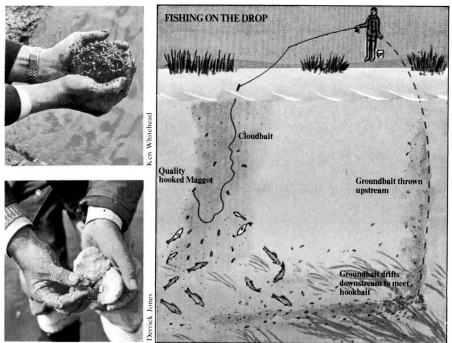

Ken Whitehead

Derrick Jones

Rod Sutterby

FISHING ON THE DROP

Cloudbait

Quality
hooked Maggot

Groundbait thrown
upstream

Groundbait drifts
downstream to meet
hookbait

wriggle out through the holes and in the right place—around the baited hook.

A swim-feeder deposits groundbait exactly where it is needed—but it does not always put enough there. This is why, when ledgering, groundbaiting the swim manually is sometimes employed at the same time as offering the hookbait samples in the swim-feeder.

Care must be exercised when groundbaiting a swim where specimen fish are the quarry. On a river, the introduction of a large quantity of groundbait will invariably attract shoals of small fish, and these can prove a nuisance.

Cloudbaiting

A form of groundbaiting which is effective in many types of waters, particularly for surface and mid-water species, is cloudbaiting. This means clouding the water by introducing minute particles which the fish will search through for more substantial food.

After taking note of the rate of flow of the water, the angler regularly throws small balls

(Top left) Balls of groundbait can be liberally laced with maggots.

(Left) A stone in groundbait aids casting accuracy and distance.

(Above) The use of cloud and groundbait.

of cloudbait into the swim. This is done upstream, so that the cloud drifts down and through the area being fished. The float tackle is cast out immediately after, following the groundbait closely through the swim.

Drip-feeding

For roach, dace and chub fishing on a small, secluded river, regular swim-baiting can be made by the use of a 'drip feed'—a tin with a few holes punched in the bottom, which is filled with maggots and hung from a bridge or overhanging branch. The steady trickle of maggots over a long period will entice fish from some distance into the swim.

As match fishermen know, regular groundbaiting of the swim is very important no matter what hookbait is used. Without it, the angler is fishing on a hit-and-miss basis.

Gravel pit fishing

Most species of coarse fish, including bream, roach, rudd, perch, pike, carp, tench and eel inhabit gravel pits. Chub, barbel, dace and grayling, more commonly river fish, will also be found. But all these species will not be found together and so, before going fishing, it is advisable to find out which fish are present so that suitable tackle can be chosen.

Study the waters

Gravel pits vary considerably in size, shape, depth and character, and to get the best from fishing them concentrate on just one or two of a group at a time. Study the waters, especially the effects of changing conditions on the feeding habits of the fish and the locations of the most populated swims.

A gravel pit rarely has a uniform depth. Instead, the bottom slopes drastically, creating shallows of a few feet and sudden deep holes of 20-30ft, perhaps more. This apparent unpredictability can daunt the angler on his first visit, but observation, a little planning and the right technique can produce good results first time.

The prime gravel pit species, bream, roach, carp and tench (but not rudd), are mid-water or bottom feeders. During the summer and early autumn they tend to feed by night in the shallows and by day in deeper water. Therefore, where possible, fish an area containing shallows and medium depths, with deep water close by. If weedbeds are present, so much the better.

A successful method, which will be explained in greater detail in later issues, is to ledger with a simple open-ended swimfeeder rig. Use this with a sturdy but sensitive 12ft rod, a fixed-spool reel, and a line strength to match water conditions and the size of the prey. A 3lb b.s. line is suitable for sizeable

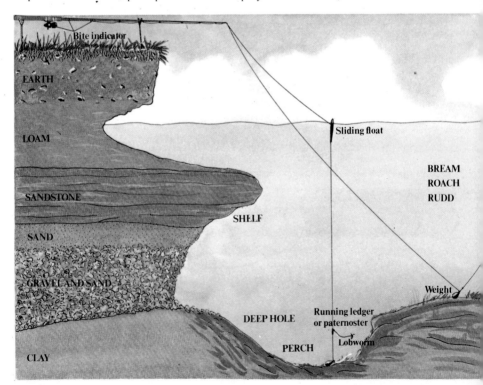

roach and rudd, 5 or 6lb b.s. for average tench and bream, and 8-10lb for shoal carp. Set up the end tackle so that there is an 18in trail between hook and swimfeeder. The latter is held running-ledger style by a plastic-plug stop. Attach an eyed hook securely to the main line. Use front and rear rod-rests and adjust the outfit so that the rod points slightly downwards to the water. A small blob of groundbait hanging on the line between reel and butt ring will serve as a bite indicator. The bale-arm should be closed for roach, rudd, tench and bream, and open for the strong-pulling carp.

The proven bait

Proven baits for this method are maggots (hook size 16-18), bread flake or flake and maggot mix (12-8), and whole or just the tail of lobworm (8-6). Make sure the groundbait in the swimfeeder is soft enough to disintegrate quickly so that after casting out and waiting for a couple of minutes, the swimfeeder can be dragged back some 18in to release samples, among which the baited

hook will settle. The advantages of this technique are that there is no need to check the exact depth fished and that the hook will be close to the groundbait, no matter how far out you cast.

When to groundbait

Throughout most of the day fish the slope leading to the deeper water, groundbaiting occasionally with balls of fine sausage rusk laced with hook-bait samples, and filling the swimfeeder with hook-bait sandwiched between plugs of softish groundbait. From evening until the middle of the night, and again from dawn until midmorning, try moving to medium-depth water. Ground-bait heavily to attract and hold the fish as they head for the shallows during these very

Gravel pits can offer varied and interesting fishing in shallows, medium-depths waters and frequent deep holes. These conditions also account for the variety of species encountered in gravel pits—perch, pike, roach, rudd, carp, tench and bream.

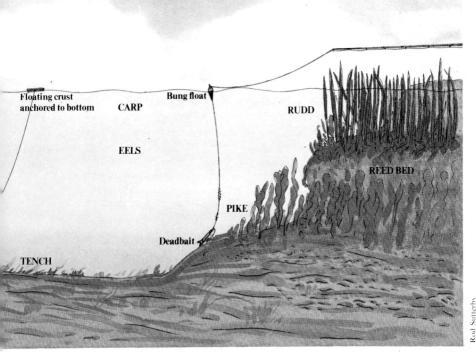

Floating crust anchored to bottom   CARP   Bung float   RUDD

EELS

REED BED

PIKE

Deadbait

TENCH

Gravel pit fishing

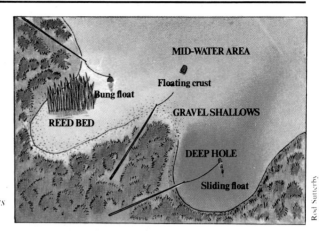

(Right) A typical gravel pit area can include reedy shallows, ledges, gravelly spots, very deep holes and medium-depth fishing. Adjust your angling style to match these different conditions: floating crust over mid-water, sliding float in deep holes, float fishing or ledgering off reedy areas. Be ready always to switch methods.

Rod Sutterby

Robin Fletcher

(Left) Flooded gravel pit at Steeple Langford, Wiltshire. An established water where the banks have been cleared and shored up with the angler in mind. A likely swim is seen at left.
(Right) The irregular contours of this recently flooded Hampshire pit provide numerous vantage points for the fisherman. Trees have been cut back to give access to the water.

important and predictable feeding periods.

How the fish will bite will depend on whether the fish are feeding boldly or just playing with the bait. Tench are notorious for plucking at the bait, causing the indicator to jerk as if a roach or rudd were nibbling. Counter this by jerking back. If the indicator moves up a little pull it back down. A little teasing of this sort often provokes a decisive take from a hesitant fish.

Buoyant baits

The shallows usually contain weed in plenty and large amounts of natural food, and it is in these areas that fish are found at night. Excellent catches can be made in as little as 18in of water. A light ledger or mini-swimfeeder can be used to place the bait on the bottom, but off-bottom techniques also work. For example, a buoyant bait such as a crust cube or a fat lobworm, free-lined or cast on a ledger trail long enough to enable it to float, will catch not only surface feeders like carp and rudd, but also tench, roach and bream who are normally bottom feeders.

Big carp are a popular quarry nowadays. In gravel pits, which are sometimes specially stocked with them, they often reach 20 or 30lb. Carp tackle includes a 10 or 11ft carp rod, line of 8-15lb b.s., and well-sharpened, eyed hooks.

The bait is fished on the bottom—free-lined if heavy enough to cast on its own; ledgered if it is a lightweight particle bait. All the baits so far mentioned will tempt big carp. Parboiled potatoes are another effective bait, and in recent years sweetcorn has proved very successful with carp and other species. Pastes can be concocted from pet-

and roach can still be caught. The two predators, pike and perch, are taken in summer on various baits and with spinners and plugs, but winter fishing will produce the larger specimens.

Ledgered lobworm

Perch gather in deep holes in gravel pits and can be caught on a running ledger or running paternoster rig baited with a whole lobworm. Place the rod on rests, leave the bale-arm open and give a run plenty of time before striking.

For pike, a sturdy purpose-built or carp rod, 10-15lb b.s. line, and a wire trace carrying two or three treble hooks, is standard kit. Good baits are dead roach, small bream, herring and mackerel and can be free-lined on the bottom or, in breezy weather, cast out beneath a sliding float to work across water with the wind. A deadbait, cast far out and retrieved jerkily to simulate the erratic progress of a sick or injured fish, makes an effective bait when searching large areas of varying depth. Pike, like carp, regularly patrol channels and shallow bars through deep water. Such spots are always worth special attention.

Advantage of float-fishing

Float fishing is also widely practised in gravel pits and has some advantages. A sliding float, an antenna or, in windy conditions, a long, wide-bodied float, can be used to search deep water under the bank for tench, bream and roach during the summer months. A float is also helpful when fishing deep water beyond a shelf on which a ledger rig would snag and so reduce bite indications, especially when the fish are shy biters.

Lastly, remember that the steep banks of gravel pits and the deep water immediately beyond them are dangerous places. Watch for crumbling banks, and note them, especially when night fishing. Remember, too, that while you may be enjoying your night's fishing, others may be sleeping. Not only is it bad fishing to create noise and disturbance, it can also lead to ill-feeling between anglers and local residents.

foods and meat products, and artificial high-protein baits can be purchased.

Carp also feed near and at the surface, and can be lured by floating crust. In breezy weather, providing the depth is not too great, a crust can be anchored in position by ledgering it on a trail equal in length to the depth fished.

During the summer and autumn months carp-strength tackle can be used for big eels— a species unjustly neglected in gravel pits, for specimens of over 4lb are often to be caught. Big eels turn up occasionally during the day, but night-time, when they are feeding in the medium depths, offers the best sport. Deadbaiting is the best method to employ for this underestimated, fighting fish.

In winter pike and perch abound. Rudd, tench and eels are less active, but bream, carp

145

Trotting

Trotting, sometimes called 'swimming the stream', is a method of float fishing in flowing water where the float and bait is allowed to travel with the current. The depth at which the bait is fished depends on the species of fish being sought and at what depth it is most likely to feed. Generally, the float and bait are cast slightly upstream of the angler and allowed to travel downstream until the end of the swim is reached. The procedure is then repeated.

When to trot

Trotting is employed when the fish are feeding off the bottom. In summer, for example, both chub and roach feed in midwater or just below the surface and, on occasions, bream feed here as well. Trotting can be successful in winter too. Specialist dace anglers fish this way almost exclusively, while both roach and chub often prefer a moving bait to a stationary one.

Clear or fairly clear waters are more conducive to good sport than coloured waters, especially where they flow fast where the bait, because of reduced visibility, is less likely to be seen by the fish.

Allowing the bait to rise

The manner in which the float and bait are allowed to travel downstream is important. Usually they should move at the same speed as the current but sometimes, when fishing with a stick float and caster, for example, the float should be held back allowing the bait to rise up in the water. This may be done either at the end of the swim or, if it is a long one, several times as it passes through.

In fast shallow water, the angler sometimes wades with the rod pointing downriver. The float, depending upon the whim of the angler (or a bite from a fish), will be checked very slightly as it travels downriver, making the bait rise and fall as it travels through the swim. This method of presenting the bait is especially effective on such waters

S. L. Ward/Natural Science Photos

S. L. Ward Natural Science Photos

(Above) Trotting from midstream demands the landing net and bait must be carried. Peter Ward is playing a dace on the Kennet. (Left) To get a clear run downstream for the terminal tackle, a long rod is necessary when dapping from the bank.

as the Avon and Kennet when barbel and chub are the quarry.

On the Upper Thames, many chub are taken by trotting the opposite bank. For this technique the float is cast well upstream of the angler and retrieved when some 15 yards below him. Bites can be expected at any time. Unlike trotting under one's own bank, or in the centre of the river, when the float starts its run almost opposite the angler, for trotting the far bank the float must begin well upstream of the angler.

Tackle is important and should be as light as possible. The rod should be a long one, 12ft, 13ft or 14ft with a 'tippy' action for roach and dace and an all-through action for such bigger fish as barbel, chub and bream. It should also have plenty of rings to prevent the line sticking to it in wet weather. Line strength varies, depending upon the species being sought, but should be between 2-4lb b.s. Although most present-day anglers prefer a fixed-spool reel there is no doubt that for trotting a centrepin is far superior for control of the tackle.

Mending the line

Sometimes, especially when fishing across river, a 'bow' will appear in the line which must be corrected to ensure that when the angler strikes the hook is driven home. This is achieved by flicking the rod back against the direction of the current thus making the line straight. This is called 'mending the line'. Because of this the line must float and although some monofilaments will float reasonably well, for perfect tackle control the line should be greased before fishing.

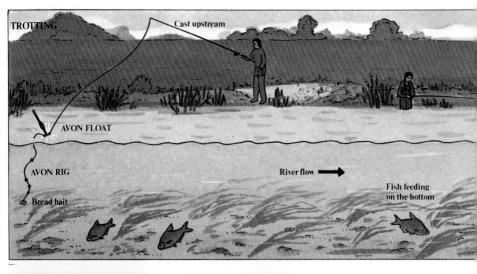

TROTTING

Cast upstream

AVON FLOAT

AVON RIG

Bread bait

River flow ➡

Fish feeding
on the bottom

(Above) A number of
modern floats are designed
for trotting. They are often
variants on traditional
patterns such as the
Avon.
(Left) The centre-pin is
ideal for trotting. Its
drum is controlled by
finger-pressure on the rim.
(Below) When trotting with
the fixed-spool reel, the
bale arm is left open.
Line is controlled by a
finger on the spool.

Hooks depend upon the bait and will vary
from a No.18, for caster and single-maggot
fishing, to a No. 6 when using big bread-
crust or flake.

The kind of float is very important. In fast-
flowing waters a float carrying between one
and four 'swan' (SSG) shots will be necessary
and must have a fairly stout tip. This will
ensure that the float remains visible even in
turbulent water. The same kind of float will
also be used for trotting bread against the far
bank for chub, and minnows for barbel.
These floats are attached to the line both top
and bottom and are sometimes known as
'Chub Trotters'.

Mike Prichard

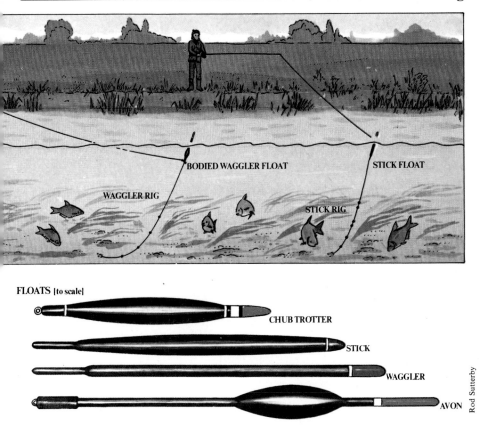

BODIED WAGGLER FLOAT

STICK FLOAT

WAGGLER RIG

STICK RIG

FLOATS [to scale]

CHUB TROTTER

STICK

WAGGLER

AVON

Rod Sutterby

In waters of medium flow, lighter floats can be used. For roach, dace and bream, one with a short, thin antenna will make for more sensitive fishing, although in choppy water it may be difficult to see all of the time. In this situation, a float with a slightly stouter antenna would be better. These floats are attached either bottom, top, or both.

'Waggler' floats

In recent years 'Wagglers' have become popular. This float has a stout body, usually made of balsa, situated at the bottom of a length of peacock quill or Sancandas reed. The 'Waggler', a heavy float even in its smallest size, takes a lot of shot and is fished by casting upstream and retrieved when below the angler. It is attached to the bottom only and fished with the line sunk.

Another popular float is the 'Stick'. Used mainly for caster fishing it consists of a tapered body made from varying proportions of cane and balsa. Best used for fishing close or fairly close in, it is shotted so that no more than $\frac{1}{8}$in of the tip shows above the surface. Like the 'Waggler', it is attached to the bottom and fished with the line sunk.

The manner in which the strike is made depends upon both the float used and the method employed. When trotting against the far bank which is more than 15 yards away, or wading with the float downstream, the strike is overhead, the rod being pulled back over the shoulder. For middle-of-the-river and close-in fishing, a sideways strike against the current is preferable. When fishing with a sunken line or with a 'Waggler' or 'Stick' float, the strike is made with the rod held low. With the 'Waggler' float, not only should the rod be kept low but the strike should be made downstream.

149

Spinning

Spinning is the art of casting and retrieving a lure designed to look or act like a small fish frog or mouse. Spinning is often a deadly method and most sea, game or coarse anglers find it necessary to spin at times. Using a variety of spinner-spoons, plugs, jigs or pirks, anglers use it for a number of different species on waters throughout the country.

Spinning is also one of the best methods of fishing for young anglers. Armed with one or two plugs, a closed-face fixed-spool reel and a decent spinning rod, the novice will learn to both cast and catch a sizeable fish.

Species caught with spinners
Most game fish take a spinner readily. Many sea fish, even flounders, fall to them, and in coarse fishing, pike, perch, zander and chub take these lures often, while other fish in the carp family (bream, carp, tench, and others), do so occasionally.

Generally speaking, spinning is a good method for the open river where there are deep pools, or for large stillwaters, gravel pits and reservoirs. One should not spin in confined spaces, as retrieval will be difficult. If the river is overhung with much vegetation, bad casting will result in lost lures.

A pike of nearly 20lb—the fish of a lifetime for most anglers—falls to a well-used spinner. As this catch demonstrates, it is not always necessary to offer a new, shiny lure in order to take a specimen fish.

Spinning is an active method of fishing and good to use in cold weather.

Choice of rod depends on the water more than anything else. On big rivers, gravel pits or reservoirs you may need a powerful, two-handed, stepped-up carp rod to throw biggish spoons, spinners or plugs a long way. In contrast, on small rivers, canals or ponds, short casts with a 7-8ft spinning rod of hollow glass for use with lines of 5-8lb b.s. may be adequate.

A certain amount of common sense is needed in choice of rod: big pike or salmon on a small river, for example, would need a powerful line, from 10lb to 20lb b.s.

The choice of reels is legion. It is possible, though, for the experienced angler to spin directly from a top-class centre-pin. With plugs you can pull off loops of line from the rod rings, while for sizeable plugs and heavy spinners you may use a multiplying reel.

(*Left*) *A spinning enthusiast with a box of spinners and lures.*
(*Below*) *A spinning rig incorporating a Wye lead to prevent the line kinking. One swivel or a plastic vane between two swivels, both rigs leaded, will also serve as an anti-kink device.*
(*Overleaf*) *The single-handed overhead cast begins with the rod tip at eye level and the line held by the fore-finger. The rod is raised smoothly to almost vertical and brought forward smartly, when line is released and the forefinger applied to the spool to check the cast.*

Bill Howes

Multipliers are accurate on short to moderate casts but difficult to cast light baits.

Other than for light spinning, closed-face reels are rarely used. For playing heavy fish they prove ineffective since the line within the housing goes through too many angles, creating considerable friction. Many open-faced fixed-spool reels are, however, superb. One with a roller pick-up and a reliable, easily reached anti-reverse switch is especially useful.

The species of fish also governs the choice of rod, reel and line. In weedy waters, like the Fenland drains, you need heavy line and a powerful rod to hold the fish. The same applies to heavy fish in small waters. On the other hand, when perch or chub fishing, a MK IV carp rod, or its lighter version, the Avon, in glass or split cane, are excellent.

Ultra-light spinning

Ultra-light spinning is proving to be increasingly popular. For this, a sawn-off length of fly rod, 5-6ft, with a line of 2-4lb b.s. is recommended. A tiny fixed-spool reel of high quality, like one of the small Shakespeares, Daiwas, or Ryobis, and small lures, almost down to big flies in size, but

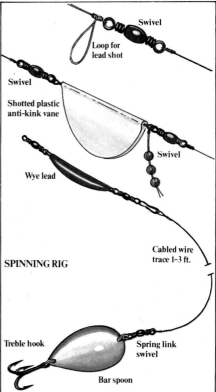

Swivel
Loop for lead shot
Swivel
Shotted plastic anti-kink vane
Swivel
Wye lead
Cabled wire trace 1-3 ft.
SPINNING RIG
Treble hook
Spring link swivel
Bar spoon

SPINNING
OVERHEAD CAST

Rod Sutterby

with diving vanes or propellors, are also necessary. You can, in fact, make your own lures on big single hooks, and catch more carp species with this than you would on conventional spinning gear.

The wide range of rods and reels provides great versatility of spinning. Lines are also varied, but a good standard line is a simple monofil, usually dyed dark in colour, and supple. Some anglers use plaited nylon, particularly on multiplying reels, but monofil generally has more stretch. Other spinning, such as trolling from a boat, may require special lead-cored lines, and some sea spinning is done with wire lines. Different strengths of nylon monofil together with appropriate weights to get the spinner down, usually prove adequate.

If a fish has a lot of sharp teeth you may need a wire trace on the line. This applies particularly to pike and zander and many sea fish, but not when spinning for game fish, perch or chub.

Cabled, supple, dark-coloured wire is better than made-up, plastic-coated, shiny traces. Add a swivel to one end and a safety-pin link swivel to the other by passing 2in of

cable wire through the swivel eye. Laying it back parallel, twist the two parts together by hand. Crimp-on sleeves can be used to secure the join, or strong glue.

Minimum of equipment

At the waterside, remember that you are always on the move, so a minimum of equipment is advisable. A small rucksack on your back is best, to hold food and waterproof clothing, and an angler's waist-coat with numerous pockets for spinners, spoons and miscellaneous items of tackle such as a spring balance, forceps for removing lures from fishes' jaws, a sharpening stone for blunted hooks, scissors and other small items, will prove useful. For landing salmon a small, collapsible net or gaff is necessary.

Always take enough clothes to keep warm. If possible wear plimsoles or walking boots rather than wellingtons or waders, although weight and heat saving on footwear is not always a good thing. Clothes should be drab, and the approach to the waterside quiet. It is a good plan to fish through the spot you intend standing at, particularly on a coarse fish water where another angler's groundbait

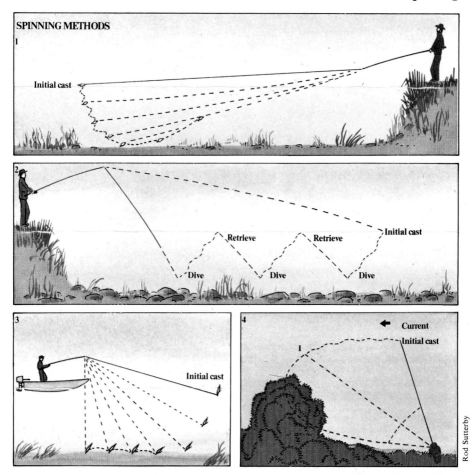

SPINNING METHODS

1

Initial cast

2

Retrieve   Retrieve   Initial cast

Dive   Dive   Dive

3

Initial cast

4

Current
Initial cast

1

Rod Sutterby

may have attracted shoal fish and predators close to the bank.

Where to cast

Where to cast? First, with a sinking spinner, find out the depth of water working on the principle of retrieving slow and deep. Cast out and allow the spinner or spoon to sink with the pick-up off, and judge the time it takes the spinner to strike the bottom. As the spinner nears the bank, raise the rod top to avoid the lure running into the slope. Casting in a fan-wise fashion, each cast being some five degrees to the side of the previous cast, is also used, but this can make for boring fishing, except from an anchored boat. It is probably better to cast where you think the predator will be.

Having explored the most likely places— ledges, sunken branches, and holes behind boulders—move on and try another spot.

Some anglers have difficulty estimating how far out the lure is. To remedy this, tie a nylon stop knot, such as a Billy Lane stop knot, to the line at a fixed length above the lure, perhaps 15ft. As the knot clicks through the top ring as you will know where the spinner is. This is particularly useful for night spinning—one of the most exciting forms of fishing that there is.

For night spinning you also need a shot clipped on the line just above the trace swivel, or if not using a trace, some 2ft up the line. This prevents the trace swivel being reeled into the end ring of the rod, or the

153

Spinning

*(Previous page) (1) The rod is held low and the spoon returned a little at a time until it bounces off the bottom. (2) With the rod at an angle of 45° the minnow is allowed to dive deep and is then retrieved. (3) From a boat the Deep Diver is retrieved rapidly as it sinks to the bottom. (4) A plug is used to reach fish beneath over-hanging trees. The plug drifts downstream [1] before the rod is dipped below the water and line slowly reeled in [2], dragging the lure in an arc beneath the tree [3].
(Right) When spinning, the angler is very visible and so should wear dull colours.*

Arthur Oglesby

spinner itself being retrieved too close to the rod tip. It should usually hang a couple of feet from the rod tip prior to a cast. Another important consideration when spinning at night is to know how far you have cast. Fortunately this is fairly easy. In daylight measure out a suitable-length cast by pulling line off the reel, then secure a rubber band round the spool before reeling the line back on to the reel. This avoids overcasting.

Colours and sizes

Spinners, spoons and plugs come in all colours and sizes. Simple spoons are egg-shaped and can be made from dessert spoons. Despite their simplicity they will take almost anything that swims. Drill a hole out at each end and by using a split ring, add a treble hook at one end and a swivel at the other. Elongated, concave-convex spoons with or without fins, are also useful.

Bar spoons are attached at one end to a bar forming an axis around which the blade spins. The tiny sizes will take trout, sea trout and perch, and the large sizes pike and salmon. They retrieve with greater vibration, but, unlike many spoons, retrieve in a more or less straight line unless the angler alters

the position of the rod end. Fly spoons are a kind of small bar spoon, while many other spinners, like some minnows, and mackerel spinners, have a hole through them and rotate about their whole length.

Plugs can be floaters (poppers or crawlers), floaters which dive to various depths, or sinking plugs. These are available in one piece, or with two or more pieces. Some plugs dive shallow, some deep. Perhaps the most versatile, all-purpose plug is the smallest. Around an inch in length, with wool, fur and feather attached, it is almost as good as the fly-type lures, and can be fished on fly rods or with ultra-light gear.

The action of the spinner in the water is essential to a successful catch. Aim to retrieve in short bursts, swinging the rod from side to side. This will vary the direction and add a lifelike flutter to your spinner. When retrieving try not to be too quick, as the lure will rise high in the water; on the other hand, one should not retrieve too cautiously for fear of snagging your lure.

Plugs and spinners lend themselves to home-making—adding, in many ways, to one of the most enjoyable aspects of fishing.

Playing and landing

Despite thousands of words of sound advice from fishing writers on the subject of playing and landing, many fish are nevertheless lost by anglers who lack this basic skill. The most common weak spots are: little or no understanding of the slipping clutch on the frequently used fixed-spool reel and not knowing how to coax out a fish that has run into weed (which can happen to the most experienced angler).

First, then, the slipping clutch. Before making the first cast, hold the rod in one hand and place one finger lightly on the edge of the spool. With the other hand take hold of the end of the line and pull as hard as possible. The clutch should now slip. If it does so before reaching maximum pressure the clutch is set too loose, while if the line breaks the clutch is too tight. With the spool set correctly it is impossible for a running fish to break the line, providing, that is, that everything else is done properly.

When a fish is hooked, immediately apply one finger of the rod hand to the rim of the

(Above) This angler has hooked a barbel while fishing the River Kennet, a tributary of the Thames, in Berkshire. He is applying vertical pressure to the fish to prevent it from taking refuge in the weeds.
(Left) Netting another Kennet barbel. The landing net is ready under the fish, which, played out and rolling on the surface, is drawn gently over it. The rod is held high to avoid tangling with the fish.

155

spool. In this way, when the rod is held at an angle of between 15 and 30 degrees to the vertical, maximum pressure is brought to bear on the running fish. The line will be almost at breaking point but, if the spool is set right, will not actually break.

Pumping and netting

When the fish stops its run, line is recovered by the process known as 'pumping'. For this, assuming the fish is stationary or nearly so, turn the reel handle, at the same time lowering the rod until the tip is at waist level. Then increase finger pressure on the spool rim and bring up the rod to its former position. Repeat the process until the fish runs again or is ready for the net.

It is now—at the point of netting—that most mistakes occur. When the fish is played out, the net is placed in the water, ready for use. With the fish wallowing or lying on the surface, bring the rod tip down to waist level once more, and, with the other hand holding the net, draw the rod back over the shoulder, maintaining strong pressure on the spool all the time. Steady the net about 12in below the surface and draw the fish towards and over it. Do not lift until the fish is over the net.

Sometimes, as the fish is drawn to the net, it will suddenly find new strength and either swim off or change direction. Let it do so for it is unlikely to take line. Keep the finger on the spool and allow the rod to take the strain.

Two important points must be remembered: first, as the fish comes over the net make sure that the rod is no farther back than 30 degrees to the vertical. If it is, you will not have complete control over the fish. Secondly, never move the net towards the fish but keep it still and pull the fish over it.

The problem of the fish that runs into weed is one that requires swift action. Some fish, especially roach and chub, however quick one's reflexes are, will manage to transfer the hook to the weed and escape. Other species, barbel and tench in particular, are not so clever and must be extracted from the weed by 'pumping'. As soon as the fish reaches the weed, use the technique de-

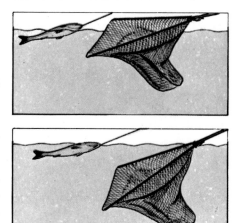

(Top) A common mistake made in netting a fish. The net is held too high and is used to scoop at the fish.
(Above) The net should be sunk beneath the fish and ready to receive it as it is drawn in exhausted.

(Left) Peter Stone unhooks a 5¼lb tench. He leaves it in the landing net to avoid unnecessary handling. If the fish is to be set free at once the landing net can simply be lowered into the water again.

P. H. Ward/Natural Science Photos

(Left) When a fish heads strongly away to the right or the left, opposite side-strain must be applied. This will give the rod a chance to work most efficiently.

(Below) Holding his rod high to bring the fish close, a Southern matchman prepares to net it. It is important to put the net carefully into the water well before the fish is drawn near.

P. H. Ward. Natural Science Photos

scribed earlier, repeating the process without stopping and keeping the finger down hard on the spool. Once the fish starts to move, keep control of the situation with continual pumping, as this will, in the majority of cases, get the fish out of the weed. This technique relies on knowing how much pressure your line will take—something that only comes with experience, and not normally before the loss of a fish.

Coaxing a fish through weed

When a fish runs into streamer weed *(Ranunculus)*, you must get downstream of it in order to extract it. Trying to coax a fish through this weed from upstream only worsens the situation. Although fish of all sorts can be forced out of 'cabbages' (underwater lilies) or various types of weedy growth, it is extremely difficult to move a fish from a cultivated lily patch by 'pumping' and many battles have been lost here.

Playing a fish on a centrepin reel is much easier than on a fixed-spool. Immediately the fish is hooked, turn the handle slowly, keeping the line tight. If the fish runs let it take line, but rest the palm of the hand lightly against the rim of the reel, facing upwards. In this way, by applying a light but insistent pressure, the fish has to fight for every inch of line but will not break it.

To sum up, when playing a big fish the important thing is not to allow the fish to take control. If this happens then it is likely to be lost. Do not hurry the playing—a sure

Bill Howes

way of losing the fish—yet do not drag it out longer than necessary, for the object, it must be remembered, is to get the catch on the bank. Maintain a steady pressure and give line only when you have to. When the fish tires or stops, even if only momentarily, take advantage and retrieve line.

Normally, one holds the rod pointing upwards, as described, but remember that fish do turn sideways and, when they do, sideways pressure must be applied. Bring the rod down to the horizontal position and keep it there while playing the fish running to the side.

Conservation

There are two ways in which coarse fishing enthusiasts commonly approach the problem of conservation: the first is by insisting that all fish they catch should be returned to the water unharmed; the second is by encouraging restocking. Yet while the sentiments are praiseworthy, neither of these practices is necessarily the best way for anglers to conserve their fishing.

Problem for the experts

The first difficulty is that most fishing waters in this country are vastly overstocked, rather than being short of fish. Adding fish to already crowded waters will only lead to stunted adults, mature fish which have stopped growing due to overcrowding and shortage of food, while only a few inches in length instead of a healthy 7in or 8in. Assessing the correct fish population for a fishing water is a problem for the experts. Fish will be examined, weighed, their age determined by 'reading' the scales, to decide whether the fish is healthy and of average weight and size for its age. It is vital not to attempt restocking indiscriminately.

The second difficulty for the angler lies in deciding when a fish should be returned to the water. Many anglers will at some time have returned a damaged or exhausted fish to the water knowing that its chances of survival were slim. So it is important to know how fish are affected by being caught and how they can best be saved from unnecessary harm.

If fish are returned to the water immediately after they have been unhooked they will have a far better chance of survival than if they are given the usual treatment meted out to them by anglers. During a match, and when 'pleasure' fishing also, a large fish is played out after being hooked until it can be brought to the landing net. By then it is weakened to the point of exhaustion.

Smaller fish are held in the hand while the

hook is removed. They are then thrown or dropped into the mouth of the keepnet. Their suffering continues, for every time another fish is dropped in they receive a further shock and their resistance is lowered a little more. Finally they are in a very poor condition and would die in a few hours if not soon released.

At the end of the fishing period the keepnet is hauled out of the water and dumped on the bank. If it is a match the fish

will be put in a metal basket to be weighed, and finally released back into the water.

By this time they have probably lost several scales and are in a state of neurosis. If they survive, it will take all of the ensuing year's growth to replace the lost scales, and if the fishery is overstocked, survival will be very doubtful. It would be better to kill them and take them away from the water.

Anglers can help in other ways: for example, if they were to bring in their fish on tackle of adequate strength in the shortest possible time, unhook them in the landing net and return them immediately to the water, little harm would be done to the fish,

Match fishermen cause fish suffering by throwing them into the keepnet. All too often this is overcrowded and shock increases each time a fish is added. In this condition they could die within hours but before being freed, with many fish irreparably harmed, the catch is weighed in a harsh metal basket.

Bill Howes

P H Ward/Natural Science Photos

particularly if barbless hooks were used.

On the Continent, matches are decided by length and not weight. As it is caught, each fish is measured and noted, then returned immediately to the water. A statutory size limit is observed and the events are closely supervised by stewards. The advantages of this system are that the fish are only handled momentarily while being measured, and that they do not spend hours confined in a keepnet with many other struggling fish. A further advantage is the avoidance of the fishes' breathing in of harmful mud stirred up by their struggles in a keepnet left in muddy water close to the bank.

Needed—a balanced population

Conservation is best achieved by maintaining a fish population at the correct level for the water. Expert advice will provide this figure. A balanced fish population will allow the fish to grow to their proper size and provide good sport for the angler.

Another way of maintaining stocks is to ensure that they have everything they need for their well-being. Fish need an adequate and continuous food supply, both when they are small and when adult. They need cover into which they can dive when danger threatens, and they require spawning facilities.

Weedbeds provide all of these require-

Rough handling during a fishing match has damaged the dorsal and caudal fins of this common bream.

ments and on all fisheries there should be plenty of weeds because this is where the fish's food lives. Fish need them for cover and in which to shed their spawn.

Reason for the close season

Weeds should never be cut until the fish have finished spawning, otherwise much of their food and a great many of their offspring will perish. Spawning is the most important stage in the yearly cycle and fish should be protected by a close season which covers not only their spawning time, but a period before and afterwards. The period before spawning is the most important. If handled in any way at this critical time, fish will shed scales. Their need for protection from disturbance at this time should be impressed on the young or inexperienced angler.

During the actual spawning period, fish seldom feed, being interested only in procreation. Afterwards they clean themselves and begin to feed in order to regain condition and start growing again. They can be handled at this time, but should be treated with care because they are in a weakened condition and any severe shocks will prolong recovery and reduce growth.

Sea Fishing

Cod

The North Atlantic cod, *Gadus morhua,* is widespread off the coasts of Britain, especially Scotland, where it comes to feed from the deep water breeding grounds round Iceland. The cod, with herring and other 'round' fish, forms a major part of the huge commercial fisheries and vast quantities are trawled each year, the cod catch itself often exceeding 250,000 tons.

Colour variation

As with many species, the cod shows considerable colour variation dependent upon area, but it is usually a green/grey speckled with brown on the flanks and top, with a white belly. The lateral line is white and very distinct. There are three dorsal and two anal fins and these, coupled with the huge mouth of the cod, all contribute to making hard work for the angler who has to reel a big one up from perhaps 35 fathoms (210ft). The cod, like many members of its family—hake, whiting, pouting, coalfish, haddock, ling— has a long barbule on the lower jaw. During spawning a female cod

162

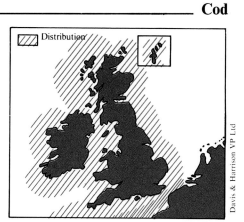

Rod Sutterby.

Habitat

Cod inhabit deep water all round the British Isles for most of the year. At spawning time, which varies according to local conditions and the kind of year, they move to shallower water, to the coast. Most cod migrate south in winter, to return north in the spring.

Bait

Wherever cod fishing is done, the best baits are fish strip, shellfish, squid and lugworm.

can release up to 9,000,000 eggs in midwater. This enormous number ensures that a sufficient percentage of tiny fish will evade the predations of other fish, birds, disease and natural disasters in order to ensure the continuity of the species.

The eggs hatch into $\frac{1}{16}$ larvae, growing to about an inch after three months. After early feeding on tiny marine organisms, the codling begin to eat fish, sandeels at first, then herring, haddock and other codling.

Fewer—but larger

It was commonplace ten years ago to take a boat not far out from Dover, Ramsgate, Deal, Hastings, and other South East Coast places, and bring in 50lb of prime cod and codling (all cod of up to 6lb are called codling). But the same does not apply today. Now fish are caught in fewer numbers throughout the year, but over a greater area, even off the West Coast, especially if one can fish deep. There, surprisingly, cod of 42lb and 43lb were taken a couple of years ago. Cod fishing seasons vary from one part of the

British Isles to another. In the Clyde the big shoals arrive during February and March, where fish of 40lb have been caught in some numbers. Off the Isle of Mull in Scotland, June, July and August are the best fishing months. On the South and East Coasts, November, December and January are the traditional months to expect cod. Down in the West Country cod are caught throughout the year, not many, but a steady trickle of big fish that have become permanent residents in the areas of wrecks and pinnacles. Most of the Scottish venues have a resident population of small and medium-sized cod which live permanently on the inshore marks, but the larger fish are seasonal visitors which

The inexperienced angler may not be able to readily distinguish between the red cod, the codling and the pollack. Colour variation in the cod derives from local water conditions. They are both distinguishable from the pollack by a white lateral line and a receding lower lip with a barbule.

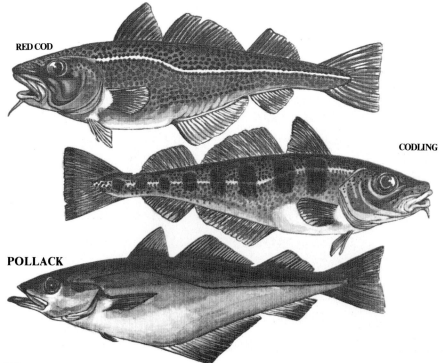

RED COD

CODLING

POLLACK

Lyn Cawley

appear either to spawn or to take advantage of a natural glut of bait-fish or crustaceans.

All this is a pointer to the 'new-look' cod fishing that exists today. The East Coast and eastern end of the English Channel were once the big cod areas, with a long-beaten record cod of 32lb coming from Lowestoft. All this has changed, the angler seeking 32-pounders going South West or North East.

Close-in cod

It is not necessary to go boat-fishing in order to catch sizable cod. There are many beaches, such as Dungeness, in Kent, and many others round the coasts where cod can be caught on beachcasting tackle. Piers, groynes and moles, too, offer close-in

deepwater fishing for the species. Notable among these is the detached mole at Dover, where numbers of double-figure cod are taken every year when there is a run of the fish. Fishing stations such as these can be found in many areas. Yorkshire offers some wonderful cod fishing at places such as Filey Brigg and up to Flamborough Head.

The current record cod caught from a boat weighed 53lb and fell to G. Martin, fishing at Start Point, Devon, in 1972. There are now both boat and shore records, the latter of which is a 44lb 8oz cod caught in 1966 by B. Jones, from Toms Point, Barry, Glamorgan. While these sizes will be admired by anglers whose usual cod (when he can catch one) is in

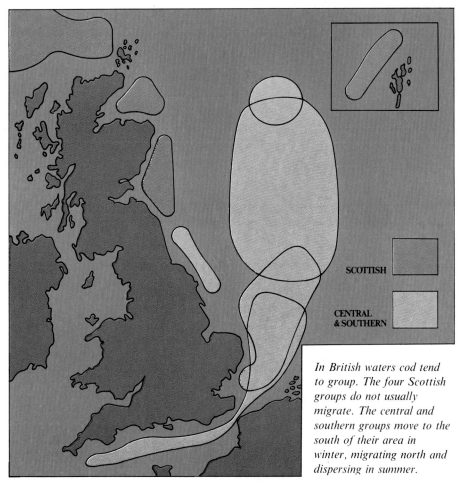

SCOTTISH

CENTRAL & SOUTHERN

In British waters cod tend to group. The four Scottish groups do not usually migrate. The central and southern groups move to the south of their area in winter, migrating north and dispersing in summer.

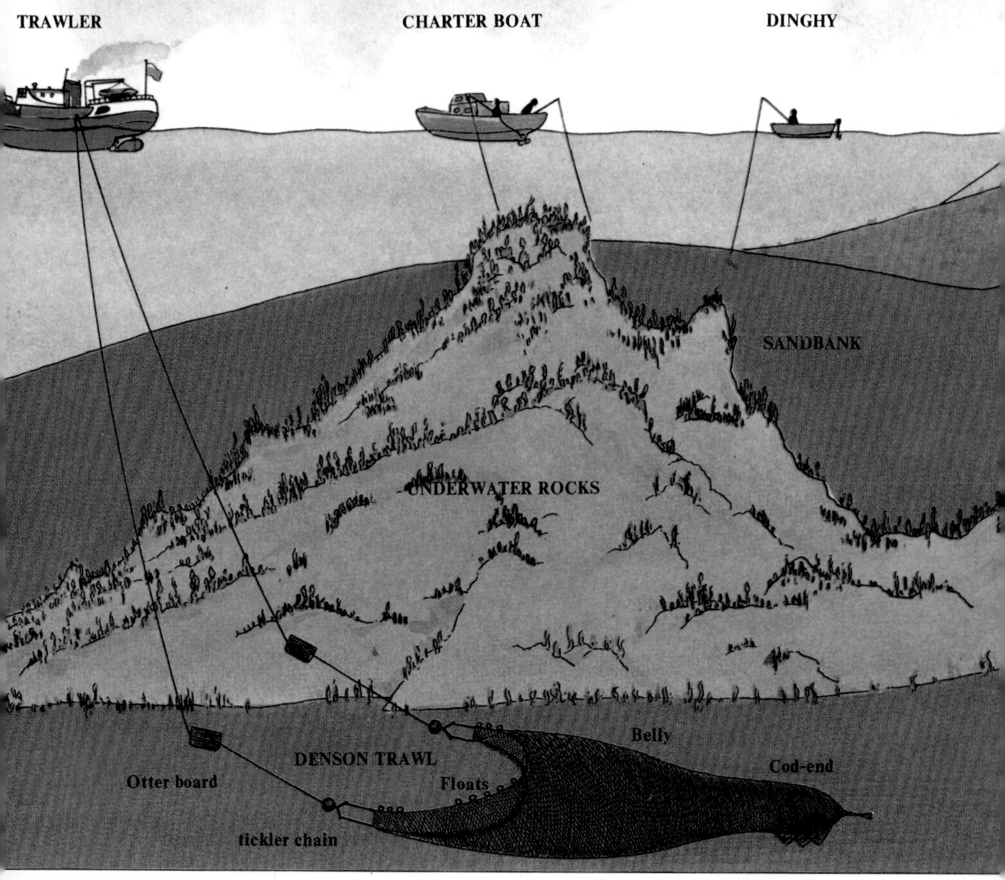

TRAWLER   CHARTER BOAT   DINGHY

SANDBANK

UNDERWATER ROCKS

Belly

Cod-end

DENSON TRAWL

Otter board   Floats

tickler chain

the 10lb region, the rod-caught records do not compare with commercially-trawled cod, some of which are known to weigh 200lb.

Feeding habits

The feeding habits of the cod are as wide as any fish. The gape of its mouth enables this fish to swallow vast amounts of edible—and inedible— matter, including white objects, which seem to attract it particularly. This habit has led to the development of white attractor spoons on cod tackle.

Many anglers over-estimate the strength of cod when choosing cod fishing tackle. This is particularly true of the average boat angler who tends to choose a really strong rod. But this is not necessary. After an initial

strong plunge or two it will come up if a steady line-retrieve is made; the large open mouth will provide most of the resistance. Despite their general greediness and large average size, cod can often be shy biters. Many an angler has struck at a tiny, twitchy bite only to find that he has connected solidly with a really big fish. On the South Coast where fierce Channel tides can make fishing difficult many cod anglers now use a wire line rather than a nylon monofilament line to get the bait down to where the fish are feeding.

Wire-line fishing

The wire has its own built-in weight and being far finer than nylon it creates less drag in the tide so that comparatively light leads can be used even in strong tidal runs. Wire-

SHORE ANGLER   ROCK ANGLER

LEDGE

EASHORE

SEABED

Rod Sutterby

England Scene

Commercial fishing trawlers will avoid the seashore, sandbanks and underwater rocks. These areas will then be left to the angler on the shore or in a boat.

Spots like Flamborough Head in Yorkshire (above) provide large winter catches of cod. Beach fishing at Folkestone in Kent (below) a popular cod venue.

Bill Howes

Cod

line fishing for cod has become something of a science and various kinds of line have been marketed in an attempt to cut down the weight, size, and thus the diameter even further. Many anglers believe wire lines to be dangerous. But they only become dangerous when they get snagged up on the sea bed and someone tries to free them by heaving on the line with his bare hands, when the wire can cut like a razor. If stout gloves are used the danger is eliminated entirely. Wire is almost essential in very deep water, where its weight takes the bait down without the necessity of using big 2lb leads.

Techniques

The techniques for catching cod include all the standard methods: ledgering with fish strips, lugworm, squid; paternostering with soft crab, whole small pouting, and so on; pirks and lures, and feathering. Cod, too, can be taken from deep water, from close off-shore marks, from piers, rocks and beaches, and from the tops of 100ft-high Yorkshire cliffs! Here the safety factor is a vital element in strong winter winds.

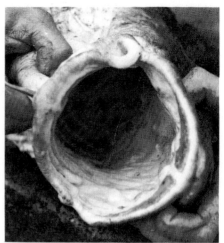

Eric Birch

The cod's huge mouth (above) allows it to scoop up many foods, including fish, crustaceans, weeds, and even tin cans and disposable cups (above right) from the sea bed. A rig incorporating a section of a plastic cup (below right) has been used with some success by cod fishermen.

Rod Sutterby

Lyn Cawley

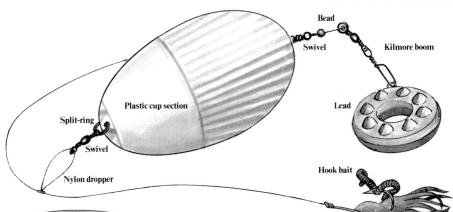

Rod Sutterby

Bead

Swivel

Kilmore boom

Plastic cup section

Lead

Split-ring

Swivel

Nylon dropper

Hook bait

Plastic cup section

A 35lb cod taken while boat fishing in winter several miles out from Newhaven on the Sussex coast. This fish was caught on the bottom with squid.

Bill Howes

169

Pollack

The author has two favourite fish: the porbeagle shark, for its tremendous endurance when fighting at the end of a line, and the pollack (*Pollachius pollachius*) because it is a fish that, when hooked, has an exhilarating first run. With the pollack, words such as 'power dive' seem accurate. This member of the cod family can be one of our sporting fishes provided it is taken over a suitable habitat and on tackle that responds to the fish's struggles.

To get the best from most sea fish, they have to be fought in shallow water. This is particularly true of the pollack, a fish of reefs and rocky bottoms, living and feeding among the tangles of kelp. The pollack comes inshore in the spring, just as the sun begins to bring warmth and fertility to the littoral waters. It is a predatory species that feeds higher in the water than the other cod-like fish. Of course, the pollack will also feed on crustaceans and molluscs but the species is particularly adapted to hunting other fish.

The pollack is sleek, well-proportioned,

immensely powerful, and built for ambushing other reef-dwelling species. It tends to shoal up according to size. Most of the inshore rock areas will have a population of smallish pollack which feed on the fry of other fish that spawn in the shallows. As summer progresses, the larger pollack come in from deeper water, feeding over the top of the reef, particularly in the late evening and into the hours of darkness. During the day, especially in strong sunlight, these larger fish sink down to the sides of pinnacle rocks, among the weeds and broken ground.

Confusion between pollack and coalfish

There is always some confusion, among novice anglers, between the pollack and its near relative, the coalfish, despite quite clear identification points. The pollack is green-brown with a dark lateral line that curves sharply over the pectoral before straightening as it continues back along the body to the squared-off tail. Among juvenile fish there can be a colour variation that is environmental. A highly coloured habitat,

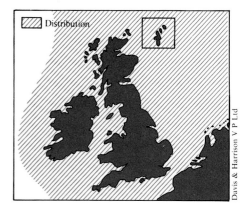

Habitat

The pollack lives over rock pinnacles and above the wrecks off the South West coast. This species also exists in brackish esturial waters and rocky areas such as Trevose Head, North Cornwall (below)

Baits

Mackerel strip, imitating small fish, is the favoured bait, but the pollack can also be taken on spoons.

Rod Sutterby

171

with a mass of red weed, for example, will influence the basic hue of the fish.

The pollack has a protruding lower jaw, an unmistakable recognition feature, indicating that it feeds by attacking its prey from below. There are three dorsal fins, as in most of the cod family, and the body is less rounded than that of the coalfish.

The coalfish (*Pollachius virens*) is thicker-bodied and is blue-black when adult but olive green before maturity. The lateral line is white and straight. The jaws are similar in length, although in the larger, deep-water specimens there is evidence of an elongated underjaw, similar to that of mature pollack. Coalfish have a barbule under the lower jaw, but you will have to search hard for this rudimentary protuberance. Another major feature which distinguishes the species is that the tail in the coalfish is clearly forked.

Both species are found over rocky ground and offshore wrecks. The coalfish seems to be more northerly in its distribution, with a lot of small fish permanently in residence on the Eastern coastline. Pollack are a South-Western species fond of the rocky coasts of the British mainland and the Atlantic shores of Ireland. Both fish come into shallow areas, but the coalfish tends to seek a slightly deeper habitat. Pollack are found in some estuaries – they can tolerate an amount of freshwater – whereas the coalfish is rarely found in a brackish environment.

Spawning period

Both fish spawn early in the year. Pollack spawn between February and May, depending on geographical location. Fish living in southern waters spawn earlier than those from a more northerly habitat. They seek deep water – of 50 fathoms or more – in early autumn, at which time the species figures importantly in trawler catches. The 'coalie' generally spawns in much deeper water in March, when as many as four million eggs are released by the larger females. The eggs are pelagic, floating and drifting on the ocean currents. They hatch into larvae about $\frac{1}{8}$th of an inch in length. These larval pollack

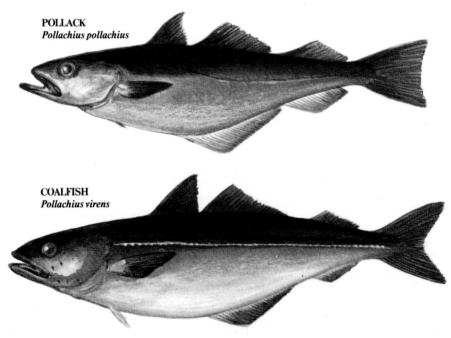

POLLACK
Pollachius pollachius

COALFISH
Pollachius virens

Ralph Stobart

Mike Millman

John Holden

(Above) The coalfish and two of the characteristics that differentiate this species from the pollack. Note the white lateral line and paired jaws.
(Right) Note how the pollack's lower jaw is protruding, an aid to a predatory fish that attacks from below. This species does not have a chin barbule.
(Left) How to recognize pollack and coalfish.

and coalfish form shoals and feed on drifting animals in the plankton stream. The tidal drift and onshore winds will move the shoals of fry into shallow coastal water, where they remain for their first year of life, feeding on copepods among the kelp and weed fronds. Both pollack and coalfish fry grow quickly and when about an inch long move out into reef areas, where the feeding is better in quality and quantity.

With the advent of West Country wreck fishing, things really began to happen, records being set and broken almost every week. The wrecks provided an untapped source of fish for the deep-anchoring techniques developed by anglers in ports like Brixham and Plymouth. The original in-

tention was to get baits down to the massive conger that fill the wrecks. Inevitably, some anglers concentrated on the layer of water over the bulk of the wreck. Giant cod, ling, pollack, coalfish, pouting and sea bream began to figure among the catches, the artificial lure making its mark as the principal method for this form of fishing.

Two basic styles

Pollack fishing divides neatly into two basic styles – letting a bait or lure down to fish, and working a moving lure across a habitat, either by spinning or trolling from a boat. In the first case, the angler is normally concerned with large fish, either from a wreck or reef. As there are a number of species that can be expected to come to the bait. the

173

Pollack

tackle is often too heavy for pollack. A technique based on a sink-and-draw working of the bait in mid-water does allow a degree of selection. To get the best sport from pollack, one must give them the opportunity to develop the powerful runs of which they are so capable.

Terminal tackle

In terms of terminal tackle and rigs, there is little to separate reef and wreck fishing. Simplicity, and a trace that gives life to the bait, are very important. You can fish a single hook to ledger rig, but I prefer a simple paternostered bait, using the weight on a 'rotten bottom' line of weak nylon that if snagged on rocks or tangled among the standing rigging of a wreck, can be broken out without losing what could be a good fish.

The trace must be long enough to give the bait an opportunity to swim naturally with the tide. Pollack will be chasing smaller fish, so anything that has an attractive, lifelike appearance will be taken. Use a 3ft trace when the tide is slack, extending this to 6ft or more when it begins to run hard.

Obviously, some consideration must be given to the length of trace that can be handled from whatever boat you are fishing from. The author incorporates a fixed boom, of twisted stainless steel wire or swivelled brass, into the rig. Its purpose is to keep the hook trace standing off the reel line when the gear is being lowered, for all too often a simple nylon paternoster will tangle the bait around the reel line if lowered too fast. A weak nylon sinker link of about 3ft is ideal. The rig is lowered to the reef or wreck and stopped immediately any solid ground or obstruction is felt, and the line is wound back a couple of turns. This will allow the bait to swim freely just above the habitat. Sooner or later, the weight will be held fast, but breaking out will only lose the lead.

Present the bait attractively. I slice off a diagonal lask of fish bait 6in long and tie it to the hook with elasticated thread so that

(Above) Feathers used for jigging lures for pollack, coalfish and ling.

Stainless Steel Wire Boom

Monofilament Trace
For Slack Tide 3ft
For Running Tide 6ft

DEEP WATER

WRASSE

RAGWORM

CRAB

(Left) The pollack lives over rocky pinnacles, reefs and deep wrecks.

Hooking a Mackerel Lask

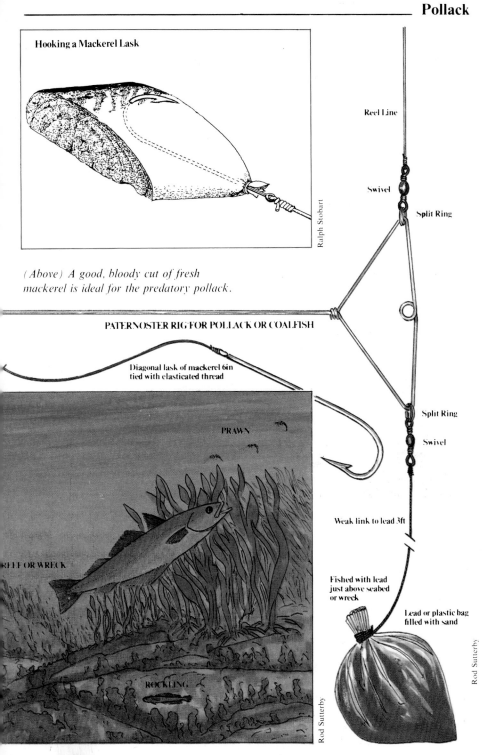

Ralph Stobart

(Above) A good, bloody cut of fresh mackerel is ideal for the predatory pollack.

PATERNOSTER RIG FOR POLLACK OR COALFISH

Reel Line

Swivel

Split Ring

Diagonal lask of mackerel 6in tied with elasticated thread

Split Ring

Swivel

Weak link to lead 3ft

Fished with lead just above seabed or wreck

Lead or plastic bag filled with sand

PRAWN

REEF OR WRECK

ROCKLING

Rod Sutterby

Rod Sutterby

175

(Above) Land's End, a fine pollack mark.
(Left) Pollack caught on a red/silver pirk.

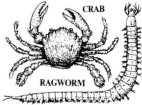

CRAB

RAGWORM

Mike Millman

the bait is not easily torn from the hook.

Pollack take a bait in a great many different ways but, once in their mouths, it will be carried back to the fish's lie. That is when the angler gets the thrill of pollack fishing. As the fish feels pressure on the line it will nose-dive back to the reef. Let it go, having previously set a reasonable playing drag to the reel. Try to turn the fish so that it does not take the rig into an obstruction.

Pinnacle rock fishing is top of the league for the pollack fisherman. Here, the prey can be smallish shoal fish swimming in groups over the tips of the pinnacles, or the solitary big specimen that hugs the sheer rock faces or loiters in the crevices. The angling style depends on the depth of water over the peaks. The deepwater reef can be fished with natural bait or pirks; the relatively shallow water reef can be trolled, or worked progressively with a lure, from a drifting boat.

Artificial lures for pollack

There are two successful kinds of artificial lure for pollack fishing – I hesitate to call them spinners because not all lures actually spin – the large metal spoon that wobbles and flashes as it curves through the water, and the bar spoon, of which the German Sprat is probably the best-known pattern. Spoons are easy to fish, whether they are being cast or trolled behind a boat, because they have weight and are, in the main,

(Right) Plump 25lb 10oz Mevagissey coalfish. (Below) Natural foods of the pollack.

Mike Millman

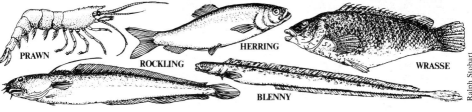

PRAWN

HERRING

ROCKLING

WRASSE

BLENNY

Ralph Stobart

designed to work without additional weight.

Unfortunately, long-distance casting demands the addition of more weight to get the spoon out to the fish, while trolling at high speed requires more weight to sink the spoon. The problem with adding either a spiral or a Wye lead to the trace, ahead of the lure, is that the extra weight dampens the action of the artificial lure. It is, therefore, best to try to avoid using additional weights, and instead to choose a heavier lure. The traditional rubber eel, made from a piece of flexible gas tubing, was one of the finest lures ever. It has now been superseded by a number of man-made fish-shaped lures with action built in. Most of them work well, but

it is worrying that when reef fishing one expects to lose gear—most of it expensive.

Colour plays an important part in pollack fishing. As an attacker from below, one would expect the pollack to be responsive to silhouette and action. There is no doubt that these two factors are of prime importance, but there are times when pollack will take only a red eel, or a white, or, perhaps, a grubby white one. Has this something to do with the amount of light penetrating the water, and possibly, the prey that the fish expect to find at that time? Experiment even by using feathered lures, to represent fry.

Avoid heavy tackle, for pollack provide superb sport on balanced, light equipment.

177

Wrasse

BALLAN WRASSE
Labrus bergylta

Wrasse are beautiful fish. In the British Isles they are found in most coastal areas, where rock, weeds, molluscs and a few fathoms of sheltered inshore water provide a habitat.

The largest and most common wrasse is the ballan. It looks something like a fresh-water carp, having one long dorsal fin set above a thick, muscled body. The fin has 19 or 20 spiny rays at the head end and 9–11 flexible rays towards the tail. The jaws are powerful, with lips designed for tearing limpets and other shellfish from rock faces. The teeth on the jaws are strong but there are no teeth on the palate. Instead the wrasse has pharyngeal teeth for grinding.

Ballan wrasse
Ballan wrasse occur in many colours, related to those predominating in their environment. Newcomers to shore fishing often make the mistake of identifying a number of different 'ballan' species because the fish vary so much. Generally, they are a greenish brown, often with a reddish belly dotted with white spots. The pectoral and pelvic fins are frequently red and spotted.

Rod Sutterby

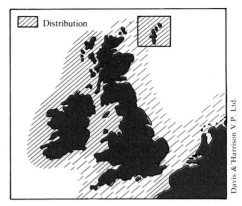

Distribution

Davis & Harrison V.P. Ltd.

Habitat

The colourful, fighting wrasse can be found wherever there are rocks and reefs holding the crustaceans and shellfish which the species feeds upon. Typical of wrasse ground is the shredded coast of Ireland's beautiful Dingle peninsula (below).

Baits

Use small worm, shellfish or crustacean baits.

Mike Pritchard

John Holden

The species favours a habitat where there is at least three or four fathoms of water at low water spring tides—probably because strong, lengthy kelps need a reasonable depth of water to grow in. These weeds provide ideal cover both for the wrasse and for the smaller creatures, such as crabs, lobsters, other crustaceans, and molluscs, on which the species feeds. Furthermore, during storms, areas of shallow water are much disturbed by strong surface movement, which drives these animals out from the security of the weeds into deeper, clean ground areas where they can be more easily caught by the predatory wrasse.

Smaller ballan tend to remain very close inshore for most of the year. Larger fish keep to deeper water, either below cliffs, where the water is often ten or more fathoms deep, or farther out to sea on offshore reefs rising clear of the seabed. In reefs, the fish live in the higher areas at depths of about ten fathoms. They are seldom found in shallow inshore areas as they need more food than such areas can generally provide.

(Above) The mouth of the wrasse, showing the strong jaw teeth present in these fishes. There are also teeth in the throat.
(Right) Rocky, weedy habitat of the wrasses.
(Below) Shellfish and crustaceans that form the food of the wrasse family.

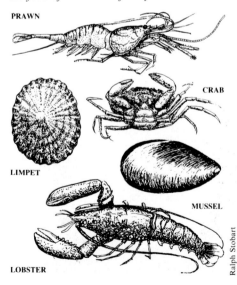

PRAWN

CRAB

LIMPET

MUSSEL

LOBSTER

Ralph Stobart

180

Ballan wrasse do not form shoals, although there may well be an enormous population on a single reef. They have definite territorial behaviour, each patrolling a small area. This may be related to their breeding habits, for wrasse are one of the few fish to build nests. They spawn in late May–July in shallow water, making the nest from pieces of seaweed and debris which they jam into crevices between rocks. The eggs are then dispersed throughout the strands of weed that comprise the nest.

Slow growth of ballan wrasse

Ballan wrasse eggs are quite large, about a millimetre in diameter, with a distinct yellow colour. The fry measure about 2in in the first winter of life. With average feeding, they grow to 7in in two years.

Occasionally, the angler will hook a brightly coloured, smaller wrasse when fishing from the rocks. This may be any one of a number of lesser wrasse species, but the commonest is the cuckoo wrasse, *Labrus mixtus (L bimaculatus)*. This fish is more likely to be hooked in deeper water than the ballan, but does occasionally come near the cliffs. As with the ballan, beginners often wrongly identify more than one species of cuckoo. This is because the sexes are completely different in colour. Males are a striking blue with an orange-red hue to the top of the head and shoulders. Females are orange-red, with three dark spots under the end of the dorsal fin.

The cuckoo wrasse rarely exceeds 14in in length, with males always slightly larger than females of the same age. Both sexes are poor fighters, but add colour to any catch.

Another small wrasse (up to 9in), the corkwing, *Crenilabrus melops*, also varies greatly in colour, although the variation is not related to sex. One identification feature that is fairly reliable is the single dark spot in the centre of the tail wrist. In addition, the

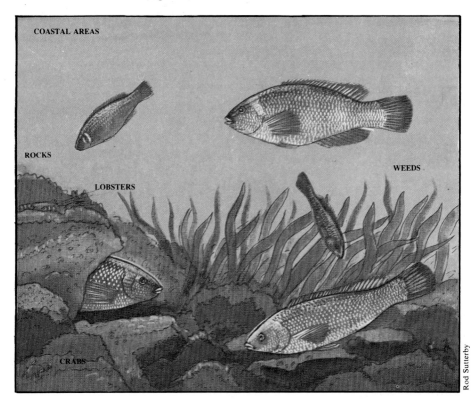

COASTAL AREAS

ROCKS

LOBSTERS

WEEDS

CRABS

Rod Sutterby

cheeks and underside of the jaws are streaked with lines of bright blue or green. The females have a protuberance just behind the vent. This is part of the egg-laying mechanism, although little is known of its precise function.

Corkwing and Goldsinny

The corkwing can be easily confused with another little wrasse, the goldsinny, *Ctenolabrus rupestris*, as both the size and shape of the two fish are similar. But whereas the corkwing is fairly brightly coloured, the goldsinny is a drab overall brownish-yellow. Nevertheless, it too has a single spot on the tail area, although this is on the upper rather than the central part of the wrist.

The goldsinny is fond of much deeper water than most wrasses, preferring depths of around 30 fathoms. It is small, averaging only 6in long, and is common only in the west of the British Isles.

Another small wrasse occasionally caught around Britain is the small-mouthed wrasse, or rock cook, *Centrolabrus exoletus*. Apart from its extremely small mouth, identifying features are its dorsal fin in which the soft rear part is slightly raised above the hard-rayed forepart, and the five spines at the leading end of its anal fin—all other wrasse have three. It also has a more northerly distribution than most other wrasse, being found in the North Atlantic and in the Baltic.

The last British wrasse is the rainbow, *Coris julis*. This is a brilliantly coloured and is common in the Bay of Biscay and down ·towards the tropics, but it is only a rare migrant to Britain and then only to south-western shores.

The rainbow wrasse is small—about 6in long—and has no scales on the head. It is alone among wrasse species in having elongated and pointed pectoral fins. The dorsal fin is set low on the body, with a raised and pointed leading edge to the hard-rayed

(*Above*) *The ballan wrasse is beautifully marked, as are all the members of the group. It is the largest British wrasse species, with a rod-caught shore record weight of 8lb 6oz 6dr, taken in 1976 from a beach in the Channel Isles.*
(*Left*) *Hooking a whole crab and lugworm, both tempting baits for the larger wrasses such as the ballan.*
(*Right*) *The kelp-strewn gullies of South Cornwall hold large numbers of the colourful wrasses.*

Ralph Stobart

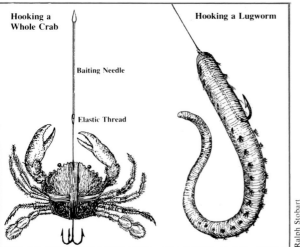

Hooking a
Whole Crab

Hooking a Lugworm

Baiting Needle

Elastic Thread

section. Colour varies, although the predominant hue on male fish is purple, to which is added bright silver blotches and a lateral silver band. Females are less bright but have the same basic coloration.

The only wrasse of interest to anglers is the ballan. They are not large fish—adults reach about 20in—but they can be powerful fighters on light tackle. The fight, like the fish's colour, is largely conditioned by its environment. Strong tides, currents that sweep around rocky headlands, and crashing wave patterns that surge into gullies and

Mike Millman

channels, all add power to the run of a hooked ballan.

Light tackle is also important in protecting the fish from hurried pressure changes. The swimbladder is not connected to the gullet, so that the fish cannot quickly equalize pressure as it is winched to the surface. This unfortunately means that a lot of splendid fish are released only to die.

Wrasse 'just give up'

A protracted fight can also bring about the death of a wrasse. It seems that they sometimes just give up life after being brought ashore. No amount of gentleness when unhooking them revives the will to live.

Wrasse can be caught throughout the year, although fishing is best between May and November, as in the winter fish move into deeper, warmer water. Nor is there any particular time of day to fish, for they can be caught throughout the entire period of daylight. This makes the species popular with anglers, for the hottest of summer days and slackest tide will produce wrasse.

Two times when wrasse do cease to co-operate, however, are at night and during hard weather, when breakers surge far up the cliff faces. Wrasse disappear into a safe hole in bad weather. Likewise, the sensible angler stays away from cliffs and ledges that are a hazard when the wind howls.

Mike Millman

Plaice

Of all the fishes caught around the British Isles, few are better known than the plaice (*Pleuronectes platessa*). It has long been a favourite with the housewife as it looks very attractive when displayed on fishmongers' slabs with its eye-catching orange/red spots. The plaice belongs to the order of fish known as Heterosomata, which means 'twisted-bodied'. These are the flatfishes which swim on one or other side of their body just above the sea bottom.

The plaice lies and swims left side down. The colouring of its right or upper side varies from a light sandy brown right through to a dark brown according to the locality and the type of seabed on which it lives. The distinctive spots, too, range in colour from pale orange to bright scarlet. Furthermore, if the seabed is chalky, then it is not uncommon to catch plaice with white spots as well as red. The underside, however, is always a translucent bluish white with thin blue streaks.

The skin of the plaice feels completely smooth when rubbed with the finger, although there are several bony knobs on the ridge of the head which distinguish it from other flatfish. The lateral line is very slightly curved in the vicinity of the pectoral fin, and the jaws are lined with very strong teeth. There are also muscles resembling a second set of jaws at the entrance of the gullet, which are used to crush small shellfish.

Plaice distribution

Plaice are found all around the British Isles, extending northwards as far as Iceland and as far south as the Mediterranean. Spawning takes place very early in the year— usually in January or February—in depths of 15-30 fathoms. The eggs float in the sea and measure approximately $\frac{1}{10}$in in diameter. A good-sized female, a fish of, say, around 3lb, produces as many as 250,000 eggs in one spawning. Depending on the water temperature, the eggs take anything from 8-28 days to hatch. The newly hatched larvae measure about $\frac{1}{3}$in, and at this stage are not flat but rounded like other fish.

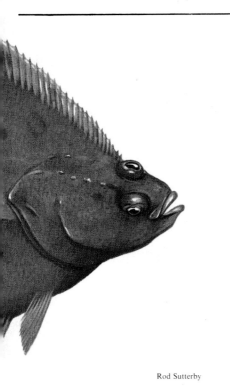

Rod Sutterby

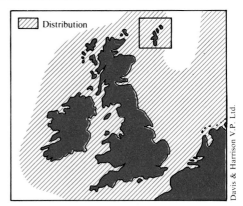

Distribution

Davis & Harrison V.P. Ltd.

Habitat

The plaice, Pleuronectes platessa, *held in high esteem as a table fish, prefers to live in sandy areas such as Morte Bay, seen below looking south-west from the rocks at Mortenhoe. It is common all round the coast of the British Isles.*

Baits

Although bivalve eaters, plaice are usually caught on lug or ragworm.

A. F. Kersting

MUSSEL BED

RAZORFISH

Rod Sutterby

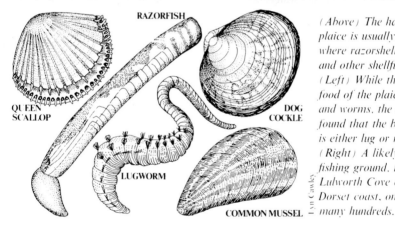

RAZORFISH

QUEEN SCALLOP

LUGWORM

DOG COCKLE

COMMON MUSSEL

Lyn Cawley

(Above) The habitat of the plaice is usually an area where razorshell, mussels and other shellfish live.
(Left) While the natural food of the plaice is bivalves and worms, the angler has found that the best hookbait is either lug or ragworm.
(Right) A likely plaice fishing ground, the beautiful Lulworth Cove on the Dorset coast, only one of many hundreds.

The larva feeds on its yolk sac for about the first week of its existence and normally not until it has exhausted this food supply does it change from its original round shape to the flat shape it will have for the rest of its life. At the same time, the young plaice begins to take in food, which at first is, of course, of microscopic dimensions.

The fish's change in shape begins with a change in the position of the eyes. The left eye moves upwards and forwards and after about ten days arrives on the upper margin of the head just in front of the right eye. A little over four weeks later it reaches its final position above and in front of the right eye. While the eyes are going through this rotating movement, the young fish begins to

take up a new position when swimming. As it has been growing, the whole anatomy of the body has gradually undergone a distinct twisting process, and the fully developed fish finally swims on its left side with both eyes pointing upwards.

Plaice growth rate

The growth rate of a plaice, though relatively fast for a flatfish, is slow when compared with that of cod, for instance. A four-year-old fish will measure only 12-13in, although this may vary slightly from area to area. Females mature some time between their third and seventh years, when they are about 9-11in long. Males mature a year earlier, between their second and sixth years.

The early life of a plaice is spent in sandy

shallows feeding on very small crustaceans called copepods and large quantities of mollusc larvae. After about six months of this diet the fish attain a length of about 2in, and at about this size they gradually move farther out from the shore, although they still favour areas where the depth is less than five fathoms. Tagging experiments have shown that plaice do not as a rule travel a very great distance, usually staying close to the area where they were spawned throughout their life. There is one fish on record that was tagged in the North Sea in 1904. It was recaptured in 1920 only a few miles from where it had originally been tagged.

After spawning

Adult plaice return to shallower waters near the shore in March and April to recover from the rigours of spawning. At this time they are thin, but after a few weeks of feeding in the rich shallows they quickly regain weight. The adult fish feed mainly on bivalve shellfish of all kinds, small cockles and mussels being firm favourites. The mussels are swallowed whole and are crushed by the jaw-like muscles in the throat; the fish then digests the contents and excretes the shell.

If there is ample food, plaice will frequent almost any type of seabed. Some of the best catches are taken in very rocky areas where they are usually feeding on mussels growing on the sides of the rocks. On sandy seabeds they search out razorfish and they will even travel up estuaries in search of cockles and other bivalves. Occasionally, too, they will eat marine worms, such as lugworms and ragworms, although these do not seem to figure very prominently in the plaice's natural diet. Therefore, it is not surprising that, although trawlers catch great quantities of plaice, rod and line anglers fishing the same area with marine worms usually fail to make big catches.

The most likely area to take plaice on rod and line is on mussel beds—but the mussels should be smallish, no bigger than an inch in length. Mussel beds appear in different areas from year to year, and they are usually

Robin Fletcher

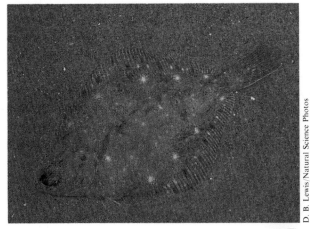

(Left) A fine example of camouflage: a plaice at rest on sand. The fish's pigment cells respond to the colour and pattern of the fish's background and imitate it to an amazing degree.
(Right) A still-fresh 6lb 8oz plaice caught by well-known angler Bill Herme.
(Below) A paternoster trace with a plastic attractor, and the same attractor used with a running ledger.

located by accident, but once found it is reasonably safe to assume there are plaice to be caught there in good numbers.

The ideal time to try for these 'flatties' is during prolonged settled weather during the summer. Clear water and bright sun make for better fishing. As the fish feed largely on bivalves, one would assume that these would be the best bait, but for some reason they seem reluctant to take them when they have been removed from their shells; and of course it is totally impracticable to try to hook the mussel while still inside its shell. Thus the angler is reduced to using less favoured, but nevertheless successful, marine worms as bait. Lugworm usually proves the best, with ragworm running a close second, although this order may be reversed in some areas. Peeler crab, too, is often used.

Size potential

Plaice do not grow to great size and the rod-caught record is a fish of 10lb 3½oz, boated by H Gardiner fishing in Longa Sound, Scotland in 1974. Professional trawlers frequently take bigger fish than this, often well into double figures, but the rod and line angler can usually count himself lucky if he takes fish in the 3-4lb range. For this reason a light hollow glass rod in the 20lb class is to be recommended, providing leads of over 12oz are not going to be used.

For terminal tackle a trace should be used when the tide is running, but paternoster

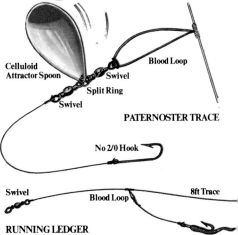

Celluloid Attractor Spoon
Blood Loop
Swivel
Split Ring
Swivel

PATERNOSTER TRACE

No 2/0 Hook

Swivel
Blood Loop
8ft Trace

RUNNING LEDGER

gear is favoured on sluggish tides or slack water. If using a trace, it should be about 8ft in length, either fished through a Clements boom or a Kilmore boom. If baiting with lugworm, a long-shanked hook, No. 2 or 1, is quite large enough. Use three hooks together, as more than one fish is taken at a time quite regularly. This is often because, even if you are holding the rod when the plaice swallows the worm, no bite is detected due to their having the nasty habit of swallowing the baited hook and remaining still. It is only when you lift the rod tip that you realize that a fish has taken the bait.

Fish caught like this are usually deeply hooked. If, however, a bite is felt it is usually

Mike Millman

Celluloid Attractor Spoon

15lb b.s.

Lugworm

Rod Sutterby

second, every time the lead strikes the seabed it sends up a cloud of 'dust' which, because plaice are very curious creatures, brings them close to the baited hooks to investigate. Fishing this way, the bite is very positive, being more in the nature of a sudden snatch rather than the gentle tap experienced with a trace. Unlike a bite on a trace, the sudden snatch should be struck immediately. Once hooked, the fish dives for the seabed and on light gear can put up quite a lively fight, diving for the bottom all the way to the boat. A landing net should be used in preference to a gaff for the bigger specimens.

Although plaice generally favour deeper water than other flatfish such as dabs and flounders, good fish can also be taken by shore-based anglers. However, whereas boat anglers will go out and fish specifically for plaice, plaice taken by shore anglers are more often caught by accident than design. Most likely areas for shore plaice are river mouths, particularly those of Devon and Cornwall. Notable fish can be caught from the shore. The 1984 shore rod caught record is 8lb 1oz.

Estuaries and bays

When fishing for plaice in estuaries, the baited spoon method is the best. By slowly recovering line the bait is kept on the move, so preventing attack by the crabs which abound in this kind of area. In addition, the spoon as it revolves flashes and disturbs the seabed, attracting fish to the area. As well as estuaries, other likely shore-based spots are sheltered sandy bays with a fair depth of water, and rocky shores with sandy gullies. For the latter, a paternoster rig is recommended, the terrain being too rock-covered and snaggy to use a spoon.

Plaice make excellent eating. A fish of over $2\frac{1}{2}$lb can be 'quarter filleted'. To do this, cut through to the bone from head to tail along the lateral line with a sharp knife and then carefully remove the flesh from the bone by cutting outwards towards the fins. Do this on both the top and the underside, thus making four good fillets. A fish in good condition will produce half its total weight in fillets.

only a light tap, tap, and should be left for the fish to gorge the bait. To avoid the temptation of striking too soon, it is best not even to hold the rod.

To attract the fish, white spoons may be added to the trace, but they must be celluloid and not metal. Celluloid spoons are lighter and even a slight tide will give them movement in the water, and it is this movement that attracts flatfish to the hooks.

Slack-water fishing

A different method of fishing should be used when using paternoster gear on slack water. In these conditions, the rod tip should be continually raised and lowered. This has two effects: first, it gives the bait movement;

Sharks

SIX-GILLED SHARK
Hexanchus griseus

Twenty-five or so species of fish belonging to the shark order have been recorded in the waters around the British Isles. One of these species, the basking shark, *Cetorhinus maximus*, although relatively common, cannot be considered as a potential angling species as it is a plankton feeder unwilling to take any bait presented by an angler.

Nine other species are nearly always found in water well beyond that fished by anglers. Since these species are bottom-dwellers which swim at the edge of the continental shelf, they too can be removed from the list of species taken by anglers. Eight species are taken with great regularity on many parts of the coast but are not considered as sharks because of their small size, or names. These are the tope and smoothhound, the spotted dogfish—lesser, greater (bull huss), blackmouthed—the spurdog, and monkfish which is also a true shark.

The remaining species are all large members of the family which are considered by anglers as real sharks. At least two of these,

the blue shark, *Prionace glauca*, and the porbeagle, *Lamna nasus*, are extremely common at certain times of the year in some places, while two other species, the mako, *Isurus oxyrinchus*, and the thresher shark *Alopias vulpinus*, make the angling press with some regularity. A recent addition to the list of rod-and-line captured species is the six-gilled shark, *Hexanchus griseus*. There is only one recorded in Britain so far.

Several other species are known to frequent our waters. Reports exist for the bramble shark, *Echinorhinus brucus*, Greenland shark, *Somniosus microcephalus* and, surprisingly, the hammerhead, *Sphyrna sp.*, which has been claimed (unsubstantiated) as a rod and line capture. Reported sightings only, without the evidence of an actual specimen, are the rigger shark, *Galeocerdo cuvier*, and white shark, *Carcharodon carchararias*.

The capture by rod and line of any of the last five, even six, species must be considered as luck rather than reward for intentional

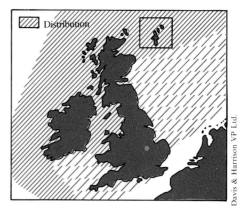

Davis & Harrison VP Ltd.

Rod Sutterby

Habitat

Sharks are mainly roving fishes, seeking their food in the expanse of deep waters. Where food fishes congregate off cliffs and rocks, sharks will often come close to the shore at places such as the Hoy area off Orkney (below).

Baits

Whole dead fish of many kinds, especially the oily ones, are excellent shark baits.

Mike Millman

angling effort and any angler trying specifically for these would spend many fruitless days before reward came his way, if at all.

Nevertheless since fortune does smile on some anglers, no description of the sharks found around Britain can be complete without them. Since all sharks conform more than most fish to a general shape or body form which consists essentially of a conical head with mouth on the underside and long tapering cylindrical body which ends in a forked tail, only those features which differentiate them need be discussed.

The hammerhead

The hammerhead is immediately recognizable because the head is flattened from above and below and extended laterally into an unmistakable shape. The reason for this strange modification is not understood. There have been many suggestions about functional adaptation. One is that the wide placing of the olefactory organs at the extremities of the 'hammer' may have given the shark a 'stereoscopic' sense of smell.

Another species, the thresher, also immediately identifies itself because of the extended length of the upper half of the tail of the fish. Again, proof of function for such a long tail is lacking. It has been suggested that the tail is used first to herd food fish into

Shark can be identified by their teeth.
These jaws show those of the mako.

HAMMERHEAD SHARK
Sphyrna zygaena

a tight pack• and then for stunning them.

Some other shark species can also be easily identified because they deviate from a general pattern shown by most sharks. Assuming that all sharks have two dorsal fins, a large one followed by a second smaller one near the tail, any shark not showing the two fins, but only a single large one near the tail, should also possess six gill openings on each side of the head and not five. This identifies the six-gilled shark.

In a somewhat similar way, the absence of an anal fin (the fin situated between the pelvic fins and the tail) means that the specimen in question is a member of the

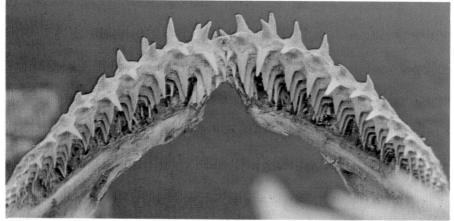

Mike Millman

Rod Sutterby

(*Above*) *One of the rarer sharks, the hammerhead.* (*Below*) *An Irish blue caught off Baltimore.*

Bill Howes

spurdog family, for all sharks which have cylindrical bodies but lack an anal fin belong to this group whether they bear spines at the front edge of the two dorsal fins or not. Such a shark would be either a bramble or a Greenland shark. Distinction between these two species is very easy, for while the skin of the Greenland shark is rough like all sharks, the bramble shark also has many large thorns similar to those on the roker or thornback ray. The English name, bramble, is therefore, very apt.

The other sharks, the porbeagle, mako, blue, tiger and white do not show any of the features mentioned above, i.e. the absence of or special development of any fins, but conform completely to the generalized picture of a fish with five pairs of gill openings, two dorsal fins and an anal fin. But body proportions, fin positions, colour and shape of teeth, are aids to identification.

Blue and tiger sharks

The blue shark has an extremely long, slim body with the upper part of the tail much larger than its lower part, narrow, long pectoral fins and vivid blue colour. A shark with a blunt, short snout and short pectorals, highly asymmetrical tail, and grey or transverse bars would be a tiger shark.

Three species remain, the porbeagle, mako and white shark. They bear the greatest resemblance to one another and are closely related. Indeed the similarity between the porbeagle and mako is so great that it was once not realised that the mako existed in British waters. A world record claim to the International Game Fishing Association (IGFA) for a record porbeagle showed that mako exist in our seas, for on examination the fish was identified as a mako, not a porbeagle, on the basis of tooth structure.

Had the captor known that the mako is characterized by very long, slim triangular teeth, unlike the triangular teeth of the porbeagle where the main triangle is flanked by one very small triangular cusp at the base, the mistake would not have been made. Again, the porbeagle tends to be much more squat or plump than the mako, and always shows two caudal keels, one large, the other much smaller and less distinct. The mako only has one keel, due to the flattening of the body just in front of the tail.

Any shark taken off Britain which externally resembles the porbeagle but has only one caudal keel should also be examined for tooth shape. If they are triangular, with serrated edges then—at long last—a British white shark will have been taken.

The blue shark is a southern species which prefers warm water. As an oceanic fish it arrives off Britain's South Coast and south and west coasts of Ireland with the coming of summer, but keeps well off shore. Its main distribution area is off Cornwall both on the English Channel side and to the north and it is only at the end of exceptionally warm summers that some may move north into the Irish Sea. Off Ireland many are found off the south and south-west and along certain areas in the west such as Galway Bay.

Floats for sharking are not the subtle things the freshwater angler uses. This is a novel screw clamp stopper.

Some may move north to appear in the autumn off the west coast of Scotland, but because the waters of the Minch (between the mainland and the Outer Hebrides) have only a northern and southern access to the open sea, few blue shark are found in that area. Most records from these northern waters come from west of the Hebrides, from the Rockall and St Kilda area.

A similar distribution exists for the mako shark. However, the numbers caught each year are nowhere near as great as for the blue since the species tends to be more solitary. Packs of mako are never encountered. All mako captures so far come from the western end of the English Channel or the northern part of the Bristol Channel.

Mako and porbeagle

The mako has so far not been recorded from Irish waters, while the porbeagle is widespread. Many parts of the coasts of the British Isles hold porbeagle with certain places in Wales and Scotland now producing specimens. So-called 'hot-spots' have been discovered off the Isle of Wight, North Cornwall, North Devon. But big catches may only be due to the great number of anglers fishing these areas. There are similar hot-spots off the west coast of Ireland.

If anglers concentrated on shark fishing many similar hot-spots would come to light, as has been proved in Shetland. Here, due to the effort of two anglers, many porbeagle have been hooked including two specimens. Comparison of the hot-spots shows that they have one factor in common. They are all tidal areas close or relatively close inshore often in association with reef areas or rough ground which are frequented by shoal fish such as herring or mackerel and to a very large extent pollack.

A similar distribution pattern appears to exist also for the thresher which may be encountered anywhere at any time around Britain. Again most records of capture come from the British south coast, but this probably only reflects the fact that there is more shark angling done in that part of our islands than elsewhere.

Mike Millman

This rug is awarded by the Shark Angling Club of Great Britain to anglers who have caught shark of 250lb or more.

So far as the other species are concerned one, the Greenland shark, is definitely cold-water-loving so that the Shetlands would be the obvious place to expect the first rod-and-line capture. Perhaps some anglers fishing for common skate will be the first to catch one of these sharks. Since both the bramble and six-gilled sharks are bottom-dwelling species of rather deep water both could be taken anywhere angling is carried close to or in water of over 100 fathoms.

Of the British species which have been recorded as rod-and-line captures the six-gilled shark is the one with potentially the largest size. The present record, taken in 1976 off Penlee Point, Plymouth, at 9lb 8oz is no indication of the ultimate size for the species, for it is known to reach 1,500lb.

Even the British blue record of 218lb, a record which has stood since 1959, is no

indication of size for the world record is almost twice that weight. But fish of that size are uncommon and may become less so for the killing of these fish (especially by British anglers) means that there are fewer fish to reach the very big sizes. This is obvious when one considers the gradual decrease in size of the average weight of blue sharks taken off our south-west coast.

The world record weight of over 1,000lb for a mako may also be somewhat on the low side, for larger specimens are known. British anglers, therefore, still have a target to aim for, for the British record weight for the species of 500lb represents only 50% of the potential weight.

Cornwall's world record

So far as the porbeagle record is concerned, Britain heads the World list with the 465lb fish taken of Padstow, Cornwall in 1976. But commercial captures suggest that it may reach more than 600lb.

As with the blue and mako sharks, the British thresher record, of 323lb established in 1982 by S. Mills fishing near the Nab Tower, off Portsmouth, Hants, is no indication of ultimate size, for specimens in excess of 1,000lb. have been caught elsewhere.

So far as the other species which have been mentioned are concerned, all with the exception of the bramble are giants, for while the latter probably does not go heavier than 300lb, hammerheads have been reported to 15ft and 1,000lb, while the tiger shark will probably reach twice that weight.

Legendary white shark

The weight and size of the white shark are legendary, with specimens in excess of 20ft and two tons having been caught in nets or by harpoon. These fish therefore make the world rod-caught record of 2,664lb taken off Australia look a little small.

In second place in the giant league must be placed the Greenland shark which in its cold waters reaches almost the same size as the white. It is an extremely sluggish species and is easily taken by hand-line and landed without any struggle. This is why it is also called the 'sleeper' shark.

Conger

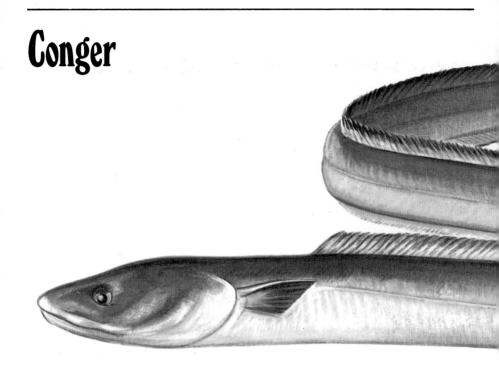

Research into the life cycle of the conger eel (*Conger conger*), has not been as thorough as that of other species. Only detailed research into sea species that are commercially useful has been carried out, and much of what has been written about the conger has yet to be proved. It does appear, though, that the conger eels seen in British coastal waters and caught by anglers are not in fact fully mature in spite of their large size. The British rod-caught record stands at 109lb 6oz, caught off Plymouth in 1976, but many larger fish have been recorded by British fishermen. There is evidence from deeper waters that the conger grows very much larger than was previously believed. In 1972 a fish of 220lb was taken in a trawl net off Denmark.

The conger is born in the ocean depths—spawning can take place as deep as 2,000 fathoms. Although it can only spawn once it is tremendously prolific, producing as many as 15 million eggs. These eggs are bathypelagic, they float freely in the sea at a great depth, and are carried on the slow-moving currents of the North Atlantic Drift towards the Continental Shelf. The larvae can take more than two years to reach the shallow coastal waters, and during that time they change, first to look like a narrow-headed leaf (leptocephalus) which is completely transparent and grows to a length of about 5in and then to the familiar cylindrical eel shape. These structural body changes (metamorphoses), are common in many fish species.

No mistaking the conger

The conger is first observed in British waters in the familiar eel shape and is sometimes mistaken for the common eel, but the differences are easy to spot. The dorsal fin on the conger starts level with its pectoral fins, that of the common eel starts much farther back along the body. The conger has scaleless skin and the upper jaw is longer than the lower one. The teeth are more pronounced in the conger and small congers stay mainly inshore and have a very

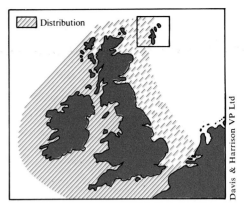

Davis & Harrison VP Ltd

Distribution

Rod Sutterby

Habitat
The conger is found in deep water and inshore. It seeks wrecks, rocks, piles or harbour walls as hiding places. The rocky cove and small harbour at Dunquin, Co Kerry, Ireland (below) provides the perfect conger habitat.

Bait
Whole small fish, sides of large mackerel, the head and attached guts, all take conger.

John Holden

Conger

(Left) A lively conger caught off Stromness, Orkney.
(Right) A mackerel head makes an attractive bait for conger.
(Far right) The British rod-caught record conger is 7ft 9½in long, has a girth of 2ft 5½in and weighs 109lb 6oz. Robin Potter hooked it over a wreck near the Eddystone reef in September 1976 and took 22 minutes to boat the giant fish.
(Below) Many charterboats have a well into which the conger can be dropped to avoid injury to anglers.

fast growth rate. There is a well-authenticated case of a 3lb conger placed in Southport Aquarium and growing to 69lb in four years, and of another which reached 90lb in five and half years.

These smaller eels are voracious feeders, living on fish, lobsters, crabs and cuttlefish. They are not solitary fish, and tend to feed in groups. In the Bay of Biscay they have been observed hunting in packs when feeding on the octopus. When an octopus is found the group of congers will attack it and grip each of the octopus's tentacles in their powerful jaws, and spin backwards to dismember it and consume the remains.

The conger is found in the coast off the southern parts of Scandinavia, as far south as eastern Equatorial Africa, and the whole of the Mediterranean. Similar species can also be found on the Atlantic coast of America, the South Atlantic and the Indian and Pacific Oceans. As they grow in size, the majority retreat to deeper water, but many large fish live in convenient caves or holes close to a good food supply. Many harbours and fish quays have congers living close at hand, and some of them can grow very large indeed. Many of the very

large shore-caught conger have come from such places, one of the most notable being taken by Albert Lander at Torquay in 1967. This fish, which weighed 67¼lb, lived among some large pipes that had been lost overboard from a barge.

In other areas the conger retreats to deeper water during the day and moves inshore at night to feed. These fish are very susceptible to changes in water temperature, and a sudden very cold spell can kill them. Generally, during the colder weather, they retreat to the depths where the variation in temperature is very small.

Male conger do not grow as large as females, and although most standard re-

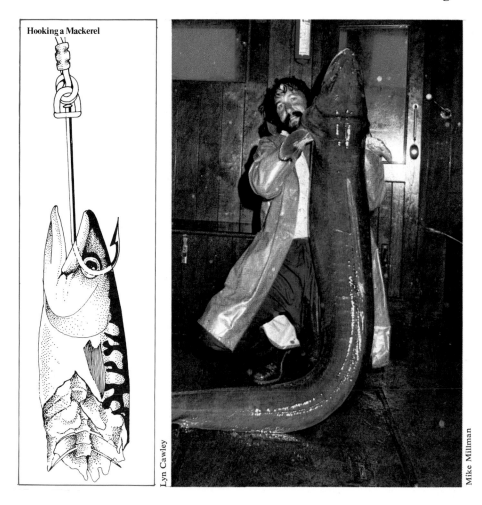

Hooking a Mackerel

Lyn Cawley

Mike Millman

ference books state that the male fish seldom exceeds 15lb, male fish have been caught weighing up to 35lb. The concensus of opinion seems to be that the male conger becomes sexually mature in about five years, but the female may take nearly ten years to develop. The conger dies before its eggs can become ripe. It would appear that the eggs need nearly a year to develop before they are fully ripe and the great depths of the ocean, with its tremendous water pressure, is a necessary factor for ripening.

If the conger is prevented from making this journey, by being kept in an aquarium for example, its body begins to change, it stops feeding, its bones become soft and its teeth fall out. The fish has adapted to a deep-water existence.

Where do conger spawn?

Unlike the common eel (*Anguilla anguilla*) there is no set time for the conger to migrate to their spawning grounds, but it is during the summer months, and although the spawning does take place in the Saragasso Sea region, the areas are never the same. It is possible that the conger has more than one area in which it spawns.

Large fish which are found inshore have already been mentioned, but the majority of big conger inhabit the deep water reefs and wrecks, and appear to be most prolific

199

Conger

in the waters of the south and west coasts of this country. Certainly far more large congers are caught from these areas than from anywhere else, but it is possible that if the wrecks all around Britain's coast were fished equally large congers would be found.

The deep-water wrecks where the largest congers are found lie mostly on a seabed of mud or sand and give the appearance of large reefs rising from a featureless plain. The tidal currents run up channel, slacken off and then run down channel. During the tidal run many fish seek the shelter afforded by the wreckage. When the tide is at its strongest the conger bites are few, but as the tide slackens, fish begin to move around the wreck, and the congers emerge from their shelter and begin to feed.

The size of these fish is completely dependent on how much food is available, and the wrecks along the coasts of the West Country are living larders for the conger. Opinions vary as to just how often the larger fish do feed, but when wreck conger do start to feed they are very voracious and will take nearly any offering that is presented to them. Even when they have been hooked and broken free from a line, they till take another bait within a few minutes.

Conger tackle

The tackle used by the conger fisherman has to be adequate to cope with a very large and strong fish, but need not be of the 'broomstick' pattern. Many excellent conger have been caught on light tackle—what is needed is well balanced equipment and the patience to play the fish out thoroughly. A large conger can be winched to the surface before it has realized what is happening. Such a fish, full of fight on the surface of the water, is not a pleasant sight, especially to the person who has to gaff the fish and heave it on board.

Large congers thrashing about in a boat are very distracting and there are many theories as to the best way to quiet them. A heavy blow just above the vent can stun the fish, and a knife driven into the skull

between the eyes can kill it, but it is not always possible to get the fish into a suitable position to do either of these things. A heavy blow may miss the fish and do damage to tackle or to the floor boards of the boat. It seems that the best thing to do is either to transfer the fish to a box where it can remain unmolested or to throw a large sack or covering over the fish, when it will lie quietly.

Where conger feed

Although the conger is generally regarded as a bottom-living fish, feeding mainly on the seabed, this is not always true. There have been instances of conger being taken on baits fished in mid-water, and it is not uncommon to see a conger swimming on the surface in rocky inlets. The conger has its own method of avoiding the 'bends', the crippling result of the sudden change in water pressure that kills the majority of deep-water fish. As the conger rises to the surface it will belch, releasing air from its stomach and equalizing itself with the water pressure as it rises. The bubbles resulting from this action are often seen on the surface when a conger is hooked. This is one of the reasons why a conger can be so full of fight on the surface, whereas other species, such as the ling or pollack, are unable to return to the bottom.

Mike Millman

(Above) A conger comes aboard. The gaff may look heavy compared with the size of the fish, but it avoids possible injury from the conger's extremely powerful jaws.
(Right) Conger diet includes crab, lobster and cuttlefish, but fish too are taken.

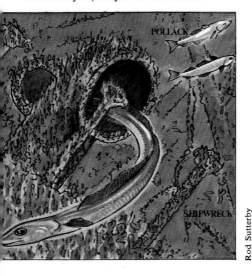

POLLACK

SHIPWRECK

Rod Sutterby

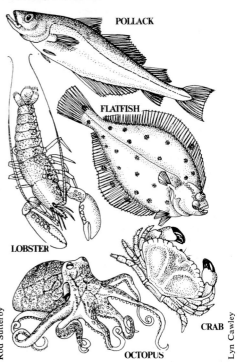

POLLACK

FLATFISH

LOBSTER

OCTOPUS

CRAB

Lyn Cawley

Mike Millman

Beachcasting rods

When Leslie Moncrieff demonstrated that his Springheel rod (which had a reversed taper butt) used in conjunction with his 'Layback' casting technique would hurl 4-6oz leads well beyond the 150 yard mark, beachcasting tournaments became a battleground for competitors, designers and tackle manufacturers, as indeed they are now some 30 years later, not only for beachcasting rods but reels too.

Ten years later a second breakthrough arrived in the form of the Swedish firm ABU's 484 beachcasting rod which had an incredibly stiff action due to its alloy butt and rapid-taper glass fibre blank. Unlike Moncrieff's Springheel rod, which through the reverse-taper butt section absorbed some of the power built up by the angler during the cast, the 484 transferred all the power into the cast and for the first time ever distances beyond that 200 yard barrier were being achieved on the tournament field by people such as Paul Kerry. This of course related to longer casts from the beach, despite a recognised reduction due to drag and air resistance from the baited terminal rig. Tournament distances have now increased towards the 300 yard mark using a 5¼oz casting lead in both the multiplier and fixed-spool reel events. And both rod and reel manufacturers are constantly striving towards greater distances still.

The impact of carbon-fibre has of course been tremendous, providing a beachcasting rod considerably lighter than the old ABU 484, with integral overfit or spigot ferrules instead of the heavyweight chromed brass, locking ferrules.

Rod construction

Top-quality modern rods have great rigidity with no hint of deflection or buckling in the lower half, due to various carbon-type braids wrapped around the blank. The actual blank is made from several different carbon cloths (to achieve the correct taper) rolled around a hardened steel mandrel and after oven-baking at high temperatures ground to a super-smooth finish. The blank is then cut and spiggoted (unless the rod is made in two separate halves each with integral corresponding ferrules or overfit joints) and a sheathing of PVC or fixed reel fitting plus duplon grips fashioned at the butt end.

Top-quality beachcasters consist of carbon tube throughout. Budget-priced carbon rods may be fitted with a (shrink-tube covered) dural aluminium butt whilst models at the very bottom of the price range

(Above) Champion long-distance caster, Paul Kerry, displays a nice catch of East Coast cod taken from the south beach at Great Yarmouth, some 150 yards out on lugworm.

203

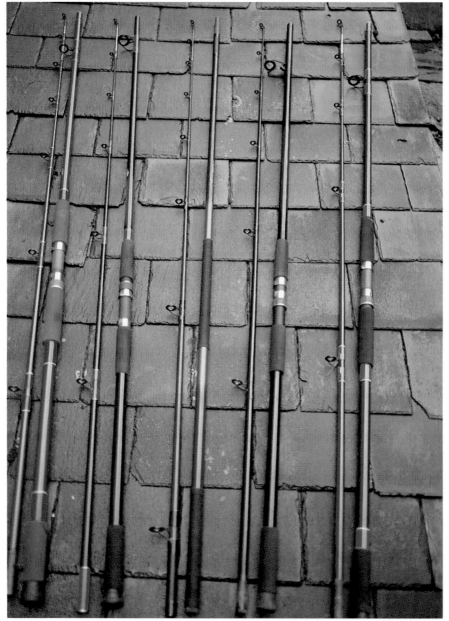

John Wilson

are still manufactured from fibre-glass blanks or a composite mixture of both carbon and glass fibres.

In addition to the more traditional screw-reel fitting sandwiched between grips of duplon plus a duplon hand grip at the butt, some beachcasters, particularly those used for multiplier reel fishing, are available with a pair of simple plastic coaster fittings which can secure the reel in any desired position.

Rod rings on the vast majority of

(Left) A selection of carbon-fibre and carbon/glass composite beachcasting rods which have hard-wearing aluminium oxide rod rings. The middle rod has no reel fitting. The multiplier reel is secured by a pair of 'coasters' at exactly the correct position for casting to suit the individual angler.

A beachcaster in action at Clew Bay, where many islands offer great beach fishing.

beachcasters (even budget models) now have lined centres of aluminium oxide which means that unlike the old stainless or hard chromed rings of yesteryear, they do not groove and subsequently cause line wear.

Top-of-the-range models are fitted with SIC (silicon-carbide) centres throughout which provides an extremely hard, yet super-smooth rod ring.

Beachcasters designed purposefully to be used with a multiplier reel will be furnished with up to 8 rings starting with a butt ring diameter of no more than 25mm, to ensure the line is supported along the rod's curvature when bent. Whereas models designed specifically with fixed-spool reels should sport no more than 4 or 5 large diameter rings tapering down 50mm to 20mm from butt to tip ring to ensure long frictionless casts.

Using small-diameter low-set rings in conjunction with a fixed-spool reel will result in greatly reduced distances, a fact which the manufacturers of many budget-priced beachcasters do not seem aware of. So many are fitted with a set of several medium-sized rings which is neither one thing nor the other. At a pinch a multiplier can always be used with a beachcaster hung with just 5 large rings for fixed-spool fishing. But a fixed-spool reel cannot be effectively used (if the cast is reduced by half) on a rod ring for use with multiplying reels. So beware.

The action, or how the rod responds to load, is controlled by its taper and the actual wall thickness of the blank be it of carbon or fibre-glass. A steeply tapered rod is faster in its delivery than one of a slow taper which slopes gradually from butt to tip. Speed and action may be further enhanced by the process of compound tapering, a design where extra layers of reinforced carbon or glass cloth is applied at certain spots along the blank. For instance, some manufacturers actually roll fibre-glass into the tip to provide maximum sensitivity to their carbon beachcasters, while others use up to several layers of varying carbon cloths to achieve the same result.

Fast taper rods bend and flick straight in immediate response to casting, particularly the well-proven pendulum cast which for both fishing and tournaments has virtually become the standard technique for achieving long distances consistently.

On the other hand slower rods which cast far enough to reach the fish (less than 100 yards say) are less sensitive to casting errors and are far more enjoyable to use, particularly when playing large fish from the shore.

Most manufacturers offer beachcasting rods in the 11½ to 13ft bracket because on the tournament field it has been proven that consistently long casting is best achieved within this range. And a 12-footer should cover most shore-fishing requirements.

Boat rods

Bill Howes

The sea angler's boat fishing rod is merely an extension to his arm, acting just like a lever, converting the pulling power of a handline to lifting strength. What has happened over half a century or so is that anglers have applied sporting techniques to deep-sea fishing.

Once upon a time anglers went to sea as onlookers at the commercial fisherman's trade, for showing interest in the professional's livelihood was a sure way of gaining a place in their boat and a real chance of coming to grips with a truly big fish. But a need grew to extend the sport beyond taking fish for the pot, resulting today in a large majority of sea species such as tope, smoothounds, dogfish and even bass being returned by their captors. There is now a growing band of boat fishermen who endeavour to return most of the fish they catch, taking just the odd fish or two for the pot, in order to conserve stocks for the future.

In the old days boat rods were made from built cane, rather clumsy and twice the weight of today's carbon-fibre equivalent, but they advanced the sport considerably from the handline stage where it began. It was believed that rods had to be strong and initially, because cane came in relatively short useful lengths, nobody wanted to introduce a metal ferrule into the middle of them. Some even had steel cores to give extra power for fighting large species. Expensive models were made of built cane whilst buget priced-boat rods were manufactured from whole cane sections joined to solid wooden handles and were exceptionally heavy.

Need for flexibility

Gradually, as other departments within sports fishing developed, it dawned on sea-anglers that what was needed was a measure of flexibility. The ultra-stiff, immensely strong boat rod failed to provide enjoyment on two counts. It failed to transmit the vibrations and thrill of a hard-fighting fish and neither could it flex to absorb a fish's powerful runs. Most of the movements of the fish resulted in a bending of the rod's entire length. With the advent of extruded solid-glass rods there was at last a material which could be relied upon for bending progressively that rarely broke, even under extreme pressure. But solid glass-rods were very heavy to hold and did not have the recovery of built cane. Nevertheless the material was inexpensive, so there was a flood (as with coarse fishing) of cheap rods on the market and although far from perfect in action these glass rods did attract many more people into boat fishing.

Hollow glass fibre

The natural progression in the glass-fibre industry from drawing out glass fibres and weaving them into a matt or cloth as it is perhaps better known, was quick. Rod manufacturers soon realised that a controllable material had at last been found and there was sufficient demand for the substantially more expensive (just as there is with carbon today) hollow glass-fibre rods for manufacturers to set up rolling plants.

The Americans led the field for a number of years but soon a British industry emerged. The simple technique (which is similar for the production of carbon-fibre blanks) involves impregnating a cloth woven from glass fibres and rolling it around a hardened steel mandrel to give it the shape and taper of the blank required. It is then bound tightly before the whole mandrel is placed into an oven where high temperatures set the glass.

After releasing the glass tube from the mandrel the blank is then ground to produce a clean, even and smooth tapered tube. Action can be built into the blank in two ways. First, through the actual taper of the mandrel upon which the cloth is rolled, and second, according to the amount (thickness) of cloth used in a particular area of the blank.

Hollow carbon fibre

With these two factors settled, a curve of almost any power and compression can be

(Above left) A quiet moment during a deep sea angling session from a trawler off the North Devon coast near Appledore. A variety of rods is in use, mostly 6ft or 8ft long. (Right) A selection of modern 'uptide' and standard 'downtide' boat rods and the reels to use with them. Notice the longer uptide rods on the left have extremely sensitive tips. (Below) For heavy duty deep sea fishing for powerful species, wire line is now popular. A roller tip ring bearing a stainless steel pulley is essential to avoid wear and grooving under friction.

Mike Prichard

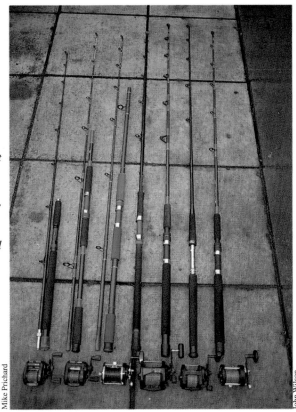

John Wilson

achieved. Now that carbon-fibre is used in the majority of fishing rod blanks manufactured in the UK a considerable weight reduction is achieved in addition to other benefits such as the incredible quick return of carbon compared to glass-fibre.

Carbon boat rods are not only light and a pleasure to use, they are almost unbreakable. They are not affected by oil, saltwater or extremes of temperature and require next-to-no maintenance. These features alone give modern rods tremendous advantage over the more traditional rod-making materials.

Selecting a boat rod

There is no standard boat rod as such, simply those which are considered a standard length (somewhere between 5½ and 7ft) also referred to as 'downtide rods' and 'uptide rods'. As their name suggests these much longer rods (between 8 and 10ft long) are used for the comparatively modern technique of uptide fishing whereby the lead is cast up and across the tide as opposed to it being lowered directly downtide from the boat's stern.

Uptide rods have extremely fine tips for sensitive bite registration with a reserve of power in the butt and permit the use of light reel lines of between 15-20lb to enjoy the fight from and subsequently land comparatively large species such as tope. They are not generally rated in line strengths but in suggested lead weight ranges. For example, 2-6 oz or 4-8oz.

Standard-length boat rods however are rated in the class of line strengths for which the power of the rod is most suited. For example, 15lb, 20lb, 30lb, 50lb and 80lb. A 30lb class rod for example will cope with lines up to 30lb, leads up to 1½lb and quite fast tides when fishing from an anchored boat. Such a rod is intended to be used for tope, big shoal fish such as cod, pollack, ling and rays up to medium size, but will still provide enjoyment with smaller fish.

A 50lb class rod enables all but the largest of common skate and conger to be hauled up from deep-water marks with a line of around

(Above) Boat rods are built to withstand strains and stresses that would destroy coarse fishing equipment.
(Right) The longer uptide boat rod is most effectively used for species like bass, which in clear water can show a surprising amount of caution.

50lb test. For a larger quarry still, big porbeagles and mako sharks, halibut and the massive common skate found off Shetland, Orkney and the west of Ireland, some anglers prefer to go up to an 80lb class rod coupled to a large-format reel and lines around 80lb test, either monofilament or dacron.

For hauling up big fish from deep-water marks the rod should have a roller tip ring. All boat rods should in fact be fitted with quality rings of a one-piece frame construction such as the FUJI range which have aluminium-oxide centres and will not groove, the only exception being when using wire lines. The entire rod should then be fitted with roller rings, otherwise grooving and excess friction will take place.

The demands of shark fishing also call for the rod to be fitted throughout with roller rings of good quality. When powerful fish repeatedly make long runs, it is imperative that the risks of line wear be reduced to a minimum. Most standard-length, downtide boat rods are fitted with a moulded rubber butt cap. This can be rested against the upper thigh for support during a lengthy battle, or better still, fitted into a specialized butt pad which covers the crotch and belts around the waist. If a butt pad is not used for playing fish such as big conger or skate etc, then severe brusing of the groin area is inevitable.

Top-quality boat rods which might also be used in the tropics when trolling for exotic saltwater spatsfish are usually fitted with a slotted butt cap that fits into specialized, 'tubed' rod holders and into the gimble of a fighting chair. This ensures the rod will not twist either during trolling or during the fight. For anglers prefering a stand-up fight, it's wise to select a butt pad that incorporates a cross bar into which the rod's slotted butt cap will fit securely.

After use, hose boat rods down with freshwater to remove all particles of salt, paying particular attention to rings and the screw-reel fitting. Boat rods are subject to more knocks and general abuse than all other types of rods. A seasonal rub down with a cleaning agent, followed by a gentle smoothing with wet and dry sandpaper will remove all the dross. It is then a matter of applying enough coats of varnish to effectively seal the whippings on the rings and give the finish the owner needs. Before varnishing, inspect the rings closely, looking for scuffing within the ring itself. Any ring which is loose should be rewhipped and any that are grooved instantly replaced.

John Wilson

Centrepin

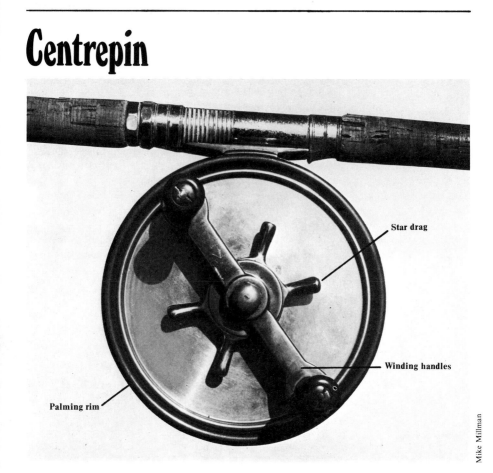

Star drag

Winding handles

Palming rim

Mike Millman

The centrepin reel

Centrepin reels for sea fishing have a history stretching back into the middle eighteen hundreds. Early models were constructed from either teak, oak, or mahagony and had brass fittings. Most were about 4 inches in diameter and the narrow spools were capable of holding little more than 100 yards of the thick hemp lines common to the period. Gradually these lines gave way to much thinner plaited lines, which considerably increased the reel's capacity. A handle on either side of the drum was often too small and allowed little or no leverage. Before such refinements as check rachets and line guards were added, Nottingham and Scarborough reels were simplicity itself. Over the years centrepins manufactured from metal and

bakelite complemented the wooden varieties and, with little change in size or design they continued to be widely used for general sea fishing up to the late 1950's.

The technique for using a centrepin reel against heavy, fast running fish, such as pollack or bass, was not achieved easily. Anticipating the fish's behaviour and changing from winding to palming the drum, when the fish demanded line, required fine judgement. The inexperienced angler often suffered the penalty of cracked knuckles from flying handles or a monumental birds nest when the reel drum overran the line under pressure. This could lead all too often to the loss of a good fish. The author remembers, as an inexperienced angler, losing five double figure pollack in a row, during a trip off the

Bill Howes

Cornish coast, for one or other of the reasons mentioned.

Fishing with a centrepin without a slipping clutch, has the advantage of putting the angler in direct contact with the quarry. Every movement of the fish is instantly transmitted to the fingers, and once a level of experience has been gained, it is certainly one of the most sporting ways of fishing. Although the use of small centrepin reels declined with the introduction of the multiplier just after the Second World War, they are still used occasionally for boat fishing.

Centrepin's comeback

In the past few years there has been a slight swing back to centrepins, and a variety of new models are now available in tackle shops.

Large diameter centrepins for heavyweight species have long been popular and with good reason. Unlike the large modern multiplier, which is fished above the rod, thereby creating certain problems of balance, the centrepin hangs below and is really more comfortable to use when dealing with outsize fish such as shark, skate and conger. Line capacity is tremendous and most nine-inch reels can hold 600 yards of 60 to 80 lb braided line and considerably more monofilament. Of many excellent reels, one of the classics was undoubtedly Hardy's Fortuna, which went out of manufacture about twenty years ago. However there are still large numbers in everyday use aboard the sharking fleets running out of Cornish ports. The Fortuna, produced in a range of sizes from

Multiplier reels

12in down to 7in, featured a silk smooth movement and a clutch or star-drag that was second to none in positiveness and strength. The reels were fitted with two-inch handles which gave all the leaverage one could wish for. The smallest Fortuna, and perhaps the most popular model, was the 7in weighing 5½ lb. In mint condition the reel is a collector's item and can easily command a price in excess of £125. It is a real thoroughbred.

Centrepin technique

When fishing with a centrepin reel, it is vital to set the drag light enough to allow a large fish to take line under pressure but when the time comes to strike or pump the fish it has to be tightened down allowing a safety margin in case of an unexpected run. If too

Many modern multiplying reels such as this Ryobi 320 have a clutch which automatically engages from free spool when the handle is turned.

much tension is used it is all too easy to tear the hook out of the fish's mouth.

The multiplier reel

The majority of boat anglers nowa days use the multiplying reel for fishing in both shallow and deep water. They range in size from 2/0 to 14/0, the latter being used to handle giant game fish. Multipliers are designed to retrieve line rapidly and have ratios between 2:1 and 5:1. In recent years, reels with automatic gearing have become popular. With a ratio range of 2½:1 to 4½:1 and in a few cases 5:1, they change down into low gear when a fish is pumped and up into a higher gear when only the line and terminal tackle is retrieved.

Another useful feature recently introduced is an inbuilt digital counter which accurately records and displays the footage of the line that is out. This can be very advantageous when fishing in deep water. Many multipliers have a rotating or bar-type line distributor which lays retrieved line evenly across the width of the spool. All multipliers have either a star or lever drag which allows a fish to take line without the handles revolving. Star drags, which are cheaper to manufacture, vary considerable in their effectiveness. Cheap reels can strip after a period of time when used for deep water fishing against weighty specimens. It is always good policy to buy the best reel you can afford. Expensive reels incorporate what are described as aircraft quality bearings set in both end plates which gives the drum a smooth, even action and reduces friction to a minimum. Lever drag multipliers are more expensive but well worth the extra expenditure. The lever does away with the on/off mechanism necessary in conventional multipliers and allows the amount of drag imposed on a fish to be adjusted constantly throughout the time it is played. This can also be done with the star drag but not with as much ease or accuracy.

Multiplier technique

The technique of boat fishing with a multiplier is easily mastered. Provided one keeps a thumb on the spool as the weight runs to the bottom, few problems will be experienced. Failure to keep the free running spool in check can result in a birds nest. It is wrong to use the audible check as a means of controlling the spool or deliberately to tighten up the tension screw which controls distance between the flanges and side plates. Both of these methods result in considerable wear if not outright damage to the reel. Before loading a multiplier with nylon monofilament, a level of backing must be wound on to take the build up of pressure nylon imposes on the spool. Without it, the reel can literally burst apart during the playing of even a moderate size fish.

The use of wire line for deep water fishing, particularly where there is a fast run of tide, is rapidly gaining ground. It does, however, require quite distinct techniques and equipment.

Multipliers with wide spools and line levelers are quite unsuitable for use with wire which requires a narrow spool with good a line capacity. Whilst medium weight multipliers manufactured for boat use can be used for casting from the shore, there is an extensive range of reels designed specifically for the purpose featuring such refinements as spool tensioners and centrifugal breaking systems. These reels can be set to suit the casting weight by dialling a number on the back plate corresponding to the amount of lead being used. When this is cast, the drum revolves at just the right speed thus preventing a tangle. This can be a valuable asset when casting at night but one still needs a measure of practice to use the multiplier correctly in the dark.

The fixed spool reel

Fixed spool reels have a part to play in sea fishing from the shore. Since their introduction in the late 1930's, constant development has brought them to a high level of sophistication.

Development is stiil going on and fixed spools are giving way to skirted spools which are vastly superior in balance, smoothness movement and gearing. Long distances can be achieved with the lightest metal lures or natural baits, they are also suitable for float work from the shore or dinghy.

Large fixed spool reels with a line capacity of 250 yards and more of 25 lb breaking strain monofilament are used extensively for surf casting. These can handle large fish quite well but the wire bale arm is often distorted as the pressure is exerted on one side only. This type has a corrosion resistant finish, hardened, free running rollers and a very sturdy drag. Most wind on the left and the crank folds flat for easy fitting into a medium-size tackle box.

Braided lines

The perfect line, that will enable an angler to fish with every style and in any type of water, does not exist as yet. Developments in recent years have given a much greater range of lines to choose from and these include nylon monofilament, braided nylon, lead-cored, steel and the traditional silk line (now only found as a fly line for the dry fly purist). Naturally each of these lines has its uses, and although the vast majority are of monofilament, there is a strong case for braided lines with certain styles of fishing.

Manufacture

Braided lines are twisted from polester fibre, a synthetic substance manufactured from raw materials which include coal, water and petroleum. It is the petroleum ingredient that in part accounts for the steady rise in price of this line over the past few years. Like monofilament, the polyester fibre is extruded under pressure, but any similarity ends here.

Braided lines are soft, pliable, and can be purchased in continuous lengths of up to 1,000 yards. Unlike monofilament, however, the line is not translucent. Nor is it now manufactured in breaking strains of less than 10lb—a great loss to the angling world. In the sizes sold, its circumference is greater than that of monofilament, and it naturally follows that less line can be wound onto a normal reel. This is a disadvantage.

Braided line possesses numerous advantages, not least its complete lack of spring. This makes it easy to wind from the spool onto the reel. it knots easily, the knots pulling firmly together without slipping,

Mike Millman

and, naturally, this makes for greater security. Regardless of the material, there must be some loss of strength with every knot that is tied, but the seriousness of this is much less acute with a braided line. The lines are hardly affected by water and have a high resistance to sunlight, mildew and rot, needing only an occasional wipe with a soft cloth to remove fine particles of grit that act as an abrasive on fishing lines.

The stretch problem

Every angler who has tried to pull his hook free from a snag will vouch for the fact that monofilament line stretches astronomically under pressure. In fact, it stretches by 17 to 80 per cent, depending on its method of manufacture. Over-stretching leads to distortion in the line's shape, and causes permanent weakness, often over considerable distances. In use, the braided line will only stretch a maximum of 10 per cent, and only does this in the period immediately before breaking occurs. Thus the risk of permanent damage is small.

This almost complete lack of stretch is a great help in preventing line from jamming on the spool of your reel, where a direct pull with monofilament line can often force one strand under others below it and bring the whole reel to a halt.

Undoubtedly, it is the stretch factor that had endeared the braided line to anglers who need a strong and reliable line for really hard work—work which includes spinning, trolling and heavy sea fishing where the extra bulk needed to accommodate the thicker line can be found in the large reels used, and where continued pulling against snagged terminal tackle will cause little or no risk of future line weakness.

While the initial outlay may cause many anglers to think twice before purchasing a braided line, there is a strong case for its use as a longterm money-saver.

(Left) A shark reel loaded with braided line.
(Right) The line in action.
(Below) The structure of 130lb b.s. braided line.

Bill Howes

BRAIDED LINE

Rod Sutterby

Wire lines

The relatively recent introduction of wire line for boat fishing has been the most important sea angling innovation of the century. It was first introduced to this country from America a little over 10 years ago, and that great sea angler Leslie Moncrieff was one of the first fishermen over here to use and popularize it. It was first developed in the States to allow big-game anglers to troll baits without the encumbrance of a heavy lead, and while it is still used over there for this purpose, it is now also used extensively in conjunction with lead or a down-rigger for slow trolling at depths of up to 100ft for salmon and lake trout in freshwater.

It was quickly realized by sea anglers in this country that here was the answer to bottom fishing in strong tides or deep water. In fact it exceeded all expectations once the correct techniques for using it had been perfected and some incredible bags of fish were taken by boat fishermen where other anglers using conventional lines had very indifferent results.

Acceptance only a matter of time

So far, fishing with wire line has still to be accepted by the average sea angler, although it is surely only a matter of time before this happens. Fishing with wire requires completely different techniques and equipment, but it is not difficult to learn. With a little practice, the average angler can become proficient in its use in a comparatively short time. Unfortunately, in the early days it quickly received a bad reputation as many anglers, using it as just another fishing line, had disastrous results.

The original wire also was of a single strand construction from Monel metal and considerable developments and improvements have been made since that was first marketed. While the single-strand wire was very hard wearing and less prone to kinking, it was much thicker than more recent lines

(Right) To catch deep-water species such as ling from a strong tide flow, wire line is sometimes used. It is then imperative that the rod has roller rigs throughout.

and rather unpleasant to use. It was followed by a single strand, stainless line which was beautiful to use but very prone to kinking, and these kinks, once formed, were all but impossible to remove.

In efforts to overcome this problem, a very flexible seven-strand wire was evolved, and while this format succeeded to some extent, the multiple stranding produced a further problem. With constant use, some of the strands were liable to fracture and where this happened, badly lacerated fingers were often the result. Apart from this, it was found in practice that salt water badly affected stainless wire over a period of time and its strength rapidly deteriorated.

The British wire line on the market has a chrome base, it is very soft, pleasant to use, resistant to kinking and completely unaffected by salt water, so it overcomes most of the problems which gave wire lines a poor reputation. The line is 'Tidebeater' (supplied by Efgeeco). A seven-strand wire line is available too, manufactured in the U.S. by Berkeley.

John Wilson

Used correctly, wire line can open up a new world to the sea angler. To hold bottom, you require a fraction of the lead compared with conventional monofilament or braided lines of Dacron or Terylene. In very strong tides, for example, and fairly deep water where you would require at least 2lb of lead on a monofilament line to hold bottom, you can achieve the same result using wire with less than ½lb. This means you are in closer touch with the fish at all times, and it is far more sporting, as, after all, the average-size sea fish of 6–7lb can hardly give of its best when it is towing a large, heavy lead.

Bite indication

Bite indication with wire is a revelation in itself: bites from small fish are registered immediately and positively, where similar bites on monofilament would not be felt at all, due to its inherent stretch. So positive is the indication from wire line that an angler experienced in its use can, even in deep water, tell you the composition of the bottom –whether it is rock, sand, shingle or soft mud –just from the feel of the bouncing lead.

The one disadvantage of wire line is that fishing from a crowded boat becomes inadvisable. When using wire you require plenty of room between you and the next angler, as it is absolutely essential to keep wire under tension at all times, and should you become entangled with another fisherman's line this is not possible. Wire reverts to coil form when tension is relaxed, and most efforts to straighten it result in kinks, so that it then becomes so weak that it will snap under the slightest pressure.

This brings us to the first and most important aspect of its use, and the one that causes most problems to novices. Never, *never* lower weighted wire to the bottom from a free spool, as if you do you will not know when the lead hits the seabed. The result will be a pyramid of coiled wire on the bottom which will come back full of kinks. Lower it under slight tension, with your thumb on the spool of the reel and you will then feel the lead arrive.

When using wire it is advisable to mount your running lead on a heavy monofilament

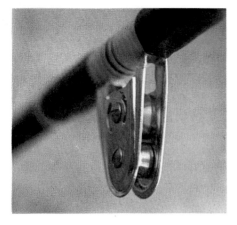

leader at least 12ft long. This should be fastened to a small, oval link or split ring that is small enough to be wound through the rod guides and down onto the reel. It will mean, in effect, that when your lead with its normal flowing trace is wound in, all the wire will be back on the spool.

If you neglect to do this and mount your lead directly onto the wire, it will be left to swing like a pendulum from your rod top when moving from one anchorage to another, and this constant motion will cause metal fatigue with corresponding weakness in the line. Wire should always be connected to the metal loop or split ring with a haywire twist. But be sure to take a double loop through the ring before commencing the twist.

A heavy leader serves another purpose in as much as it provides a small degree of stretch between the angler and a heavy fish. Without this cushioning effect, it is all too easy to tear the hook free.

The tackle required for wire is a reel with a large diameter, yet narrow, spool such as a Scarborough, Alvey or, ideally, a Penn Master Mariner. Normal multiplying reels with wide, small diameter spools are useless as these coil the line too tightly and it will then require a heavy lead to straighten it. For the same reason, you should use a rod with a soft action and flexible top, and it is absolutely essential that it is fitted with a roller top or better still, roller guides all the way down the rod.

(Above left) A roller-type intermediate ring for wire-line fishing.
(Above) New-type boat ring by Fuji with an aluminium oxide guide for wire fishing.
(Below) Ordinary ring damaged by wire line.

Mike Millman

Finally, one word of warning to those fishing from an anchored boat, or more especially from a drifting boat. Never attempt to free wire with your hands should it become snagged on the bottom. It can cut through flesh like a hot knife through butter. Loop the line round a stanchion or stem post, and let the boat pull it out. It is also sound practice to use a trace of slightly lower breaking strain than the wire so that if you do have to break out, you will only lose a hook or part of the trace and not many yards of relatively expensive wire.

Sea hooks

No item of the sea angler's equipment is more important than the hook which, after all, is in direct contact with the fish and so has to withstand all kinds of strain.

Despite this, hooks often receive scant attention. Many anglers will cheerfully part with £100 for a rod, reel and line, and then go out of their way to buy cheap hooks, which are brittle, poorly finished and often quite unsuited to the job they are expected to do. Others purchase good hooks, but then allow them to become rusty and blunt, with points that will hardly penetrate the softest mouth.

Hook manufacture

Before we look at the most popular hooks for sea fishing, it is as well to examine the method of manufacture that produces a good hook. Most are made from high-carbon steel wire. One machine straightens the wire from a large coil and a second cuts it to the appropriate length. The 'needles' obtained from this operation are then ground to a rough point, and another grinding imparts a fine hollow-ground point. The blunt-end of the shank may now be 'pennelled' or tapered by grinding, which allows the eye to be closed up smaller.

A steel chisel cuts a barb in the needles as they move round a rotating drum, the angle and the depth of the incision being determined by the setting of the chisel. Different fishing methods call for this variety of barb.

The next step is bending, which is carried out round a mandrel or cylinder. Variations on the angle of the bend are numerous, and each style of hook and size has its own.

The eye is now formed. It is either left straight or can be set towards or away from the point. Some hooks, for example, those used in mackerel fishing, are flattened in the shank, while others have grooves for whipping on flies or feathers. For extra strength, large hooks can be brazed, as are the Mustad Seamaster range, which are used

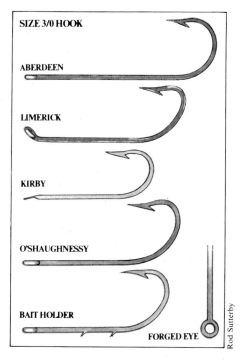

SIZE 3/0 HOOK

ABERDEEN

LIMERICK

KIRBY

O'SHAUGHNESSY

BAIT HOLDER

FORGED EYE

Rod Sutterby

for shark and game fishing throughout the world. This kind of hook is also subjected to anti-corrosion tests in a salt spray chamber in accordance with internationally agreed standards. To minimize corrosion, hooks are plated with either bronze, tin, nickel or even as has been known, gold.

Hook size

Treble hooks, which are now wisely used for pirk fishing over deep-water wrecks, are also brazed. As much of the work is done by hand, the cost can be considerable. Hardening and tempering by heating, and then cooling with oil, give maximum strength and resilience. Finally the hooks are scoured in revolving drums filled with an abrasive, and then polished in a similar way with a mixture of sawdust and oil. These operations together produce a hook that can be relied on to perform perfectly.

A fair proportion of anglers are confused

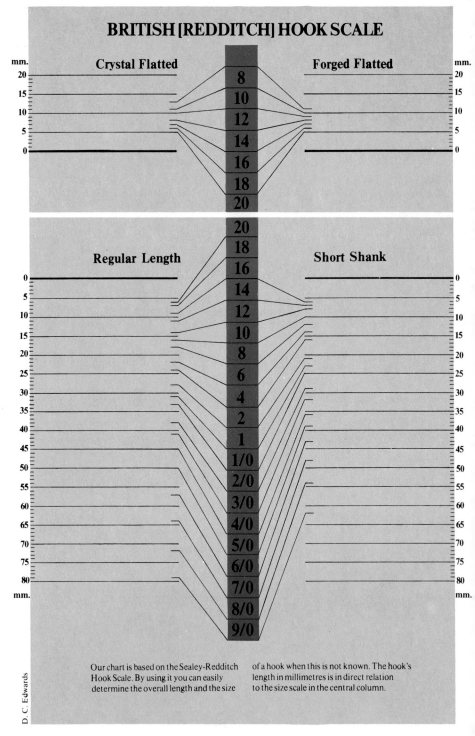

BRITISH [REDDITCH] HOOK SCALE

Crystal Flatted   **Forged Flatted**

Regular Length   **Short Shank**

Our chart is based on the Sealey-Redditch Hook Scale. By using it you can easily determine the overall length and the size of a hook when this is not known. The hook's length in millimetres is in direct relation to the size scale in the central column.

D. C. Edwards

by the multiplicity of hook sizes, which largely stems from the traditional use of private scales. The world's fish hook manufacturers now use only the British (Redditch) scale.

Hook style

So much for hook manufacture and sizes. This still leaves the bewildering array of styles of hook. For sea fishing this can be reduced conveniently to around half a dozen kinds. Among the most popular is the razor sharp, straight eyed Aberdeen hook which has a long shank made from light wire. Perfect temper prevents any straightening despite the extra leverage from the shank. This hook is used extensively for estuary fishing, particularly for bass, plaice and flounders. As it is so fine in the shank of wire the Aberdeen is most suitable for baiting live sandeel and prawn.

Shore anglers who fish from the precipitous rock ledges of the north Cornwall coast also swear by them for spinning with

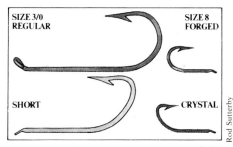

SIZE 3/0 REGULAR — SIZE 8 FORGED — SHORT — CRYSTAL

Rod Sutterby

deadbaits for fast-moving mackerel, garfish, pollack and bass. Some will argue that it is the only hook for saltwater fishing. That is a bit sweeping, but every self-respecting sea fisherman should be equipped with a range of Aberdeens between the sizes No.1 and 4/0, with the emphasis on No.3/0.

For general bottom fishing three kinds stand out—Limerick, Kirby and O'Shaughnessy. The Limerick is well suited to use with a paternoster for bream, whiting, pouting, cod and ling, its pull being direct and its penetration excellent. For ledgering there is little to choose between the other varieties, which have a wide gape between

the point and the shank, but the O'Shaughnessy is the strongest and particularly suitable for holding conger eel.

The conger is a fish that demands and receives respect from beginner and expert alike. In the past decade the development of deep-water wreck fishing has produced some enormous congers, some over 100lb in weight. To cope with the strength and sawing motion of the conger's jaws and to withstand prolonged battles, a hook must be durable, and this is where the forged eye hook comes into its own. In conger fishing for the big specimens, finesse goes out of the window. Eels over 50lb have a large appetite, and the experts think little of offering a whole bream weighing as much as 3lb. Such a bait, intended to attract huge fish, requires a forged hook of either No.10/0 or 12/0 attached to a couple of feet of cable-laid wire. No matter how much pressure this kind of hook receives, it will not straighten out as a conventional conger hook may well do.

Another hook that has become a favourite in recent years is the 'bait holder', which is designed with two slices in the shank to prevent the bait slipping down to the bend. The design has its disadvantages, though, as the wire needs to be thick, penetration is only average, and worm baits are literally ripped to pieces by the sharp edges. Worst of all, the nicks in the shank reduce the strength of the metal by at least 50 per cent.

Care of hooks

No article on hooks would be complete without reference to the care of them. While most are sharp when they leave the factory, handling can easily dull them, and so it is essential to examine each one before it is used, and from time to time while fishing. Any with a slightly turned point and those lacking needle sharpness should be gently honed with a good stone. Soft Arkansas whetstone, used with a light oil, is perfect for the job. Hooks that show signs of irreparable wear must be discarded after each trip. Failure to observe this simple rule could lose you the fish of a lifetime.

Sea leads

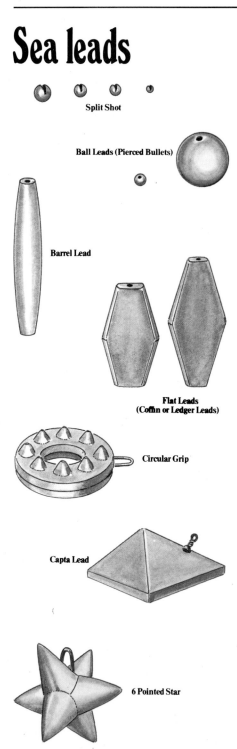

Split Shot

Ball Leads (Pierced Bullets)

Barrel Lead

Flat Leads
(Coffin or Ledger Leads)

Circular Grip

Capta Lead

6 Pointed Star

Leads for sea angling range from split-shot to bombs weighing as much as 4lb which keep a bait on the bottom in deep water during fierce tides. There are many different types and each performs a specific task.

Shore fishing

Split-shot, the indispensable weight used in freshwater fishing, also plays a vital role in saltwater, where it is used in float fishing and drift-lining for such species as pollack, mackerel, garfish and the wily mullet. Shot is available in a variety of sizes and should be gently crimped on to the line with pliers.

Ball leads (also known as pierced bullets) and barrel leads, which are designed to run freely on a line, range from ¼oz to 3oz. These leads are correct for making up the sliding float rig used to suspend a bait close to the bottom in almost any depth of water. The 'slider' is popular with anglers seeking wrasse, pollack and bass over rough ground. Barrel leads weighing up to 6oz are sold in many tackle shops for bottom ledgering but they roll around on firm sandy ground and tend to twist the line. These larger sizes, therefore, make a poor type of lead and are best avoided.

Leads for muddy ground

For ledgering on muddy ground in tidal rivers and estuaries where the water is shallow, flat leads are by far the best. Although they make for poor long-distance casting, those with a thin profile sink to the bottom more slowly than bombs and consequently do not penetrate more than a few inches into the ooze. Extensions of the smooth, flat weight are the Circular grip, Capta and the Six Pointed Star. These are useless as casting leads but they hold well on firm mud, shale and sand – even when the tide pours out of rivers in spring tides.

The long-casting beach fisherman requires a variety of weights ranging in size from 2oz to 10oz which offer minimum wind resistance. Across the years numerous

(Left) Beachcasting: the shape and weight of lead selected is important.

Mike Millman

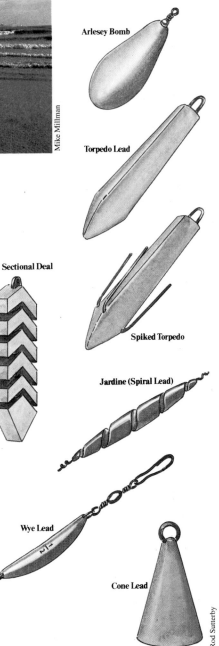

Arlesey Bomb

Torpedo Lead

Sectional Deal

Spiked Torpedo

Jardine (Spiral Lead)

Wye Lead

Cone Lead

Rod Sutterby

patterns have evolved and present-day beach fishermen even with bait attached think nothing of casting up to 200 yards out where the bigger fish roam.

The long-distance lead

Aerodynamically the reknowned Arlesey bomb is the best lead for reaching great distances. A swivel at the narrow end ensures the reel line does not twist during the cast, but once on the sea floor the smooth bomb is a poor holder and is easily rolled around by the tide.

One compromise is a torpedo with four flat sides and with its weight concentrated at the pointed end which prevents the lead turning over in flight. From this lead came the spiked torpedo, featuring four or five soft wire arms embedded in the heavy end. These dig into the sand and prevent the lead from moving in all but the roughest weather. Under retrieving pressure however the arms bend backwards and the lead can be wound in easily. The now little-used sectional Deal beach lead is made up from five 2oz pieces moulded in a V-shape which fit together on a central bar fastened into a pointed bottom section of 4oz. Each piece simply lifts off the bar to give six casting weights in one.

Breakaway leads

The modern equivalent of the above lead is in fact a complete kit or system manufactured by the Gemini Tackle Co. The Gemini system 100+ comprises separate

223

Sea leads

Mike Millman

torpedo-shaped weights of 3,4,5,6,7 and 8oz, to which various end arrangements can be added. Included in the kit are the long and short breakaway wires, plus extra-long fixed wires.

Quite simply, the very end of each lead has a ¼in long, ⅛th-diameter screw thread, on to which is screwed various colour-coded plastic nose cones which accept the removable spring wires. It is a unique system which gives the option of no less than nine different combinations from the standard four wire breakaway grip to fixed extra thick wire designed for use in big tide races. The leads can of course be used as a plain nose cone without wires, or with extra long breakaway wires for uptide fishing.

The original breakaway lead bombs devised by the Breakaway Tackle Co. of Ipswich are still as popular as ever and the bestselling beachcasting leads in the UK. They are available in 3oz, 4oz, 5oz, 8oz and 10oz sizes and operate via a plaster collar which retains the four sprung wires until a hefty pull is given, either by a cod running off with the bait (usually hooking itself in the process) or by the angler wishing to retrieve the lead. Breakaway leads are available with both long and short tails (the stem to which the trace is joined) and there is an optional plastic breakaway which can be added via an oval split ring to a breakaway lead, providing no less than 8 wires to find purchase instead of the usual

four. A handy addition for really strong tides.

Spinning

For spinning from the shore, the weight must hug the line and present the minimum resistance to air and water. A spiral like the Jardine takes a lot of beating. It has a continuous groove running from end to end and twisted wire spirals at each end through which the line is wound. Jardines come in weights from 2oz to 8oz, the lighter versions being the most suitable for general spinning work with natural and artificial sand eel or fish strip baits. The banana-shaped Wye lead fitted with a link swivel is also excellent for spinning. As with the Jardine, nothing should be placed on the line between the lead and bait. Both these types are suitable for working ultra light metal lures or for increasing casting range with heavier models. Where possible however it is always better to purchase a long casting

Irish Tourist Board

224

'pirken' of the correct casting weight rather than add lead.

Leads for boat fishing

Many types of leads and many different techniques used in shore fishing have a use when working from a boat in shallow water. Float work is exactly the same but for drift lining when the boat is set at anchor in a fair run of tide, the weight must be increased to get the bait down below, for which plain bombs or torpedoes are ideal. For downtide ledgering at anchor cones both plain and wired are used in a variety of sizes from 8oz up to 3lb. Ledger cones can be rigged with a 'rotten bottom' by tying a small swivel to the eye with light nylon. If the weight gets caught up in a rock crevice or a wreck steady pulling will free the trace end. This is a big comfort when expensive wire traces are in use. For uptide ledgering at anchor, breakaway leads are much preferable to all other types.

Offshore fishing

In offshore fishing the angler faces the combination of deep and fast-running currents particularly during spring tide periods, and the actual type of reel line is a most important factor when fishing in more than 20 fathoms. Monofilament creates much less drag than dacron line and so less weight is required to hold bottom. In water 35-45 fathoms deep it is impossible during spring tides to keep even 3lb of lead on the bottom. This is one reason why many charter boat skippers drift-fish during new and full moon periods. So it is as well to remember this when booking a deep-water fishing trip because working a heavy pirk on the drift can be a hard, extremely tiring business.

Trolling for bass and pollack is a popular and often rewarding way of fishing. The size of the lead depends very much on the strength of tide, speed of the boat and how deep the fish are running. For deep work 1lb is about right and for shallow fishing 8-12oz should be used.

Home-made leads

Factory-made leads are now very expensive. The alternative is to buy die-cast aluminium moulds and lead from a scrap-metal dealer and make your own. The unit cost is less than half the price of shop-bought leads, which over a period of time is a worthwhile saving. Lead-weight making should be done in a shed, never in a kitchen. Unless approached correctly it is a dangerous business and children must be kept safely away from the operation. Lead pipe should be cut up into small pieces and melted in an iron ladle over a gas ring until melted. When ready for use the metal is poured slowly into the block which should be gripped lightly in a vice. Moulds must be absolutely dry before use or the molten metal will spit in all directions when it strikes the aluminium – which could be very dangerous. After allowing a few minutes for the casts to set the mould can be removed, split open and the lead dropped to one side. After a dozen or so leads have been fashioned the block becomes very hot and must be left to cool for at least 10 minutes. Needless to say, gloves should always be worn throughout.

(Above left) Jardine leads are probably the best shape for sea spinning from rocks or the shore.
(Left) A small codling taken on a simple trace and bomb-shaped lead.
(Right) A box of large leads made for a week's exciting charter-fishing in the Plymouth area.

Len Cacutt

Sea swivels

One of the most useful, but most neglected accessories for the angler is the swivel. It is primarily used to prevent fishing line from becoming twisted, and whether the angler employs any of the various forms of spinning, or merely retrieves a deadbait, the turning action of the bait spiralling through the water will be transferred to the line. If monofilament is allowed to twist, it begins to kink, and at best becomes a tangled mess—at worst the line weakens so badly that it will break at the first strain.

The only preventative is the use of one or more efficient swivels mounted between the line and lure, working in conjunction with an anti-kink weight or vane. Such devices are attached to the reel line by means of a bloodknot or grinner knot. But efficiency is difficult to achieve in a swivel. Early traces had two, three or more swivels, operating on the principle that the more that were added, the better the chance of at least one working. Those early mechanisms were in the form of an open, oblong box with eyes mounted through each end. A little corrosion or rust plus an accumulation of grit and mud quickly impaired their efficiency.

One basic principle

Today, the angler has the choice of several types of swivel, all working on the same basic principle but with varying refinements. The plain barrel swivel is the most popular and probably the tackle dealer's best seller especially since many anglers simply ask for 'a swivel' and leave the choice to the assistant. Its construction is simple, with two eyes (through which trace and line are mounted) allowed to revolve independently on their separate beads of metal carefully shaped to fit the inside of the barrel. The free rotation of the eyes depends on tolerances left when the thin metal is compressed during machining: nine times out of ten, the tolerances are adequate and the swivel revolves freely. The tenth case is where

trouble sets in, and before leaving the shop it is worth checking each swivel that is purchased, and again before fishing.

An improvement on the plain barrel is the American Berkley swivel. It differs only in that a good grade of metal is used and the eyes are flattened slightly at the terminal ends to ensure that trace and line stay in place, free from a natural tendency to pull to either side when an unequal strain is applied. An improvement in efficiency which costs little more, is the Hardy Ball Bearing swivel. Again, there is the barrel type of construction but with exacting tolerances and incorporating small ball-races that ensure that the eyed pieces revolve freely.

One swivel remains in this category—the Diamond swivel, in which the loops are not round but diamond-shaped and are fastened by means of an expanded link. Usually

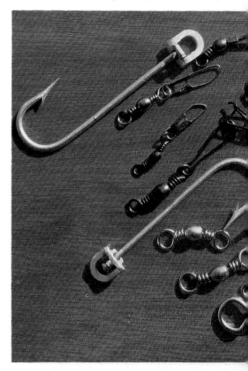

manufactured from fine steel, they appear rather flimsy, but in fact are equal in strength to other types. They are considerably lighter and rarely jam.

Swivels for freshwater fishing are usually made of brass or blued steel. However, these materials are not strong enough to withstand the strains placed upon them by the rigours of saltwater fishing. For this reason the usual material for swivels for the heavier forms of sea fishing is stainless steel as it is not only tougher and more resistant to bending, but is also not attacked by saltwater, even so they should be checked at regular intervals.

Sea water is very abrasive too, because of the particles of sand suspended in it, so the rather open construction of a barrel swivel will allow sand to enter and cause damage to the moving parts. This is not very important if the swivels are bought cheaply and thrown away after use, as is often the case with sea anglers who fish for the smaller, weaker species around our coastline, so that it is not too serious if a swivel jams.

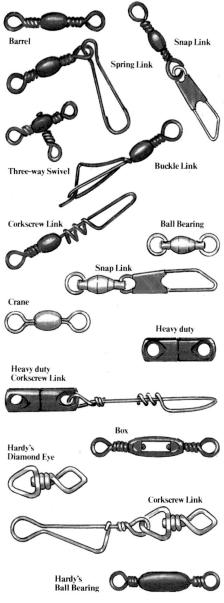

SWIVELS AND LINKS

Barrel

Snap Link

Spring Link

Three-way Swivel

Buckle Link

Corkscrew Link

Ball Bearing

Snap Link

Crane

Heavy duty

Heavy duty
Corkscrew Link

Box

Hardy's
Diamond Eye

Corkscrew Link

Hardy's
Ball Bearing

Rod Sutterby

Mike Millman

(Above) There is a wide variety of swivels available to the angler, catering for the demands of different waters and species. (Left) A selection of the swivels and booms needed by the sea angler if he is to cope with the sea's powerful fishes.

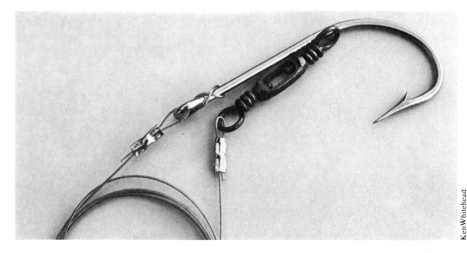

KenWhitehead

Matters can be very different if you are fishing for big conger eels, skate, or shark, and the angler who is lucky enough to fish for such hard-fighting, powerful species as marlin, or broadbill swordfish, or the very biggest sharks, should never use anything but the very best tackle, including swivels which are engineering marvels.

These swivels will be made of stainless steel or a really hard alloy not affected by sea water. All moving parts will be machined to very fine tolerances, so that it is almost impossible for abrasive particles to enter and will probably be grease-filled as a further protection. Miniature ball-races can be built in to ensure the smoothest possible rotation by minimizing friction, and modern developments have produced swivels which are far in advance of the simple barrel-type device.

One kind of swivel stands on its own, and that is the three-way swivel which is most frequently used in forming the float paternoster for fishing a livebait. Constructed in the barrel style with an extension eye standing out from its side, it is prone to distortion and weakness if the bait gets caught and extreme pressure is applied as the angler pulls to break free. The only precaution against this weakness is to recognize it and replace the swivel immediately.

Link swivels are a means of quickly attaching (or detaching) a lure to a trace, or

to a line. Ideally they should be simple to open and close—even with wet, cold hands—and strong enough to grip without collapsing when extreme pressure is applied.

Plain link swivels with two overlapping half-clips seem to find greatest favour among anglers, despite the fact that they are difficult to open when needed and often slip open without warning to shed either lure or trace during use. An improvement is the safety-pin link, where an open steel loop doubles back to fasten—as the name suggests—into a metal clip. Providing the clip is secure and there is sufficient overlap on the pin to fit snugly into it, this is a safer and more convenient unit than the plain link.

At first sight the diamond-link looks a flimsy affair of a single wire loop doubling back to clip over itself. But in practice it is strong, simple and easy to clean.

How many swivels to use?

How many swivels should be used when fishing? Generally, the fewer the better: every swivel requires a join either to the line or cast, which weakens it. On most occasions just one is enough, provided that it has been properly maintained and is used with an efficient anti-kink vane. But there are arguable exceptions to this rule. Some would say that the choice depends upon the length of the trace: a short trace needing two swivels, one at each end. A longer trace needs a third.

Mike Shepley

Sea booms

Due to the enormous resistance they create, particularly when casting, both beach and boat sea fishermen have in recent years switched from the heavy, old brass boom paternosters to the much lighter, more practical type. Whilst stainless-steel booms, particularly the French boom, are of course still sold and some sea anglers swear by them, the greater proportion now use plastic-type booms of one kind or another.

Shore-fishing booms

The idea of a boom is to ensure the bait is separated from the trace to alleviate tangles and enhance natural presentation by way of a paternoster. Today's specialist beach fishermen go one step further in reducing casting resistance by not using a boom as such, simply a trace link some 24-30in above the lead to which the hook line is tied.

The trace link is a swivel sandwiched between two swivelled beads and provides the ultimate long-range single-hook paternoster because the hook is held tight to the thicker (45-60lb test) shock leader during the cast by a plastic hook clip, sometimes also called a bait clip. The clip itself is retained on the trace by a length of narrow gauge tubing. To stop the clip from riding up the trace during the cast a nylon stop knot is tied immediately above. A 15-20mm gap from plastic clip to the stop knot allows for trace line stretch during casting. The clip is fixed on the wire of leads with long tails (as opposed to the shock leader trace) by easing the tubing over the eye and sleeving it down before wedging the clip in.

Another DIY paternoster rig similar to the above is made by Delta Tackle consisting of plastic line stops which are actually glued on the shock leader trace with Loctite adhesive, sandwiching between a swivel to which the hook link is tied.

With both the above rigs slackening of the trace on impact with the water ensures the hook's instant release from the plastic clip

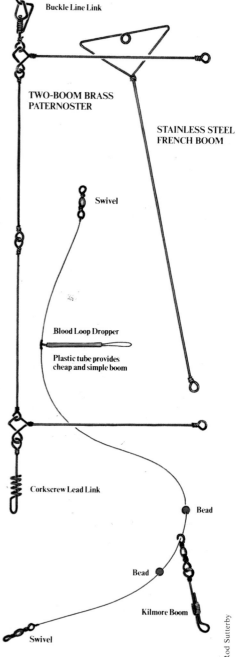

Buckle Line Link

TWO-BOOM BRASS PATERNOSTER

STAINLESS STEEL FRENCH BOOM

Swivel

Blood Loop Dropper

Plastic tube provides cheap and simple boom

Corkscrew Lead Link

Bead

Bead

Kilmore Boom

Swivel

Rod Sutterby

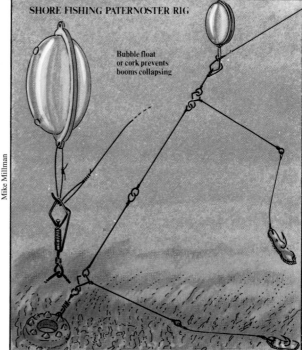

SHORE FISHING PATERNOSTER RIG

Bubble float
or cork prevents
booms collapsing

Mike Millman

Rod Sutterby

*(Above) A pollack rig based
on a French boom, 20ft
trace and artificial eel.
(Left) A two-boom brass
paternoster, stainless steel
French boom, and the
useful Wessex ledger.
(Right) A bubble float or
cork aids bait presentation.*

whereupon the bait comes to settle naturally on the sea bed, in addition to having increased dramatically the casting distance.

For those not interested in distance casting, or who may wish to offer two (or more) hook baits instead of one, there are numerous plastic mini-booms available, such as the Mustad, knotless paternoster (in both short and long formats) or the Cox and Rawle pro rig system comprising two interlocking cylindrical nylon tubes which sleeve anywhere on the shock leader trace. Between these two halves, either a swivel or short plastic boom fits into the recess enabling neat, adjustable paternoster rigs to be constructed easily and quickly. Five-inch long booms are also available.

Booms for boat fishing

There are several booms designed specially for ledgering directly downtide. The best known is the Kilmore, consisting of a loop of wire leading to a swivel and lead attachment. The loop through which the line is passed can be plain or fitted with an inner

'lined' ring. The major disadvantage of the Kilmore boom is that the lead hangs from the bottom of the boom causing the trace, which hangs past it, to tangle either when the rig is descending to the bottom or between rebaiting and casting when the lead naturally swings freely.

The clements boom is designed to prevent such tangling and has a large eye at both ends through which the reel line passes. From one end hangs the swivelled lead attachment, and so long as this attachment hangs farthest (towards the rod tip) away from the hook trace the lead will hang at right angles to the line and prevent tangles. There are numerous improvements all based on the clements boom now available, such as the red, zip slider, the Ashpole sea boom and the Eddystone nylon sea boom. Each provides a tangle-free running ledger slider through which the reel line can be pulled by a fish running downtide with the bait. A cushioning bead should always be used between boom and the trace swivel.

Sea booms

Specialized uptide ledger booms are also available. These are made from strong black nylon and are up to 6in long with a reinforced collar at the lead-link end, easily separating lead from the trace link in a 'cantilever' fashion. Again it is imperative to use a buffer bead, as the trace swivel could damage the end of the nylon tube.

Extra-long anti-tangle booms up to 12in long are also used when drift fishing over wrecks or rough ground using artificial rubber eels for cod, pollack or coalfish etc. Mustad's Tubi Boom is available in both 200mm and 300mm lengths through which the line runs with a simple lead link at the angled end. Long, anti-tangle booms are easily made by sleeving a bored swivel bead (of the correct diameter) over a length of the rigid tubing used by carp anglers and adding a link to accept the lead.

As with uptide booms the tubing must be stopped against the trace (6-12ft long) by a cushioning bead. Care must be taken when lowering the rig downtide so the long trace does not double back over the reel line and tangle with the rubber eel.

This is achieved by casting with a smooth underarm swing. The trace will then straighten out as the lead descends and not flip back, provided line is allowed to peel smoothly from the reel under gentle thumb pressure.

Boat anglers specialising in this form of drift fishing using lightweight rubber and plastic artificial eel-like lines, should equip themselves with a comprehensive stock of swivels, swivel beads, rigid black tubing of varying diameters and even some 2-4 oz designer leads, more commonly used by their freshwater counterparts. Making up a custom trace to suit the circumstances is the a simple matter.

The single-eyed Kilmore boom, and variants on the double-eyed Clements boom, designed to prevent line and trace from tangling.

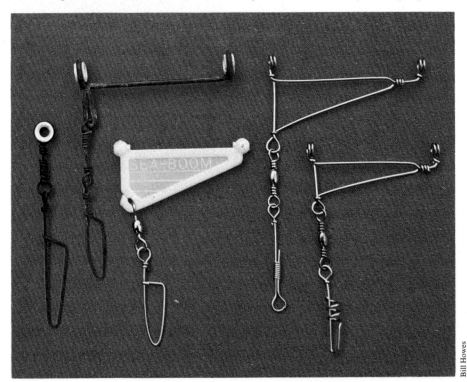

Sea fishing clothing

Whether fishing from the end of a breakwater, estuary mouth, the beach or from a boat anchored well off-shore, the sea angler is invariably a long way from home and a change of dry clothing. So a complete duplicate of everything stored in the boot of the car is nice to have in reserve should you get a soaking.

Something worth remembering as a general rule is to go sea fishing wearing more layers of clothing than the weather forecast dictates rather than less because you can always take some off. But if you don't take it with you, it cannot be put on.

Summer conditions

During the very warmest of summer conditions a tee-shirt or sweat shirt, plus jeans or moleskin trousers is an ideal base together with a high-necked fisherman's smock. These are usually made from sailcloth-type, close-weave material and excellent to put on should a chilly wind suddenly spring up.

Shelter can often be found at the end of the pier but when situated miles along the beach or out on an open boat, body temperature quickly reduces in even the lightest winds. So take a polo neck sweater along too. In case of rain a set of lightweight waterproofs is imperative, either jacket and over trousers in PVC, or bib-and-brace style chest-high trousers covered with a jacket that has an integral clip-on or zip-on hood. The latter are especially useful and take up little space in the tackle hold all. Footwear depends entirely upon location and while an old pair of trainers is ideal for boat fishing in warmer weather to provide grip on a slippery deck, beach fisherman will require PVC or rubber wellington boots at least. Lightweight waders with soft, flexible uppers are ideal, allowing you to stand in the surf to cast or retrieve fish and yet not feel uncomfortable during a long walk.

For total protection against both the

Irish Tourist Board

Tackling up while the boat heads for the mark. Keep fishing and other gear tidy. Extra clothing should be kept dry in the cabin, but ready for use.

evening's chill and rain, or night fishing during the summer months, a one-piece waterproof suit made from coated nylon, Gortex or Silcatex etc, with an integral or zip-on hood is recommended.

You can wear several layers of sweatshirts and jumpers underneath or invest in a one-piece thermal undersuit made from warm, fleecy polyester fabric with elasticated cuffs and ankles which doubles up for winter fishing.

Winter conditions

To go over the one-piece thermal undersuit

(Below) Lifejackets must all conform to British Standards specification BS 3595. The angler is also wearing good shoes for boat fishing and waterproofs. (Below right) When fishing from the beach you must keep feet warm and dry. The one-piece suit is ideal.

Ken Whitehead

which is imperative for cold weather fishing from a boat or the beach, there are several choices of suitable waterproof and windproof garments.

For ease of casting movement, the beach angler usually prefers a one-piece light-to-medium-weight lined suit with integral hood, elasticated cuffs, storm flap pockets etc. To keep the feet warm in the coldest weather thermal boots such as Skeetex, or Sunbridge Hot Foot Boots are indispensable. Such boots are however only knee length so care must be taken in the surf. In addition they are rather tiring when there is a long walk ahead. So a quality pair of thermal socks and thigh waders with light uppers are still widely used by many beach fishermen.

The boat angler needs to be rather more warmly clothed and in addition to thermal boots a heavily lined one-piece suit with integral hood and storm cuffs is worn over a thermal undersuit (also with an integral hood) to provide maximum protection from the wet and extreme cold. Beneath the thermal undersuit simply wear jeans and two loose fitting sweatshirts or a thermal vest and sweatshirt combination. A mistake often made when dressing for cold weather, is to smother the skin with tight-fitting clothing. This prevents air from circulating around the body and once stale, air drops in temperature; a point well worth remembering. Some anglers find that a loose-fitting tracksuit is more comfortable beneath the one-piece thermal undersuit.

In recent years floatation suits have become extremely popular with boat anglers. These are available in practical designs of tear-resistant, waterproof material, protected by a zipped and velcro-fastening front with the floatation provided by heavy-duty cell foam that can support a person of up to 200lb in the water.

Moreover the closed cell-lining has superb thermal qualities so the angler is kept

Irish Tourist Board

both warm and safe. Floatation suits are available in various highly visible colours such as yellow, orange and red and in either one-piece or two-piece formats. With the latter, crotch straps should be used with the bouyancy jacket otherwise it could ride up over the head should the angler fall overboard into the water.

An alternative in floatation garments is the floatation vest made from heavy-duty cell foam. This is also available in highly visible colours and is worn on the outside over both summer or winter clothing. For ease of movement and maximum protection whilst fishing some boat anglers prefer to wear a fully lined ¾ length floatation jacket (which also supports a 200lb person) which comes with crotch straps to prevent it riding

up over chest-high trousers, or bib-and-brace unit worn beneath.

As there are so many options it is best to try each out along at the local specialist tackle dealer to see which is most comfortable and practical for the individual needs. Whichever combination you choose don't forget after every trip when it is smeared with bait and fish slime, to sponge down thoroughly with warm fresh water and leave to dry. There is nothing worse than attempting to put on damp and stinking clothing, especially when making a boating trip well offshore in rough seas.

Once upon a time hands were the most difficult part of the body to keep warm but now there are several excellent designs of neoprene gloves and gauntlets available which provide warmth in the most severe weather.

When long periods of waiting are expected between bites, neoprene gloves are best. For the sensitivity of casting or continually operating the reel as when drift fishing etc there are two ideal types. Those in which the tips of the forefinger and thumb peel back and stay back (held by patches of velcro) and those in which the same have been removed. The exposed finger and thumb tips remain warm because the rest of the hand inside is insulated by the neoprene even when wet, just like a wet suit (from which neoprene gloves were derived.)

Acrylic mittens also make excellent fishing gloves. Those which have a pull-over top quickly convert to warm gloves for those long waits between bites.

Lastly it is a proven fact that anglers lose most of their bodily heat via the head so a hat of one kind or another is imperative if you wish to stay warm. Unless wearing a thermal undersuit with an integral hood or an oversuit with the same, wear a simple woolly bobble hat which can pull down over the ears to alleviate the chill from biting winds or wear a fur-lined peaked waterproof cap which has pull-down ear flaps. And take a scarf along to provide additional comfort around the junction between collar and hat.

Lugworm

D. B. Lewis Natural Science Photos

The lugworm, *Arenicola marina*, is one of the most popular of all baits used in sea angling, particularly with anglers fishing the East Anglian and Kent coasts. It is a smaller species than that other very popular choice of sea anglers, the King Ragworm, but when used from beach or boat it can be one of the deadliest baits for cod.

Ninety per cent of the sea fish found around the British Isles will usually take this bait readily, and besides being ideal for cod, it is particularly useful for the smaller varieties of flatfish – plaice, dabs and flounders. Many inland sea anglers prefer to buy a day's supply of lugworm from their local tackle shop, but anybody can dig an adequate supply for himself.

The best environment

The lugworm prefers sheltered beaches with a good depth of top sand and where the sea has a low salinity. River estuaries, therefore, provide the best environment. One never has to travel far along the British coastline to encounter such habitats –

Whitstable, Dale Fort, St Andrews, Millport, the south coast of the Isle of Man, Clew Bay on the West Coast of Ireland, are just a few of the many well-known areas where the lugworm can be dug in numbers. Size and colouring can vary considerably from area to area – in some cases there is a marked difference between the worms dug from the same sandy bay – due to environmental factors.

The common lugworm is often known as the 'blow' lug to differentiate it from the black lug which is very thick-skinned and requires gutting to prolong the time it will keep, and from the Deal yellow-tail, a worm peculiar to the south side of the Stour Estuary in Kent.

Lugworm live in a U-shaped burrow in the sand, the entrances of which are marked at one end by the tell-tale spiral casts and at the other by a depression in the sand known as the blow hole, through which the worm draws its food. Into the tunnel fall particles of sand mixed with water and organic

236

matter, all of which the worm eats. The organic matter is digested and the sand is excreted, forming the cast at the other end of the burrow.

For digging the common lugworm the ordinary flat-tined potato fork is the best tool; a spade chops too many worms in half. Lugworm casts are found on any sandy beach below high water mark but, normally, the nearer to the extreme low water mark the greater the number of casts to be found and the bigger the worms. If the sand is covered in casts no more than 2 or 3in apart, then worms can be dug by trenching, that is, digging the sand as one would the garden. However, if signs are few and far between, 'singling' is best. This involves removing the sand between the blow hole and the cast, thus uncovering the worm after about three forkfuls. The burrow is lined with mucus from the worm's body, giving it a bright orange colour rather like rust, and enabling the angler to see exactly which way the burrow is running at each forkful.

(Above left) The lugworm, showing the gill fronds in the centre part of the body, and the hard bristles, or chaetae.
(Below) The asymmetrical casts of the common lugworm, different from the spiral-coil casts of the Deal yellow-tail.

G. E. Hyde

The worms should be removed to a clean wooden box or plastic bucket. Never use a galvanized pail as the zinc kills the worm very quickly. When sufficient worms have been dug, they should be washed in clean sea water to remove all particles of sand as well as any worms pierced by the fork. These should be put into a separate container for, although they will live as long as the whole worms, the blood exuded by their wounds has an adverse effect on the others.

Storing lugworm

When you return home, the worms should be placed on clean, dry newspaper in a single layer, with another piece laid on top so that the bait is sandwiched between two sheets of paper. If the weather is cold, the temperature not rising above 4.4 C (40 F), and the worms are stored in a garage or outhouse, they will stay in good condition for 4-5 days. In the summer, when temperatures are high, this life is reduced to less than 36 hours unless the worms are refrigerated. Another method of keeping worms alive until required is to place them in a well-aerated saltwater-filled aquarium. With this method care must be taken to remove any dead worms immediately, before they can pollute the water.

Unfortunately, the peak of autumn cod fishing coincides with the time when lugworm is most difficult to obtain, for it is spawning. Although the actual day it occurs varies from colony to colony, in nearly all areas spawning takes place between the last week of September and the middle of November. Lugworms are not hermaphrodite (having characteristics of both sexes) but sexed male and female. The eggs of the females and the sperms of the males begin to accumulate from mid-summer onwards, moving around in the body fluid and giving the worms a milky appearance. If a worm is broken this fluid will be found to be rather sticky and slimy.

When the worms are ripe, the spawn of both sexes is released onto the sand, where fertilization occurs. If the worm survives the spawning it will go right to the bottom of its burrow and remain immobile for two or

Lugworm

Digging for lug. Tedious but necessary when bait costs are considered.

three weeks while it recovers. During this period it eats very little, creating no tell-tale casts to mark its presence, so that sands that previously appeared to contain millions of worms, now seem completely barren.

Four or five days after spawning, the larva hatches. About 1/100in long, it is pear-shaped, opaque, and bears no resemblance to the adult worm. By early spring it has taken the form of the adult and is found high in the sand, working its way downwards as it matures. At two years old it spawns for the first time and usually lives to spawn a second time, at three years, this time the lug dies.

The Deal yellow-tail

There is evidence that adult lugworm will come out of the sand and swim freely in the sea. This phenomenon usually occurs in the early spring. The Deal yellow-tail is probably a sub-species of *Arenicola marina,* although many authorities believe it to appear different simply through environmental factors. However, the worm behaves entirely differently from the common lugworm. The cast, instead of being a haphazard spiral, is perfectly symmetrical, and the worm burrows to a greater depth than the common lug.

The yellow-tail is generally larger, and when dug appears very limp, seeming, to the uninitiated, to be dead. It also has the peculiar habit of coiling itself into a circle when held in the palm of the hand, whereas the common lug will only bend slightly. The best way of keeping the yellow-tail – its name derives from the bright yellow stain it leaves on the hands – is in clean sea water.

Another sub-species is the black lug, which is even bigger than the Deal yellow-tail and has a very thick skin. It often lives in a mixture of mud and sand, where the most successful way of obtaining it is to use a small, long-handled spade, digging straight down from the cast and following the trail until the worm is sighted. It is rarely possible to trench for this worm.

Roll them in newspaper

Immediately after digging, the intestines and blood should be squeezed out through the head end and, to keep them in perfect condition, the worms should be rolled singly in sheets of newspaper. The black lug is large enough to provide several small baits from a single worm, although for cod fishing a whole worm should be threaded on the hook. Because it is tough, it makes an ideal bait for beachcasting.

Common lug can be threaded either singly or doubly, depending on size, when beach fishing for cod, but for boat fishing it is usually better to hang them from the bend of the hook, just passing the hook in and out of the body where the sandy tail section joins the fat part. The number of worms put on a hook depends, first, on the size of the worm and, second, on the size of the fish expected. When fishing for varieties of small flatfish, a largish worm may be broken in half to provide ample bait for a small mouth.

Ragworm

Just as the soil of the countryside is a home for many kinds of earthworm, so the seabed provides sanctuary for many kinds of marine worm. One of the commonest species is the ragworm, of which several kinds exist.

The ragworm differs from the lugworm in that it tapers very gradually from head to tail and is much fleshier. Most ragworms are bright red and all varieties have hundreds of 'legs' down each side of the body. The head is armed with a pair of bony pincers which the worm can thrust out and retract at will and a large worm can inflict a painful bite on the unwary angler.

Where the ragworm is found

King ragworm is probably the most common and the most sought-after for bait. The angler can obtain two large, or several smaller baits, from a good-sized specimen which can be over 2ft long. The worm is found close to the high-water mark but the nearer one goes to the low-water spring-tide mark, the more prolific it becomes—although this varies from coast to coast as does the worm itself. The best localities are estuaries where there is a mixture of river mud and shell, where it lives in a U-shaped burrow, the sides cemented with mucus from its body. Once it has dug its home the worm can propel itself through the tunnel with its many 'legs'. The bait-digger seeking this worm treads the ground carefully, watching for a water-spout pushed up when the burrow is compressed by his boot. If worms are scarce it pays to locate both entrances to the tunnel and remove the soil between, looking for the tell-tale burrow. In some areas you may have to dig to a depth of 2ft or more to secure the worm. Where there is an abundance of worms, and each footfall produces several jets of water, 'trenching' is the best method. A good day's supply of bait can be obtained from one hole.

At spawning-time the king ragworm changes its bright red colour (with a pale green back) into a slate green and, when broken, exudes a slimy, milky liquid. During this season, which varies from area to area but is usually in spring, the worm is of very little use as bait. One interesting fact, however, is that during the breeding season, large numbers of worms leave the safety of their burrows and swim freely in the sea. If,as often happens, there is a sudden on-shore wind, great numbers are thrown up by the breakers onto the beach, either to die in the sun, or be swallowed by seagulls.

All worms deteriorate very quickly in high temperatures and, once dug, they should be dried and cooled as soon as possible. Whole, undamaged worms should be wrapped singly in newspaper and stored at 2°C in a refrigerator, where they can be kept in good condition for more than a week. Damaged worms should be separated and used first.

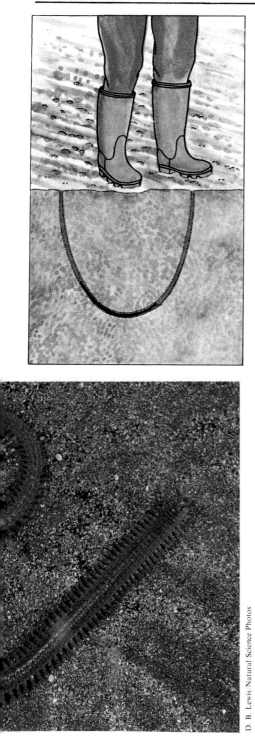

(*Above*) *The ragworm's mucus-lined burrow.*
(*Left*) *The ragworm,* Nereis (Neanthes)
virens, *strikingly coloured.*

But if keeping is not important—perhaps all
the worms are going to be used next day—
they will keep perfectly in a box of
vermiculite (insulating granules).

Mounting the bait

King ragworm can be an extremely
effective bait, particularly for bass and
pollack. For these fighting predators, worms
up to 1ft long can be used whole. Secure just
the head on the hook, leaving the rest
trailing. Mounted in this way it is very lifelike and pollack and bass rarely bite short.
They have insatiable appetites and take the
whole worm into their mouth before making
off with it. The largest worms can be cut in
half and baited in a similar way. Other
species that prefer ragworm to lugworm are
flounder, thornback ray, dogfish and
smooth-hound.

White ragworm is a variety which has

241

become very popular over the past few years, particularly with beach anglers. It is smaller than the king ragworm, one 8in long being a good specimen. Because it is a very localized worm it cannot be dug in sufficient numbers to ensure regular commercial supplies.

The white ragworm lives in sheltered bays where there is an abundance of soft yellow sand, although it is sometimes found in the same area as king ragworm if there is fine surface gravel. A relatively shallow-burrowing worm, the white ragworm is rarely found more than 9in deep, and often only 2in or 3in, below the surface. Because it gives no indication of its whereabouts, digging must be 'hit or miss', the search limited only by choosing the right kind of ground. No visible change occurs in the white ragworm during the breeding period but, like other varieties in the species, it comes up from the sand and swims freely in the sea.

Preserving the white ragworm

The white ragworm does not keep as well as the king ragworm and the most useful preservative is a plastic bucket full of fresh seawater. As well as being much smaller than its cousin the king ragworm, the white ragworm is also more delicate, and a fine gauge wire hook is recommended to avoid damaging the worm.

Rockies are another small member of the family and, as the name implies, they are found in chalk rocks among deposits of mud

and sand in sheltered bays. These deposits tend to fill the natural crevices in the chalk outcrops and the worm lives in these, so that a pick-axe is more useful than a fork for prizing this bait from its habitat.

Rockies and Maddies

Rarely exceeding 5in or 6in, the rocky is a very active worm with bright red colouring. To keep it at its best, put it into a box of fine grit dampened with seawater. In a refrigerator it should remain active for three or four days. As with the white rag, a fine wire hook is recommended to avoid undue damage when baiting. Presented in this way white ragworm will catch the same species of fish as the king ragworm.

Maddies are the smallest member of the family, rarely growing to more than 3in in length. They are most likely to be found in estuary and harbour mud, living like the king ragworm in burrows lined with the mucus from their bodies. Because the mud is smooth, the tunnel entrances appear as large pin-pricks on the surface. When the area is trodden upon the tiny holes emit small spouts of water. Maddies appear to live in colonies for it is not unusual to dig as many as 30 worms with one forkful. Its small size and soft environment make it a delicate worm and one very difficult to keep alive for more than 24 hours. It is highly esteemed as bait for mullet fishing, particularly in and around harbours and, fished on a small hook it is an excellent bait for garfish.

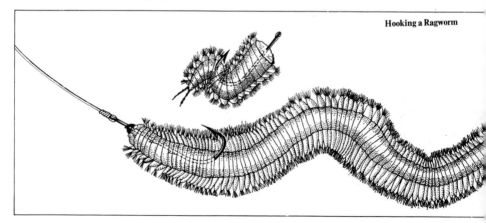

Hooking a Ragworm

Ken Whitehead

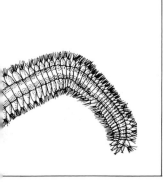

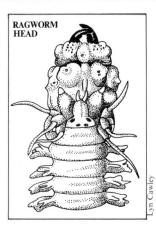

RAGWORM
HEAD

Lyn Cawley

(Above) Differently coloured from the specimen shown on the previous pages, but still the familiar king ragworm, Nereis virens.
(Far left) Two ways to put ragworm on the hook.
(Left) Top, or dorsal view of the head of the king ragworm in its protruded form. The eyes can be seen as four dots just before the body segments begin.

243

Mackerel

TWO HOOK TROLLING RIGS

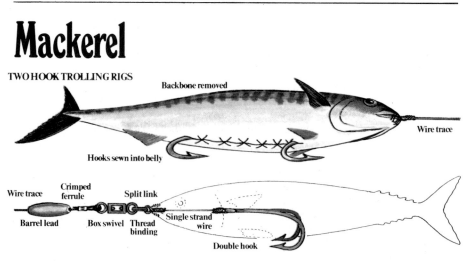

Backbone removed

Wire trace

Hooks sewn into belly

Wire trace · Crimped ferrule · Split link · Barrel lead · Box swivel · Thread binding · Single strand wire · Double hook

Of all the fish species inhabiting Britain's coastal waters, there is none with a more mixed reputation than that enjoyed by the mackerel. Although some rate them highly for a variety of reasons, there are those who dismiss them as 'dirty eaters', or as being too easy to catch or not worth eating. But as a fish bait, a fresh mackerel has no equal.

What makes the fish so attractive as a bait? In short, it is the mackerel's abundant body juices, rich in oils and vitamins, a characteristic shared with the herring and salmon. Fish are able to detect these juices by the sense of smell which all species, to a greater or lesser degree, possess. Because of its attraction, it is important that mackerel is used only when in prime condition.

Feathering

Mackerel may be taken in various ways, although the majority are caught by boat anglers using sets of hooks dressed with feathers. 'Feathering' is a good method, as up to six hooks can be used and, on occasions, a greedy mackerel will be caught on each, thus providing a plentiful supply of bait. Some fishermen advocate other methods, such as highly efficient sets of Norwegian lures, in which metal alternates with rubber tubing cut to imitate the eel.

No matter how efficient the lure may be, however, it will not produce results if fished at the wrong depth. It is important to

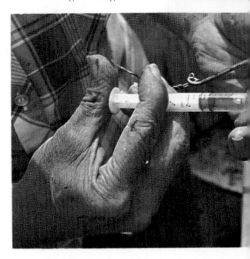

(Above) Two trolling rigs, one using a double hook, the other with singles in tandem. (Right) The attraction of mackerel lies in its rich and oily flesh. (Below) Injecting a mackerel head with pilchard oil as an added attraction for conger. (Far right) A mackerel tail fished on a running ledger with a wire trace is one of the standard methods used by anglers concentrating on conger.

244

remember that the mackerel, not possessing a swim bladder, can move surprisingly fast and so a shoal can change depth very rapidly. If several anglers are on board it is advisable for them to fish at different depths until a shoal is located. When very calm conditions prevail, as is often the case at first light, watch for sudden turbulence on an empty patch of sea—this could well be caused by mackerel just below the surface.

Mackerel as bait can be fished in a variety of ways, and methods of presentation attractive to most species can be found. Two important considerations must be borne in mind, whatever style of fishing is to be employed. First, the bait size and pre-

sentation should be appropriate to the quarry and its manner of feeding; secondly, the bait and hook should be matched in size.

Apart from its other advantages, the mackerel's shape and bone structure make it an ideal bait form. It can be cut in different ways according to requirements. The section adjoining the caudal or tail fin provides on each side a near-triangular patch known as a 'lask' or 'last'. This is recommended for bream, whiting, and other small species. Remember, though, that while various species may be of roughly similar size, their mouths are quite dissimilar—a fact to be considered when selecting hooks and cutting bait to match. An over-large bait can mask the barb so that hooking the fish becomes virtually impossible.

Alternatively, a side or flank can be offered, either whole, halved or sliced into strips to resemble small fish. To hook a half-side or strip of mackerel, drive the hook right through the fish and then twist this to allow

RUNNING LEDGER RIG

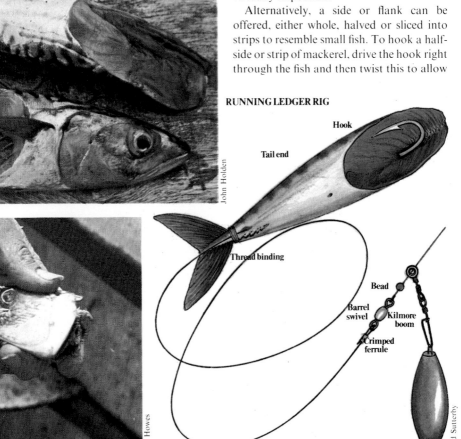

Mackerel

the hook to come through again in a different place. This ensures that maximum benefit is gained from the oily flesh.

A whole side of mackerel can be held in position and presented in an attractive manner by whipping a small hook onto the trace a couple of inches above the main hook. The top of the bait is then supported, the lower portion being free to move with the current to simulate a small live fish.

A mackerel sliced diagonally across its body from just below the gill cover on one side to a point near the vent on the other, makes an ideal top bait, as indeed does the head complete with entrails. To obtain the latter, the fish should be cut around the 'shoulders' so that the head comes free with the innards attached. Here again, the important thing is to exploit the fish-attracting juices. This bait is excellent when float-fished. To secure it, pass the hook through the head adjacent to the eye.

Conger can often be lured by a whole mackerel. Use a baiting needle to draw the

(Above) For large fish such as cod, needing large hooks, a whole side of fresh mackerel is ideal. Thread the hook through. (Above, right) A side of mackerel cut into strips will bait a dozen hooks.

(Below) Fresh mackerel on a running ledger. Note the breakaway casting lead.

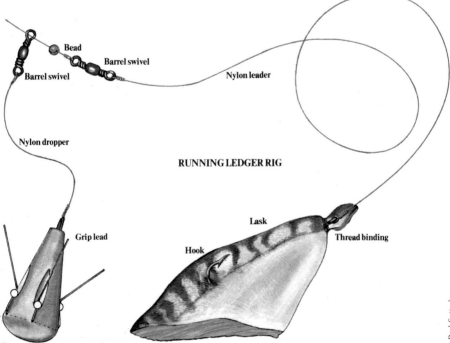

Bead

Barrel swivel

Barrel swivel

Nylon leader

Nylon dropper

RUNNING LEDGER RIG

Grip lead

Lask

Hook

Thread binding

John Holden

hook into position. Some anglers draw the hook up to the vent, others prefer it to protrude from the bait's flank. Whichever method is used, slash the skin in several places to release the blood and oily juices.

When using large baits of this kind, the tide's motion will frequently cause them to spin and so impart an amount of twist to the trace. To overcome this, use at least one, swivel between the reel line and hook.

For most sea anglers the mackerel is a summer species. This leads to an obvious question: what does one use when fresh mackerel are not available as bait? In some areas, the South West for example, mackerel are caught professionally throughout the winter, weather permitting, and can be bought fresh from fishmongers. In other regions, though, when the fish have travelled to inland fishmongers via the wholesale market, and then, after being bought as bait by the angler, they can be very wrinkled, unattractive specimens.

For anglers with a deep-freeze, a great saving can be made by catching early morning mackerel and then freezing them for later use. But fish which have been dead for hours, and lying in the sun in an open boat, do not freeze properly for when unfrozen they will rapidly deteriorate into a soft and useless mass. At one time the alternative solution was simple—use her-

ring. This species was cheap and plentiful. They are still an excellent bait, but over-fishing has led to a scarcity and high prices.

Having dealt with the mackerel as a bait, let us return briefly to its defence in other spheres. The mackerel is not a 'dirty eater' but is a predator which chases and kills other fish, although there is a period during spring and early summer when plankton become its prime diet.

Competition for food

That mackerel can be easy to catch cannot be denied. This is certainly true of most, if not all, shoaling species. The competition for food can be so great that individuals will throw themselves on anything attractive, as witness the savagery with which a pack of spurdog will dispute possession of a bait, or the way whiting will snap at potential food. The larger the shoal the greater the competition, and nowadays there are few species to be found in greater abundance than mackerel.

A mackerel long-since caught and stale is a sad offering as a table fish. But one fresh from the sea is a real delight. Unfortunately, no fish becomes soft and unappetizing more rapidly, and so remember that mackerel caught on a summer's morn, subjected to the heat of the day and then taken, perhaps, on a long journey home, will be stale and far from the tasty dish they can be.

Squid and cuttlefish

The flesh of squid, cuttlefish and to a lesser extent octopus makes super bait to tempt many species of sea fish. They belong to the class Cephalopoda, and are cylinder or sac-shaped molluscs with suckered tentacles surrounding the mouth and joining the head. The eyes are conspicuous, and the mouth is equipped with horny jaws like a bird of prey's beak.

Squid have a 'quill' or backbone closely resembling plastic, while the shell of the cuttlefish is a familiar sight on beaches.

The squid is most commonly used as bait, as its distribution in the Atlantic, English

cleaned by severing the head and cutting evenly down through the centre of the body to the tail. It should then be opened and laid out flat, and the stomach removed in one easy movement. With care you can do this without bursting the ink sac which has an acid content irritating to human skin. Squid wings are useless as bait and can be thrown away. Finally, it needs thorough washing using two changes of fresh water, and then the bait is ready for freezing.

If you are preparing a number of squid at the same time, it is a good policy to pack them in polythene bags holding just enough

(Left) A large cuttlefish. (Below and right) Stages in the preparation of a squid for bait. Keep the head separate as conger bait.

P. H. Ward/Natural Science Photos

Channel and North Sea brings it within range of trawlers operating at ports dotted around the coastline. Cuttlefish are frequently caught but in nothing like the numbers of squid. The octopus is a rare catch in British waters, but a few are hooked by anglers fishing on very rough ground for more conventional species.

Advantages of squid bait

Squid is the cleanest bait to use in sea fishing as the flesh is firm, cuts cleanly and easily, and can be presented attractively in a variety of ways. Above all it keeps well, and a supply laid down in a freezer can stay perfectly fresh for two years. This applies if you follow simple rules. The squid must be thoroughly

for a day's fishing. Failure to do this will almost certainly result in wasted bait, as once thawed out it cannot be refrozen.

Freeze the heads separately

Squid heads make a great bait for conger, ling or any other large species, and should be frozen separately. If they are mixed in with the bodies of the squid and taken out on shore trips when small fry are the quarry, it is likely that only the tentacles will be used, which is wasteful.

Take a word of warning however. The freezing compartment of a domestic refrigerator is only suitable for keeping small quantities of squid for short periods.

If you do keep it there, make sure the lady

'MURDERER'

Rod Sutterby

Squid are rarely caught on rod and line, but they can be taken with a 'murderer'. It is used like a pirk or jig.

of the house knows about it. Disasters can occur when a refrigerator is switched off for de-frosting, and the squid is left in the top.

Squid caught on rod and line

Although most squid are obtained from commercial sources, they can be caught fairly easily on rod and line during the winter months when they shoal in vast numbers particularly at the western end of the English Channel. Between October and March they can be a problem in deep water as they snatch at baits put out for pollack and coalfish with a 'take' that is similar to those of both species. The similarity ends after the take however, as they let the bait go a few feet from the boat, even after making a number of powerful dives giving the impression that they are securely hooked.

For a reason that has never been clear, the squid is seldom caught on normal tackle. It is

10 fathoms deep. The average weight is 2-3lb, but specimens to 10lb are not uncommon. In fact, it is generally the larger squid that are caught on rod and line.

All fish will take squid, and some species particularly relish it. Heading the list are red and black bream, which are caught in their thousands on very thin strips about 3in long offered on fine hooks to paternosters, or a single hook on a flowing trace.

Change a frayed bait

As the squid is so tough, it is possible to catch several bream on the same strip of bait. As soon as the edges show signs of fraying however, it must be changed. Hundreds of conger eels to 100lb are also taken on squid head, or a whole squid hooked through the body and ledgered close to a wreck or on rough ground. Similarly it is a great favourite with the ravenous ling.

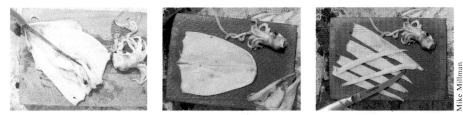

Mike Millman

a crafty fish. To outwit them, the angler uses a murderer—a weighted body about 4in long fitted with two rings of needle-sharp points at one end of the lure. Jigged about 10ft below the surface, it will hook any squid that strikes at it on one of the many points. When the catch is lifted over the side, watch out for the ink which the squid will pump out.

The squid cannot be used as bait immediately after capture as the flesh is jelly-like and almost transparent, to the extent that you can see its vital organs. Six hours after death the flesh changes to the familiar white rubbery texture.

Most rod-caught squid are taken within a few feet of the surface, but in water less than

A strip of squid about 10in long and 1in wide cut to resemble a fish, makes a fine trolling bait for bass. Mounted on a long-shanked hook and worked astern at about three knots, it will dart about in a realistic manner and soon find a taker.

For shore fishing on storm beaches, squid is ideal bait as it stands up to long casting and can take any amount of battering from heavy surf. Many flatfish enthusiasts use it extensively as a bottom bait for turbot, plaice and dabs, although it has never been much good for flounder.

During the winter months, monster mackerel have a definite liking for a thin strip of squid, and give great sport on light tackle.

Sandeel

The sandeel is not only one of the best baits for sea angling, but a very important part of the food chain for most species of fish. Three varieties are found in British waters: the greater sandeel *(Hyperoplus lanceolatus)* which can be easily identified by the black spot on the sides of the snout, the sandeel *(Ammodytes tobianus)* and the smooth sandeel *(Gymnammodytes semisquamatus)*.

They have elongated bodies and no spiny rays in the fins. The upper jaw is extensible and shorter than the lower, and the tail fin is forked and separate from the dorsal and anal.

When and where to find sandeel

Sandeels shoal in very large numbers but are seldom seen in daylight as they lie buried in the sand. They emerge after dark, and the light from a torch will often reveal what appears to be a solid shimmering mass in the shallow water of sandy estuaries. Sandeels are generally caught by towing a fine-mesh seine net from a small rowing boat off sandy beaches, or by digging and raking in the sand on the beach. The latter is best done at low tide right at the water's edge, as the eels like to hide in very wet sand. If there is a freshwater stream running down the beach this is also a good place to search.

The speedy sandeel

Most sandeels are dug for at night when it is customary to work by the light of a pressure lamp. Once an eel has been lifted out of the sand it must be picked up immediately as it has the ability to tunnel back extremely quickly. In fact, a 7in eel, when placed on very firm sand, can disappear beneath the surface in less than two seconds.

Collecting by hand will produce about 30 eels in a couple of hours—more than enough

Mike Millman

(Above) To keep sandeels alive it is necessary to use a portable pump to aerate the water. The fish need a high level of oxygen to remain alive.
(Below left) Sandeels and artificials.

bait for a day's fishing. A seine net, however, will trap as many as 10,000 eels in a single run of less than half an hour. The net is weighted at the bottom with rolling leads and supported by cork floats which keep it upright and level with the surface. It is paid out from the stern of a rowing boat which slowly describes a circle about 50 yards out from the beach. One end of the holding rope is kept onshore by a member of the three-man team, and when the net has been completely laid, the other end is brought ashore. The seine is then pulled smoothly in until the bag is clear of the water.

During sorting, a careful watch should be kept for poisonous weever-fish, which are frequently caught during sandeel operations. Eels over 5in are retained and the rest quickly returned to the sea.

Keeping sandeels alive during transportation was a problem until quite recently. Sandeels depend on a high level of oxygen in water and, if this falls below a certain level, they die within a few minutes. Fortunately,

small, battery-operated air-pumps are now on the market, and can run as long as 30 hours on a couple of 1.5-volt dry cell batteries.

A reliable aerator

The Shakespeare company produces a reliable pump which is light and compact and currently retails at £15. A matching heavy duty PVC livebait-carrying bag costs about £6. The bag, which holds a gallon of water and becomes rigid when full, is perfect for keeping bait in good condition. It also features a water level gauge that indicates the maximum volume of water that can be aerated by this motor-pump. In many ways this outfit is one of the best contributions to angling for many years.

As sandeels are plentiful in the summer but extremely scarce after October, livebaiting during the dark months will necessitate keeping a stock of sandeels at home. All you need is a large glass tank of the type sold by shops catering for tropical fish enthusiasts, a couple of filter boards, and a mains air pump. A tank 3ft long by 1ft wide and 18in deep holds enough water to keep 200 eels alive for a long period. The bottom of the tank should be covered by 8in of sand for the eels to bury in, and it is advisable to remove 10 gallons of water every so often and replace it with a new supply of seawater. Sandeels do not require feeding as they filter plankton from the water and find other forms of marine life in the sand. To supplement their feeding, add a few large pieces of seaweed to the tank from time to time.

The courge

Before the introduction of air pumps, the angler had to use a floating courge to keep sandeels alive. For hundreds of years they were made professionally from wickerwork in a variety of sizes, but the trade died out in the 1920s. They were pointed at both ends with a trap door in the top and could be towed behind a sailing or rowing boat so the eels were maintained in an almost natural environment. The modern equivalent is a wooden box, with one pointed end and many small holes, which allow the passage of

Mike Millman

water. It can be towed behind a slow craft without damaging the eels, but is usually placed in the water on a tether, when the boat is either drifting or at anchor over a mark.

During the journey out, the eels are kept fresh in a plastic drum to which buckets of seawater are constantly added. Some boats with glass-fibre hulls have livebait tanks built in at the water-line. A constant change of water can be obtained by simply opening a sea-cock. With this refinement, both eels and other fish can be kept alive indefinitely.

Catching sandeels

During boat fishing trips in deep water, sandeels are occasionally caught by accident on feathers intended for mackerel. To fish for them selectively, however, you need to be over sandy banks where there is a fast run of tide. Such a place is the Skerries Bank off the Devon coast, renowned for its turbot, plaice and dab fishing. Between the Skerries Buoy at the eastern end and Start Point at the west, the banks are covered by varying depths of water. Sandeels swarm in millions here, and

(Above) A wooden courge. Attached to the boat and left floating, the holes allow seawater to pass through and keep the sandeels alive and fresh.
(Above right) Old-fashioned wicker courges, once universal, are now being replaced by the holed wooden boxes.
(Right) Two methods of baiting sandeel.

if you drop a set of feathers half a dozen times, you will collect enough for a good day's sport.

Many sandeels to 1ft in length are foul-hooked, but are considered too big for live use. Instead, thin even strips cut from just behind the head to the tail are used. When livebaiting, most expert sea anglers prefer eels with a light brown back, as these are livelier than those sporting a dark green hue.

To bait a sandeel, hold it firmly but lightly between the fingers and thumb, throat outwards. Put the point of the hook through the bottom lip and nick it into the soft skin of the belly just behind the head—this is the

Bill Howes

Mike Millman

normal way of offering it in a fair run of tide. When fishing in slack water, however, it is often better to simply hook the eel through the top of its body, in front of the dorsal.

Hooks for sandeels

Hooks must be long in the shank, needle-sharp, and fine in the wire—a description that fits the Aberdeen perfectly. Live eels must be offered on a very long trace, which allows them to swim around in a natural manner. The movement is enhanced if nylon monofilament with a b.s. of no more than 12lb is used.

Trolling with live or dead sandeels over rocky ground can be a rewarding business,

and big catches of pollack and bass are made. Of the many species partial to sandeel these two predators head the list, and even medium-weight fish of these species completely engulf a fair-sized eel in a single attack.

For shore fishing from rocky stations the live eel is best used with float gear, but the float should be sufficiently large to withstand the eel's thrashing without going under.

The eels can also be offered successfully as a spinning bait if you are fishing deep water from rocky ledges. This is general practice on the north coast of Cornwall, where the main quarry is bass, pollack and mackerel.

253

Rubber eels and lures

For more than a hundred years, rod and line fishermen have used artificial lures to catch sea fish. Long before the start of this century, ingenious minds dreamed up many different types of baits that twisted, wobbled or travelled through the water with an undulating motion. The earliest lure was made from a length of wide rubber-band, one end whipped to the hook shank. It bore a remarkable resemblance to a living worm.

Sophisticated lures appear

From this beginning, more sophisticated lures soon evolved. Two types in particular, known as Brook's Double Twist Spinning Eel, and Captain Tom's Spinning Eel, were the first to be made from lengths of india-rubber pipe. This was pushed onto a large hook to form an 'elbow' at the bend, which caused it to spin when worked through the water at speed. Small brass swivels attached to the hook eye prevented the line from twisting to any great extent, and the top end of the pipe was securely fastened to the shank with stout thread.

In 1948, rubber gave way to plastic and the first modern eels appeared. The

A selection of modern, colourful lures for sea fishing. Their success depends upon movement to attract fish.

'Mevagissey', produced by Alex Ingram, was made by a dip-coating process. Early models featured a long, soft, curved tail, which plugged into a hollow body. When viewed from above, the lure had a natural-looking action, but it tended to spin, which caused the reel line to twist. One day, watching a jet landing with its braking parachute extended, Alex noted that this chute oscillated, and he realized that if the action could be incorporated into a sandeeel, its movement would be much improved. Over a period of time, various prototypes were tried out in the rugged conditions of wreck and reef fishing at many sites in Britain, until the 172mm Red Gill lure finally emerged that was to revolutionize sea fishing.

In the late 1960s dip-coating gave way to injection moulding, and improved plastics produced a much better eel. Modern PVC resists ultra-violet radiation and the effects of saltwater, so that lures now have tremen-

(Left) Three models in the well-known range of colourful Toby lures. (Below) A group of lures which the bass angler uses to attract his particular prey.

Steve Bicknell

dous durability. A boat angler fishing off Falmouth, who kept careful records of each fish he caught, noted that 199 pollack fell to the same Red Gill lure. Gradually the range has grown, and the latest is the 210mm Thresher, designed for wreck fishing.

Eddystone artificials have certainly made their mark on the sea angling scene since their introduction in 1974. Less sophisticated, but with a devastating tail action, they are now in wide use, and account for large numbers of big fish. Some models designed for spinning have a metal head plugged into the conventional plastic tail. This enables the lure to be cast a considerable distance, without the need for a spiral lead on the trace. Eddystone trolling lures with exceptionally long and very thin tails are also used with great success by anglers seeking bass and pollack.

Movement—the secret of success

No matter how good the design of an artificial sandeel, its success is totally dependent on one thing—movement. All have a negligible action of their own, and only movement imparted by an angler gives a lure 'life'. Unfortunately, this is not always realised, and one sees artificial sandeels being used garnished with a strip of mackerel, squid or—incredibly—a natural sandeel. Anything on the lure's hook will completely ruin its action.

Soft plastic can easily become deformed, too, if not handled with a reasonable amount

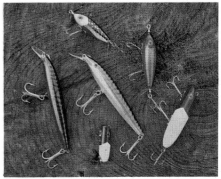

Mike Millman

of care and it is therefore important not to crush eels into a tackle box.

Plastic lures are available in a wide range of colours, but divers tell us that below 30ft, even in clear water conditions, colour (as we know it) begins to disappear. At 100ft it has gone altogether. So what is the point in painting artificials so attractively—most are used in depths of 40 fathoms (240ft) to which no light penetrates. The clue is surely in the phrase 'Colour *as we know it*'. The human eye may perceive quite differently from the fish's eye.

During 1972, a year when many outstanding pollack and coalfish were caught in deep water, red lures accounted for the greatest number, including the present British record pollack of 25lb. Lures of other colours were being offered in an identical manner, but got a very poor response. Consequently, red lures were so much in demand that supplies

ABU RAUTO

Rod Sutterby

Bill Howes

ran out in the tackle shops, and stocks finished in green, yellow and blue were quickly given a coat of red paint.

Recent studies have shown that lures coloured deep purple with a blue head, and dark red with a gold belly are currently catching extremely well.

Profusion of metal lures

So far we have dealt only with plastic lures, but there are a great many manufactured in metal. This type is used extensively for shore spinning, and, to a lesser extent, trolling from small craft over inshore grounds. The range of shape and colour is bewildering. The newcomer to sea angling is easily confused by the profusion of different types, all of which profess to catch fish when, regrettably, most are designed to catch anglers. A recent estimate of the number of plastic, wood and metal lures originating in North America came to almost 4,000 kinds. While many are obviously the result of detailed study into the habits of certain species, the majority are completely worthless. It is a sad fact that many tackle shops in Britain now carry artificials that are equally ineffectual. Before parting with your money, therefore, take advice from anglers with experience in artificial lure fishing.

Spinning is now a very popular method with shore anglers. Development of suitable tackle has kept pace with the sport and hollow glass rods, fixed-spool and multiplier reels handle lures of ⅛oz up to 4oz. All the

beginner needs is a 7ft rod, a fixed-spool reel and 10lb b.s. line—£12 buys a good-quality outfit from a reputable manufacturer.

Among the most successful metal lures for spinning are Toby, Droppen, Spinflasha and Wingflasha, which have accounted for many fine bass, pollack, mackerel and garfish. In addition to the spoon used as a spinning bait, a spoon may also be used as an attractor for such species as bass, flounder and plaice. In this instance the fish is attracted by the spoon and takes the conventional bait. It is used by experts when working in estuaries and tidal rivers. Spoons take many forms—what is right in one place can be a complete flop in another. Many are home-made from brass, copper and occasionally plastic. Inventors pay great attention to the overall shape, thickness and twist of the blade, and to the colour, which many consider vital.

Swedish model

A commercially produced spoon that takes a lot of beating is ABU's Rauto. Among its captures in deeper water have been record cod on 6lb line, and much heavier fish on stronger tackle.

The search for new and better designs in both plastic and metal goes on. Many fish, especially bass, are becoming familiar with the appearance of current designs of plastic sandeels and show an added wariness, but there is little doubt that British manufacturers, who lead the world, intend to stay one jump ahead.

Peeler crabs

Many people believe, quite wrongly, that the peeler crab is not a crustacean, but, like all other crabs, it belongs to that group of creatures. These have their skeleton on the outside of their body and their muscles and organs inside it. Growth is only possible by changing shells, and this is done by growing a new, larger shell, which has at first to be soft in order to fit beneath the existing hard shell. When the new, soft shell is fully formed, just before the old one is discarded, the crab is known as a 'peeler'.

Common shore crab

Of the many varieties of crab found around our coasts, the best, and most widely used, for bait is the common shore crab *(Carcinus moenas)*. The young crab starts life from an egg which hatches in the upper layers of the sea. At this stage the larva bears no resemblance to the adult, but in a few weeks it undergoes five moults, after which it sinks to the seabed and takes on the characteristic form of a crab.

During the crab's early life moulting takes place frequently during the summer months, when the water is warm, but the process occurs less frequently in winter and as the crab matures. At the half-grown stage it will shed its shell twice or even three times a year, whereas the adult will change its shell very infrequently—probably every second year.

Immediately after casting off its shell the crab becomes what is known as a soft back or soft crab. At this stage it is defenceless and so hides itself, but a new shell begins to form straight away. After a few hours the shell is

In their peeler state crabs make a fine bait for many kinds of fish. A rocky coast has an endless supply of this bait.

Ken Whitehead

Peeler crabs

P. H. Ward/Natural Science Photos

like parchment but the crab is still not at its best as a bait.

The colour of the common inshore crab varies greatly according to its locality, but it is most often a greenish-brown, sometimes with distinctive markings on the top of the shell or carapace. The crab approaching maturity adopts a much redder hue, so earning the nickname 'red belly'.

A short time before shedding takes place the new shell beneath has so cramped the crab's muscles that much of the power leaves its legs and claws. This is when the angler will find the vulnerable creature hiding under seaweed, around rock ledges, in soft sand and mud around rocks, harbour walls and breakwaters—anywhere which provides protection from strong tides and from natural enemies.

Artificial sanctuaries

Professional peeler crab gatherers often place broken roof tiles on the mud flats in estuaries or half bury tins in mud or sand to provide artificial sanctuaries—and thus traps—for the crabs. Gathering becomes much easier as these shelters are laid in straight lines, so decreasing the amount of walking needed.

(Above) Cornwall's rocky coast is ideal for gathering crabs for bait. Bass, like crab, are found feeding close inshore here.
(Above, right) Crabs can be hooked in different ways, while the legs alone also attract fish to the hook.
(Right) Small crabs can be bound to hooks by the use of the elasticated thread.

Of course, not every crab gathered in this way will be at the peeler stage. The only way to tell if it is suitable for bait is to carefully remove the end joint from a leg and see whether the segment has not been removed at all because the new skin is completely formed. If this is the case, the crab can go into the gatherer's bucket. It pays to collect more than will be needed for a day's fishing for they will be at different stages of moult and some can be kept for use when ready.

Having returned home, the angler should examine the bait carefully, selecting for use first those whose carapace has started to crack from the underside of the shell or those with a shell which has started to lift. The rest should be placed in a bucket of wet seaweed—bladderwrack is best—and kept in a cool place. These crabs will live up to two

258

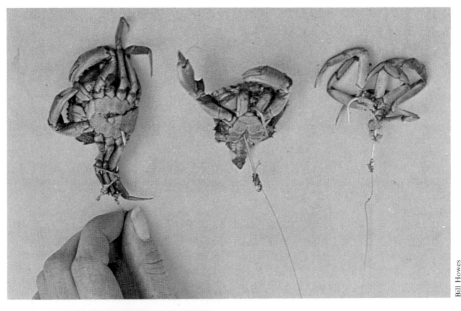

Bill Howes

Ken Whitehead

Many anglers hold that the peeler crab is the supreme sea fishing bait, while others criticise it because of the preparation needed. With care, however, several fine pieces of bait can be obtained from one crab. First remove the eight legs and two claws from the body and then, using the thumbnail, remove the carapace. With the aid of the thumbnail, or a knife, remove as much of the shell from the underside as possible.

Small baits

The crab can be used whole, depending on the size but, more often, the body is cut crossways in two or quartered to provide four small baits. Anglers often discard the legs and claws but these, hooked in a bunch like worms, can prove a deadly bait. By carefully removing the four segments one at a time from the legs with a gentle twist and a pull they can be peeled off. The claws can be dealt with in the same way.

When starting a day's fishing it is advisable to leave the peeler crabs in a bucket of sea water for a while as this makes them softer and easier to peel. Beachcasting crab puts considerable strain on this soft bait and so the whole body or segments should be tied to the hook with elastic thread or wool.

weeks, continuing the shedding process, but at a much slower rate than in their natural state. It is advisable to inspect them daily, removing any dead and renewing the weed after about a week.

A deadly bait

Peeler crabs are highly attractive to all sea fish but are especially deadly with bass and cod. Inshore boat fishing and beachcasting will both produce good results with this irresistible bait. The cod is greedy and is relatively easy to hook, but the bass will often suck the bait from the hook and so demands the angler's full attention.

Shellfish

In the sea, molluscs are a very important link in the food chain. Most important to the angler for bait are mussels, cockles, limpets, winkles and whelks. Many fish—the plaice is a typical example—will feed almost exclusively on baby molluscs, preferring 'seed' cockles and mussels. It is not surprising, then, that many species of shellfish have been used by the sea angler for many years.

Mussel as bait

The mussel, which is a bivalve, or two-shelled creature, has been a very popular bait for years, particularly on the East Coast. It is very easy to gather but it does require some preparation as it is virtually impossible to bait with the seed mussel upon which the fish are feeding.

There are about eight species of saltwater mussels found round the British coasts, but the horse mussel is the one generally used as bait by anglers. The young mussel begins life as part of the plankton before settling on the seabed and securing itself to rocks, stones, pier piles and similar spots with a series of very strong threads named the byssus. These threads, often called the 'beard', hold the mussel firmly to its rocky anchoring point even in the strongest gales. Mussels are sometimes found in great clusters and it is possible to gather a bucketful in minutes. It pays to be a little selective, picking out those with clean shells and leaving the barnacle-encrusted specimens, which are not usually as plump and juicy as the younger ones. The easiest way to remove the animal from the shell is to immerse in boiling water, which forces open the shell. The flesh is then removed by scooping out with a knife. Salt may be sprinkled on the bait to toughen the flesh and so make it stay on the hook. For beach fishing, a good method is to put three or four of the prepared mussels in a very fine-

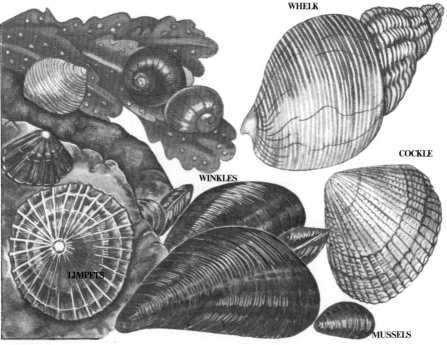

WHELK

COCKLE

WINKLES

LIMPETS

MUSSELS

Rod Sutterby

260

1 *Limpets must be prised away from their bases by the use of a knife.*
2 *Single mussels are not big enough as bait, but a bunch makes an attractive offering.*
3 *By turning rocks over which are covered at high tide one can usually find a plentiful supply of hookbait from the animals which live there.*
4 *The whelk has a massive shell which has to be cracked open before the creature can be used as a hookbait. Once on the hook, however, its muscular foot holds it securely to provide an excellent bait.*
(Left) Most shellfish make good baits and the sea angler should be prepared to experiment with them.

Ken Whitehead

mesh hair-net, which is attached to the hook and enables the bait to be cast a greater distance without flying off. Used this way, the mussel can be a deadly bait for cod.

Cockles as bait

Cockles are another variety of bivalve which will take many different species of sea fish. They are used extensively in Scotland, particularly on the Clyde. Cockles may take longer to gather as they have to be raked out of the sand in their preferred habitat of sheltered bays without strong tides or heavy surf. This bait requires no preparation other than the opening of the shell and the removal of its contents. Rather than cracking them open with a heavy blunt instrument, which will damage the animal inside, it is better to take a cockle in each hand, and where the

shells are hinged, lock one into the other and give a sharp twist. This breaks the hinge on the weaker of the two and allows the creature inside to be hooked out with the thumbnail. It is not a very large bait singly, but half a dozen or so on one hook make a very respectable offering.

The limpet is another mollusc, cone-shaped and dark brown in colour, which the angler can gather himself. They can be detached by prising them off with a knife or similar implement. The animal is then exposed and removed from the shell with the thumbnail, to reveal orange disc-shaped flesh and a blackish patch. Used singly on a small hook it is a good bait for flatfish, particularly dabs, while several on a large hook will attract most other species.

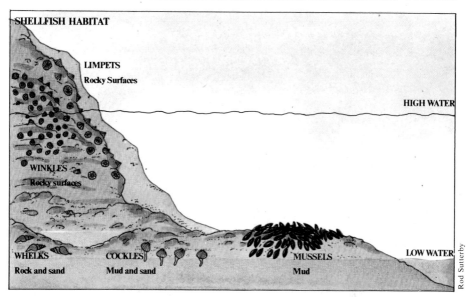

SHELLFISH HABITAT

LIMPETS
Rocky Surfaces

HIGH WATER

WINKLES
Rocky surfaces

WHELKS   COCKLES   MUSSELS   LOW WATER
Rock and sand   Mud and sand   Mud

Rod Sutterby

(Above) There is an abundance of marine life to be found where the shore is rocky, leaving small pools as the tide recedes. All shellfish here can be used as bait.
(Left) Barnacles and limpets carpet these rocks. When the tide comes in and covers them the limpets roam over the rocks seeking food. The mussels do not move, but their shells open and food particles are filtered from the gills to the mouth.

Unfortunately, its soft texture means that it cannot withstand forceful casting and is likely to be mutilated very rapidly by any crabs in the vicinity.

Where the winkle is found
The winkle, a member of the snail family, is among the smallest of the univalve molluscs. It can be found on most coastlines below the high-water mark and prefers a rocky bottom with good weed covering. The shell is smooth and ranges in colour from brown to black. The winkle is not widely used as a bait but fish are caught on it.

The main problem is that of removing the fish from the shell. If boiled first, this is done with a pin, but with a live winkle it is necessary to crack the shell with a hammer or any other blunt tool. As they are small,

several winkles are needed to make an adequate bait, but their toughness means that they remain on the hook for a long time and are not thrown off on the first cast.

The common whelk is much larger than the winkle and its flesh is greyish green. Large specimens can reach over 3in in length. They are to be found on seabeds of mainly stone and gravel and near the low-water mark at spring tide, but in considerably fewer numbers than the winkle. Professional fishermen take large quantities in baited pots from the deeper water and will usually sell a few to the angler. Again, the only successful method of removing the flesh while alive is to crack the shell, but one whelk makes a large bait, thus saving work and time in bait collecting.

Whelks are not really sought after as a bait by anglers, although commercial fishermen bait their longlines with them very effectively. Their success, however, can probably be attributed to the fact that a longline is left for several hours undisturbed and that the whelk is so tough that it will remain on the hook until eaten by a fish. For the rod and line angler it is best as a bait for cod and pouting as these two species are not particularly fussy.

Pirks and jigs

(Above) Pirks attract fish by the movement of their appendages as the lure is worked through the water.
(Right) A home-made 'baby octopus' cut from flexible plastic, with the head cleverly constructed from a drilled, painted, bullet.

In recent years pirking or jigging for free swimming fish such as pollack, coalfish and cod, has gained ground with deepwater boat anglers, and the method is now in wide use. It entails fishing with a weighted lure, invariably fitted with a treble hook. Pirks take many forms and range from lead-filled pipes, already chromed or painted in a variety of colours, to old plated car door handles or to sophisticated stainless steel and chrome-finished models from Scandinavia. Home-made pirks are cheap to produce, but the professional type can cost over £5.

Jigs

Jigs are generally smaller lures, often with coloured feathers set in a metal head rather than the all-metal body of a pirk. They are

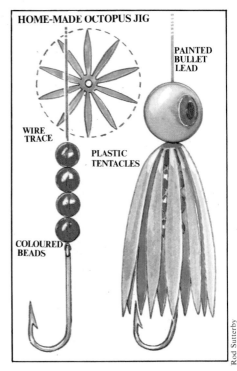

HOME-MADE OCTOPUS JIG

PAINTED BULLET LEAD

WIRE TRACE

PLASTIC TENTACLES

COLOURED BEADS

264

used in a similar way to pirks and range from 4oz to 26oz, the weight varying with the depth of water and the strength of tide. In general terms, few of less than 12oz are used in more than 20 fathoms of water.

Pirk fishing with heavy lures in the deeps requires a great deal of physical effort, which few anglers can keep up for more than half an hour. It is only with daily exercise that one builds the arms and shoulders to cope with the strain. Skippers who habitually fish wrecks in the Western Channel have the necessary physique and can keep a 26oz pirk going for hours on end, catching on average a hefty fish with every other drop. Tackle for this very specialized and rugged aspect of sea angling is a stout 7ft fast-taper hollow-glass rod, with plenty of power in the butt section. Matched with a top quality high-geared multiplier of at least 6/0, filled with 50-80lb b.s. monofilament line, such a rod will suit all occasions. Braided line is never used in this style of fishing because it creates too great a drag in tidal flowing water.

(Below) Pirks can weigh as much as 26oz, so fishing with them can be exhausting. But for wreck fishing, the fluttering, flashing pirk will attract big pollack in numbers. Sea anglers should always carry a selection, kept brightly polished.

When out with charter parties, most skippers stand high on the craft's bows, well out of the anglers' way, and hurl the heavy lure as far as possible, allowing it to flutter unchecked to the bottom. When this is done over a wreck which holds a big fish population, the pirk is often grabbed on its way down while still high above the wreckage. If not, it should be retrieved from the bottom ultra-fast, until contact is made.

Spring tides help cover ground
For really good fishing the boat must drift and cover as much ground as possible. West Country charter skippers, who have brought pirking to a fine art, enjoy the greatest success during big spring tides, when the flow of water carries their craft along at a speed in excess of four knots.

Pollack and coalfish are fast-moving predators, much attracted to what appears to be a tasty meal swimming for its life. Both species invariably take the lure with a sideways slash and the treble hook usually embeds itself on the outside of the fish's jaw. Quite a few become foul-hooked in the head area, in front of the dorsal fin.

Although small pollack in the 4-6lb class go for pirks, it is more often specimen size fish up to the record size of 26lb that are caught. A few years ago the author hooked a monster of 23lb 4oz on a large Intrepid

Mike Millman

(Left) To catch big cod from deep water you need a comprehensive range of pirks from 4-20oz.
(Above) Home-made pirks. A yellow lead model and a tube filled with lead, both pirks drilled for split-rings and trebles.
(Right) Mike Millman with an excellent 20lb pollack taken on the lure seen protruding from the mouth of the fish.

John Wilson

Flectolite pirk, at a depth of 42 fathoms. At that time it ranked as the fifth biggest pollack taken on rod and line, although coming from such deep water it had no chance to show its true fighting ability. Even so, pumping it up was not without effort.

It must be remembered, from a purely sporting point of view, that deep water pirking has little to offer. Tackle must be on the heavy side if the lure is to be worked correctly—and most fish are hauled unceremoniously to the surface without having time to make any adjustment to the sudden change in pressure. Unfortunately, not every angler is concerned about the sporting aspect. Growing numbers only want to catch fish, and that is a sentiment fully supported by those angling skippers who keep the bulk of the catch and sell it.

Anglers fishing pirks from conventional positions in a boat adopt a quite different approach to the quick retrieve method of the boatman in the bow, and instead work the rod with a pumping action, as one would with feathers. While it is effective if not more than six anglers fish at a time from just one side of the boat as it moves across the wreck, this method does not match the fast-retrieve system.

Baited pirks

The effectiveness of large pirks can be increased by adding 1ft-long, coloured plastic streamers (which serve also to hide the hook) and of course natural baits. A

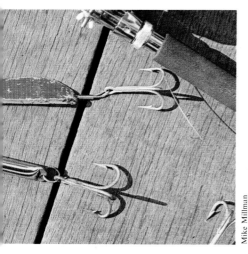

Mike Millman

whole side of mackerel or cut squid does nicely. Both these baits are particularly good for ling, which hunt close to or on the bottom. Many outsize fish have been caught on baited pirks, including several weighing over 40lb from marks in western waters. Although one would not deliberately offer a baited pirk for conger, it is interesting to note that the former British record eel of 102lb 8oz, caught by Ron Thompson off Mevagissey, Cornwall, in 1974, was hooked by this method. Other conger weighing around 50lb have ended their days in the same way, in both deep and shallow water.

Pirking over reefs

Pirking over reefs and open ground, where the species are less numerous, is a different proposition. Here the drift fishing technique is even more vital to success. Cod are caught on pirks worked close to the bottom, particularly where the ground is mud or shale. In shallow water, pirking can be done from small boats or dinghies with much lighter tackle and baited lures of 4-6oz. The sporting element is high—cod hit lures hard and put up plenty of resistance by continually trying to bore down towards the bottom. Between 1970 and 1973 pirking for cod at the Ganntocks mark in Scotland produced dozens of specimen fish, some weighing over 45lb. Since then, the run of cod coming into the Clyde from the Atlantic

to spawn in January and February has shrunk noticeably. This is probably due to commercial trawling, which has been understandably heavy in the area. Despite this, good fishing is still to be had, with plenty of cod reaching double-figure weights.

The majestic halibut is in the true heavyweight class. The largest species of flatfish in the world, it frequents the Pentland Firth off the northern tip of Scotland and waters around Orkney and the Shetland Islands. Large shiny pirks of up to 3lb, fitted with tough, forged No 12/0 (and larger) treble hooks, connected to wire lines, have taken several monster fish.

Pirking for halibut

Drifting these large, purpose-made pirks close to the bottom in very deep water, where the tide is strong, is the most successful method for halibut. Landing a fish safely is another matter. Obviously, tackle in the 80lb class is needed before you stand any chance. But with a fish that can weigh 400lb, there is nothing unsporting about it.

Harbours and piers

Mike Millman

Fishing from jetties, harbour walls, piers and groynes into deep water has almost all the benefits of boat angling without that dreaded scourge of the angler afloat— seasickness!

Around Britain's varied coastline there are quite a number of seaward-projecting structures, providing an attractive habitat for a wide variety of sea species. Fish drawn to the security and food stocks of deepwater wrecks, rocks and reefs are also attracted to the underwater structures of piers, jetties, harbour walls and groynes, especially those in a good depth of water at all states of the tide. These provide abundant marine life in a natural state without suffering a drying-out process twice a day as the tide recedes.

Piers give moral support
Seaside piers have long been the favourite fishing stations for elderly, comfort-loving sea anglers, small boys and beginners who initially require the moral support and companionship of other fishermen as they make their first unsure casts.

One great advantage to young anglers fishing from above-water structures is that they can learn to operate their tackle by

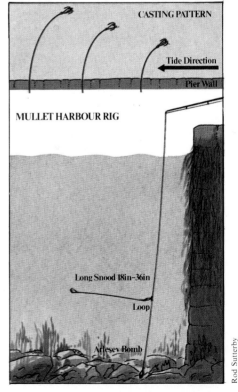

CASTING PATTERN

Tide Direction

Pier Wall

MULLET HARBOUR RIG

Long Snood 18in–36in

Loop

Arlesey Bomb

Rod Sutterby

(Left) Many tiny Cornish hamlets have harbours that are ideal for mullet and bass fishing. This is Charlestown, near the town of St Austell.
(Below) Harbour walls demand that anglers use casting patterns that respect all other anglers' fishing areas. Mullet fishing is best done by a long-snood rig.
(Right) For those anglers who suffer from sea-sickness, piers are the answer.
(Below right) With the paternoster, midwater and bottom species can be fished for using different hooks and baits such as lugworm and small dead sprats.

Bill Howes

lowering it rather than casting. This eliminates 'crack-offs' and tangles when using multiplier reels.

The tackle should be powerful enough to cope with the conditions—such as the strength and height of the tide—as well as being strong enough to land the fish when caught. When float fishing for bass, for example, on the lower deck of a pier, it would be inadvisable to fish with 'open-water' tackle—a light spinning rod, a fixed-spool reel and 5 or 6lb line. The first good bass hooked would immediately dive for cover among the old barnacle-covered iron girders and smash such tackle. For such a snaggy angling situation, a stout beachcasting rod, a powerful multiplier or centrepin reel, and 15 to 20lb b.s. line is effective.

Where double figure cod weights are expected and a long haul-up has to be made, because the powerful rush of the tide makes dropnetting impractical, a stout pier rod about 9 or 10ft in length or a heavy duty beachcaster is needed, together with a powerful reel and strong line of 25 to 35lb b.s. Such tackle may appear to be on the

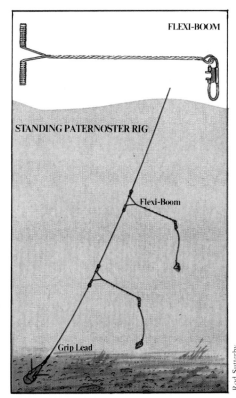

FLEXI-BOOM

STANDING PATERNOSTER RIG

Flexi-Boom

Grip Lead

Rod Sutterby

Harbours and piers

(Left) A number of fish species can be caught from piers and groynes. Bass, pollack and cod are taken in good numbers, but of them all, the mullet must be favourite. It is the speciality of the harbour angler, unknown by those who prefer the deep sea.

Mike Millman

(Right) One of the main problems about fishing from piers and groynes is that of getting large fish up from sea level. Your rod, reel and line will play the fish while it is in the water, but do not winch it up many feet to your level. Always have a drop-net ready for immediate use.

Bill Howes

pulley-hauling side, but it must always be remembered that with difficult shore fishing the strength of the tackle must be geared to overcome hazardous tackle handling, rather than just the fish itself.

Some seaward-projecting structures, however, present the gentlest of tides and sandy-bottomed fishing positions, necessitating the use of the very lightest of tackle—almost that used by the coarse fishing matchman. This is particularly true when fishing for harbour mullet which require a very subtle, silent coarse fishing approach.

A great deal of successful pier or harbour wall fishing can be done with the simplest of inexpensive tackle and a few fundamental terminal rigs. Provided the angler, who need not necessarily be highly skilled, studies the fishing conditions carefully, and presents the right bait when the fish are in a feeding mood (which could be at a certain state of the tide or during the hours of darkness—or both) good fishing can be had.

Long casting from piers is seldom necessary or absolutely vital to the making of good catches. Usually fish will be found

lurking in search of food around the underwater structure, right below the angler's fishing stance. A standard length 'pier rod', about 8–10ft long, will prove adequate when used in conjunction with a multiplier, a fixed-spool or a sea size centrepin reel. Short boat rods can also be used for pier and harbour wall fishing where the 'haul-up' is more or less perpendicular and there are no obstacles. If masses of rocks surround the fishing station and projections of various kinds present a definite hazard to the landing of a hooked fish, a longer rod will be of great assistance. This will enable the angler to steer his catch clear of the snags and haul it up, either directly with his tackle, or land it by means of a drop-net operated by one of his companions.

Match tackle with species

Line strength and hook sizes need to be matched to the size and species of fish expected. When the fishing ground is not 'tackle-hungry', for example, the pattern and weight of the lead used will be dictated by the strength of the tidal flow and the nature of the bottom which is being fished over. For

270

general pier and harbour wall type fishing locations, where the usual catch may consist of the flatfish species—dabs, flounders and a possible plaice or two, small codling, whiting, wrasse, pollack, coalfish and the odd thornback ray and 'strap' conger eel—the main reel line could be fixed at a sensible 24lb b.s. and the rest of the terminal tackle scaled down in steps to minimize tackle losses. The reel line to lead link in such cases would consist of a length of 20lb b.s. and hook links or snoods of nylon 16lb b.s.

Paternosters are pier favourites

The favourite bottom fishing terminal rig for piers has always been the paternoster, where one or more wire booms are mounted above the lead. This method, if three booms are used with a hook dropper suspended from each one, gives the angler a chance to experiment with three different kinds of bait and the fish have a varied 'menu' to choose from. Hook sizes should always match the size of the bait being used so that it can be mounted correctly and neatly presented.

Vary baits and hook sizes

Where both large and small fish species are expected, the bait offerings and hook sizes can be varied so that a bottom-feeding flatfish can take a lugworm offering on a 1/0 hook and a double figure cod can engulf a small dead sprat mounted on a size 6/0 hook higher up the terminal trace.

Winter fishing from piers, harbour walls, groynes and jetties may necessitate the use of stout rods and strong line to combat rough weather as well as the energies of the fish. In the warmer spring, summer and autumn months, however, a great deal of fine sport can be had by employing light, fine tackle techniques.

Coarse fishing 'specimen hunting' gear is admirably suited to the pursuit of large bass, which in summertime, especially at night, forage around piers and harbour walls. Likewise, light float fishing tackle will account for the ultra-shy mullet, garfish and mackerel which sport around at dusk and after dark in the vicinity of groynes and jetties, especially if quantities of waste food,

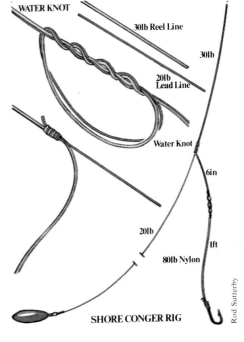

WATER KNOT

30lb Reel Line

30lb

20lb Lead Line

Water Knot

6in

20lb

1ft

80lb Nylon

SHORE CONGER RIG

Rod Sutterby

A shore fishing conger rig. The water knot is used to attach the 20lb b.s. leader to the 30lb reel line. A swivel leads to the 80lb hook trace.

vegetable matter or fish offal find their way into the water from fish quays or factories on the waterfront.

To avoid accidents and loss of life it is important that all shore anglers, particularly those fishing from angling stations above deep water, observe certain safety rules. Always observe strictly the rules of the pier or harbour wall so far as overhead casting, line strength and sinker weights are concerned. In rough weather, when waves are apt to break over the fishing station, leave the place well alone. On some piers, Tilley lamps and lanterns are banned because they constitute a navigational hazard when shone seawards.

Be careful when using a dropnet from piers or harbour walls with no guard rails and when climbing down perpendicular iron ladders or negotiating steep, weed-covered stone steps.

Harbours and estuaries

Fishing tackle, baits and methods used on exposed harbours and estuaries are similar to those used to cast from beaches and rocks on the open coast. With tide races and cross currents at their strongest at many harbour entrances, tackle must be even heavier than would normally be required for seafishing. Most harbours and estuaries, however, are quiet places where long distance casting and specialized tackle are unnecessary. For the beginner there are mackerel, garfish and flatfishes; for the more experienced angler the challenge of shy mullet and heavyweight conger eels.

Harbour fishing

To fish in harbours—or anywhere else for that matter—it is necessary to determine the fish's role in the environment. The next step is to use a suitable bait at the correct depth and location. It is pointless, for example, ledgering a strip of mackerel for mullet feeding on surface plankton. If mullet were taking pieces of bread from just below the surface you could assemble very light float tackle, bait with a flake of bread and cast near the feeding shoal. As mullet are shy it pays to cut line diameter to the safe minimum of about 4lb breaking strain; the rod and reel can be correspondingly light—a freshwater specimen rod and fixed-spool reel. The same tackle used with slightly stronger line would be suitable for the wrasse and pollack found closer to the seabed. Substituting worms and pieces of crab or fish for the bread should give excellent results.

Mackerel, garfish, bass and pollack are midwater predators that hunt their victims rather than waiting for them to drift past on the tide. They respond to bright, flashing movement and vibration which can be duplicated by a spinner of some kind. Artificial lure fishing is particularly good for these species when their activity cycles are at a peak; at dawn and dusk. Simple,

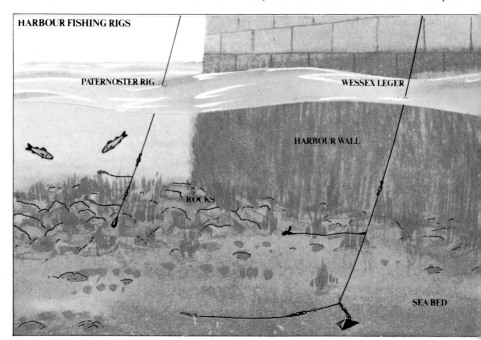

HARBOUR FISHING RIGS

PATERNOSTER RIG

WESSEX LEGER

HARBOUR WALL

ROCKS

SEA BED

lightweight tackle—freshwater tackle, for example—is perfectly adequate; even a simple handline may suffice. Successful lures range from spinners and spoons to feathers or even a strip of silver foil draped around a bare hook. The abundance of species that take either float-fished or spun baits probably explains why harbour and estuary fishing is so popular with holidaymakers and beginners. If a survey were taken, we would perhaps find that 90% of the seafish caught along the British coast are mackerel, small pollack and wrasse, bass and flatfish hooked from harbours during the holiday season.

Natural baits

Normal shorecasting tackle to throw the baits well out, so that they lie on the open ground, can be a helpful method. Worms, fish strips and sandeels attract rays, flatfishes, bass and even huge monkfish.

Fishing at night, when the fish are more active, is usually the best time when fishing off harbours. This is especially true when fishing for conger eels which hide during the day and are rarely tempted to feed. As soon as the sun goes down they creep out of the

Mike Millman

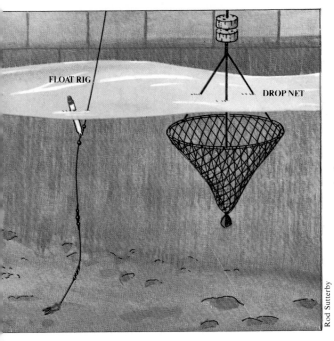

FLOAT RIG

DROP NET

Rod Sutterby

(Above) The tiny harbour of Coverack, Cornwall. Many kinds of fish will come into this bay.
(Left) Many fish species, large and small, are attracted to the areas below harbour walls. In the summer, holidaymakers drop unwanted food down, fishermen throw small-dead fish and discarded bait into the sea. Offal may be thrown overboard from coastal vessels tied up. All this, plus the presence of natural food living on the weed and in crevices in the walls, encourages fish to stay. Drop-nets are used for hauling up large fish which may fall off the hook.

Harbours and estuaries

rock piles and weed beds and sport is brisk until dawn. Conger eel fishing is a rough, tough sport. Casting out a chunk of really fresh fish on strong tackle, wait for a bite, then be prepared to join in a tug-of-war—which the eel wins more often than not. But it is fun, offering chances to catch one of the biggest species the shorefisher encounters.

Estuary fishing

The species found in estuaries are usually the same as those in harbours and the angler may not be faced with long casting. There are, however, so many different types of estuary that it is impossible to generalize. The vast Essex Blackwater is little different from the open coast, having beaches, sandbanks and channels as well as creeks

Spectrum Colour Library

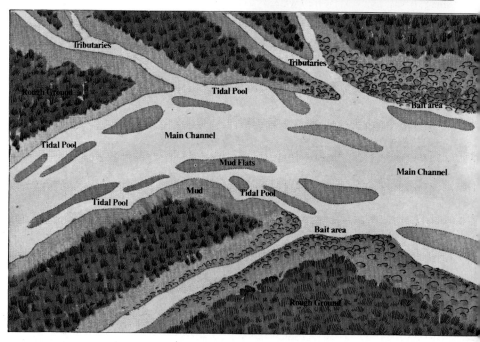

(Top photograph) Looking across the estuary of the Tweed from Berwick-upon-Tweed. On the far side lies Tweedmouth. It is a typical estuary, with prolific bait-gathering areas on acres of rich mudflats.

Estuaries are the homes of many species of fish. Bass, mullet, eels, gobies, garfish, flounder can all be fished for in the shallow, food-rich waters. Sea trout are found here on their way upstream to spawning grounds.

Off the main channel, mullet and trout, and eels too, will lie waiting for the tide to bring in food. The whole area is a natural food larder for all species and sea and land birds take full advantage of low water.

274

and mudflats. Some of the West Country estuaries, on the other hand, are no more than inlets used as harbours. As with successful fishing in harbours and from open shores, an understanding of natural history is important. If there are pilings, quays and backwaters, light tackle harbour techniques are best. Where there are sand spits and shingle beaches washed by surf, fish with standard casting tackle.

In estuary fishing the most significant factor which makes it different from other branches of seafishing is the fact that all estuaries are a confluence of fresh and saltwater. How they mix is crucial to the ecology of the area and therefore to the fishing. If vast amounts of freshwater pour into the estuary, as happens in a fast running spate river that tumbles from the mountains to the sea in a short course, seawater is swamped. The effect is to build up a saline gradient where the sea makes most headway in mid-channel but has little effect closer to the banks, where the water is brackish.

Some fish—flounders and mullet—are attracted to brackish water, but most of the truly marine species are repelled. To catch them you must fish from a boat in mid-estuary. Where saltwater dominates a sluggish freshwater flow and pushes it well inland, salinity is high even close to the banks and fishing is better for the truly marine species (cod, bass, plaice, whiting, conger eel) that require a high salt content.

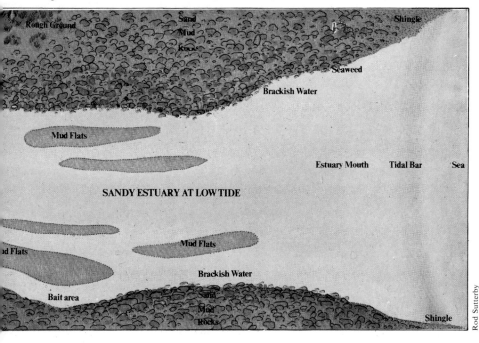

SANDY ESTUARY AT LOW TIDE

Rod Sutterby

The main channel will hold the stronger bass, where they can feed on the lugworm and ragworm washed out of the mud and sandbanks by the force of the tide. Crabs, mussels, clams, cockles abound here.

As the estuary widens the water-flow slows and it is more shallow. Areas of weed hold small marine organisms such as shrimps and fish larvae. Still brackish, the water here has a greater salt content.

Many river mouths and estuaries often have tidal bars, where ridges of sand or shingle build into the barriers that prevent the passage of craft. mackerel and garfish can be caught in this area.

Off-shore fishing

The off-shore fishing grounds round the British Isles have something for everyone. There are large skate, halibut, shark and conger, as well as cod, tope, ling, and a wide variety of lesser fish, all of which provide good sport on rod and line.

The secret of off-shore fishing is to know and understand the various species and their favourite habitats. For example, it will be a waste of time fishing over rocky pinnacles for tope. This small shark lives mainly by hunting flatfish and pouting, and usually confines its activities to flat, sandy or shingly ground. But pinnacle rocks are a good place to bottom-fish for conger, ling and cod. In mid-water around the pinnacles you will find the free-swimming fish such as pollack and coalfish.

Vital decision

Deciding where fish should be found is vital. Like people, fish will be found where the most food is available. Around wrecks or weed-covered reefs, for example, there will be a thriving population of small fish, crabs, prawns and immature lobsters. These creatures form the food of bigger fish, such as cod, ling and pollack.

All fish have good times and lean times. During the summer, shoals of mackerel and sand-eels provide a superabundance of food for larger species, and during the winter months, along the south and east coasts, huge shoals of sprat and immature herring drift inshore followed by packs of hungry cod, pollack and spurdog. This is good for the fish, but at times they can become so glutted with food that they completely ignore the bait, or are hauled sluggishly to the surface, their throats jammed with sand-eels or freshly taken sprats.

Seasons for sea fish

Anglers find that fish come and go through the seasons. In West Country and Scottish waters, huge influxes of coalfish and cod appear to mix with the ever-present pollack and ling. This leads to bumper catches. On the South and East Coasts, fish stocks have declined and anglers now rely on migratory species such as bream to provide good fishing. Off the Sussex coast, it is the April influx of good-sized black bream that everyone looks forward to, while a little later in the year, and farther along, off Hampshire and the Isle of Wight, anglers can find bass and tope, and perhaps even heavyweight cod during the winter. The same pattern applies right around the country with various species becoming predominant according to latitude.

Anglers seeking large fish—over 50lb —have more of a problem. There are fewer of them and as a rule their distribution is very localised. The conger is an exception, being widespread in southern waters. Halibut also grow to a large size, but fishing for them demands a trip to the Pentland Firth.

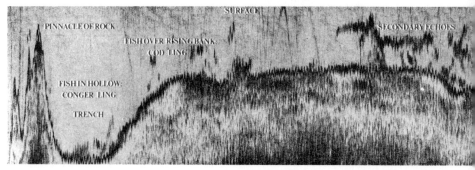

276

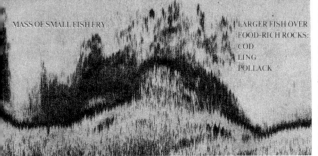

MASS OF SMALL FISH FRY

LARGER FISH OVER
FOOD-RICH ROCKS:
COD
LING
POLLACK

(Above) This angler is
holding his rod carefully
away from the gaffing
operation to avoid tangles.
The monkfish is being properly
gaffed in the jaws to prevent
its edible parts from being
damaged. A fish-box is handy
to receive the fish.
(Left) Echo-sounders tell you
where to fish.

277

Off-shore fishing

As basic equipment, the off-shore angler will need a 6ft boat-rod. Longer rods are used, but as baited hook is dropped straight down over the side and there is virtually no casting to be done, length is not necessary to provide leverage for distance casting. Most boat anglers use the very effective multiplier reel which has a fast rate of line retrieve (useful when winding in from deep water), good braking, and a ratchet which enables the angler to prop his rod securely and adjust the brake to a correct tension so that a bite will be registered by the 'clack' of the ratchet. For off-shore fishing, line breaking strain (b.s.) should be about 20lb, although a stronger line should be used if you are fishing specifically for conger. In shallow water, when fishing for flatties, or out deeper for black bream, a lighter line will be adequate. But the 20lb b.s. line will stand a great deal of punishment if a sizeable conger is hooked.

One of the most effective terminal tackles is the running ledger, with the sliding boom holding a lead of sufficient weight to hold the bottom. This will depend on the strength of the tide. Leads come in all the standard shapes—grip, torpedo, bomb, Capta—and all do their job well when used at the right time and place. The running-ledger rig with boom, swivels, a two-yard leader and end hook, will work well on practically all types of sea-bed, except rocks. Here some form of paternoster is necessary. With this rig, the angler will feel the weight hit bottom but know his hooks are placed above this. If care is taken to keep the sensitivity to a fine degree, with the lead keeping just in touch with the bottom, the hooks will not snag.

Try to keep your terminal rig as simple as possible. Apart from making the task of tackling-up quick and easy, it also helps to avoid a lot of wasted time when you have to unravel a tangle.

Tackling-up

Tackling-up is the first job, while the boat is heading out to the mark. First make sure that any items of gear not needed immediately—extra clothing in case of

(Above) The ledgered bait will sit close enough to lure fish from the wreck.

The off-shore seabed with its varied grounds and their fishing methods.

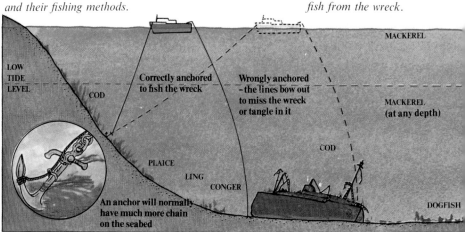

LOW TIDE LEVEL

COD

Correctly anchored to fish the wreck

Wrongly anchored – the lines bow out to miss the wreck or tangle in it

MACKEREL

MACKEREL (at any depth)

PLAICE

LING

CONGER

COD

An anchor will normally have much more chain on the seabed

DOGFISH

a squall, spare rods, food and drink—are all stowed away in the cabin, or somewhere out of sight. When fish are coming aboad there must be no unwanted gear to get in the way, especially if a conger is thrashing about in the boat.

Boat-owners do not look kindly on anglers using seat-boards or the gunnel for cutting up bait strips from mackerel or squid. Always use a baitboard and a sharp knife. Mackerel taken on feathers specifically for bait should be left in a bucket of seawater or in a keepnet over the side in order to be kept fresh. This lively fish is by far the best bait for almost every type of sea fishing, and in the spring and summer a bout of feathering as soon as the boat is at anchor is advised. Sometimes a boat can halt on the

way out and be allowed to drift over a likely area for as long as it takes to get sufficient mackerel for the day's fishing. But don't assume that mackerel will always be around. So a standby bait—herring, squid, lugworm or ragworm - should be acquired before setting out. Most sea angling centres have tackle shops nearby which open early all through the week so that anglers can buy frozen baits and odd items of tackle.

Wait before dropping down

When the boat anchors, wait until the craft is steady before dropping down the lines. It may take a few minutes for the boat to sit right in the tide. Sometimes a small sail may have to be hoisted to hold the craft steady in the tide if the wind is coming from the side. The stern corners are the ideal places from

(Above) Paternoster tackle on the drift over sandbanks presents bait attractively.

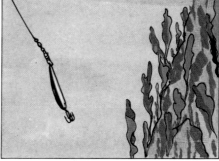

Above) The pirk is a lure that works well while drifting over rocky pinnacles.

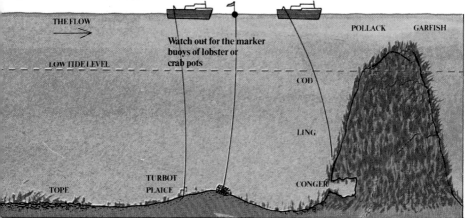

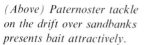

Off-shore fishing

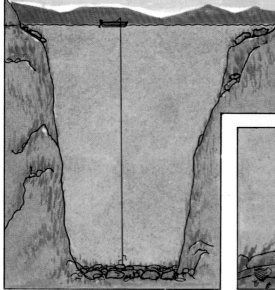

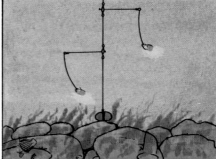

(Above, below) The many sea lochs of the Western Isles are usually so deep that fishing at anchor is impossible. Here, drifting is necessary, with paternoster tackle to avoid snagging bottom.

Rod Sutterby

which to fish. From these places the lead can be of just enough weight to get the bait down, and then allowed to work out with the tide, but always being kept in contact with the seabed. The anglers behind them must have heavier weights to avoid tangling. The successful off-shore angler will adjust his tackle so that he is in constant touch with the bottom. He will not allow his lead to bounce up and down in the sand or mud because this will set up vibrations and echoes in the water that may well keep fish away. The ideal method is to be able to 'feel' the seabed all the time, and be able to differentiate between the small tugs and pulls of the tide and anchor-rope, and similar sensations from fish.

Don't snatch!
Different species of fish have different 'bites'. But as with other forms of fishing, it is not necessarily the biggest fish which give the strongest bites. Some large cod will give tentative pulls at first, but this fish has a very large mouth, so a hurried snatch by the angler may well pull the bait out of its mouth. Wait. Let the take develop, and strike when the cod has taken the bait, turned, and is swimming away. The hook will then be set properly and the fish can be

played to the boat. Keep alert for bites at all times, but do not be misled by the very similar twitches which the tide can exert on the terminal rig. Experience will teach you the subtle differences.

Before setting out, whether in your own boat or not, be sure to have enough food and drink for the trip, a thick pullover and some weatherproof clothing. The day may be fine and the forecast good, but things can change rapidly in the long periods that sea anglers stay out—and especially if the fishing is good.

Remember not to anchor in a busy sealane; watch for the onset of a sea-mist; keep an eye on the sky. Squalls can blow up in minutes and the time taken to up-anchor may be just enough for real trouble to develop as the wind rises and turns a calm sea into a heaving and dangerous place for a small boat.

Be very careful to watch for the approach of bad weather. At sea, even close inshore, conditions can worsen very quickly. Do not hesitate to up-anchor and head back if this happens.

Seaway Code

Once you have fallen to the lure of sea fishing you may want to own a boat. But the sea does not allow many mistakes and before setting out in a boat of your own be careful to make sure you have a lifejacket. The *Seaway Code* is a useful little booklet giving helpful advice on safety for sea anglers, and can be obtained free from the Department of Trade, Room 505, Gaywood House, Great Peter Street, London SW1P 3LW.

Many fine pollack like this can be caught in the pinnacle-strewn waters off the rocky coast of Cornwall. A fish-box holds fresh mackerel caught for bait.

Len Cacutt

Wreck fishing

Mike Millman

Wreck fishing is the most spectacular branch of sea angling and it provides anglers with the opportunity to consistently catch specimen fish. Reasonable catches are occasionally made from wrecks lying close to shore, but their accessibility can lead to overfishing and the numbers of fish living in them is drastically reduced. The best action is now found on sunken hulks lying more than 20 miles out, a distance which can only be reached in good weather conditions by skippers operating large, fully equipped, licensed charter-boats.

Some wrecks lying within ten miles of the shore are pin-pointed by using shore markers, but this is a chancy business. One skipper who made a success of this type of operation was Colin 'Fishy' Williams of Mevagissey, the 'man with the magic eyes', who had the incredible ability to anchor

(Left) Typical catch from a wreck mark. (Below) The Decca Navigator and echo-sounder of a wreck charterboat.

right over hulks when the land was nothing but a mere haze.

The alternative is an electronic Decca Navigator, which receives a continuous stream of signals from shore stations. These are displayed as numbers on green, red and purple dials, which give an accurate cross-bearing of the boat's position in relation to 'lanes' on a special Decca chart listing hundreds of wrecks plotted by hydrographic surveys. Each hulk has a set of coordinates and when these are known it is possible to position the boat right over it.

Secret wreck marks

All charter skippers keep a record of the numbers and jealously guard them. Every year new wrecks are discovered by accident and as each is likely to be sheltering hundreds of fish, it is understandable that skippers prefer to keep such information to themselves. Some skippers go to great lengths to preserve the secrets of such a mark, only visiting the place when no other vessel is in sight. They then keep a vigilant

Mike Millman

(Left) Sunlit seas and a hardened sea fisherman battling it out with a big conger hooked over a south-coast wartime wreck. Maintaining pressure is imperative to retain the eel. (Below) Wartime wrecks produce the biggest hauls of cod, conger and especially ling such as this pair of beauties taken in 180ft of water off Alderney in the Channel Islands.

John Wilson

look-out during the time the boat is anchored over it, and should another charter boat be spotted they leave the area quickly.

Finding the wreck is one thing, anchoring accurately is something else. Many West Country skippers have brought this to a fine science and before letting the anchor go are able to take into account direction of tide, wind strength, and how the hulk is lying on the bottom.

Sometimes the anchor is dropped 600 yards uptide of the mark but, by the time the warp has taken up, the craft is close enough for baits to drop right back into the wreck where the fish are likely to congregate.

Dominant wreck species

While many different species are found on wrecks, the sport is dominated by conger, ling, pollack, coalfish and bream, all of which fall into three distinct categories. Conger and ling are taken on heavy-duty tackle and big baits ledgered on the bottom. The pollack and coalfish fall to medium-weight gear, artificial and natural baits, between the wreckage and the surface, although the bottom 10 fathoms is usually the productive zone. Black and red bream are caught by using more sensitive tackle or baits dropped right into the wreckage.

The techniques for catching each group will be discussed in turn.

Conger and ling reach enormous weights and over the past ten years records have gradually crept upwards. The record conger

John Wilson

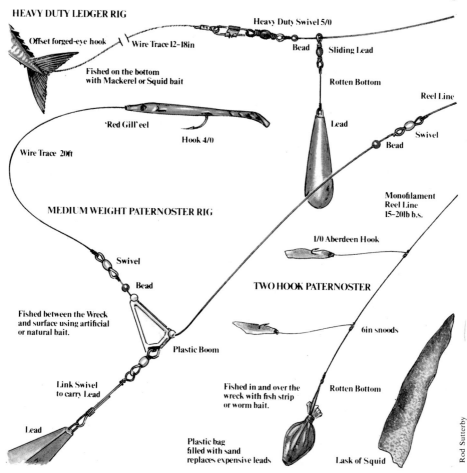

HEAVY DUTY LEDGER RIG

Offset forged-eye hook

Heavy Duty Swivel 5/0

Wire Trace 12-18in

Bead

Sliding Lead

Fished on the bottom
with Mackerel or Squid bait

Rotten Bottom

'Red Gill' eel

Lead

Reel Line

Hook 4/0

Wire Trace 20ft

Swivel

Bead

MEDIUM WEIGHT PATERNOSTER RIG

Monofilament
Reel Line
15-20lb b.s.

1/0 Aberdeen Hook

Swivel

Bead

TWO HOOK PATERNOSTER

Fished between the Wreck
and surface using artificial
or natural bait.

6in snoods

Plastic Boom

Link Swivel
to carry Lead

Fished in and over the
wreck with fish strip
or worm bait.

Rotten Bottom

Lead

Plastic bag
filled with sand
replaces expensive leads

Lask of Squid

Rod Sutterby

is now a giant 109lb 6oz, to the credit of
Bristol angler Robin Potter, who was fishing
22 miles south of Plymouth. Britain's biggest
rod-caught ling fell to Henry Solomons of
Brixham, at a mark four miles south of
Dodman Point, Cornwall, and weighed 57lb
2oz. Stout tackle must be used to deal with
such fish successfully. The right combination
for this heavyweight section of wrecking is a
50lb-test rod with a 6/0 multiplier and
monofilament line. Braided lines are unsuitable for deep-water fishing as their drag
demands the use of heavy leads.

There are many good British-made
hollow-glass rods available, but when it
comes to reels only the American Penn
Senator and British Tatler models stand up

well to the terrific punishment wrecking
imposes on fishing tackle.

Terminal tackle for these rough and tough
fish is a ledger rig of good quality wire 12 to
18in long, ending in a 10/0 hook, preferably
of the offset forged-eye type. A stout 5/0
swivel connects this to the reel line, and also
stops the sliding lead from running down to
the hook. It is good practice to use a rotten-
bottom to hold the lead. This also obviates
the need for a costly running boom.

Old or fresh bait?

Both conger and ling are catholic feeders,
and will accept almost any fish bait, although
the majority are caught on mackerel or
squid. It is a half-truth that conger only take
fresh baits, as many 50-pounders are taken

285

on mackerel three days old. But fresh bait increases one's chance of success.

The take from an outsize conger can be quite gentle in spite of its bulk and strength. It often mouths the bait for some time before actually taking it, and only experience will tell you when to strike. But never be in a hurry, for many conger hooked in the lips break free. When the rod tip tells you of the eel's presence the slack line should be wound in slowly until contact with the fish is made.

Get the conger into clear water

Once the hook has been struck home you must pump the conger into clear water above the wreckage. At this point, never give line, so the risk of being broken up must be taken. Later, line can be given under pressure through the slipping clutch. Conger weighing more than 50lb make continuous power-dives in an attempt to regain the wreck, while fish to 80lb have been known to dive back from the surface through 40 fathoms, despite a tight clutch and thumbs on the spool.

Ideally, conger should be brought to the gaff in an exhausted condition. Failure to observe this important rule puts the catch at risk, and can be very dangerous for the chap wielding the gaff.

Ling feed quite differently and wolf big baits without any regard to caution. As soon as a bite is felt, the hook can be driven home, and the fish dragged away from the bottom. Fish weighing 30lb and more give a good account of themselves, but providing the hook has a firm hold, the issue should never be in doubt. After a few wreck trips the difference between conger and ling bites can be easily detected.

Wrecking for pollack and coalfish is tremendous fun. Both species are grand fighters and the line-stripping plunge of even a 15lb pollack is one of the most thrilling experiences in sea fishing. During the summer, most are caught on medium-weight tackle from anchored boats. The usual rig is a single 4/0 hook to a 20ft trace, worked from an 8in wire boom, or the recently introduced plastic variety. The boom effec-

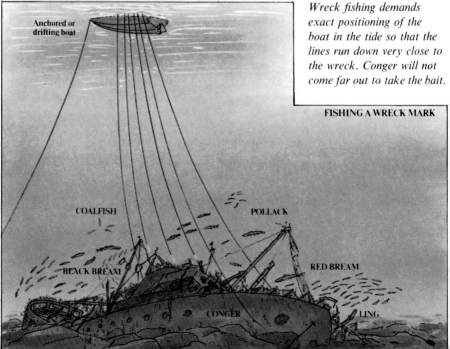

Wreck fishing demands exact positioning of the boat in the tide so that the lines run down very close to the wreck. Conger will not come far out to take the bait.

FISHING A WRECK MARK

Anchored or drifting boat

COALFISH

POLLACK

BLACK BREAM

RED BREAM

CONGER

LING

Rod Sutterby

tively keeps the trace from tangling with the reel line during its long journey to the bottom. It is then steadily retrieved until the bait or artificial eel is taken. At this point the fish will make its characteristic plunge, and line must be given or a break is a certainty.

The coalfish is a better fighter because it is less affected by changes in water pressure. On the average it will make at least half a dozen tremendous runs before reaching the surface, and the fight is never won until the fish is safely in a net. Pollack, on the other hand, are much affected by the 'bends' and when pumped up too quickly arrive lifeless at the surface.

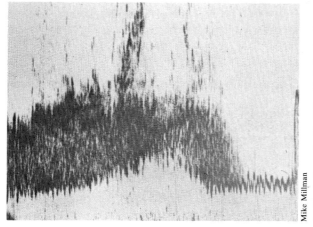

(Above) A stomach pad is essential for helping the angler to fight strong plunges of big ling and conger hooked on wreck marks. The pad provides a pivot for the rod and takes much of the severe strain put on the angler's back and arms.

(Left) The rising streaks above the trace of this deep-water wreck show that there is a massive build-up of fish hovering above it.

Between November and March, females are heavy with roe, and so many fish congregate on deep-water wrecks that echosounders and fish-finders (sophisticated enough to normally pick out a single specimen) record what appears to be a solid mass. Most of the winter wreck fishing is done on the drift, after dan-buoys have been dropped to accurately mark the wreck's position in relation to the tidal run.

Spring tide = frenzied feeding

For several reasons, the best catches are made during spring tide periods, when the fast run of water stirs the fish into frenzied feeding activity. In this mood they strike fiercely at natural baits and various kinds of lures without hesitation. Big tides also ensure fast drifts across the wreckage, which makes it possible to get in as many as 30 productive drifts during a single tide.

Drift fishing is most successful when not more than six anglers work at a time. A charter-boat moves sideways down the length or across the hulk, and the lines stream out naturally from one side only. Working from the wrong side, the lines go under the keel. Apart from the obvious danger of cutting off, it is extremely difficult to have direct contact, and bring up the fish. Lines also tangle with those streaming away correctly, and much valuable fishing time is lost. It is a fact that too many leads plummeting down at the same time frighten fish, and the catch is often smaller when a 10-

Wreck fishing

strong wreck party are active all at once.

Most winter fishing is done with heavy-weight nylon paternosters rigged with artificial eels on short snoods. For a two-hook rig the nylon must not be less than 60lb b.s., and if three artificials are being used, which is typical rod-and-line 'commercial' practice, the strength is stepped up to 80lb. Even this can be snapped like cotton as two fish tend to run in opposite directions after taking the lures simultaneously.

Crude but effective

While the method of fishing is perhaps a trifle crude, it takes considerable skill to get the best out of it. The lures, weighted with at least a pound of lead, are allowed to plummet at high speed to the bottom. Quite often they are grabbed by fish swimming as much as 8 fathoms above the wreckage. When this happens, the multiplier is thrown into gear, and the full weight of possibly three specimen-sized fish comes on to the rod. The sudden, violent jerk is usually

enough to drive the hooks home, but it is as well to strike a few times yourself to make absolutely sure. At this stage, the slipping clutch is set to give line under pressure as the fish will immediately plunge downwards.

Successful winter wrecking on the drift depends greatly on the skill of the skipper. He must set each drift up to take advantage of the wreck's position and know exactly where the high parts are. As he watches the sounder, a constant stream of instructions is shouted back from the wheel-house, and the anglers must be ready to respond instantly to such orders as 'Up 50ft!' or 'O.K. We're over, drop back 50!'

Failure to heed the warnings will almost certainly result in the loss of quite valuable tackle. Repeat that a few times during the day, and winter wrecking becomes a very expensive business. Large pirks, or jiggers as they are also termed, fitted with large forged-eye treble hooks are used effectively for wreck fishing throughout the year, but a

Mike Millman

288

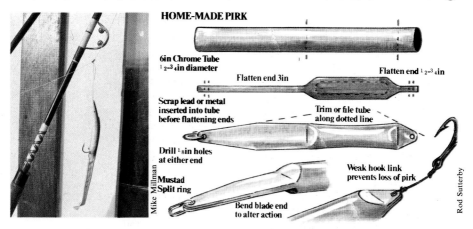

HOME-MADE PIRK

6in Chrome Tube
1 2–3 4in diameter

Flatten end 3in

Flatten end 1 2–3 4in

Scrap lead or metal
inserted into tube
before flattening ends

Trim or file tube
along dotted line

Drill 1 8in holes
at either end

Mustad
Split ring

Weak hook link
prevents loss of pirk

Mike Millman

Bend blade end
to alter action

Rod Sutterby

(Above) An artificial eel on a short snood for winter wreck fishing for pollack. (Above right) Two rigs for wreck-fishing. (Below left) The 'Conqueror' will become a great conger 'hotspot' for future anglers.

great deal of stamina is required to work a 26oz lure correctly for long periods. Charter-boat skippers, seldom short on physique, have developed this type of fishing to a fine art. Their method is to stand high on the bows, well out of the anglers' way, and cast the lure as far as possible, letting it run unchecked to the bottom. If it fails to attract a fish on its way down it is retrieved at an ultra-fast pace with a high-geared multiplier until it finds a taker. The largest pollack are taken on pirks, the author's best specimen weighing 23lb 12oz, which is not far short of the national record. Unfortunately such a fish hooked on a weighty pirk is quite incapable of achieving its fighting potential.

Tough on man and tackle

To cope with winter wreck fishing, tackle must be heavy, and it is customary for 50lb class hollow-glass rods and 6/0 to 9/0 multipliers to be used. Its tough on equipment, too, as many would-be record breakers have found to their cost, when a rod has cracked under the strain, or a multiplier has jammed. Anglers also suffer: after the first dozen drifts and perhaps 20 big fish, stomach, arm and back muscles start protesting. More than a few men have been

exhausted to the point of giving up fishing, although down below fish were almost queueing up to get on a hook.

Normally, summer's black bream tend to stay around wrecks until well into December. The red bream record stands at an incredible 9lb 8oz, a fish hooked by Brian Reynolds of Plymouth, off the Dodman Point, Cornwall in 1974. By comparison the heaviest black bream is some way behind at 6lb 14oz, and was caught by John Garlick of Torquay in Lyme Bay off the Dorset coast, in September 1977. Both species are voracious feeders and many outsize fish have been hooked on large conger baits.

To get the best of bream fishing a most useful rig even for deep-water sport is a two-handed spinning rod matched with a light multiplier, for example the ABU 6000C or the slightly heavier Penn Long Beach 65, or Garcia Mitchell 624 models. End tackle can be a two-hook paternoster with 6in snoods made up from 15 to 20lb b.s. monofilament and 1/0 Aberdeen hooks.

For bait, squid is the best; it cuts well into thin strips and is very durable on the hook. Quite often several bream can be caught on the same bait, but as soon as the edges show signs of wear it should be changed. Other good baits for bream are mackerel strip and worms. All bites must be struck very quickly as sea bream have an uncanny knack of being able to strip hooks clean and can quickly eject those they consider suspicious.

Beachcasting

John Wilson

Obtaining maximum distance when beachcasting is all about transferring the compression built up in the rod tip by the caster's technique to the lead weight. Sloppy rods absorb much of this power, whereas rigid, fast-tip rods create the velocity for maximum casting distance.

As air resistance and other drag factors increase with speed it makes sense to use relatively heavy sinkers of between 5 and 6oz for long-range casting. To maximize on distance a monofilament reel line of between 15-18lb test is ideal, to which is knotted an 8 or 9 yard shock leader of 50-60lb test mono. This alleviates sudden snap-offs which would occur for instance if just a 4oz lead was tied direct to 15lb line and wound up on a fast-taper beachcaster for long-range casting. An unattached lead zooming down the surf line towards other anglers is a horrifying accident just waiting

to happen. So don't tempt fate by using a shock leader below 50lb test and ensure all knots are firmly tied to good-quality lead links and swivels.

Just one hook is best and casts a great deal further than a two- or three-boom paternoster, particularly if it is held tight to the trace with a hook clip to minimize air resistance. Some simple and easy-to-make rigs are described in the chapter on sea booms.

The reel line can be much thinner in diameter than the shock leader because it does not suffer during the compression build-up of a cast and in effect undergoes little strain in fishing, unless the rig becomes caught on the bottom and you need to pull for a break. Another factor worth considering is that if a heavier or larger diameter reel line is used,creating greater water resistance, a heavier lead is required

Bill Howes

(Left) Champion tournament caster, Paul Kerry of Norwich, demonstrates his skill with the pendulum cast from the south beach at Great Yarmouth, a prolific local cod hot spot during the winter months.

to hold bottom. This could mean reduced casting potential beyond weights of 6oz.

For distance casting, say 150 yards plus, there is actually little to choose between fixed-spool and multiplier reels, except that upon retrieval the latter is smoother and can easily be wound against weed due to the line going directly around the spool and not at right angles via the bale-arm, which creates friction despite a roller in the bale-arm unit. Because it takes practice to achieve long distances using multiplier reels, the beginner is probably wise to start off with a fixed-spool reel. Then, once the casting technique itself is mastered, a multiplier reel can be tried.

Apart from routine maintenance the only thing to remember about fixed-spool reels is to fill to the brim with line or potential casting distance is greatly reduced. Friction from the spool's lip quickly cuts down casting range, once line level falls below ¼in from the lip of a fully loaded spool. Correct loading therefore could add up to 50 yards to the cast.

If considering a multiplier reel choose the best you can afford. Those fitted with a level-wind mechanism will ensure the line is wound evenly back and forwards across the spool rather like a cotton reel and this helps provide long, trouble-free casts. To help alleviate over-runs the spool should be controlled by gentle thumb pressure when the lead reaches the top of its trajectory and commences its downwards passage towards the sea.

By far the most effective cast to use from the beach is the well-known pendulum cast. Designed for maximizing on distances for casters on the tournament field, this rather athletic cast which demands perfect timing, has allowed beach fishermen to consistently achieve long casts using standard tackle and a baited hook.

The cast is made with the feet apart standing left-side on to the sea with the left foot (assuming the caster is right-handed) at around three o'clock and the right, upon which the angler's weight is concentrated, at around five o' clock. With the lead hanging on a 6-8ft drop it is swung up the beach away from the angler at around head height (to build up momentum) and allowed to swing back pendulum-style (hence the name of this cast) actually passing behind the angler to his right. To emphasize this

Beachcasting

THE SOUTH AFRICAN CAST

THE LAYBACK CAST

(Right) Leslie Moncrieff's original 'Layback' casting style used a stationary sinker and a very long rod handle. Now, tackle has shorter handles that allow greater power transfer. The stationary lead is given its swing (1,2 and 3) and under the stress of the power stroke (4) the rod is thrust forward to position (5). So in both basic beachcasting styles the over-the-shoulder power stroke is all-important.

movement the angler simultaneously pushes down on the butt with his left hand and with his right moves the rod slightly over to the right.

When the lead reaches the top of its swing behind the angler's right ear the rod tip is swept down and around into a horizontal half-circle, winding the tip up to increase lead speed at its final release point, which occurs once the angler pivots round and faces the sea. Weight is now transferred from the right over to the left foot as the rod is swept forwards on the final stroke, sending the lead skywards on its trajectory towards the horizon. This necessitates

pulling down with the left hand whilst pushing firmly forwards with the right. Ideally it should be one fast, fluent, powerful yet rhythmic motion. Any sudden lurch or jerk within the cast is liable to cause either premature or late release of the lead and most certainly an instant break-off or over-run if using a multiplier reel. Fixed-spool reels are of course much more forgiving.

The best type of rod for pendulum casting is one made from an 11½-12½ft fast-tip rigid, carbon-fibre blank. Any cushioning which occurs during the rod's wind up will lessen the velocity at which the lead is propelled

(Left) In the South African cast the sinker lies behind the angler. (1) The shoulder swing begins at (2), with the weight transferred to the left foot. Note that the sinker is still to the rear (3). At (4) the power stroke begins, arms pushing and pulling, putting strong compression on the rod (5). At (6) the line is released and the sinker can speed away, the angler aiming the rod-tip at the lead to keep friction to a minimum.

Rod Sutterby

rather like trying to fire an arrow from a bow made from a spongy garden cane.

One of the most important factors is actual handle length, or more precisely the distance between butt grip and the reel fitting. If it is too short full leverage can never be applied during the power stroke of the cast. If it is too long the rod tip cannot follow through on the last part of the cast and premature release is inevitable if using a multiplier reel.

Where the beach shelves up quickly behind the angler and pendulum casting cannot be practised, the relatively simple South African cast is useful to know. The lead and terminal rig is simply laid out on the beach behind the angler and then suddenly swept over the shoulder with a twist of the upper body and shoulders together with a push/pull of the arms as the diagram illustrates.

If using a reasonably soft, old-fashioned beachcaster with a long handle the 'lay back' cast will easily put your bait out over the 100 yard mark. Follow the directions in the illustration from the lead in a stationary position and lean to transfer all your weight from the right to the left foot (assuming you are right-handed) on the power stroke and follow through immediately.

293

Sharking

Most anglers assume that since sharks grow to a size much bigger than fish they normally catch their equipment must be scaled up and that it should be heavy and strong. Many anglers buy rods and reels with which they could fight and land fish many, many times greater than any that have been landed in this country. Many charter boat skippers also provide over-heavy tackle for those anglers without, who hire them for sharking.

Heavy tackle is not needed

Heavy boat rods, extremely large reels loaded with 130lb b.s. line are well beyond the requirements of any of our sharks since none make the fantastic 400-to-600-yard-runs of marlins and tuna for which such equipment was developed. Only very long runs require such heavy lines for the pressure of the water on the line during a long curving run (or its resistance as such a length is being moved through the water) would break a lighter line. Since the average angler can only produce a pull of 25lb with, say, a 7A, no angler would ever need a line much heavier than 30lb b.s. Moreover, the weight in water of any of our sharks cannot break the line, for the weight of the fish in water is only a fraction of its weight in air.

A fighting porbeagle comes to the gaff after being hooked from a shark-boat off the coast of North Cornwall.

Considering the fighting qualities of the various species liable to be taken, and the weight to which they go, the following types of tackle are recommended so that each would allow the fish to give the best sport:— blue shark—30lb-class tackle; porbeagle 50lb-class tackle; mako and thresher, as well as large porbeagle 80lb-class rod and reel. Each one of these tackle classes can be reduced to a lower one with increasing experience in catching shark. The terminal tackle, because of the size of baits used and the size of the mouth of sharks, should consist of large 6/0 to 10/0 good-quality hooks, attached to a biting length of 2 to 2.5mm diameter braided wire, because a shark's teeth are liable to cut through anything else.

The shark's abrasive skin

The biting length, 2 to 3ft long, should be attached to a further 10ft of slightly thinner, similar wire or long-liner's mono-filament nylon to withstand the abrasive action of shark skin.

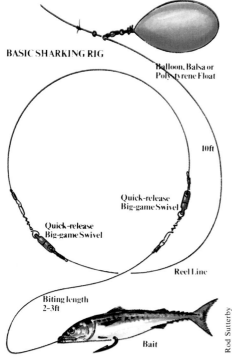

BASIC SHARKING RIG

Balloon, Balsa or Polystyrene Float

10ft

Quick-release Big-game Swivel

Quick-release Big-game Swivel

Reel Line

Biting length 2-3ft

Bait

Rod Sutterby

(Above) Standard sharking rig. (Below) Sharking tackle: 10/0 hooks, wire traces, balloon floats, 80lb reel, harness, butt pads.

Bait in shark fishing consists of whole fish used either singly if the fish is large, or in number if they are small. The favourite bait is mackerel which as a shoal fish probably represents the commonest natural food of sharks. However, any other species may be used and many sharks have been taken on pouting or pollack. Various methods of mounting the bait are used with the head or tail pointing up the trace. Each method should ensure that the bait does not come off when first taken, for sharks rarely swallow the bait at once. Natural presentation is not essential, for the movement of the bait should give off the erratic vibrations of an injured or sick fish.

Bait—the off-the-bottom rule

Since sharks are usually mid-water or surface-fish, the bait should be fished off the bottom. This is achieved by attaching a float, either a balloon or square of polystyrene, to the line once the depth set for the bait has been reached. The float should always be as small as possible so as not to produce resistance once the bait is taken. This off-the-bottom rule on bait presentation is not absolute, for many sharks are taken with the bait on the bottom fished as a flowing trace.

John Wilson

TROLLING RIG

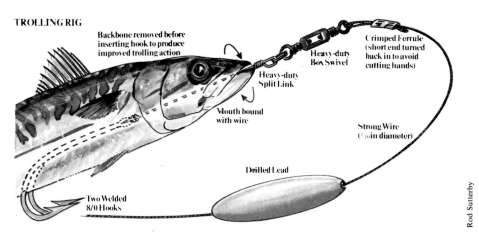

Backbone removed before inserting hook to produce improved trolling action

Crimped Ferrule (short end turned back in to avoid cutting hands)

Heavy-duty Box Swivel

Heavy-duty Split Link

Mouth bound with wire

Strong Wire (¹⁄₁₆in diameter)

Drilled Lead

Two Welded 8/0 Hooks

Rod Sutterby

The method of fishing depends very much on the area, the wind and tides, and both drifting and fishing at anchor are successful. In each case, the use of rubby-dubby is almost essential, especially if blue shark are sought. A good brew of rubby-dubby helps to bring the fish to the boat. Any shark swimming through its trail of fine particles will follow them to source and find the bait. The presence of the fine, oily particles of food prompts the shark into feeding.

Trolling for porbeagle

Recently, trolling a mounted whole fish bait for porbeagle has been successfully tried off Ireland. This is a standard method for mako in many parts of the world and would probably bring good results in British waters. But its one drawback is that only some four baits can be fished by this method. Its obvious advantage is that a much greater area can be covered. Line must be paid out as soon as the bait is taken so that the fish has a chance of swallowing the bait before the hook is set. No rules can be made about striking. While some sharks will take the bait with a rush, others will play with it before taking it properly, or perhaps leave it alone. In every case, should a strike be missed it is advisable to retrieve the bait slowly with frequent stops. This may induce the shark to have a second go, providing always that the hook is not bare.

Similarly no rules are possible about the

Mike Millman

type of fight to be expected. In many cases it will not start until the fish has been brought to the side of the boat for the first time. After this anything may happen, long runs away and towards the boat, periods of inactivity or deep soundings. Two species, the mako and the thresher, will make long runs and will often clear the water completely in repeated, spectacular leaps. But the fish will tire slowly and come to the side of the boat. At this stage it may suddenly sound, or stop fighting altogether. On being brought to the surface such fish have often been found to be dead. Once a fish is really tired, then, and only then, should be the time to bring it inboard

(Above left) Before mounting on the double-hook, the fish's backbone should be removed. The bait will then have a good, realistic action while being trolled.
(Left) Beneath the burgee of the Shark Angling Club of Gt Britain, five small flags indicate the number of shark that had been caught in the day's outing.
(Right) Two gaffs are needed to lift this defeated porbeagle into the shark-boat.
(Below) Trolling for porbeagle, using a group of teasers—mackerel with their backbones removed. This method was first tried, with success, by Kevin Linnane and Mike Prichard.

Bill Howes

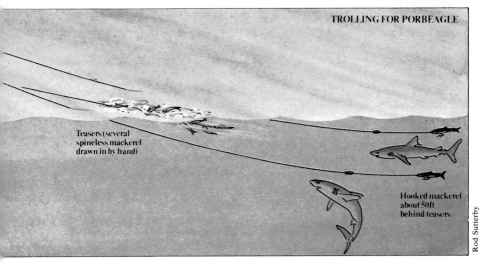

TROLLING FOR PORBEAGLE

Teasers (several spineless mackerel drawn in by hand)

Hooked mackerel about 50ft behind teasers

Rod Sutterby

FLYING GAFF

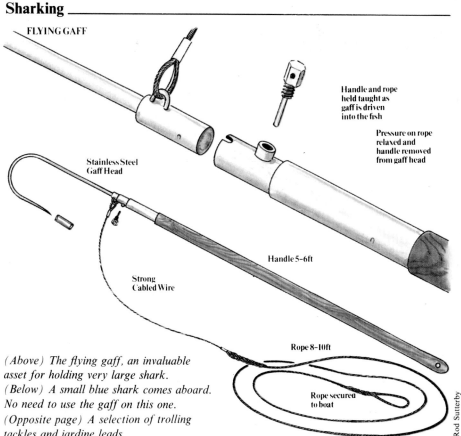

Handle and rope held taught as gaff is driven into the fish

Pressure on rope relaxed and handle removed from gaff head

Stainless Steel Gaff Head

Handle 5-6ft

Strong Cabled Wire

Rope 8-10ft

Rope secured to boat

Rod Sutterby

(Above) The flying gaff, an invaluable asset for holding very large shark.
(Below) A small blue shark comes aboard. No need to use the gaff on this one.
(Opposite page) A selection of trolling tackles and jardine leads.

Mike Millman

for a lively shark can do great damage to an angler or a boat. Always fight a shark in the water—not in the boat. Small sharks can easily be lifted into the boat by hand if the freeboard of the boat is not too high.

The flying gaff

The use of flying gaffs, those which have detachable handles where the head itself is attached to or carries a rope, is essential, since most gaffed shark thrash about wildly. They are then easier held at the end of a rope and there is less chance of injury from the handle which may break or be moved around erratically by the thrashing fish. A noose passed over the tail of the fish lying at the side of the boat can also be used to tether the fish. This is probably the best method as it always allows the fish to be returned to the water uninjured, necessary if anglers are to continue to enjoy their sport.

Sea trolling

Trolling or towing a bait, natural or artificial, behind a moving boat to catch fast-moving predatory fish, has been practised for centuries. There exist in museums in North America polished stone rigs used by Eskimos as long ago as the 15th century.

Up to the late 1950s trolling was one of the principal fishing methods used by sporting anglers in British waters. Then, when charter boats fitted with sophisticated electronic equipment came onto the scene, sea angling underwent massive changes. The opportunity to make large catches quite easily from an anchored boat on wreck marks proved too great an attraction for many anglers, and trolling, or whiffing as it is sometimes termed, was almost forgotten. To be fair to trolling, the method was only suitable for the angler with his own boat, or with access to a small craft, so perhaps it was

natural that the new sport of wreck fishing became so popular.

At present, however, there is a definite swing back to the use of small boats, for anglers tire of four-hour runs out to a mark and do not welcome the high cost of a day's fishing. Besides, certain species—bass, for example—could never be caught from a charter boat with ten anglers aboard, and so devotees have continued to fish as their forefathers did, although technical advances are making a great difference to the catches.

Varied baits

Baits for trolling are very varied. Small whole mackerel and sandeel are widely used, as are mackerel and squid strip. Marine worms are used to a lesser extent. Bright metal lures fitted with treble hooks are popular, but their effectiveness is largely restricted to shallow water fishing for

Mike Millman

299

(Right) Two very good trolling baits. The squid is mounted on a double hook, with strong threads providing struts to ensure that the wings adopt a natural attitude. The 'cocktail' rig consists of a red plastic squid and a dead herring mounted close behind it.

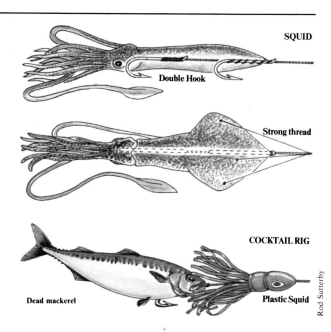

SQUID

Double Hook

Strong thread

COCKTAIL RIG

Dead mackerel

Plastic Squid

Rod Sutterby

mackerel, pollack and school bass. In deeper water the artificial eel is now generally used with great success. Lures of this type have come a long way since the introduction of the first models, which featured a plastic body and a tail made from the rubber ring of a jam jar. Thirty years of steady development have brought considerable manufacturing expertise, yet improvements continue to be made.

Red Gill

Red Gill, the brainchild of Alex Ingram of Mevagissey, is now a fourth generation lure. His latest innovation is a specially shaped hook, fitted to the large Thresher model, which prevents the body of the lure being detected and pushed up the line, when a fish strikes at it. Of the five models offered the 172mm size is by far the most successful.

In the last couples of years, however, the Eddystone Eel, produced by David Beer of Plymouth, has proved a serious rival. It has a much softer tail made from ultra-thin plastic, which gives a faster action, making it particularly suitable for trolling at slow speeds without losing its attractive motion. The Eddystone Eel is available in a number of sizes, but the medium model of 190mm gives the best results.

A new lure, the Eddystone Troller, which has an all-through action will possibly be the best yet. This lure was the result of an enormous amount of research, done with the cooperation of the expert bass anglers who fish Eddystone, Britain's top bass mark. The spectacular catches are made over the gullies close to the lighthouse itself, where giant bass, some weighing as much as 20lb, are common. But catching them has proved impossible so far.

Artificial eel

The best rod and line capture made on an artificial eel is the British record bass of 18lb 14½oz taken by Roy Slater in 1975. The biggest fish are extremely wily, and refuse to be tempted by anglers' lures, but hundreds of fish weighing between 7 and 14lb are taken each year. To contact them requires a thorough knowledge of the reef, for the only way they can be caught is by trolling the lure at least 100 yards behind the boat, taking it right through the jagged gullies. The rocks on either side rise to within a foot of the surface, and even a slight knock against the gneiss rock will hole the stoutest craft.

The bass anglers at the Eddystone, rightly known as the most dangerous reef in the

Curved Jardine Lead

No. 3 Swivel Link

TROLLING RIG

Red Gill Lure and Hook

Four Turn Blood Knot

Red Gill Hook

Rod Sutterby

(Left) Swivels are an essential part of trolling rigs. Without them lines will become hopelessly twisted.
(Overleaf) Trolling off the unmistakable Eddystone rocks.

average weight. The best patterns for trolling are those whose centre of gravity is below the level of the line, which prevents twisting or kinking. A curved jardine lead is mounted by running the line around a continuous groove and spiral wires at the ends of the lead. This kind can be changed without cutting the line and is very popular for that reason.

Trolling for pollack

Trolling for large pollack on offshore reef marks requires a similar approach. During the day, the fish swim near the bottom, so trolling is best at first light and in the late evening when they rise to within a few feet of the surface. As with the bass, it is vital to work the bait a long way behind the boat, where it is well out of the way of engine noise and propeller turbulence.

Working a lure for these 'race' pollack is an exciting sport, and records prove that trolling is one of the deadliest methods for making big catches. An indisputably classic haul was made many years ago, when Captain and Mrs H Millais trolled rubber eels 6ft below the surface at $3\frac{1}{2}$ knots, off Sennen Cove in the far west of Cornwall.

Their first session, in the early evening, produced 24 pollack and coalfish, weighing 269lb, which included a pollack of 21lb and a 20lb coalfish, at the time the biggest ever caught on rod and line. The following evening saw a repeat performance, when 34 fish totalling 416lb came to the net. The best specimen was a coalfish of 23lb 8oz, which was to hold the British record for a great many years. While these were exceptional catches, there are many instances of hundreds of pounds of fish being taken, at times in a matter of hours.

Shallow water

Fishing shallow water close to a rocky shoreline can be very rewarding, especially during the later months of the year, when

English Channel, fish alone, and this presents problems. To leave the tiller or wheel for just a moment in the turbulent waters when the boat is under way, even at three knots, is asking for trouble. To avoid it, rods up to 15ft long and fixed to special holders mounted in the stern are used. When a bass hits the lure, the length of the rod first cushions the powerful strike and then its spring back, combined with the boat's forward speed, drives the hook home. At this point the boat's engine is knocked out of gear, leaving the angler free to net the fish.

The experts have tended, in the past, to use lures of their own design, jealously guarding their secrets. Tempers have risen sharply when lines have crossed and one angler has wound in and seen the other's lure. Home-made varieties are now less common but a few anglers still modify commercial lures in various ways in the hope of gaining the edge over rivals.

Usually two rods are used at once, and these are matched with multiplier reels filled with 35lb b.s.monofilament line and 25ft traces of 25lb b.s. The size of lead depends on the strength of tide, speed of the boat, and depth the lure is to be fished, but 1lb is the

Spectrum Colour Library

bass and pollack hunt inshore. The best places to search for them are in the tide rips off headlands. Fine examples that spring readily to mind lie close to Berry Head, in Devon, and Rame Head, Dodman Point, and the Lizard in Cornwall, at all of which big catches are regularly made.

It is best to troll in the early morning, and locals who specialize in this type of fishing are generally afloat by 6.30am and reckon to have half a dozen good bass in the bag by breakfast. The same trolling tactics are used for fishing close in, but it seems that natural baits, particularly sandeels, catch better in shallow water. Used in a live state, and trolled at very low speeds, success is assured.

Hooks
Eels should be mounted on long shanked fine wire hooks such as the Aberdeen, by passing the hook point through the fish's bottom lip and then nicking it into the soft skin on the underside just behind the head. Presented in this way on a long trace, the eel can swim naturally and will live for some time, thus avoiding the need to change the bait.

Although discussing trolling, it is worth mentioning that live sandeel mounted in the manner described, but offered on a split-shotted 20ft long drift line, as the boat moves along with the tidal run, is a superb method of attracting bass and pollack.

Lifelike movement
Returning to trolling with dead sandeel, it is essential for the eel to be very soft and flexible, so that its movement in the tide will be lifelike. This is best achieved by gently bending the fish backwards and forwards until the backbone is broken in a dozen places. Some anglers prefer to use a thin strip from the length of the sandeel, which is hooked through once at the thickest end of the piece. It is essential to cut the strip evenly, using a thin-bladed, razor-sharp knife. Any suggestion of a jagged edge will spoil the movement and this will be instantly spotted.

Sea birds are a good indication of fish feeding near the surface, constantly wheeling and diving over the water. Find them, and you stand a good chance of coming home with a fine catch.

Mike Shepley

Feathering

MACKEREL FEATHERS

Hooks dressed with feathers are often used to catch mackerel, pollack, cod and whiting. Less commonly, bass and garfish are taken by 'feathering'. The tackle is set among a shoal and jerked up and down to simulate the erratic movement of small fish. The use of several feathered hooks helps create the impression of plentiful food. Once a shoal has been located a greedy mackerel, whiting or codling can often be taken on each hook.

Boat or pier

This technique has been employed for generations in Scottish and North Eastern coastal waters, but has now spread to the South. Feathering is most frequently practised from a boat, using either a rod or a handline, wherever shoaling occurs. Pier anglers, again using either tackle, can also take advantage of incoming shoals.

The rig for feathering consists of up to six feathered hooks on traces or 'snoods' of about 5in, which are attached to the reel line. A line of 15-20lb b.s. should be used, for with a fish on every hook it will have to take a considerable load when being reeled in to a boat or a pier. The snoods should also be strong enough to avoid losing any fish when hauling in the catch and should be set 9-10in apart so that they do not tangle. A fairly heavy lead should be used at the end of the reel line, for a smaller weight may take a long while to sink, by which time the shoal may have moved on, the feathers not having had a

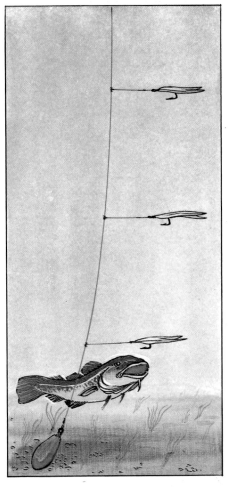

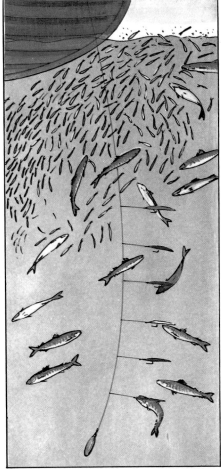

Rod Sutterby

Bill Howes

(Left and above) Mackerel can be taken in large numbers on six-hook feathered traces. The feathers, coloured, resemble small fish.
(Right and above) Cod feathers come from white chickens. While they can be 'worked' in the way mackerel feathers are pumped up and down, cod can be caught by allowing the feathers to stream out. Some commercial fishermen have feather winches.

Bill Howes

(Left) When you find them, mackerel come inboard in large numbers. Those that are not needed for bait can be gutted and taken home. Do not, however, assume you will catch enough for the day's fishing, so take a standby bait along, such as frozen fish, squid or lugworm. (Right) Both mackerel and cod feathers can be bought quite reasonably from your local tackle shop. But feathered traces can be made simply. The whip-knot is an easy one to tie by following our numbers from 1 to 5. When the line is pulled through the last winding, make sure that all the turns are close and neat before pulling both ends tight and cutting off.

BAITED FEATHER RIG

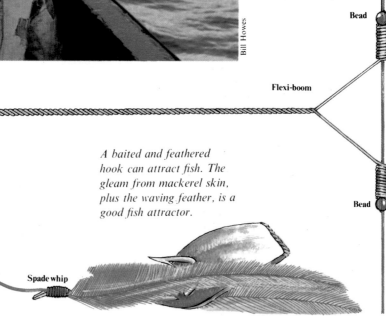

Bead

Flexi-boom

Bead

A baited and feathered hook can attract fish. The gleam from mackerel skin, plus the waving feather, is a good fish attractor.

Spade whip

Feathering

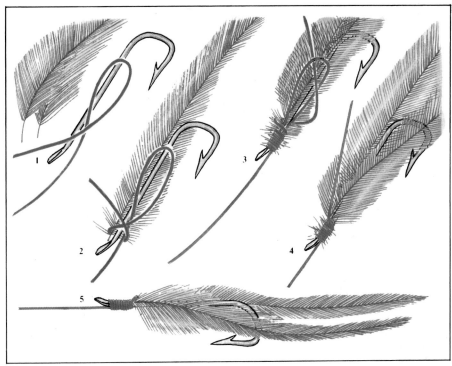

Rod Sutterby

chance to attract them. For mackerel a size 1 or 1/0 hook is suitable; for cod a larger hook, a 3 for example, is recommended.

When fishing for mackerel as bait (which is hard to beat for its appeal to many species) a six-hook rig will provide a plentiful supply. A group of boat anglers must remember though to be careful when swinging these multi-hook rigs in board, especially in a wind, for painful accidents and lost fishing time can result from lack of forethought.

Three feathers only
The taking of large catches of mackerel in this way—and they are extremely easy to catch—is regarded by some as unsporting, and is very wasteful if, as is often the case, many fish are killed when not needed for bait or food. This is all the more serious when the mackerel, like other species, is being depleted too rapidly by the growth of commercial fishing.

In any case, when the acquisition of bait is not the objective, the sport achieved with a single feather, especially one made to one's own design, is much more enjoyable. Combine this rig with a lighter rod and line for best effect. Single feathers provide a good opportunity for experimentation and, with practice, for fishing selectively. Bass, for example, have been caught on a lure made from a salmon fly to which two white feathers are added.

When fishing for larger species such as cod and pollack, it is impractical to use more than three hooks as the weight of these fish makes them considerably more difficult to boat than mackerel or whiting.

Traces of feathers can be bought ready-made from tackle dealers, but it is cheaper to make them yourself, using chicken feathers. These, taken from the neck, where the length and quality are best, are used in their natural white or can be dyed, usually in bright shades of blue, green, orange or red. They are whipped firmly onto sea hooks of a size appropriate to the fish sought, and are then ready to be attached to a snood made from the reel line.

307

Weather

Weather plays a vital role in every aspect of sea angling, and to treat it with less than total respect is asking for trouble. Most commercial fishermen, like men who work the land, can predict with uncanny accuracy what the weather pattern is likely to be half a day ahead, simply by looking at the sky. Unfortunately, it takes years of experience, and ordinary folk must rely on more down to earth methods of forecasting, and what is known as the Beaufort Scale or Wind Force.

This was devised in the early 19th century by Sir Francis Beaufort, a British naval officer and hydrographer, and classifies wind speeds ranging between Force 0—Calm, and Force 12—Hurricane. This is now the standard scale used in meteorology, and gives a good guide as to what conditions may be expected in the open sea. A knot is the measure of the speed of ships and is equal to one nautical mile, or 6,080ft, per hour.

It should be realized that the Beaufort wind scale chart can only be a guide as to what might be expected in the open sea. Should the direction of wind be against the run of tide, even a moderate Force 4 can put up a much fiercer sea locally. Facts such as this must always be taken into consideration

Weather condition	Wind speed	Wave height
Force 0 Calm. Sea like a mirror.	Less than 1 knot	
Force 1 Light air. Sea has a series of ripples.	1–3 knots	Not more than 3in.
Force 2 Light breeze. Small short waves appear. Crests have a glassy look and do not break. Usually good fishing weather.	4–6 knots	About 6in
Force 3 Gentle breeze. Large wavelets seen. Crests begin to break. Foam of glassy appearance with a few 'white horses'.	7–10 knots	About 2ft
Force 4 Moderate breeze. Small waves becoming longer. 'White horses' constant.	11–16 knots	3½ft
Force 5 Fresh breeze. Moderate waves very much longer in form. 'White horses' everywhere. Spray starting.	17–21 knots	6ft
Force 6 Strong breeze. Large waves with extensive white crests form. Abundant spray.	22–27 knots	9½ft
Force 7 Near gale. Sea heaps up and white foam from breaking waves blown in streaks along the direction of the wind.	28–33 knots	13½ft

Force 0: A flat-calm Skye seascape, but sadly rare in those rugged waters.

Force 1: Gentle ripples, light air—but note the Warm Front cloud pattern.

Force 8 Gale. High waves of greater length. Edges of crests begin to break in spindrifts. Foam blown in well-marked streaks along direction of the wind.	34–40 knots	18ft
Force 9 Strong gale. High waves, dense streaks of foam blown along. Crests of waves begin to topple, tumble, roll over. Heavy spume affects visibility.	41–47 knots	23ft
Force 10 Storm. Very high waves with overhanging crests. Resulting foam, forming great patches, blown into dense white streaks. Surface takes on a white appearance. Violence of the sea becomes heavy and shocklike. Visibility much affected.	48–55 knots	29ft
Force 11 Violent storm. Exceptionally high waves. Small and medium sized vessels might be lost for a time behind the troughs. Sea completely covered with white foam. Everywhere the edges of the wave crests are blown into froth. Visibility badly affected.	56–63 knots	37ft
Force 12 Hurricane. Sea a maelstrom of spray and foam. Becomes completely white, affecting visibility very badly.	64 knots or more	In excess of 37ft

Force 2: A pleasant breeze on a hot summer's day. No weather trouble.

Force 4: White horses everywhere here, looking out from Weymouth Harbour.

when embarking on a deep water outing, or indeed on any kind of boat fishing trip.

Influence of the land

The contour of the land can also have a big bearing on the condition of the sea, even miles offshore. For example, a near westerly gale in the western English Channel will keep water angling boats operating out of Fowey, Looe, Plymouth, Brixham and Torquay tied up to the quay, but their counterparts at Falmouth and Mevagissey will be afloat over wreck marks lying in the vast area of Falmouth Bay. The reason is the influence of the Lizard Peninsula, which stretches out for miles, almost due south, from the Cornish coast. This gives so much shelter that it is possible to fish in comparative comfort 10 miles off the land, while just a mile to the east the sea will be a maelstrom of white water.

Estimating wind force

In estimating wind force from the appearance of the sea, factors such as depth of water, swell and the effect of heavy rain, which tends to flatten the sea, must be noted. The latter can easily give a false impression of the sea's true state. It is also impossible to estimate the wind at night by sea criteria. Near land or in enclosed waters with an offshore wind blowing, wave height will be much smaller and the waves steeper.

If you make a booking for a deep water trip on a licensed craft operated by a professional skipper, the worry of whether conditions are suitable for fishing can be left

to him. Above all, do not question his decision to cancel the trip you have been looking forward to for months. He will have done so with great reluctance after taking detailed advice from the local meteorological office. Remember that he makes a living by going to sea and that staying tied up to the wharf unnecessarily will not pay the rent and keep an expensive boat with hired electronics in operation.

Through thousands of deep water angling trips in the past decade the sport has retained a 100 per cent safety record—professional skippers want to keep it that way.

Don't chance it—stay at home!

Unfortunately, the same cannot be said for privately owned craft. Every year anglers lose their lives in boating accidents, simply because they did not have the common sense to stay ashore when bad weather was forecast. Indeed, many are stupid enough to set out in conditions that are already dangerous—an act which all too often puts at risk the lives of those engaged in subsequent rescue operations.

Small, open boats are unsafe in winds of Force 3 and upwards, and under these conditions should never be taken outside sheltered water.

Most local authorities and harbour masters post detailed local weather forecasts outside their offices. A forecast can also be obtained from the nearest meteorological office or by dialling the GPO Telephone

Bill Howes

Richard Jemmett

Force 5: Wind on tide a mile offshore. A nasty sea, time to head home.

Force 8: No hope of getting out as huge waves break on shore. Stay at home.

Weather Service, the number of which will be in your local telephone directory. You can find out about sea conditions by telephoning your local coastguard, who will also be listed in the Post Office telephone book.

Shipping forecasts

Shipping forecasts for the 28 areas comprising the British Isles are broadcast on BBC Radio 2 (1500 metres) 200kHz at 0033, 0633, 1355 (1155 on Sundays) and at 1755. Gale warnings are also broadcast on this frequency as soon as possible after receipt and repeated, following the next news summary, on the hour.

Forecasts for inshore waters (up to 12 miles from the coast) are broadcast every evening on BBC Radio 4. The times on both medium wave and VHF frequencies vary around 2345 in different parts of the British Isles. Full details are given in the local editions of the *Radio Times*.

Only a moderate north-westerly, but rocks are a dangerous place now.

Special reports

Special forecasts for small boat users are broadcast on Radio 3 medium wave (464 metres/647kHz) on weekdays at 0655 and Saturday and Sunday at 0755.

Weather forecasts and gale warnings are also broadcast by Coast Radio Stations at times and on frequencies shown in the *Notice to Ship Wireless Stations* issued free by the GPO on application.

Information on local weather and sea conditions is given on the following BBC local stations (see panel at right).

RADIO STATION	VHF (MHz)	MED. WAVE (metres/kHz)
Bristol	95.5	194/1546
Blackburn	96.4	351/854
Brighton	95.3	202/1484
Carlisle	95.6	397/755
Cleveland	96.6	194/1546
Humberside	96.9	202/1484
Medway	96.7	290/1034
Merseyside	95.8	202/1484
Newcastle	95.4	206/1457
Solent	96.1	301/998

Small boats

(Left) This is the correct way for two anglers to sit in a boat while fishing. All undue movement must be avoided. Waterproof cushions are necessary for long periods on hard seats. (Below) Always sit in a small boat so that your weight is balanced. If it is at one end or the other a wave may swamp it. The rowing-boat is suitable only for inshore fishing.

Ken Whitehead

A sea angler's first tentative trips should be confined to sheltered waters and made under the guidance of someone with experience.

If you are planning to buy a dinghy you will want to know what size of boat is adequate for sea trips and how many people can be carried safely. There is a simple rule of thumb to follow when making your choice. For use in fine weather and inshore waters, the minimum length of any boat should be twice your height. The breadth, or beam, should never be less than one third of the length, while the internal depth should be about an eighth of the length. Obviously a man of 5ft weighing only a few stone is a much safer load than one of, say, 6ft 6in, of twice the weight. A small boy may be safe in an eight-footer when a big man would be in constant danger of upsetting the same craft.

Size of boat

How many people will a boat carry? Take the largest person in the party and apply the above rule. You will then need to increase the length of boat required by roughly 1ft for each additional passenger. More than three anglers should not go out in a small boat.

Boat handling and seamanship are acquired with practice and experience. But there are basic principles which help the novice. Of prime importance is 'trim', that is,

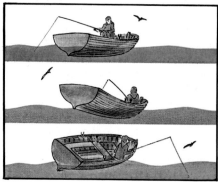

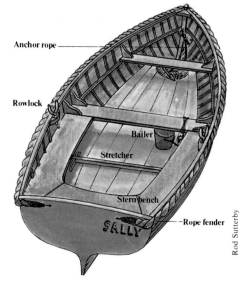

Anchor rope

Rowlock

Bailer

Stretcher

Stern bench

SALLY

Rope fender

Rod Sutterby

disposing the load in a boat so that she rides evenly in the water, neither down at the bow or stern, nor heeling to one side or the other. Never allow anyone to sit on the bow or sides of the boat. As far as possible keep weight out of the ends of the boat and she will lift easily on the waves. It is unwise to make any violent move aboard a boat; calm action and forethought are recommended. And keep the boat tidy. Stow your rods and tackle away until you are ready to begin fishing.

Launching

To launch from a beach—and no two beaches present the same problems since wind, tide and surf are constantly changing—you should copy the methods used by locals. On a simple shelving beach of shingle, with only small waves running, two men will bring a 12-14ft boat over the shingle on greased boards, stern first, until it is almost afloat, with waves reaching along almost half her length. One man will take his place in the middle of the boat with oars ready to push-row as soon as the boat floats, while the other waits for a 'smooth', pushes the boat far enough to be able to turn and head out to sea.

If the shore does not slope sufficiently to float the boat quickly, it will be necessary to launch bow first, with both men walking into the water pulling the boat until it floats. As the water deepens, one boards and rows from amidships to keep the boat heading into the waves while his helper steps aboard. The bow-first launch is again best when the beach is very steep so that the boat can be run down, with anglers already aboard, oars at the ready, by helpers who stay ashore.

If an outboard motor is to be used, the boat should be kept under way during the launch, using the oars, until the motor has been started and can take over, or the boat may turn and drift back into the surf should the motor prove obstinate. Outboard motors are now very popular, but the beginner should still learn to row proficiently at the outset, and see to it that his dinghy is provided with well-fitted rowlocks and oars of adequate size. He is then able to return safely if the engine fails.

Even if you do not intend to fish at anchor you must carry one and keep it ready for use. In the event of engine failure, broken oars or the like, the anchor is the only means of bringing the boat to a halt and countering wind and current. Be sure that the anchor is a good one with plenty of cable attached. The wind blowing offshore may leave a decep-

This small rowing-boat is suitable only for two of these anglers. Overcrowding is very dangerous and fishing impossible.

Bill Howes

Small boots

(Left) Two anglers working well together while fishing from a small boat in Lough Carrane, Co. Kerry. (Right) A fleet of small boats launching off the beach and a groyne at Folkestone for a day's sea angling. (Below) Offshore winds can drag an anchored boat out to where the water is too deep for the anchor to be of any use.

Irish Tourist Board

tively smooth sea close inshore. Farther out it may blow stronger and can carry even an anchored boat out to where the sea roughens unless there is enough cable to give the anchor a good hold, and still more in reserve to pay out should it drag into deeper water. Three times the depth of water is the accepted guideline to cable length. The reserve should be led back over the prow to the middle of the boat and secured with an easily released hitch and neatly coiled. You can then handle the rope without moving forward. A 7lb anchor and 30 fathoms of 1½in circumference rope will suffice for a dinghy in ordinary longshore conditions.

Always anchor from the bow, not the stern. The combined weight of an outboard motor and downward pull of the cable, were the anchor to snag, could quickly submerge

the stern. It is good practice always to have your anchor rope clear and ready to slip should an emergency require you to move in a hurry. If, when doing so, you tie a buoy to the end of the rope before releasing it—an inflated plastic fender will serve—you will be able to return and recover the anchor when the danger has passed.

Essential equipment

A good compass must be taken, and once at anchor, or if visibility begins to deteriorate, take a bearing of the nearest safe landing place in case of sudden thick fog. In fine weather it will be possible to 'fix' your position, if not too far offshore, for you will be within sight of prominent buildings, hilltops and other natural landmarks.

An effective bailer with lanyard attached, is another essential. The lanyard may either

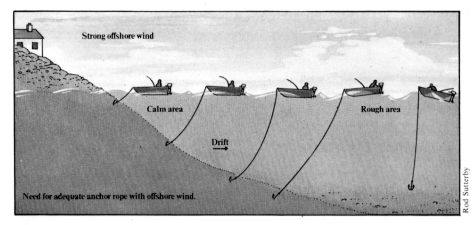

Strong offshore wind

Calm area

Drift

Rough area

Need for adequate anchor rope with offshore wind.

Rod Sutterby

Bill Howes

be tied near the deepest part of the boat or a loop slipped over the wrist to stop it being lost overboard while bailing. Lanyards should also secure the rowlocks and even the outboard motor, which could disappear overboard if its clamp is loosened.

When at sea it is essential to keep a good lookout at all times. It is the unwritten law of the sea to go to the aid of anyone in distress. You can call for help yourself, but do not fire off *red* flares unless you are in real danger of drowning. If you have merely got into some difficulty which requires a tow home or other simple help—not the Search and Rescue Services—set off a white flare. All the information you need about safety equipment and so on is contained in 'The Seaway Code', obtainable free of charge from Coastguards, libraries, and seasport clubs.

Weather conditions

Pay attention to weather conditions both when you are afloat and before setting off. Even if the sea is calm, the sun shining and there is only a gentle breeze blowing, you should telephone the local weather station for an assurance of continuing good weather. The whole scene can change very rapidly. Consequently, the small boat sea angler should never venture far from a safe landing place or secure haven.

Acquaint yourself with tides and the strength and direction of tidal stream. It will greatly effect the time needed to travel out or home. A most useful item is the 'Pocket Tidal

Stream Atlas', obtainable from agents for the sale of Admiralty charts. This shows graphically the strength and direction of tidal streams at any hour, before and after high water at Dover, in various areas of the coast. The time of high water at Dover is published in the daily press or is available in Tide Tables, which will also show the time of high water in your locality and tackle shops usually have these. Sometimes it is possible to leave after high water so that the current helps you on your way to the fishing ground, and fish for an hour or two until the tide turns so that the stream will help you home.

To bring the boat back onto gently shelving beaches the outboard motor can be kept running to bring the boat through the surf, but the bow must be kept as light as possible and the boat headed straight into the beach. The bow painter rope should be held ready by someone who remains back in the boat, ready to go forwards as soon as the boat is safely grounded but not a moment sooner. It is courting disaster to have someone forward, as his weight will depress the bow and swing the boat broadside onto the beach to be swamped by the waves.

Haul the boat up the beach out of the reach of the sea. If you are short of help on a long beach, carry all the gear up first to lighten the load. Where there are no greased boards or rollers, take out all removable parts including the bottom boards, turn the boat upside down and carry her!

Cruisers

When an angler wants to go sea fishing with greater comfort and safety than is possible in a dinghy, he will look to the many excellent inboard-engined launches which have been designed and built for the purpose of angling. Faced with a confusing number from which to choose, he will do well to make the acquaintance of sea anglers who own such boats in his locality. Thus he may learn of the advantages and shortcomings of at least some of the designs, and may find that one is a favourite for local conditions. Beware, though, of anyone who is trying to sell his boat to you. Even if he is completely honest, he may be unaware of incipient decay or a defect which only a qualified marine surveyor can detect.

Generally speaking, motorboats suitable for sea angling are those based on workboats and the semi-open types built for inshore professional fishermen. Those between 18ft and 30ft are the most popular. Boats of such size built specifically for 'cruising', with the maximum amount of sleeping accommodation, will not suit the keen angler; the cockpit will be too small, the area of her top-hamper exposed to the wind will make her unhandy, and space to work the anchor will be very restricted.

It is possible, of course, for the owner of such a craft to enjoy a spot of fishing while cruising, and he can sample the varied sport available while on his annual holiday, but his priorities will be quite different from the serious angler. On the other hand, boats of over 22ft can easily provide two berths in a forepeak and still have plenty of open space for half a dozen men to fish with rod and line.

Photo: Bill Howes

An armada heads out from Westport Quay towards the great complex of islands, where fishing is always possible.

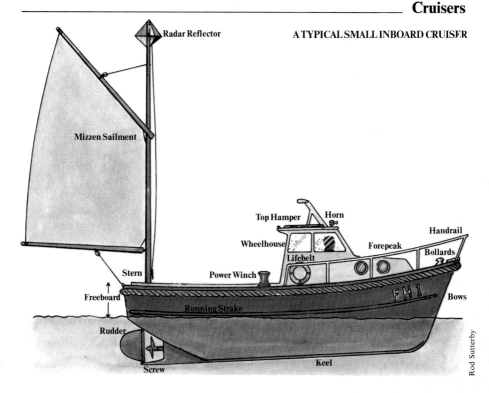

A TYPICAL SMALL INBOARD CRUISER

Radar Reflector

Mizzen Sailment

Top Hamper

Horn

Handrail

Wheelhouse

Forepeak

Bollards

Lifebelt

Stern

Power Winch

Freeboard

Running Strake

Bows

Rudder

Screw

Keel

Rod Sutterby

The forepeak combined with steering cab will add greatly to the comfort by providing shelter from cool breezes which prevail in the best fishing season, and protection too, for navigational equipment. The area affected by wind will tend to make the boat lie awkwardly and sheer about when wind and tide are in opposition, so a mizzen sail will prove helpful in restoring the balance.

The heavy anchors needed by these bigger boats will tax the strength of the crew, especially in deeper waters. With an inboard engine, now almost universally diesel, a power winch eases this task.

For the novice owner

To gain experience before making a choice, and to get some idea of what is involved in working a boat, the novice owner will do well to book places in some of the boats which take out angling parties. Even though he may be an experienced angler, such trips will enable him to note what goes on, making a friend of the boat-man who is often an angler bitten by the sport to such an extent that he has taken up the job full-time. Skippers are often willing to let you help to work the boat. But do not make a nuisance of yourself.

Join a club, too, where boats are available or owned by fellow members many of whom will be able to give good advice. Some clubs and Local Authority evening classes will give instruction in seamanship and navigation.

Having acquired a powered boat our angler will have to get used to handling her before venturing out to sea, delighted with his new plaything—a marine Sunday motorist. For he will soon discover, perhaps before he succeeds in leaving the quay, that a boat does not react in any way like a motorcar.

He may swing the wheel, intending to steer away from the quayside, only to find that the bow does not move out, but that the stern swings in towards the wall, dragging along and preventing the bow from moving out. It is essential that he study the principles which govern the behaviour of a motorboat. The

Cruisers

type of boat most commonly in use will have a long straight keel with a hull of moderate displacement, a single screw, and a rudder which will most probably be controlled by wheel steering. It is of first importance to discover the 'hand' of the screw as this has a very important effect on the movement of the vessel at low speeds. Because the blades are alternately in different depths of water the bottom blade is working in denser water and a greater degree of *pressure* is obtained there than in the upper blade thus pulling the stern *sideways* as well as pushing forward. This effect is greatest when the boat is

(Previous page) Angling cruisers need special features not always found on pleasure craft. First is plenty of room at the stern. Secondly, a powered winch for the anchor rope, worked from near the stern, is another important necessity, for skippers of charter-boats do not always have a crew. (Below) How to manoeuvre away from a quay.

stationary before it has had time to respond to the forward thrust of the screw. Its effect dies out as the boat gathers speed. When the screw is left-handed (it revolves anti-clockwise as viewed from astern) it will tend to thrust the stern to the left and vice versa if it is right-handed. With practice this allows the boat to be turned short round and manoeuvred in confined spaces when the natural turning circle of the boat at cruising speed is too great.

Turning with left-handed screw

To turn neatly round with a left-handed screw, let go the mooring and drift clear of it, engage for ahead and open the throttle to give a short burst, closing it again before the boat gathers way. You will find that the stern has begun to swing to the left and the bow to the right. Repeat this and you will increase the swing. You may let her begin to move ahead a little if it is necessary. When the boat moves ahead with the rudder in the central position, and the water flows evenly on both sides it has no effect, but when it is moved

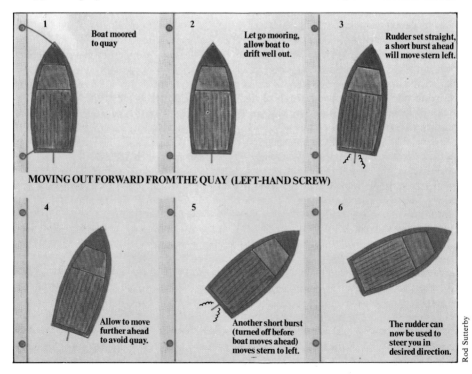

1 Boat moored to quay
2 Let go mooring, allow boat to drift well out.
3 Rudder set straight, a short burst ahead will move stern left.

MOVING OUT FORWARD FROM THE QUAY (LEFT-HAND SCREW)

4 Allow to move further ahead to avoid quay.
5 Another short burst (turned off before boat moves ahead) moves stern to left.
6 The rudder can now be used to steer you in desired direction.

Rod Sutterby

318

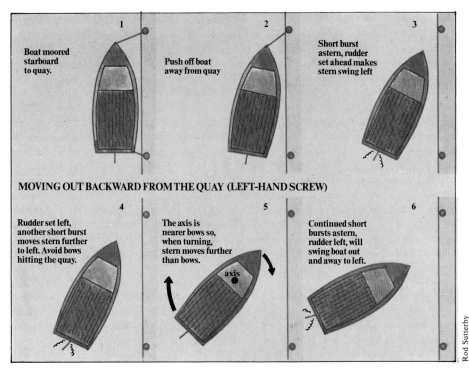

1 Boat moored starboard to quay.

2 Push off boat away from quay

3 Short burst astern, rudder set ahead makes stern swing left

MOVING OUT BACKWARD FROM THE QUAY (LEFT-HAND SCREW)

4 Rudder set left, another short burst moves stern further to left. Avoid bows hitting the quay.

5 The axis is nearer bows so, when turning, stern moves further than bows.

axis

6 Continued short bursts astern, rudder left, will swing boat out and away to left.

Rod Sutterby

over to the right, pressure is built up on the forward side which will cause the stern to move to the left and further increase the movement of the bow to the right. Now with the boat swinging nicely but beginning to move ahead it may be necessary to check the forward movement. With throttle closed as the boat slows, engage the gear astern and put the rudder to left. Open the throttle again and the thrust from the screw (pushing water forward onto the back of the rudder) will help you keep the stern swinging to the left, as will the force of the water flowing past the rudder as the boat moves astern. The amount of movement, both forward and astern, must be carefully restricted so as to allow the swinging movement to be the greatest. This routine is best tried out where there is plenty of room and little wind.

Applying the technique

Having mastered the technique it can then be applied to get neatly away from alongside a quay. If the boat is lying right side to it, a touch ahead (with the left-hand propellor),

(Above) Backing away from a quay by means of a left-handed screw. First push the boat off; then a short burst, with the rudder straight to swing the stern out. When in motion, turn the rudder left. Short bursts of the engine will pull the craft away.

will begin to swing the stern away. When her stern is far enough out to keep the bow from scraping along the quay, go astern with the rudder to the left. If the boat has a right-handed screw the very opposite applies and the boat would need to be lying with its left side to the quay to obtain this effect and the rudder put to the right.

It will help the initial outward swing of the stern when leaving the quay if the bow is held by keeping fast the 'bow spring', while the first touch ahead is given to stop the forward movement, allowing the ahead time to be prolonged thus getting the maximum effect from the sideways thrust of the screw. Only when the stern is well out should the rope be freed and the screw reversed.

This method of getting away from the quay is particularly useful when the wind is blowing onto the quay, for it is one of the peculiarities of boat behaviour that when she is going astern the *rudder* has less affect than when going *ahead* but her *screw* has *more*. It will pull her astern to windward better than it can push her bow out against the wind. If caught between quays with the wind astern and an obstruction ahead and your boat refuses to turn short enough to get her round into the wind, put her in reverse. Then, as she begins to move astern, the pivot point will move right aft and the bow blow away from the wind, letting the screw take the boat stern-first to windward out of trouble.

Effect of wind and current

Angling launches and workboats are often fitted with a large fender around the bows to facilitate this manoeuvre by protecting the stem from damage should it bear on the quay. The wind and current, if any, will affect manoeuvring when coming alongside and you will have to judge which will have the greater effect. When approaching with the wind from ahead its effect varies with the height of the bows and depth of the forefoot. The slower the boat, the more the wind will catch the bow and blow it off course, and with too great an angle of approach will blow the bows onto the quay. The gear must be put into neutral at a point where the boat will soon stop, lying at an angle of about 20° with her bow just off the quay. The rudder should then be put over to force her stern towards the quay and the screw put slow ahead when she will drop nicely alongside as the gear is again put to neutral. *Do not* do this with a burst or you will induce the sideways action of the propellor which may overcome the force of the rudder.

Berthing in following wind

If the wind is from *astern* as you approach your berth, take plenty of room; carry on well past the spot, turn, then approach head-to-wind. If the current is stronger than the effect of the wind, approach head-to-current

but take care to watch the way the wind is affecting your approach. The bow rope should be passed ashore and secured first, the stern rope following as soon after as possible.

Do not let your crew throw ropes until you are quite sure you are going to complete the manoeuvre successfully, for it is better to go off and approach again if you have muffed it. A rope secured ashore too soon will inhibit this, while if it misses, it may get around the screw, when you will be really in trouble.

It is not possible to include even the fraction of all you should learn in this short article, but finally you would be well advised to register your boat with H.M. Coastguard Yacht & Boat Safety Scheme. All you need to do is fill in a simple post-paid card obtainable from the Safety Scheme 'Issuing Authority' at clubs, harbour offices, marinas or Coastguard Stations, and send it back to the Coastguard. It will be retained at the Coastguard Rescue Headquarters for your area.

Bill Howes

Game Fishing

Salmon

The Atlantic salmon (*Salmo salar*) is one of the most mysterious fish in the world. Considered by many to be king of fish, its reputation as a great and powerful fighter, its great stamina and unusual life-cycle is still fascinating despite our increased knowledge.

Egg fertilization

The salmon egg or 'ova' is generally laid by the parent hen fish in November and December. Scooping out a hollow or 'redd' in the stones she quietly lays her eggs while an attendant male covers them with milt. Fertilization of the covered eggs takes place fairly quickly and it is not long before the female uses her broad tail to cover the fragile eggs with loose stones. Unless disturbed, or subjected to excessive floods, the eggs are safe from predators and silting and it will only now be a matter of approximately 90 to 120 days before the new life is born.

The salmon starts its life as a minute egg—the size of a small pea—nestling under loose stones and gravel in the upland waters of the classic salmon rivers or small Highland

Salmon

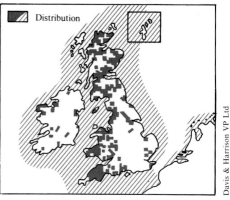

Rod Sutterby

Habitat

The salmon, Salmo salar, *is sought by the angler as it makes its way upstream to spawn in the area where it began life. The River Barrow (below), rising in the Slieve Bloom Mountains, is such a water.*

Bait

The range of salmon flies is enormous. Popular patterns are Brown Turkey, Hairy Mary. Worm, lures and shrimps are also used.

Salmon

(Left) Salmon parr (the large fish here is perhaps a trout parr) can spend four years feeding in a river before going down to the sea as a smolt. In the sea, the salmon feed well on fish and crustaceans. At between three and five years the smolt is known as a grilse. It is then ready to return to its home redds to breed. (Right) The Spey, shown here at Castle Grant, is one of the great classic salmon rivers of Britain.

Kinns & Ward/Natural Science Photos

burns. Approximately 12 to 15 weeks following fertilization, depending on water temperature, a minute fish or 'alevin' will emerge from the egg. It is then sustained for the next six weeks on a small yolk-sac attached to the underside of its body. Once this has been absorbed, the fish must fend for itself. Now, many mortalities can occur.

Once the yolk-sac is absorbed the initial problem for the infant salmon or 'fry' is that of finding food. Early spring can be cold and cheerless. Natural food in many upland, acid streams will be at a premium and the salmon faces the first battle for survival. Sadly, the ravages of nature will kill off a large number of the hatching stock; but those which do find food and resist the attacks of numerous predators still have many pitfalls ahead to overcome. Slowly, however, cheerless spring gives way to softer summer. Hatching flies dance on the water and the salmon 'parr' feed on every available morsel of food to come their way. Another freshwater winter still lies ahead when food will again be at a premium and the small parr must be ever-watchful for herons and a host of other hungry predators.

Given survival and a bit more luck, at the end of a two-year sojourn in the upland streams the young parr slowly acquires a silvery coat. It is now fast approaching the 'smolt' stage. With the first warming of the upland waters—frequently in May—the smolt will instinctively drop downstream to the estuaries and the wide open sea. This too is fraught with danger from predators and unknown pollutants in the lower reaches of many of our rivers. Further losses will occur, and only a few will attain the sanctuary of the deep sea and be lost in its vastness.

Sea-going migrations

This at least was the way it was thought to be until a few years ago. Today, we know some of the sea-going migration routes which British salmon take. It is known, for instance, that many go to the rich feeding grounds off the coast of Greenland. Also, once at sea, a smolt is known to increase its weight by 15 times in less than a year. Thus a small, insignificant fish of five or six ounces can quickly become one of five or six pounds. At this stage of its development it is known as a 'grilse' and it is now capable of reproduction and of making its way back to the river of its birth. Depending on circumstances, however, many of the fish will continue to rove the seas for another year. This may enable them to double or treble their weight and thus reach maturity. A great deal depends on water temperatures and availability of food; but a two-year sea life salmon should reach eight to·10lb. Some salmon,staying up to five years at sea, reach weights of at least 30 or 40lb and more.

Arthur Oglesby

Many of our migrating salmon go north. Some are reputed to go under the Arctic ice—which, mercifully, protects them from the destructive tactics of the commercial fishermen to which they often fall prey.

The urge to reproduce

At some stage in their sea journeys the salmon will develop the overpowering urge to come back to the rivers of their birth, find a mate and reproduce the species. Salmon behaviour in this respect is not uniform and a great deal will depend on the individual river from which the salmon have originally come. On such rivers as the Tweed, Tay, Spey, Dee, Wye and Eden—a lot of fish return in the early spring. Some rivers will, however, have fresh fish in January, but it is little more than speculation why fish enter one river then and others in summer or autumn. Not all salmon are destined to spawn in November or December. What induces a spring-running instinct in one salmon and an autumn return in another still remains a mystery. Much inconclusive speculation has been generated on the why's and wherefore's of salmon behaviour, but the fish remains enigmatic, with a strong disposition of pleasing itself!

The salmon's trials begin

History provides a lot of clues of when salmon are likely to enter a specific river system. On most rivers of the British Isles the first trial the fish must undergo is to run the gauntlet of the various netting and trapping systems operated in or near the estuary. Sustained high water in the rivers during the early months will ensure good passage for the fish with minimal loss to the commercial operators. At times of low water the fish tend to rove the estuaries waiting for adequate flows and may thus be more likely to suffer capture by the nets on every ebb and flood of the tides. Of course it makes sense for man to crop this valuable resource; but it also demands responsible behaviour from those who take the crop. Unfortunately, the high price of salmon encourages the illegal element to flourish and salmon will continue to be in jeopardy as a species until greater protective measures are introduced.

Shortly before entering the river, the salmon ceases to take food, though the reason for this is unclear. Some authorities say that salmon simply lose all desire for food and that, as a result, the stomach occludes and the fish become incapable of digestion. Others claim that nature causes the gut to atrophy so that food cannot be taken at all. Whatever the real reason, there is little doubt that salmon in freshwater do not feed in the full sense of the word. Living in freshwater the salmon suffers a slow deterioration. But even if the salmon did show a desire to feed in freshwater, few of our classical salmon rivers contain sufficient food to sustain them anyway. Certainly on capture in freshwater, nothing is ever found in the salmon's stomach.

The salmon's power and beauty

On entering the river the salmon is beautifully arrayed with a bright silvery mantle—an object of power and beauty, in its prime for both sporting and culinary purposes. Apart from a malignant and spasmodic disease known as Ulcerative Dermal Necrosis (UDN), the next predator in the chain is the angler. But, as the fish do not feed in freshwater, angling is a very inefficient method of catching them. There is

(Inset, below) Driven by a powerful and instinctive urge, the salmon comes in from the sea to run upstream, heading for its birthplace. Hazards, such as commercial fishermen, rapids, pollution—and anglers—await the fish.

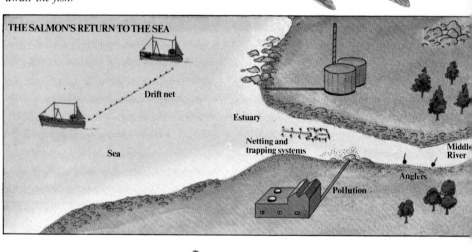

THE SALMON'S RETURN TO THE SEA

Drift net

Estuary

Netting and trapping systems

Sea

Pollution

Anglers

Middle River

Spawning Male
Three to eight years

(Left) Burrishoole Fishery, Co Mayo, typical of the waters that salmon ascend in order to spawn.
(Below) Life cycle of the salmon. The alevin feeds on the attached yolk-sac until all the nutriment has gone. The tiny fish must then find its own food. After two years in the parr stage the fish, now a smolt, heads for the sea, where it will feed on the rich diet of the salt-water fauna. Once back in freshwater it will not feed.

Irish Tourist Board

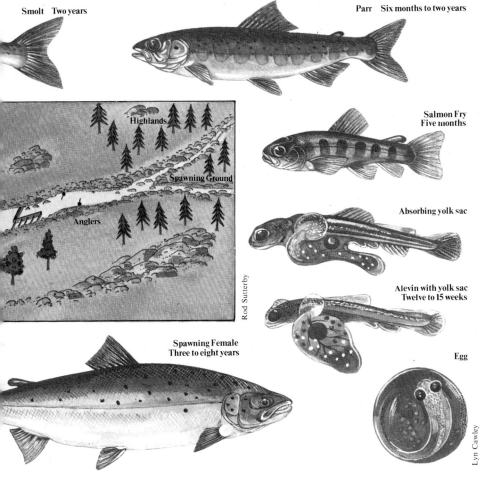

Smolt   Two years

Parr   Six months to two years

Highlands

Spawning Ground

Anglers

Salmon Fry
Five months

Absorbing yolk sac

Alevin with yolk sac
Twelve to 15 weeks

Rod Sutterby

Spawning Female
Three to eight years

Egg

Lyn Cawley

327

Salmon

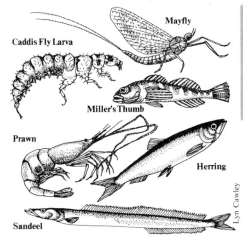

Caddis Fly Larva

Mayfly

Miller's Thumb

Prawn

Herring

Sandeel

Lyn Cawley

(Top) A salmon ladder on the River Tummell, near Pitlochry, Perthshire. (Above) A popular salmon fly, Jock Scott. (Left) The salmon's natural diet. (Right) The ghillie, just as pleased as the angler, unhooks a fine Irish salmon.

G. L. Carlisle

Irish Tourist Board

no known bait that will induce them to *feed*, but there are several lures which will, on occasion, induce salmon to take them into their mouths for sufficient time to become hooked. Many fisheries demand a high standard of sportsmanship from their anglers and rents to fish the better beats or stretches are now quite high. In the final resort, however, is is the angler who takes the minimum crop of salmon. Yet it is the same angler who shows greatest concern for the survival of the species. In terms of licence dues, rents and rates, the angler pays a high price for his sport, the highest in all fishing. He also makes the largest financial contribution to the good husbandry of salmon.

On their first entry into freshwater the salmon may be lethargic or active depending on water temperature alone. Cold water induces sluggish response from the fish. Most will be content to move slowly and to stay in the lower reaches of the classic rivers.

Fresh-run salmon

Angling tactics involve making the lure or bait move slowly and at a good depth; but there is always the chance of sport with fresh-run fish. Within 48 hours of their entry into freshwater, the parasitic sea lice will begin to drop from their host. There is no specific time for sea lice to stay alive in freshwater, for they have been known to survive under laboratory conditions for up to seven days.

Most anglers accept the 48-hour theory, so it is a sure sign that when a fish is caught with sea lice on it, it is as fresh a fish as possible.

Experience the best guide

As water temperatures rise, and always provided there are adequate river flows, the fish will be induced to run quickly through the lower beats and into the middle and upper reaches. Here they may be induced to take small flies or lures fished near the surface and they can be much more active. Sometimes it is possible to catch them 50 miles upstream of the estuary with sea lice still on them, but there can be no hard-and-fast rule. Only long experience of a specific river over the seasons will give a glimmer of a clue as to where the fish might be and when.

Despite these movement patterns, there comes a time when all the salmon requires is to be left in peace and quiet. Most will settle up in pools and known lies for long periods throughout the summer. Joined by later-run fish or small summer grilse, most will ignore the flies and lures offered by anglers. While the stock of fish in the pools gradually

increases, the salmon will slowly be burning up energy and losing body weight and girth. By November the salmon having survived the wiles of man and nature will be a sorry-looking creature. The flesh will have wasted away to provide the essential milt and ova which it will shed on the redds. Males will compete with other males for the best spawning placed and the most attractive partner. Some redds will be overcut and nature will also exact a high toll. Following the spawning act, many of the females will drop back into quiet water and recover.

The possessive male

Many male salmon, however, will stay near the redds and fight off other intruders. Many will succumb and die; but, unlike the Pacific salmon, which dies following spawning, there will be many survivors slowly dropping back downstream as spawned salmon or 'kelts' to return to the sea once again. Here, many of these weak and emaciated kelts will fall to marine predators such as seals, and only a few will survive to make the journey again and repeat the act of spawning.

Brown trout

It could be argued that the brown trout requires little introduction in these days of supermarkets and freezer stores where it is displayed for sale. Most people will have met a hatchery-bred fish on the end of a fork.

Intensive hatchery fish farming, however, should not be condemned. Anglers want to fish waters where there is a good head of quality fish and the restaurateur needs plate-sized trout for the table—the hatcheries supply them both.

Breeding and culling

By selective breeding, and culling out the younger fish for the 'table market', the breeder produces fast growing, healthy fish for planting out as fingerlings or 6in yearlings. Fortunately the stocking authorities also like to plant a good supply of 10-12 in stock fish as well as a sprinkling of two- or three-pounders. All this keeps the fishery healthy and the angler happy. A single season in the wild turns these hatchery-bred fish into tough, hardy, flavoursome and sporting fish.

The brown trout, *Salmo trutta*, is indigenous to Europe, North West Asia, and North Africa. It shows a remarkable diversity of shape and coloration, often according to locality. It can be categorized into two distinct forms which differ chiefly in life style but also in size and colour. The sea-trout is the migratory form. Like the salmon it spends part of its life in the sea feeding well, and putting on weight. It then returns to the river of its birth as it becomes ready to spawn. Once it has done so it drops back to the sea until next year.

The brown trout is the non-migratory form which lives in rivers and lakes. The steeper gradients of the rivers where brown trout survive best are often a long way from the sea, and in many rivers they are separated from the sea by the slower sluggish zones which trout tend to avoid. Often mild pollution also bars the way to the sea. In any event the brown trout has been separated from the sea for many generations and has adopted an entirely freshwater mode of life.

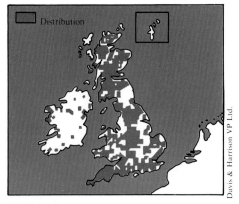

Distribution

Davis & Harrison VP Ltd.

Habitat
The brown trout, Salmo trutta, *is found in fast, clear waters and streams, but it can flourish in lakes and reservoirs.*

Bait
This fish can be caught by all natural baits, but on many waters a fly-fishing-only rule is imposed.

(Below) A quiet, limpid backwater of the River Test, renowned for its quality trout fishing.

Rod Sutterby

British Tourist Authority

Brown trout

The migratory and non-migratory trout are the extreme forms in terms of habit and appearance but there are several distinctive variations which appear in particular locations. These were indeed once considered to be separate and distinct species, or at least sub-species, and were even given scientific names to distinguish their specific status. More recently these fish have been shown to be capable of interbreeding to produce fertile progeny, and they are now regarded as variable members of the same species, now known throughout its indigenous range as *Salmo trutta*.

Local variations

Nevertheless local pride runs high, and the local names persist. Anglers anxious to sample the sporting qualities of these variations will not be disappointed by the Gilaroo trout of the Irish loughs, nor the Loch Leven or Orkney trout of their respective localities.

Where the water has not been ruined by pollution, abstraction, sewerage or canalization, brown trout are to be found in most river systems. They live in the swifter steep gradients where rocky, gravelly or stony bottoms and the swift flow produce the high oxygen requirements of the trout, and provide the kind of spawning facilities upon which their future stocks depend. The

(Above) Fishing for trout in early summer from a quiet bank of Rutland Water in Northamptonshire.
(Below) The natural food of brown trout includes a wide variety of insects, molluscs and crustaceans.

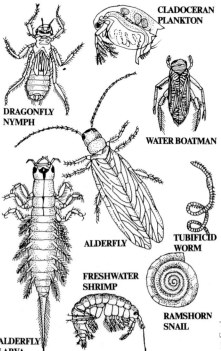

CLADOCERAN PLANKTON

DRAGONFLY NYMPH

WATER BOATMAN

ALDERFLY

TUBIFICID WORM

FRESHWATER SHRIMP

RAMSHORN SNAIL

ALDERFLY LARVA

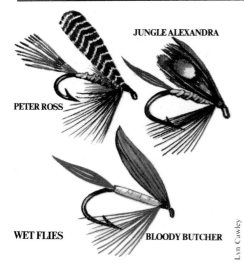

JUNGLE ALEXANDRA

PETER ROSS

WET FLIES

BLOODY BUTCHER

Lyn Cawley

(Above) Popular wet flies for catching trout include the Bloody Butcher, that was first tied some 150 years ago, the Peter Ross and the Jungle Alexandra.
(Below) Cross-section through a reservoir showing the trout's habitat and food.

slower, sluggish, muddy-bottomed reaches inhabited by coarse fishes are not favoured by trout although the coarse fish angler seeking roach or bream will occasionally take a trout on his worm.

Trout are very much at home in the typical moorland stream or the rocky beck as well as in the traditional chalk streams of Southern England. They also do well in lakes and ponds where the conditions are suitable. The intensive reservoir building programme that has taken place during the post-war years, however, has led to a total redistribution of the species throughout Britain. Many fine new waters have appeared in regions such as the South East and Midlands where few suitable rivers remained for trout. Most of these new waters have been extensively stocked with trout, and good trout fishing is now probably more plentiful and cheaper than it has ever been.

Waters rich in calcium produce prolific weed growth, and this in turn stimulates the growth of numerous insect, mollusc and

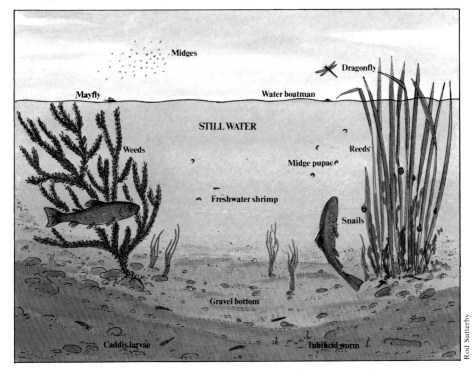

Midges

Dragonfly

Mayfly

Water boatman

STILL WATER

Weeds

Reeds

Midge pupae

Freshwater shrimp

Snails

Gravel bottom

Caddis larvae

Tubificid worm

Rod Sutterby

Brown trout

crustacean stocks. In such waters the generous food supplies favour big, fast-growing fish. Blagdon and Chew reservoirs are good examples and the angler confidently expects to take fish between 2lb and 3lb. With luck he hopes to get the odd four or five-pounder. If he is especially favoured, and suitably skilled, he may net a fish over 6lb or 7lb. The chalk streams of the South also produce excellent fish. The Avon, Kennet, Test and Lambourne rivers are typical examples. In Ireland, Lough Inchiquin and Lough Rea are well known for their high quality of fish. At the other extreme the tiny becks and streams of some northern and western districts produce small, mature, but game and crafty trout up to 8in long.

The rainbow trout

Owing to wise stocking policies most reservoirs in southern England will provide anglers with average fish of about a pound. The occasional two pounder will be taken, and once or twice in a season a three-

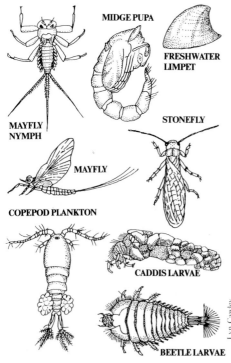

MIDGE PUPA

FRESHWATER LIMPET

MAYFLY NYMPH

STONEFLY

MAYFLY

COPEPOD PLANKTON

CADDIS LARVAE

BEETLE LARVAE

(Above) A typical stretch of fast-flowing trout river at Teesdale.
(Left) A selection of the brown trout's natural food found in fast-flowing waters.
(Below) A cross-section of a highland stream showing the natural habitat and food of the brown trout.

Moss

Caddis larvae

Lyn Cawley

334

(Below) Artificial flies come in hundreds of different dressings, but generally dry flies are not so highly coloured as wet flies. Olive Dunn, Sedge and the Dark Sedge are examples.

OLIVE DUNN

England Scene

SEDGE

DARK SEDGE

DRY FLIES

Lyn Cawley

pounder will be recorded in the book. This is good trout fishing by any standards. A bonus for the trout fisherman has been the introduction, alongside the native brown trout, of the American rainbow trout, *Salmo gairdneri,* into most stillwaters. So you may catch either species, and the chief distinguishing feature is that the brown has no spots on its tail.

Brown trout spawn at somewhere between two and four years of age. The eggs vary not only a great deal in size, but also in their incubation period. Research indicates that the time varies according to water temperature. It ranges from 21 weeks at 2 C (36 F) to four weeks at 12 C (54 F). Losses are staggering during this incubation period, and during the first year of life. Estimates vary, but the general view is that of 10,000 eggs produced only about 250 fish survive to the end of the first year. Growth rates vary too. A year-old fish may be between 1in and 5in long, a two-year-old between 4in and 9in, and a three-year-old between 6in and 13in. Hatchery fish have been recorded surviving to 12 years old, but the general run of fish is estimated to live to four or five years before it dies naturally, or is caught by the angler.

Fortunately for the angler the feeding habits of trout do not differ as widely as their growth rates, incubation periods, and maturation ages. Most trout, wherever they

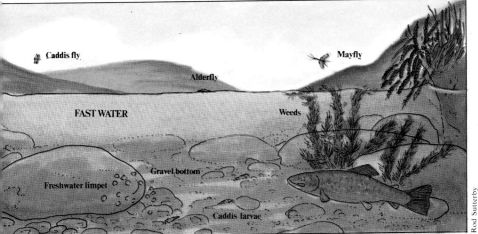

Caddis fly

Mayfly

Alderfly

FAST WATER

Weeds

Gravel bottom

Freshwater limpet

Caddis larvae

Rod Sutterby

Brown trout

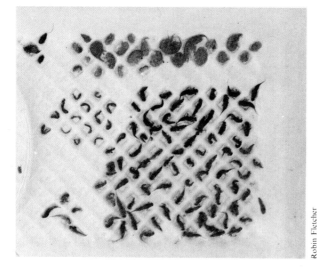

(Left) In order to match the tied fly with the natural on which the trout has been feeding waterside autopsies can be carried out. This can be done either by gutting the fish and emptying the fish's stomach contents into a dish, or by the use of a marrow-spoon inserted down the trout's throat. Here the stomach's contents clearly show that this fish has been feeding on freshwater shrimp, top, and various beetles and insect larvae.

Robin Fletcher

live, obtain most of their food from or near the bottom. They certainly supplement this staple diet with water-borne flies and insects living in or on the surface, or alighting temporarily upon it. They are not fussy about what they eat when hungry and will snap up almost anything which moves, providing they can manage to swallow it. They can be extremely fussy when food supplies are plentiful, and then the angler is hard put to please them.

Trout's haven and base

In rivers the fish tend to select a 'lie' which becomes their territorial base. It usually offers a haven from predators, and is protected from the full force of the current. They have their own territory around this base, and forage freely within it. The stream brings along food supplies regularly, and they probably feed rather more on the surface than their reservoir counterparts. Such a fish will defend its territory from intruders, and each fish in a particular reach knows its own place in the hierarchy or pecking order. If the big fellow succumbs to the angler his place will not be empty for long. The next in succession will occupy it and others will move up in the queue.

Anglers generally know such spots in their own river, and have the advantage that they can often stalk a known fish in a known

place. The disadvantage is often the very clear nature of the stream which discloses any careless move to the fish, and unfortunately 'puts him down'.

The reservoir angler often has the advantage of somewhat coloured water, and a profusion of bankside weed and vegetation. His fish rise less often, but nevertheless patrol their territories, usually giving away their rising spots. Their territories are larger, and may be vacated from time to time as the fish cruise up the wind lanes, or around the margins, in their search for food.

Although trout can be taken on many baits, including the lowly maggot, worm, spinners and lures, the artificial fly is the offering most used to attract this game fish.

Wet and dry flies

Trout are taken on dry and wet flies. The basic difference between these is that the hackles on the dry fly stand out, making it float on the surface, while the wet fly's 'wings' sweep backwards and it is fished below the surface. Wet flies and dry flies come in hundreds of different dressings and the number is added to every season. Some flies represent nothing more than the fly tier's whim and fancy—but they catch trout. Other flies represent small fish, insects and their larvae, spiders and freshwater shrimps (*Gammarus pulex*).

336

COLOUR VARIATION

Lock Leven Trout

Trout Parr

Golden Trout

(Left) Many fish species can vary a great deal in their coloration, even between the members of their own species. The nature of their habitat often dictates their colour. Trout parr always carry a row of distinctive purple-blue patches on their flanks. (Below) Refraction elongates this trout's jaws.

Lyn Cawley

F. Dalgety Camera Press

Rainbow trout

The rainbow trout, *Salmo gairdneri* is a native of the Pacific coast, rivers and lakes of the North American Continent, ranging from the Bering Sea in the north, to the southern Californian coasts in the south. Since 1884 the species has been introduced to suitable waters all over the world with varying degrees of success. In Britain it has rarely bred successfully and in most cases now exists only as a result of continual re-stocking from fish farms which have successfully bred the species by modern stripping techniques.

Rainbow's American habitat

In its American habitat the rainbow fills a niche comparable to that occupied in Britain by our native brown trout. Similarly it exhibits numerous .variants (each once believed to be a distinct species) and provides a similar range of migratory and non-migratory fish. Its growth rates vary widely according to type and environment, and it provides excellent sport for anglers. Brown and rainbow trout, are however, of quite

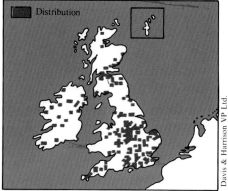

Distribution

Rod Sutterby

Habitat

The rainbow trout, Salmo gairdneri, *is a North American species introduced into the waters of Britain in the 19th century. The fish has become established in a few waters where the conditions are right for natural breeding.*

Baits

Artificial flies according to time, place, season and water conditions.

Rainbow trout

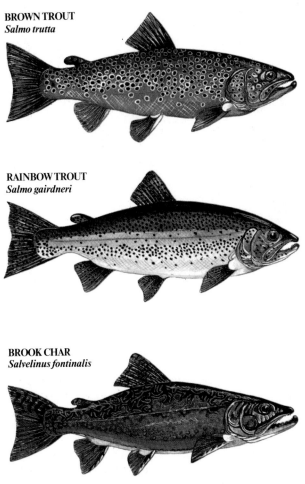

BROWN TROUT
Salmo trutta

RAINBOW TROUT
Salmo gairdneri

BROOK CHAR
Salvelinus fontinalis

VOMER BONES

BROWN TROUT

RAINBOW TROUT

BROOK CHAR

Lyn Cawley

(Above) Teeth in the upper jaw (called vomerine teeth) are an aid to identifying brown trout, rainbow trout and brook char.
(Left) Related species.

different species—although related to the *Salmo* genus.

Generally a far hardier fish than the brown trout, the rainbow can withstand high temperatures, low oxygen levels, and murky waters. It is also a far more active fish, being a free riser to the fly and living and moving in loose shoals, with a strong urge to migrate upstream for spawning, falling back into lakes or lower reaches for the rest of the season. At the extreme it is anadromous, like sea trout, migrating from dense to less dense water to breed, and enters freshwaters only to spawn.

In appearance it is similar to the brown trout apart from a distinctive wide lateral band of iridescent magenta along the middle flanks. It is usually black spotted, and the spots, unlike those of the brown trout, grow more quickly. Rainbow trout grow to a larger maximum size than the brown trout. It also spawns later than brown trout, and is therefore in excellent condition in British waters at the very end of the season.

Early work on the rainbow
The history, literature and taxonomy of rainbow trout in North America is every bit as confusing as that of its British cousin, the brown trout. Nineteenth century American and European zoologists identified and named a variety of species of trout. In Europe, for example, Gunther described

Bill Howes

G. L. Carlisle

(Above) What is the function of the adipose fin? This fleshy appendage seems to serve no purpose, and when removed as a check during population studies it does not affect the fish or grow again.
(Left) The head of a rainbow with the hook still lodged in the angle of the jaws.

species *Salmo gairdneri*. All trout were subsumed under this heading with the single notable exception of the brook trout, which in fact turned out to be a char and now enjoys the separate specific title of *Salvelinus fontinalis*. The char is, however, still commonly known in America as a trout but can be distinguished from the rainbow by its green-brown colour with lighter 'worm-track' patterns on the back, and reddish tinge on the underside. Examination of the vomerine bone on the upper palate will also provide distinguishing features. Rainbow trout have single rows of teeth set in a 'T' shape. Chars, on the other hand, bear only a group or cluster of teeth on this bone. The North American brook trout has also been introduced to some waters in Britain and these should not be confused with either brown or rainbow trout.

some ten different species each with its own scientific name, while in America a similar number of trout were similarly described by authorities, and named.

During the early part of the present century the zoological view that a species should be regarded primarily as a breeding unit, despite minor physical differences, gained ascendancy. It was shown under laboratory conditions that all the known British trouts were able to produce fertile progeny when cross-bred. More than anything, this led to their re-allocation to a single species *Salmo trutta*. The same sort of study of species in America resulted in an all-American trout being classified into the

Feeding habits

Rainbows normally feed on a very similar diet to brownies. When young they exist on daphnia, cyclops and other infusoria, but

Rainbow trout

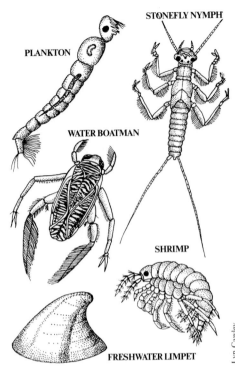

STONEFLY NYMPH

PLANKTON

WATER BOATMAN

SHRIMP

FRESHWATER LIMPET

once past the alevin stage quickly graduate to shrimp and insects, and on to snail and fish fry in addition within a year. Not only are rainbows more prone to rise than brown trout, but they are far more active in their search for food, ranging between the bottom and the surface continuously and taking good advantage of midges, nymphs, mayflies and their larvae, and in the evening on sedges and daddy long legs. In waters where coarse fish fry are plentiful, rainbows soon get used to supplementing their diet with such delicacies. It is not unusual for anglers to find fish of 14in with roach of three or four inches in their stomachs. Such fish become as predatory as pike, and as rainbows move in loose shoals they are sometimes seen driving

(Left) The natural food of the rainbow trout. The fish will also take flies and insects that fall onto the water.
(Below) The rainbow's natural habitat.
(Right) A quiet section of Blagdon, with Bill Howes trying for an April fish.

Lyn Cawley

WATER BEETLES

WEEDS

FRESHWATER SHRIMP

Rod Sutterby

shoals of small fish into the shallows where they hunt them down voraciously.

At the other end of the scale, rainbows often rise freely in boisterous weather, feeding well on the surface during high winds, following the wind lanes in large groups and fearlessly rising under the bows of the angler's boat. They will often cruise upwind in such conditions, dropping into the depths when they come to the far shores, and then feed earnestly in mid-water, or on the bottom.

When to use the dry fly

In calmer weather, when the surface is like a millpond and the angler despairs of getting his wet flies to work without creating a heavy wake, the rainbows will often rise maddeningly at midges and other small flies on the surface, ignoring the wet flies offered by the fisherman. Then the dry fly is often useful. Takes are sudden, and the rainbow is usually moving fast when it hits the fly. Smash-takes occur in these conditions, even when the cast is realistically heavy. It behoves the angler to

ensure that his rod is not left pointing at the fly so that such a take is absorbed by the rod when the fish often hooks itself.

The traditional wet fly method

Under normal conditions, with a light popple on the water, and a gentle breeze, the angler is able to fish without the wind interfering with his casting. The broken surface of the water will prevent fish spotting the angler's movements too easily, as well as covering up his mistakes when working the fly. In such conditions the traditional wet fly method is a joy, both from the bank or from a boat. A team of three wet flies is used with a long cast which, fished slowly, presents them at different levels, often enabling the angler to locate the best depth. Sometimes it also indicates the 'taking' fly. Medium casting from the bank, or short lining from a boat can be very productive.

When the fish are dour and not showing, the angler must fish the water, covering as much territory as he can to get fish moving, or locate moving fish. A lure is sometimes

Rainbow trout

successful and several patterns should be tried at various depths and different speeds. Sometimes the angler is reduced to 'scratching the bottom' with a leaded lure fished slow. Alternatively, a flasher fished fast may be used. Rainbows can often be tempted when high water temperatures have caused the brown trout to go completely off feeding. They will also move quite fast from comparatively deep water to a tempting fly realistically fished on or near the surface, following it until it is about to break surface.

The buzzer rise

When the buzzer rise occurs in the evening, fish will sip delicately at the nymph or smash at it, leaping out of the water and landing on the nymph with a boil. In late summer, when the sedges are on the water, rainbows will take boldly and hearteningly.

When fish are hooked high in the water they will often leap and splash on the surface from the moment they are hooked. Sometimes it is essential to get the rod point

(Above) Rainbow trout in the 'wild'—which are not stock fish put into waters from fish breeding ponds—do not achieve the high growth rate of the fish produced at Avington. This rainbow, caught from the Wye, one of Britain's leading game rivers, is typical of the fish which breed naturally.

down into the water to sink the line so as to absorb their acrobatics.

Most reservoir anglers welcome the rainbow and the exciting sport it offers in a hundred subtly different ways in different conditions. It can be as coy as the brown trout, and loves to cruise on the surface on hot days, sipping in the green pea-soup which the water often becomes in these conditions. Then it can be maddeningly difficult to tempt.

The increasing use of fish farming is essential if stocks are to be maintained in the face of increasing pressures from anglers, to say nothing of pollution, water abstraction, and commercial netting. These occur on

(*Left*) *A 15lb stock fish which fell to the sunken wet fly. Selective breeding can achieve weights not possible in the wild colonies.*
(Below) A typical three-fly team for use on reservoirs. A worm fly lure and Price's Orange Streamer are also shown.

Alan Pearson

DADDY LONG LEGS

THREE FLY TEAM

3ft 6in

WORM FLY LURE

3ft 6in

Second Dropper
or Bob Fly

2ft

First Dropper

Dry Fly

PRICE'S ORANGE STREAMER

3ft   2ft

Nymph

Point Fly
Wet Fly

Rod Sutterby

both sides of the Atlantic, and as stocks are regenerated from selectively bred fish-farm introduction, it is possible that the local variants will gradually disappear.

In Britain the continual existence of the rainbow is heavily dependent upon the fish farmer. In the vast majority of British waters rainbows become spawn-bound and fail to breed naturally. They can only be maintained by stocking.

Breeding colonies

The exceptions are the Derbyshire Wye, the Chess and the Misbourne, where rainbows have established breeding colonies. They also breed in Blagdon Reservoir in Somerset co-existing with the brown trout.

Rainbows are very suitable for introduction to reservoirs because they live only for four or five seasons, and can be stocked in a range of sizes. In most farm conditions a one-year-old fish may be between 4 and 8in attaining between 6 and 12in in its second year. A third year fish may be between 9 and 16in, and a fourth year fish between 14 and 20in. These are average figures and can be exceeded with suitable feeding and water conditions. A few years ago a 10lb rainbow was exceptional. Recent introductions at Avington fisheries, where fish of 20lb are being produced on high-protein diets, indicate that selective breeding has vastly improved future catches.

Sea trout

Until recent times it was thought that the sea trout, *Salmo trutta* as it was originally classified, was an independent species, while brown trout were known as *Salmo fario*. Scientific opinion now is that they are both of the species *Salmo trutta*. Even as long ago as 1887 it was asserted that there existed only this latter species of trout in Britain. This uncomplicated classification may satisfy those with a scientific turn of mind, but it does nothing for the angler who finds vast behavioural and environmental differences between the sea trout and the non-migratory 'brownie'.

What, then, is a sea trout? Sadly, a satisfactory answer is not forthcoming and we must accept that the sea trout, for want of factual information, is nothing more than a migratory brown trout. Just what induced the initial migration is little more than pure speculation; but there is on record the scientific opinion that all the family *Salmo* were of marine origin and that it was the last Ice Age which caused some to be landlocked

and others to develop the migratory instinct, perhaps as long ago as 100,000 years.

As with the salmon, therefore, the sea trout's origins are not fully understood. It follows a very similar life pattern to that of the salmon, and there was a time when our sea trout were simply called salmon-trout. Obviously, all the *Salmo* species had similar beginnings and for this reason many angling novices have difficulty distinguishing one from the other. There are differences, however, some subtle, others appreciable.

Sea trout's spawning time

Sea trout usually begin their spawning in October. On average, they are two or three weeks earlier than salmon, but there is no hard and fast rule. November is probably the month of greatest activity but some fish, according to one authority, may spawn throughout the winter. He adds that, although ripe (ready to spawn) sea trout, which have not begun to shed ova or milt, may be seen in January, and very occasionally in February, their spawning

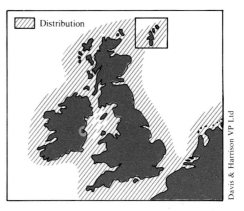

Distribution

Habitat

The sea trout ascend rivers to spawn. Below, silhouetted against an orange sunset, are Leslie Moncrieff and John Goddard, fishing somewhere along the 109-mile Ring of Kerry, a scenic route in South-West Ireland, where prime sea trout fishing may be enjoyed.

Baits

There are numerous sea trout flies, but the species may also be taken on lure and worm.

Rod Sutterby

Sea trout

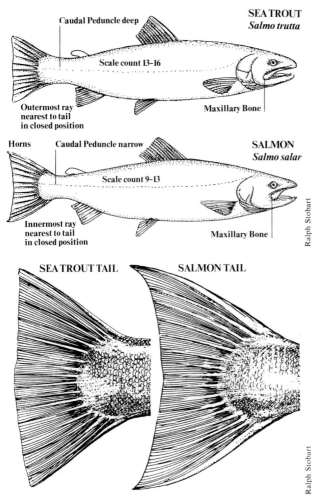

SEA TROUT
Salmo trutta

Caudal Peduncle deep

Scale count 13-16

Outermost ray
nearest to tail
in closed position

Maxillary Bone

Horns   Caudal Peduncle narrow

SALMON
Salmo salar

Scale count 9-13

Innermost ray
nearest to tail
in closed position

Maxillary Bone

SEA TROUT TAIL   **SALMON TAIL**

Ralph Stobart

*(Above left) Salmon and
sea trout identification points.
(Left) The 'wrist' of
salmon and sea trout. Sea trout
cannot be tailed by hand or by
an appliance.
(Above) A salmon and
three Spey sea trout.*

Ralph Stobart

season is generally shorter than that of the salmon, and much shorter than that of non-migratory trout.

Sea trout prefer smaller gravel than salmon for the construction of the redd in which the eggs are laid and fertilized, and, like salmon, find sand and mud unsuitable. Some will spawn in water barely deep enough to cover their backs, and they may be found in many small Scottish Highland burns with access to the larger river systems.

As with the salmon, it is the female sea trout which, with broad sweeps of its tail, makes the redd. Females are said to be able to produce 700–800 eggs for each pound of weight, but this is only a very rough guide. Like salmon, and depending on water temperature, a period of 90–120 days elapses before the eggs hatch. Much the same behavioural and growth pattern as in young salmon then occurs (see earlier chapter) but once the young sea trout smolts hit the tideway they tend to tarry, moving backwards and forwards on every ebb and flow for a much longer period than their salmon counterparts.

After feeding and growing for 2–5 months, some of the smolts which descended in spring to the sea return in summer or autumn to the river. Here they are known by different

Arthur Oglesby

return as mature sea trout. Others, sadly, tend to regard sea trout merely as vermin. It is a sad fact that a river can only offer limited life-support systems. The man with his sights set on fishing for salmon, therefore, may consider sea trout as undesirable alien contenders, as mere juveniles, in a limited larder.

Sea trout—or salmon?

The anatomical differences between salmon and sea trout, although subtle, soon become evident. There is, of course, the undisputed scale count from the lateral line to the shoulder, but the tail is the main guide, and usually produces instant recognition. In salmon the tail is slightly forked and even when stretched still shows a concave shape. In sea trout the wrist of the tail is different and the tail itself is almost square or convex. All salmon may be picked up by the tail, but if an unidentified fish slides out of the hand it is a fair bet that it is a sea trout. To the trained eye, there are several other identifying factors, but for the novice the tail is the best guide.

Following a return of the young fish to the sea, many classic rivers will experience the first runs of mature sea trout. On the Spey, for instance, it is quite normal to find fresh sea trout as early as April. But the main runs may still be to come in May and June and it frequently happens that the bigger sea trout run the river earlier in the season. Not all these fish will be destined to spawn the following winter.

More nomadic than salmon

There is little doubt that most sea trout endeavour to spend some part of their year in freshwater. They are much more nomadic in their migrations than salmon. Indeed, only a very small percentage of salmon will ever make more than one freshwater migration. Many die as kelts and of those that do reach the sea again quickly, some fall to marine predators. Sea trout, however, have been known to migrate into freshwater as many as ten times, although there are few facts on the number of times successful spawning may take place.

names—finnock (and variants), whitling, herling, sewin, sprod, peal, among others— according to locality.

Why these small fish spend autumn and winter in their rivers of birth is not known. It is known that only few perform the reproductive act and that most come and go as the whim seizes them, either individually or in shoals; but that the longer they stay in freshwater the more their appearance and condition deteriorate. Many anglers seek them for sport and the table during early spring in the River Spey, for instance, which can be simply heaving with finnock up to the end of April. This seems to be the time when they make for the sea once more.

Finnock and herling

A usual weight for these fish is about 6–8oz, and so anglers may be forgiven for knocking them on the head. It is, however, difficult to establish the legality of this practice. Some anglers are of the opinion that the finnock, herling, or whatever, should be put back to migrate yet again to the sea, ultimately to

Sea trout

Mature sea trout weigh from 1lb to over 20lb but today it is quite an event to catch one over the 10lb mark. Scandinavia has produced some of the largest sea trout captured, while the Dovey in Wales has yielded at least two specimens of over 20lb. Until March 1969, the British rod-caught record was a fish of 22½lb caught by S R Dwight in 1946, coming from the River Frome in Dorset. Now, the record is open, with an acceptable minimum claim of 20lb.

Like salmon, the returning sea trout does not need to take food in freshwater, but, unlike salmon, does occasionally take food and seems to have a digestive mechanism adequate for this. But since sea trout do not seem to increase in length in freshwater, despite some feeding, they might be expected to suffer less from their stay there than salmon. The species, however, even maiden sea trout, do deteriorate after leaving the sea; and in many districts ripe fish at spawning lose as much weight for length as salmon.

Using up stored tissue and fat

There is little doubt, therefore, that the entire process of staying in freshwater calls upon the sea trout to use up much of its stored tissue and fat. Whatever food it might occasionally take, it certainly does not get sufficient to sustain it. Sea trout which have

Arthur Oglesby

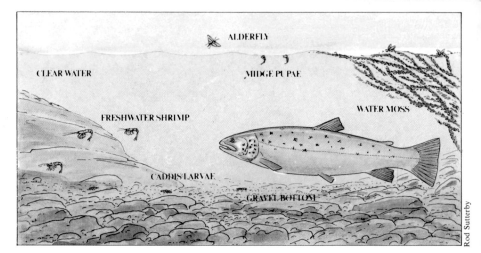

ALDERFLY

CLEAR WATER

MIDGE PUPAE

WATER MOSS

FRESHWATER SHRIMP

CADDIS LARVAE

GRAVEL BOTTOM

Rod Sutterby

350

---

run the river in April or May can be quite sorry-looking creatures by the end of September, and all sporting anglers will return such fish to the water with as little injury as possible.

On some rivers, of course, the sea trout do not begin to run until July or August. This can be a time when low water might frustrate easy passage up the river. In this respect sea trout are much more tenacious than salmon, and may frequently be seen moving through water barely sufficient to cover their backs.

Like salmon, the sea trout must have water of high purity. Sadly, suitable environments are continually being eroded and there are only a handful of worth while rivers in England today. Wales is better, but we look to Scotland for the majority of good rivers. Although more esteemed for its salmon fishing, the Spey is possibly the most prolific sea trout river in the United Kingdom. The Tweed gets good runs of big sea trout which few people ever seem to catch. The small rivers of the West Coast and the Isles abound with sea trout, but they are fickle and shy fish.

Superior to the salmon?

As a sporting fish, they are highly prized by anglers, many of whom are of the opinion that good sea trout are not only more sporting than salmon, but superior on the table. Unless the water is high and slightly coloured, the fish can be very difficult to catch in daylight. Night fishing with a fly is the epitome of sport, and on the classic streams it is the most practised method.

The sea trout, therefore, does not yet have to face the pressures now being made on salmon resources. With modest amounts of good husbandry, it seems to be a fish which can take reasonable care of itself, but it must never be seen casually as an indestructible resource. Unless something is done and done quickly, about the erosion of the suitable environment, the sea trout and the salmon may well pass into history as two of the greatest, but extinct, sporting fishes.

Arthur Oglesby

(Above left) Sea trout jumping, River Esk.
(Above) Dunbar Pool, on the Spey at Castle Grant.
(Left) The sea trout habitat is clear, pure water, fast and rich in small insects eaten when the fish is in the parr stage.
(Right) Natural food of the sea trout in freshwater is small insect life and crustaceans, while in the sea the species feeds on fish such as sandeel, pilchards and sprats.

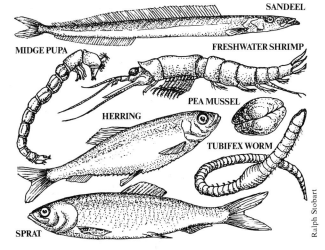

SANDEEL
MIDGE PUPA
FRESHWATER SHRIMP
PEA MUSSEL
HERRING
TUBIFEX WORM
SPRAT

Ralph Stobart

Trout rearing

During the early days of trout rearing, in the latter part of the 19th century, it was only the native brown trout which was reared, and all these were sold for restocking. Now, however, the accent is on the American rainbow trout because of its sporting qualities and the comparative ease with which it is reared. In recent times great advances have been made in the production of rainbow trout and in addition to restocking, the rainbow is becoming increasingly popular as a table fish.

The main difference between brown and rainbow trout, apart from their colour and shape, are growth rate, lifespan, and time of spawning. In the wild, native brown trout spawn during November, December or January, according to weather conditions and geographical location. There are two kinds of rainbow trout—one which spawns in the spring and one which spawns at about the same time as the brown trout. In captivity, rainbow trout can be induced to spawn at almost any time of year.

The methods of rearing trout are the same, irrespective of species, except that rainbow trout grow much more quickly than brown and have to be graded more often. They are not usually predatory when young, as are brown trout.

Conditions for breeding trout

Trout cannot be reared in any pit or pond, they must have an adequate supply of water of the correct chemical quality and temperature. It should be free from pollution, injurious metal salts with no silt or mud in suspension. Borehole water is usually preferred, but where river water has to be used, care must be taken to keep any silt away from eggs and young trout. Older fish are able to withstand a certain amount of mud or silt. The water used should be fully saturated with oxygen, and should be alkaline. A neutral pH value of between 7 and 8 is preferable, but slightly

acidic water may be used if no other is available. The most suitable water temperature is about 15°C or slightly lower. Very cold water will put trout off the feed and high temperatures may kill them.

Important stages in the life of a trout are: the eyed egg, the alevin, the fry and the yearling. At each of these stages, trout require very precise water flows and temperature ranges.

Brood fish are usually kept in a special stewpond, and some time before they are fully ripe they are transferred to holding tanks where they can easily be removed for

(Below) Typical earth-banked stewponds for trout rearing. The water must be free from pollution, saturated with oxygen, alkaline. Ideal temperature is 15°C (59°F).

(Above) A circular fry tank at Packington Fisheries hatchery cleaned out and ready for use. The automatic fry feeder dispenses pellets at regular intervals.

spawning. Eggs from hen fish are stripped into a clean bowl containing no water and are afterwards fertilized, by introducing milt from male fish. Hen fish are usually completely stripped of their ova, then returned to another pond to recover. Male fish, however, may be used several times. After the milt has been added, the eggs are gently stirred and clean water is added to the bowl. After a while, the excess milt is washed away with successive changes of water and the eggs are placed in a receptacle and covered with water.

Hatching the eggs

The newly fertilized or 'green' eggs will noticeably swell. They are then transferred to incubators, remaining there until they hatch. Care must be taken to ensure that the water temperature does not fluctuate while the eggs are incubating, otherwise they will die. Any unfertilized eggs must be removed immediately and all through the incubation period dead eggs must be taken from the incubator trays. This is called 'egg-picking' and is one of the most important jobs in trout rearing, for if any eggs become infected with fungus, the infection will rapidly spread throughout the tray.

On hatching, the little trout, known as alevins, have a yolk-sac attached to the abdomen. They feed on this for some time, and when it has been used up the fish are termed 'ready to feed fry'. This 'swim-up' stage is a very critical one in trout rearing because it is sometimes difficult to get the fry to take food.

At the swim-up stage the fry are usually transferred to fry tanks, which may be rectangular or circular and are usually made of either plastic or concrete. The important thing is to ensure that the water velocity is not too great. Care must be taken to check the water temperature, pH, filters and screens regularly. Until the fry have settled down, these checks must be done several times a day; once the fry have adjusted to the new tanks the checks must be done at least once a day.

Eric Birch

Trout rearing

In modern hatcheries fry are fed automatically with finely processed artificial food. Automatic feeders are made up of a hopper containing the food and a timing system which allows small quantities of food to fall on the water at regular intervals. It is essential to keep the fry tanks clear of faeces and uneaten food.

The fry remain in their tanks until they have outgrown them and then transferred to larger tanks or ponds. Here they may be fed either by hand or by machine. Automatic feeders used on ponds or larger tanks are much larger than those used on the fry tanks, but the system is the same. When the fry reach the yearling stage, they may be induced to use labour-saving devices known as 'self-feeders'.

These self-feeders may be mounted above tanks or allowed to float on specially designed, buoyant floats. This type of feeder relies on a pendulum positioned at one end in the food hopper, while the other protrudes into the water. Trout activate a nylon button at the end of the pendulum

(Above) Teeming trout fry in a circular tank. These small fish are fed either by hand or automatically. The water must be kept perfectly clean, clear of all uneaten food and well oxygenated. It is the most important aspect of trout rearing.
(Below) When they are large enough the trout are released into outdoor ponds. Here they can be fed by hand on pellets which supply a complete diet.

and food falls from the hopper into the water. This system avoids waste because the fish feed only when they are hungry.

Rainbow trout take more readily to self-feeders than brown trout and it is often necessary to feed the brown by hand or by automatic, pneumatic feeders which eject measured amounts of pellets at regular intervals.

Trout need protein, carbohydrates, minerals, fats and vitamins in their daily diet, and modern pellet feeds provide all that is necessary. Some pellets contain a very high proportion of protein, but for general restocking purposes about 40% is sufficient. All commercial pellet feeds are quite satisfactory and they are available in two main types. All fry pellets are of the sinking type, but for larger trout, floating pellets make the fish feed at the surface and it can easily be seen if the fish are taking their full ration.

The earth pond system

Many trout farms use the earth pond system which allows the trout to take a proportion of natural food. Snails, shrimps and other animals, such as caddis larvae, water beetles, midge larvae and those of pond and lake olives enter the ponds with the incoming water, particularly when this comes from a river or stream. This is an advantage because when the fish are released into angling waters they will be able to recognize their natural prey. If fed exclusively on pellets, they may take a little longer to become acclimatized to their new surroundings.

Any dead trout should be removed immediately from the stewpond or tank, otherwise fungus may spread through the whole stock. Healthy fish are able to throw off diseases, but the more they are crowded, the more likely they are to contract one of the many diseases to which they are susceptible.

Growth rates of brown and rainbow trout differ greatly. Browns grow comparatively slowly and continue to do so for 10 or more years in angling waters. But

Hungry trout operating a Grice and Young pendulum feeder. This avoids food wastage for the feeder only releases food when the nylon button of the pendulum is nudged by the fish.

Eric Birch

rainbows rarely live longer than five years, and in some waters the cocks do not survive their third year. This is due to their high metabolic rate: they use up all their energy during rapid growth. Without pushing them too much, brown trout can attain a size of 10in during their first year, though rainbows are able to grow to over 2½lb in the same period.

It is now possible to produce rainbow trout to double figure weights in two years by giving them plenty of space, an abundance of highly oxygenated water and as much food as they will eat. In ideal conditions they will eat at such a rate that their skin outgrow their scales and these stand out at right angles to their bodies for a short while.

The latest method of trout rearing is to employ floating cages in large lakes which solves the problem of eliminating waste products and also ensures an adequate supply of oxygen. Many fishing clubs and water authorities now employ this system because it is more efficient and cheaper than other methods.

Trout records

Stuart Linnell

A once-famous angling magazine, the 'Fishing Gazette', published between 1877-1966, contains many accounts of the capture of huge trout. On one occasion there was an upsurge of large estuarine 'bull' trout in Scotland (individual weights of more than 20 lb were claimed). Occasionally, giant migratory trout from the Kentish Stour were mentioned, the famous 'Fordwich Trout' of Izaak Walton's day. Between the two World Wars, a group of British fly fishermen discovered the huge sea-trout of Sweden's River Em, specimens of which exceeded 30 lb. New Zealand's Lake Taupo produced massive rainbows and even English chalk streams like the Kennet yielded the occasional trout of more than 10lb.

One thing in common

All these great trout had one thing in common: they had grown large by natural feeding. The migratory trout of the Stour and Em, for instance, fed on shoals of small fish in the shallow bays at the mouths of their parent rivers. The capture of such wild fish could be envied as an exceptional angling feat, as they required great angling skill.

A new development in trout fishing came with the establishment of the big reservoirs. When land is newly flooded the food is particularly rich, so trout grow quickly. But they are artificially introduced, and as the big lake settles down, the food supply diminishes

and competition with other species, notably coarse fish, increases. There is, therefore, a temptation to grow the fish to greater weights in breeding ponds before releasing them into the lake, in order to compensate for these two disadvantages. Even so, because the lakes are not often restocked, and because of the large unfished natural reserves of some lakes and the ability of the trout to spread out, there is still a degree of wildness in reservoir fish. The capture of large trout from such waters is a notable achievement.

But a more recent development in trout fishing is a cause of some disquiet so far as sporting standards are concerned. This has to do with the release of fish, which have already been raised to a large size by concentrated feeding techniques, into small areas of confined water. They do not have enough space to avoid being caught within a short time after their introduction, and the situation becomes ethically questionable when one reads descriptions of the techniques employed to catch them. It seems as if it hardly matters what fly is used if, only hours before, a human has been the source of a pellet shower.

So the angler has a moral problem; obviously he wants to catch these big fish, but at the same time, knowing the confrontation is rather artificial, he has to

(Left) Alan Pearson with the record rainbow trout. Caught in May 1977 at the Avington Fishery, Hants, it weighed 19½ It was taken with a Buff nymph on a size 10 hook and a 6lb b.s. leader. (Right) Netting a rainbow at Loch Avielochan, near Aviemore, in Scotland. The 15-acre loch is stocked every season with both brown and rainbow trout.

Bill Howes

convince himself that the apparently missing element of wildness is actually there. He also assumes that as not every fish can have come through the previous winter, those that did must have greater intelligence than other fish. But fish possess absolutely no intelligent reasoning powers, as any zoologist can prove. They do possess two qualities: an instinct for self-preservation in their native habitat, and the ability to be conditioned.

The justification?

The protection and food provided in the breeding ponds effectively conditions the fish to be more tame. Even though such fish are huge, the angler really knows that to hook one is a far less satisfying experience than that of a small boy who catches his first small roach or perch. So, to justify his action, the angler deceives himself and begins to believe in certain fallacies. One of these is that, when released, rainbow trout become wild almost immediately after having sampled a natural insect or two. Stocking a fishery himself, the author knows that, even as late as three weeks after their introduction, the stomachs of the trout are either empty or contain miscellaneous rubbish. The trout can be seen roaming around in shoals, desperately trying to find the daily ration of food pellets to which they were accustomed. Driven by sheer hunger, they will seize almost anything that moves,

be it an unrepresentative lure or a close imitation of a fly.

Friend—then enemy

It has been said that such fish, becoming wild almost immediately, recognise Man as an enemy. But perhaps only an hour or two before their release he has been the friendly provider of food! Newly released rainbows in chalk streams, where they can easily be seen, take up the most unprotected positions. It is some time before they react warily to people passing. Of course, many such fish are taken within minutes of stocking and are given neither time nor space to become natural feeders.

If you believed most anglers you would become convinced that every good fish taken had wintered through from the previous year, maybe with someone's fly in its mouth to prove it. But taking into account the lack of space and the weight of the fish, plus the short life span of the rainbow trout, most of these claims can be disproved.

The author's own experience highlights the truth that large rainbow trout, stocked in enormous numbers in small areas of water, are extremely easy to catch. A small chalk stream I fish in Normandy flows through a rainbow trout farm, the owner of which is successful in raising fish to great weights. Unfortunately, the bank of one of his pens broke down and a shoal of the bigger fish escaped into the river. I was dry fly fishing with a new, ultra-light carbon rod and spent a short time catching these fish. Every time a fly passed over, a fish took it. It was then just a question of time, with the rod bent almost to breaking point, to pull in the trout, unhook it and let it go. The pleasure soon palled, and we moved upstream to fish for the wild half-pound brown trout that the river produces. These 'brownies' are quite different from rainbows. They tend to live in the hardest places to fish, protected by stones or overhanging branches. They resist the 'wrong fly'. In short, they are a more challenging quarry than the largest rainbow.

Problem of perspective

It is difficult to place these new trout conditions into perspective. No criticism of those who grow the fish is implied, since trout fishing would simply not be available to most anglers if they were only able to fish for wild trout. The new trout also provide a new type of fishing which many people enjoy, even though it is expensive and less skilled than fishing for wild trout. But the automatic acceptance of such fish into the record lists should not be allowed. Press sensationalization of recent catches does nothing to inform the public. Because wild fish, similar in size, have been caught in the past, people simple assume that another big wild fish has been caught by an angler. They do not know what conditions were which enabled the angler to take it.

All record fish claims should arise from similar conditions, that is, a wild fish should be caught in its natural habitat. After all, no sea specimen hunter has the opportunity of seeking a cultured prey in an enclosed area. With very few exceptions, too, coarse fish are wild fish from wild places. Even reservoir trout have the opportunity for some natural growth, because of the infrequent stocking periods and wide dispersal areas.

The 'instant rainbow'

Fly fishing has developed as a sport dependent on a balanced mixture of physical and intellectual skills. Those who enjoy using these skills are now becoming dissatisfied with the growing artificiality of certain aspects of stillwater trout fishing. Although we have have not yet adopted the American term 'dude fishery' to describe fishing conditions, knowledgeable anglers are using their common sense and experience to put into perspective the record claims of captors of the 'instant rainbow'.

(Some years ago a situation arose concerning the brown trout. The record committee made a separate class of trout record, known as the 'cultivated' variety. As cultivated trout were hand-reared they would grow larger than wild fish. But the idea was dropped. Will this new development lead to a similar move? 'Wild' rainbow records could reflect the naturally growing fish, while the selectively bred giants would be listed separately. Editor.)

Fly fishing for trout has a pleasure all of its own. It is a combination of expertise and cunning, required at every stage of fishing, whether it is wet fly or dry fly. From casting and controlling the fly, to hooking and playing the fish, and finally landing it successfully, the angler must be always alert and match the legend of the trout as a furtive yet intelligent creature.

Ardea Photographics

Salmon disease

The salmon population of our rivers is seriously affected at present by a widespread epidemic of a disease now known as ulcerative dermal necrosis (UDN). As the name implies, the disease causes ulcers in the skin which result in the tissue dying. Fish with UDN are recognized by the greyish-white patches of fungus which usually appear first on the head and afterwards along the back and sides of infected fish. The fungus is, however, a secondary infection which takes hold after the primary infection—probably a virus—has struck.

Secondary infection

To the average angler, fungus is just fungus, and there is a tendency to report that fish are suffering from UDN because of the outward appearance of patches of greyish-white growth. But there are many associated diseases that have similar symptoms and have species of the common *Saprolegnia* fungus growth as a secondary infection. UDN is an ambiguous title given to an unspecified disease. It would be better called

simply the 'salmon disease', and when the research workers have had another few years in which to experiment, we shall perhaps be given more specific titles for the various ulcerative fish diseases.

Salmon appear to contract UDN while out at sea, and it is only when they enter freshwater that the fungus, *Saprolegnia*, takes hold. The worst time for infection is during the colder months of autumn and spring, but, unfortunately, hot weather does nothing to 'burn out' an epidemic.

At first it was thought that the disease was caused by a bacteria called *Cytophaga columnaris*, since this was isolated from affected fish, but exhaustive tests did not confirm this and eventually the disease was given the name 'ulcerative dermal necrosis'.

It is the secondary infection that kills the fish, and not the disease itself. In the few instances where no secondary infection has occurred, affected fish have recovered.

On its own, scientists were unable to grow the unknown fungus found on affected fish,

(Left) The diseased patches on the snout of this salmon from the River Lune are typical of UDN. It is the head which develops those dirty white patches of fungus which eventually spread to the rest of the fish's body.
(Right) Again, it is the head of the fish which has been attacked. This brown trout has had the scores and fungus removed. While some coarse species, including roach, seem to be affected it is not yet certain whether UDN is responsible or a related form of it can attack coarse species.

Arthur Oglesby

but it readily grew in association with *Cytophaga columnaris*. This suggested that the disease may be the result of an association of two organisms and not a single one as previously thought.

Research has produced a great deal of evidence to suggest that UDN is infectious, but so far there is no firm scientific proof. One fact has emerged out of all the research: the current outbreak did not spread by infection but was rather a simultaneous outbreak in many places.

UDN epidemic

The present epidemic of UDN began in the south and south-west of Ireland during the autumn of 1964. In the spring of 1966 it appeared in English salmon rivers and was later confirmed in Welsh and Scottish game fishing rivers.

The disease spread rapidly, and in 1968 outbreaks among mature trout were confirmed in many reservoir fisheries, some of which were fed from rivers where UDN occurred. But other fisheries had no direct link with affected waters.

UDN was confirmed in Germany during 1972 and, in 1976, broke out in the Baltic, affecting salmon and sea trout. Also in 1976 a report from Scandinavia stated that an outbreak of what appeared to be UDN was affecting grayling, huchen (Danube salmon), brown and brook trout, pike and whitefish. Starting in spring, it quickly spread.

When it became obvious that the disease might become a serious threat to game fish all over the British Isles, steps were taken to try to restrict its spread by encouraging anglers to disinfect tackle, clothing and boats, although no one quite knew what they were trying to protect against. Serious attempts to contain the disease gradually diminished as the spread continued. Anglers had to live with the fact that UDN was here and it looked like staying for some time.

The immense losses of salmon from UDN do not seem to have placed the species in danger of extinction, because infected fish have been able to spawn successfully, even though research suggests that the mortality rate of salmon from infected parents is much greater than those of clean fish.

Apparently UDN does not affect coarse fish, and yet coarse fish stocks, particularly perch, have been severely affected by a similar disease. Roach have also suffered losses and the cause still remains a mystery.

Eric Birch

Salmon rods

Salmon rods may be divided into two main types; spinning rods and fly rods.

Spinning rods

The choice in spinning rods depends on the size of the water being fished. For instance, to spin for salmon in small rivers with lures of up to an ounce in weight an 8-9ft rod coupled to a medium-sized fixed-spool reel or baby multiplier holding at least 100 yards of 10-12lb line is ideal.

Those which have a trigger-finger grip at the bottom of the reel fitting are designed specifically to be used in conjunction with a multiplier reel – they cannot double up to be used with fixed-spool reels. Therefore, if you wish to use both reels on the same rod, you must first ensure it has a standard reel fitting.

While budget-priced spinning rods are still available in hollow fibreglass, carbon-fibre is more responsive and much lighter which makes casting and retrieving all day more enjoyable.

The rod should have a tip-action with some backbone in the butt section to control powerful fish like salmon and be fitted with a screw-reel fitting.

The best rod rings for spinning have hardened centres to minimize line wear. Modest-priced rods will have rings which have aluminium-oxide centres. Top-of-the-range, slim-profile carbon-spinning rods come fitted with silicon-carbide rings which are the very best available. On rods used with multiplier reels which sit on top there needs to be plenty of rings to ensure the line

Irish Tourist Board

(Above) A prime Irish salmon spinning and fixed-spool combination.

(Right) Modern 13-15ft carbon-fibre salmon fly rods and reels.

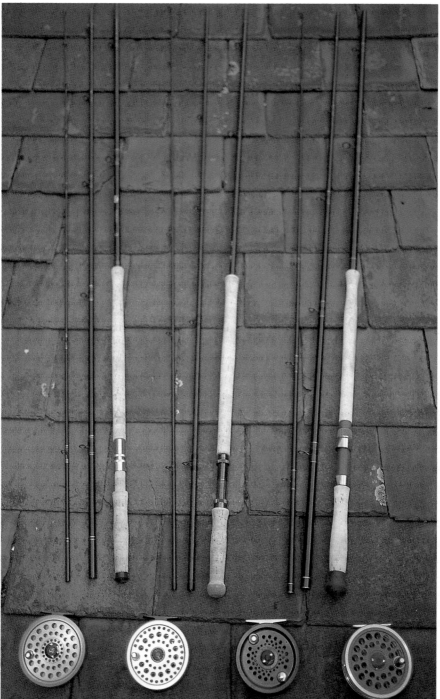

John Wilson

Salmon rods

(Left) In terms of salmon rods, this spinning outfit, in use at Ballynahinch, Co Galway, is quite short. It would be differcult to control a large salmon with its rod.
(Right) The angler here is holding the rod well up in order to keep in touch with his fish. Any slackness of line at this stage could lead to the fish jumping off the hook and being lost.
(Far right) Having beached his salmon, caught from the Lune at Newton, Don Oliver is using the correct tailing grip to pick the fish up.

Irish Tourist Board

follows the curvature of a heavily bent rod without making contact with it.

For larger rivers a length of between 10-11ft is required with the reel fitting set reasonably high up the handle for long, double-handed casting. Top-quality big river carbon spinning rods should be capable of handling a variety of lures of at least up to 2oz and lines of the 12-20lb test bracket.

Most manufacturers of quality rods suggest a range of line strengths and line weights (written just above the handle) for their salmon-spinning rods, so be sure to choose one that fits your purpose.

Avoid sloppy, inexpensive rods which may seem powerful enough in the tackle shop because, when a sizeable salmon heads off downstream with the help of a strong current, the chances of ever being able to bring the salmon back up again could be limited. This is fine, provided either the bank is clear and you can get below the fish, or you have a sturdy rod.

Most long (10-11ft) spinning rods also double up nicely for both worm and shrimp fishing. When presenting the shrimp, on float tackle especially, a long rod is necessary for close control of the float as the bait is trotted down the run, otherwise bites could be missed. Most salmon-spinning rods double as pike rods and are excellent for spinning in saltwater from the rocks for species like bass and pollack.

Fly rods

When fly fishing for grilse in small rivers necessitating relatively short casts of less than 10-12 yards, using small patterns of salmon flies, a single-handed 9½ -10½ft carbon rod capable of dealing with lines in the sizes 8-10 range is ideal. Many such rods are wrapped in 'Kevlar' for its shock-absorbing qualities which ensures the blank does not fracture under extreme strain. To accompany the rod a large 'trout'-sized wide reel is required that will comfortably hold 100 yards of backing in addition to a full 30 or 35 yard fly line.

This outfit should prove equal to the salmon encountered in all small waters, plus of course sea trout and when long-distance casting from the shoreline and from a boat when reservoir trout fishing.

Such a rod will also double up for catching mullet in wide river estuaries and even tropical saltwater sportsfish like the fast-

Arthur Oglesby

moving bone fish which can show a surprising turn of speed over shallow flats. It is
probably the most useful and versatile of all
fly rods.

Double handed fly rods vary from 12-16ft
long and top-quality models are also
produced in lightweight carbon-fibre. The
ideal all-round length would be a 14-footer
capable of handling lines in the 10-11 size,
but much depends on the sheer size of the
particular river being fished.

Not only have carbon-fibre double-
handed fly rods incredible strength, their
slimline profile is a great advantage in
windy conditions for slicing through air-
resistance and placing the fly accurately.

Most double-handed rods have a heavy
action that may be felt right through from
the comparatively thickish tip to the butt. A
tip with this fairly rigid action is required
(unlike most trout rods) because of the need
to mend the line or straighten it out. This
need arises when the strength of the current
varies at different points across the stream
and the line is pulled into a bow shape as it is
carried downstream. This in turn carries the
fly back across the flow at an unnatural
angle, making it unacceptable to the salmon.

The fisherman must then roll the line to
'mend' it as the bow shape not only presents
the fly unfavourably but also lessens the
effectiveness of a strike should there be by
an odd chance, a take. A heavy-tipped rod
enables a weighty length of double-tapered
line to be lifted off the water and 'mended'
with reasonable ease.

Whilst the principal material for salmon
fly rods is now hollow carbon-fibre there are
still many built-cane rods in use. Some
salmon fishermen actually prefer a rod of
built cane, particularly a model with spliced
joints. These are so called because the
sections are spliced together with binding
tape, forming an incredibly strong joint. The
spliced joint is of great value in Spey
casting, a form of roll cast employed when
obstructions behind the angler prevent a
normal back cast.

The Spey-style expert exerts a twisting
force along the rod but spliced joints resist
the tendency to twist and become loose, so
losing ring alignment. This is indeed a
problem with most modern spigot-jointed
double-handed salmon fly rods and
constantly checking the joints throughout a
long day's casting is imperative.

Reservoir rods

The purpose of a rod in any type of fishing is to act as a guide for the line and as a spring for hard-fighting fish. But in fly fishing the rod must also be supple enough to cast a fly which is virtually weightless. The line is weighted according to the type of fishing it is purposefully designed for and so rods will differ according to the weight of line they can carry. A suitable rod is vital for reservoir fly fishing.

Fly fishing for trout in both concrete or brick bowl and flooded valley-dammed reservoirs has become one of the most, if not the most, popular choice amongst British game fishermen. Huge numbers of anglers now regularly fish these prolific waters from the banks and from boats. And reservoir fly fishing demands two basic types of rod; a two-piece distance casting rod of 9½-10ft powerful enough to cast efficiently from both shore and boat into the high winds often present on reservoirs, and a three-piece (two-piece models are available) 'Loch-style' rod of between 10½-12ft with an easy action for boat fishing. Without question, no one rod can perform both functions, so a choice has to be made between the two distinct actions.

At a pinch, however, should you be limited to travelling space, or only the very occasional outing, telescopic fly rods, or better still, 4 to 6 piece rods suitable for general fly fishing are available. Deluxe models with positive actions made from lightweight reinforced carbon fibre are even available from a few of the top manufacturers. At a price. Nethertheless, such rods should only be considered for reservoir work as a last resort, because the decision will always be between a casting tool or an easy action Loch-style fly rod.

Distance-casting rods

The best material by far for ease of casting, due to its quick return and narrow profile (compared to hollow fibre-glass) is

Carbon-fibre fly rods. The Farnborough, for reservoirs, is second from bottom.

lightweight carbon fibre and many specialist 'reservoir tools' are now wrapped in an extra braid of carbon, or with 'Kevlar' to make them less prone to fracture from the rigours of single- and double-haul casting. A reservoir 'distance rod' should be capable of casting weight forward and shooting head lines in sizes 8 - 10 but still allow the angler to enjoy the fight of all sized trout. The best choice is a tip-actioned rod. To alleviate line wear and aid casting, top-of-the-range models have single leg rings with silicon-carbide centres. But even budget-priced fly rods these days come fitted with single leg Fuji-type rings with hard-wearing, non-grooving aluminium-oxide centres.

Base your choice of distance-casting rod on sound advice from an experienced tackle dealer who goes reservoir fishing himself and you won't go wrong.

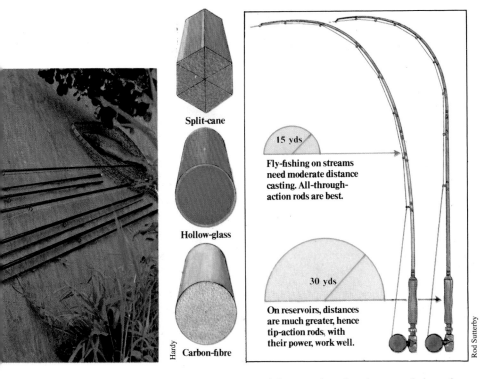

Split-cane

Hollow-glass

Hardy   Carbon-fibre

15 yds

Fly-fishing on streams
need moderate distance
casting. All-through-
action rods are best.

30 yds

On reservoirs, distances
are much greater, hence
tip-action rods, with
their power, work well.

Rod Sutterby

Loch-style rods

The same applies in choosing a suitable rod for Loch-style drift fishing, where long casting is not required. The line simply needs to be picked up once the team of flies have been retrieved and laid down again in one easy movement, ahead of the boat, shooting a few yards of retrieved line in the process. Powerful casting is simply not required which is why much lighter double taper lines in sizes 4 - 7 are used for this technique and comparatively longer rods with an easy 'forgiving' all-through action. Though old-fashioned and rather heavier than carbon-fibre, three-piece built cane 'Loch style' rods are still seen in use on many reservoirs. Their owners would no doubt insist that a cane rod lays the line down better, especially in windy conditions.

The majority of Loch-style fishermen however use three-piece carbon rods which are extremely light and a joy to use. Some manufacturers offer a choice between modern single leg and the more traditional stainless steel snake rings on their carbon Loch-style models. There is little to choose between the cork handles and screw fittings on modern fly rods.

Top-of-the-range models usually have either gun smoke Fuji-type, satin finish or even rosewood screw reel fittings, but this is purely cosmetic. Choice of the rod should not be decided upon by window dressing. Its most important asset is its action.

However, a useful addition that many manufacturers make to certain models of their Loch-style rods, is a push-in or screw-in, 4-5in extension handle. These are cork-covered and quickly convert the rod's butt for double-handed casting.

As reservoir fishing revolves around messing about in boats and working along gravel or concrete banking, protecting your rods is of paramount importance. A pair of rods will easily slip inside the rigid plastic (3 in dia) tubes sold in tackle shops, which are available in lenghts to 6ft and can be cut down to the desired size with a hacksaw.

Brook rods

Fly fishing in brooks and small rivers places a premium on accurate casting at short range. This is the basis of all brook fishing, but when selecting your rod it is important to consider the differences between brooks.

A brook running over flat country, or, if on hilly ground, with low banks, can be fished best with a short flexible rod. The shorter the rod (within reason) the more line will be in the air when casting, flexing the rod better and producing greater casting accuracy. A good choice would be a 6½-7½ft rod, designed to carry a No. 4 or No. 5 line.

This is the kind of rod usually recommended for fishing small rivers and brooks, but on water with either high, steep banks, or trees and bushes that impede the back-cast it may impose a severe handicap.

In such circumstances it may be preferable to use a much longer rod of 9ft or so, to keep the back-cast above the obstructions, or, if it is flexible as it ought to be, to permit easy, accurate casting where no back-cast is possible, however high the line is thrown.

Matters are sometimes complicated by the fact that quite small brooks, capable of naturally producing trout of only modest size, are nowadays stocked with much bigger fish. No great problem exists if the banks are clear and the stream is relatively free from obstructions, but if there are bridges, culverts and bankside trees or bushes which prevent the angler from following a hooked fish up and down the stream, then stronger tackle will be necessary.

This tackle includes a more powerful rod, which, in conjunction with a strong leader, allows the angler to put more pressure on a big fish, stopping it before it goes through a culvert, or too far past a bankside tree, beyond which the angler cannot follow.

Heavy line

This poses a problem; the powerful rod is less able to throw an accurate short line. Some compromise is necessary. This involves using a heavier fly line than would normally be chosen to fish a small water in order to flex the more powerful rod, and also choosing a rod in a material that is more tolerant of under-loading. Split cane and carbon-fibre fall into this category, fibreglass does not.

Some small streams run through tunnels of trees and can only be fished by wading, using a very short rod. In this situation it is best to use the top section of a 9ft split cane rod plugged into a separate handle, making a rod with a total length of about 5½ft.

Other brooks are so narrow that, except in a few places, casting is impossible and all the angler can do is to lower a fly straight down or, if he uses a leaded pattern, swing it like a

A small stream, the River Teise, in Kent. On this day there had been a drop in water level, giving very coloured conditions. So well-known all-rounder Geoffrey Bucknall is using the wet fly fished just below the surface on a slow-sinking line. The trout from this rich little brook come well if they reach a pound in weight.

Bill Howes

369

pendulum to the place where he wants it to drop. Paradoxically, this calls for quite a long rod, 9ft at least, and preferably longer still, to allow the angler to keep well back from the water and avoid scaring the trout. In such waters it is necessary to use quite a short leader, often as short as 3-4ft, otherwise the weight of the fly line will pull the fly up to the tip ring of the rod directly it is released. In places where the brook widens and proper casting is possible, the leader can be lengthened to the usual 6-7½ft.

Dense bushes

On a stream with very dense bushes, where fishing is only possible by poking the rod through branches and lowering the fly, the only answer is to use the longer rod and a level nylon monofilament leader approximately twice as long as the rod. This allows a leader fly to be drawn up to within ½in of the tip ring while the rod is pushed through the branches, after which the nylon is paid out, allowing the fly to fall into the water.

Before embarking upon this procedure, it is sensible to decide how a fish is to be landed if one is hooked. If it is small enough, it can be hauled up to the tip ring, but if it is too big for that, a landing net will be necessary and unless it can be worked through the jungle to where the trout can be netted, the whole operation is impossible to bring to a satisfactory conclusion.

Whatever kind of brook one intends to fish, it will almost certainly include at least some parts where, for one reason or another, a normal overhead cast cannot be made. The chosen rod should therefore be capable of roll-casting easily and accurately. If it will not, it will prove a handicap to some extent on almost every water, and on some it will be almost useless.

It has to be remembered that it takes time and practice to obtain the best results from any rod. The fly fisherman whose experience has been confined to reservoirs, lakes and larger rivers where long casting is necessary, should practise with his brook tackle until he can roll-cast, throw a very high back-cast into a convenient gap and pull out a forward

cast at an angle to it, and even cast a line with a curve in it to put a fly round a corner.

When fishing small streams, the rod will often be nearer to the fish than in any other kind of fly fishing, so it is as well to avoid white or yellowish rods, and to remove the shine from others, either by rubbing the high-gloss varnish down with oil and pumice powder or applying an extra coat of matt varnish.

To sum up, there is no ideal rod for every sort of brook. You have to pick one, or perhaps more, to suit the water or waters you intend to fish. Do not make the mistake of thinking that cheap, poor-quality tackle is suitable for little waters. In fact, these are more demanding of quality and above all, versatility, than any other trout water.

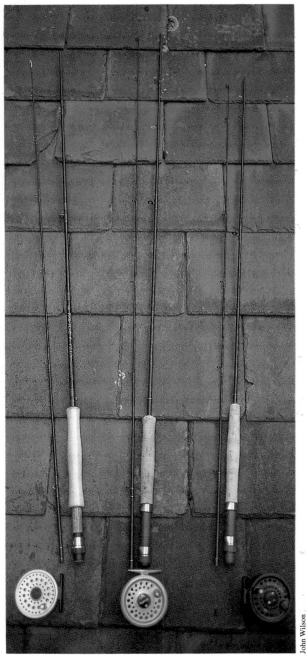

(Below) These short 6¹⁄₂-7¹⁄₂ft carbon-fibre brook rods are purely for small stream fishing with lines in sizes 3-5. Note the small lightweight reels which accompany them.

(Above) An angler worm-fishing on the River Towy, in Wales. Perhaps it does qualify for a better title than stream, but its pure, tumbling shallows offer the same attractions.

John Wilson

Fly reels

While all anglers agree that a casting reel must be properly designed if it is to work efficiently, many feel that the fly reel is a very unimportant tackle item. This may be because in fly fishing the reel has no influence on the cast, whereas when spinning the reel has a dominant effect on distance. But the fly reel is an item which warrants careful thought, because a fly reel often does more than a fixed-spool when playing a fish.

There are several reasons for this, and one is the faster runs made by game fish when compared with most coarse and saltwater species. Fly lines are thicker than monofilament so a fly reel empties quickly and as the line pile gets smaller so the spool turns faster. Under these circumstances, if the spool is a poor fit within the reel frame it will jam and the fish will be lost.

Three basic types of fly reel

Fly reels form three basic types: the single-action type where the drum moves one revolution for every turn of the handle (on a well-filled trout reel this recovers approximately 8in of line); the multiplier type where the drum performs perhaps two revolutions (thereby recovering approximately 16in of line) for every turn of the handle, and the clockwork or automatic type where the spool is driven by a spring. This spring winds itself up when you take line from the reel.

The basic function of any reel is to hold a sufficient quantity of line for the type of fishing being practised. Because fly fishing is not all the same, an angler practising one method of fishing may have a different reel requirement to another. Any of the three different types will cover all methods (providing the size, and therefore the line capacity, is right) but some methods may not fully utilize all the advantages of the more sophisticated reels. An angler fishing another method would be helped considerably by these additional features.

To illustrate this, imagine an angler fishing

(*Above*) *Two single-action fly reels, the Hardy Husky and Perfect models. The Perfect has the ball-bearing race and check and regulator mechanism exposed.*
(*Right*) *Basically, the fly reel must carry enough line for the angler to hook and play his fish. Reels in the Hardy Lightweight range are shown here.*

wet fly downstream on a small brook, where the trout average 8oz and where the record for the water is under 1lb. The angler makes short casts. He carries little slack in his hand and there is no need to give line when a fish is being played. Clearly, such a situation imposes minimal demands upon the reel.

A simple, single-action model will do all that is needed, for the reel does little beyond serving as a convenient line store. The multiplier and the automatic would also be suitable but in the situation described their more sophisticated features would not be fully used.

Problems on chalk streams

Now let us imagine a different situation. Our angler is fishing a dry fly on a southern chalk stream. The distances he will cast will be greater and sometimes he will switch quickly from short to long. Because he is casting upstream he will often have a lot of slack

line. The size of the fish varies from an average of 1lb, but there is a good chance of a three or even a five-pounder. Due to the clear water a fine leader is used, so when a hooked fish makes long runs our angler sometimes has to follow.

Advantage of the multiplier
Again the single-action reel could deal with this but anglers find that in this setting the quicker recovery afforded by a multiplier is an advantage. Other anglers may find that an automatic reel gives them still more advantages, for the automatic recovers line even faster than a multiplier. Close control can be vital, particularly when you have to get up off your knees, quickly wind up the slack and then follow a big fish down river.

Now visualize an angler wading the shore line of a large reservoir. He is casting about 25 yards and working his flies back by bunching the line in his left hand. When the flies are two-thirds of the way back a fish takes. The angler wants to get the fish under proper control as quickly as he can but has about 16 yards of slack line to deal with.

Again the single-action reel will cope but it will take so long to wind up the slack (over 60 turns) that some anglers ignore the reel completely and resort to stripping in the line to try to keep in touch with their fish. Many highly experienced anglers find this less than satisfactory, and again use either a multiplier or an automatic to wind up the slack to get them more quickly into tight-line control.

The reel's important function
These examples show the very different settings which exist in trout fly fishing. There are lots of others, but those described show not only that the reel has an important function, but also how the requirement varies.

The average single-action reel is around 3½in in diameter. With the aim of getting the fastest possible recovery, the spool is sometimes so narrow that you cannot get your finger between the flanges to control the spool when the fish runs. This can be a problem and is something to watch out for. To overcome this the spool edge is

Garcia Mitchell

(Above) In controlling a fish of this size the angler may need a reel that allows a quick recovery of line, but this single-action reel has done the job.
(Above right) The Hardy Flyweight takes a DT-4-F with no backing.
(Below) An advanced fly reel, the Garcia-Mitchell 710 Automatic, which takes a WF-6-F and 70 yards of backing.

Garcia Mitchell

sometimes swept up and over the outer edge of the reel frame. This 'exposed rim' makes a readily accessible braking surface but it is not without hazards.

The rim is vulnerable to bangs and knocks (aluminium is a soft material and dents easily). If the rim gets distorted it can bind on the frame and the reel will jam. Equally, the 'wrap over' flange is a trap for dirt and grit. One grain can make the reel stick.

The design of the multiplying fly reel is virtually the same as the single-action, except that the handle is not fastened direct to the spool but is connected by a train of gears. These gears impart the multiplying action where one turn of the handle drives the spool round more than once.

Advantage of high gear-ratio

To get the quickest possible recovery a high gear ratio would seem to offer the best advantage, but beware of reels that are over-geared. The highest practicable ratio is less than 2:1 for when you go higher (faster) the gears work against the angler to such a degree that it becomes almost impossible to turn the handle.

Most single-action and multiplying fly reels have a permanent click-check to stop the spool over-running. On the best reels the tension of this check is adjustable to suit the breaking strain of the leader being used. The adjustment is made either by a milled screw, an adjustment cam, or by moving the click spring across an adjusting rack. Each method works equally well. Another feature found on better-grade reels is the facility to change spools quickly, so affording the opportunity to switch lines (floating/sinking, and so on).

The automatic reel

The automatic reel has no handle and line is recovered by a spring. The spring is wound by the action of pulling line from the reel. When the angler wants to recover line he releases a trigger and the line is rapidly wound back (20 yards is rewound in approximately five seconds). Some anglers find the extra weight of the automatic a disadvantage, but the enthusiastic user will tell you that the greater control he has over hooked fish more than compensates for the extra weight.

Care is needed when purchasing an automatic as some of the reels available are too small and will barely handle the most popular size lines in use today. They accept a size 4 but will not handle a double taper 6 plus a reasonable quantity of backing. Again, make sure that you choose a reel with the facility to change the spool. This gives

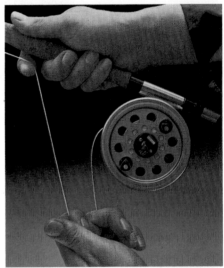

(Above) The Hardy Viscount 150 mounted on a Bruce and Walker salmon rod.
(Right) A Japanese fly reel, the Diawa 734, which can carry line up to AFMTA 9 (see Flylines chapter).
(Below right) A lightweight Ryobi magnesium fly reel – an ideal partner for today's carbon-fibre fly rods.

you all the advantages of having several reels when you want to switch from one type of line to another.

Any fly reel, whether it is a single-action, a multiplier or an automatic, should be fitted with a well-designed guard. Without this, the action of stripping out line will quickly wear a groove in the reel frame and soon both the reel and the line will be damaged.

There are so few moving parts in a fly reel that maintenance is hardly worth mentioning. An occasional spot of oil on the spool spindle takes care of the revolving parts and a liberal smear of grease on the check pawl is all that is needed. With the automatic, follow the maker's instructions regarding oiling.

Beware of dismantling the re-wind mechanism because if the spring is disturbed getting it back can be tricky. Better to leave it alone and let the maker's own Service Centre check it over every two or three years.

John Wilson

Fly lines

In the early days of fly fishing, lines were made of plaited horsehair. This was later replaced by a mixture of horsehair and silk, then by pure silk, plaited, tapered and dressed (impregnated and coated) with linseed oil.

The oil-dressed silk line was in universal use for three-quarters of a century, until it was replaced by the modern plastic-coated fly lines which consist of a plaited dacron core with a coating of polyvinyl chloride (PVC). For sinking fly lines, the PVC is impregnated with powdered metal, the quantity used determining the rate at which the line sinks.

Plasticizer

PVC is a hard material unless it contains a suitable 'plasticizer', which is introduced during manufacture. With time this is lost from the line, which then becomes hard and cracks. The loss of plasticizer is accelerated by heat and by greasing the line. Fortunately it can be restored by the use of special replasticizing grease such as 'Permaflex'.

A wide variety of line is now available, identified by a code known as the AFTM (American Federation of Tackle Manufacturers) system. This code tells you the kind of taper the line has, the weight of the first 30ft of the line, and whether the line is a floating or a sinking one.

So-called 'level lines' are of the same thickness all along their length; they are little used and their only merit is that they are cheap. They are designated by the letter L.

Double taper lines

'Double taper lines', designated DT, have both their ends tapered for more than 10-12ft, giving a fine end which falls more lightly on the water. The idea of a double taper is that when one end is worn, you can reverse the line on your reel and use the other end. These lines are usually 90ft long.

'Forward taper lines', otherwise known as 'weight-forward' (WF) resemble the first 30ft or so of a double taper with 40ft of very fine fly line attached. (In fact there is no actual attachment, both core and coating are continuous.) This allows more line to be 'shot' through the rings when casting. Recently, lines have been introduced with the first, heavier part longer than 30ft. These are called 'long belly lines'.

'Shooting heads' are similar in principle to 'forward taper lines', but instead of the fine shooting line being a continuation of the

Line Coding—Association of Fishing Tackle Manufacturers

Number	Weight (in Grains)		
1	60 (54–66)	**Abbreviations**	
2	80 (74–86)	**L** =Level Line	
3	100 (94–106)	**DT** =Double Taper	
4	120 (114–126)	**WF** =Weight Forward	
5	140 (134–146)	**ST** =Shooting Taper (or head)	
6	160 (152–168)	**F** =Floating	
7	185 (177–193)	**F/S** =Fast sinking, wet tip	
8	210 (202–218)	**VFS** =Very fast sinking	
9	240 (230–250)		
10	280 (270–290)	**Examples**	
11	330 (318–342)	**ST–8–S** =Shooting head No 8 Sinking	
12	380 (368–392)	**DT–6–F** =Double Taper No 6 Floating	

(Left) The AFTM coding for fly lines classifies lines according to weight, while abbreviations either side describe their type and performance.
(Right) When accuracy is demanded the double taper (A) is most suitable, while the forward taper (B) allows the angler to cast into wind. The shooting head (C) gives long-distance casting. Sinking lines (at foot) give varying sinking rates.

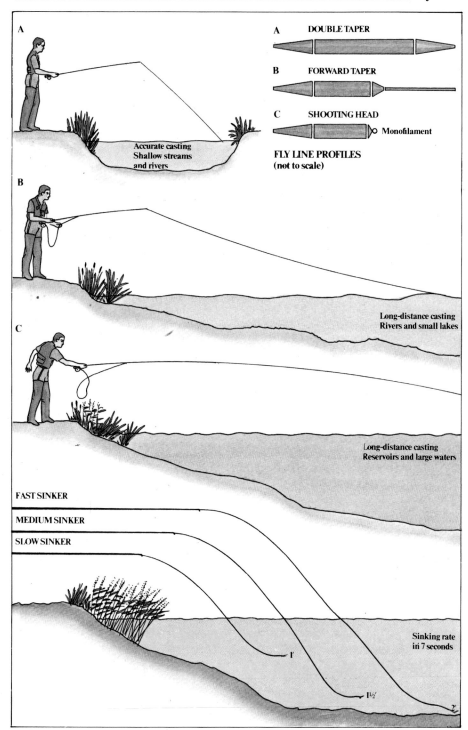

A

A   DOUBLE TAPER

B   FORWARD TAPER

C   SHOOTING HEAD

Monofilament

FLY LINE PROFILES
(not to scale)

Accurate casting
Shallow streams
and rivers

B

Long-distance casting
Rivers and small lakes

C

Long-distance casting
Reservoirs and large waters

FAST SINKER

MEDIUM SINKER

SLOW SINKER

Sinking rate
in 7 seconds

1′

1½′

2′

Fly lines

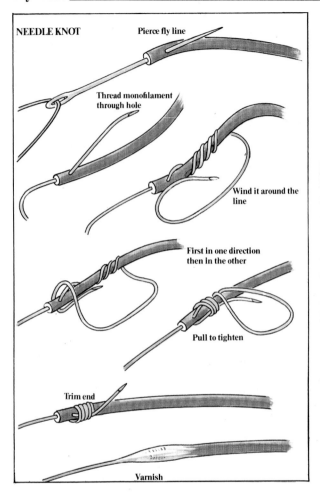

NEEDLE KNOT — Pierce fly line

Thread monofilament through hole

Wind it around the line

First in one direction then in the other

Pull to tighten

Trim end

Varnish

Knots in fly lines must not impede the passage of the line through the rod rings. Use the Needle knot (left) to join the line to the backing and the Double Grinner (right) to link the fly line with the leader.

PVC-coated fly line, it consists of nylon monofilament attached to the fly line by a special knot. This allows even more line to be 'shot' in casting, and as the fly line is usually cut from a 'double taper', shooting heads are much cheaper than either 'double' or 'forward taper lines'.

Shooting heads

Good tackle shops will usually sell halves of 'double tapers' for making shooting heads, which will need a further reduction in length, usually to 30-36ft.

All these lines can be of various floating or sinking qualities. There are floaters, slow sinkers, medium sinkers and fast sinkers, as well as floating lines with sinking tips. They

are all available in a range of weights, numbered 3 to 12. The more powerful your rod, the heavier the line it will need.

Let us look at some examples of coding. A line coded DT7F is a double-tapered floating line, weight No. 7. A WF9S is a forward taper sinking line, weight No. 9 and so on.

The reason why the weight number refers to the first 30ft or so of the line, is that 30ft is about as much as an average fly caster can control when he whips the line back and forth in false-casting. Good casters can handle more, but in practical fishing there is no advantage in having more than about 45ft, which only very good casters can handle.

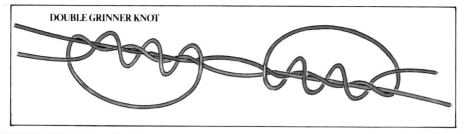

DOUBLE GRINNER KNOT

Bill Howes

lake and reservoir fishing when wet flies and lures of various kinds are needed. Slow sinkers sink at a rate of about 1ft in 7 seconds; medium sinkers 1ft in 5 seconds; fast sinkers, or as they are sometimes called, 'Hi-D' lines sink at about 1ft in 3 seconds. By counting the seconds after casting, you can decide how deep you allow your line to sink before starting the retrieve.

Backing line

For most kinds of fly fishing, your fly line needs backing; that is, some monofilament or braided, uncoated line is wound on to the reel first, and then the coated fly line is attached to it. Flattened monofilament of about 25lb b.s., or special monofilament sold for backing purposes, is cheaper than braided backing line, and easier to connect securely to the coated fly line.

Monofilament backing line is attached to the fly line with a needle-knot. The same knot can be used to tie a short piece of ordinary round-section monofilament to the other end of the fly line, to which in turn the tapered leader (cast) is knotted with a three-turn blood knot or a Double Grinner knot. All these knots are very secure, and have the advantage of being able to pass easily through the rod rings.

The pale-coloured lines are easier to see against dark reflections but harder to see against a ripple or a bright reflection. In certain conditions, such as in bright sunshine or against a dark background of rocks or trees, pale lines being false-casts in the air can scare fish. When lying on the water's surface all lines viewed from below look dark, regardless of their actual colour.

Fly lines are expensive, so it is sensible to take good care of them.

When you buy a rod you will find that its maker has specified what size line it will carry. Remember that this refers to 30ft of line in the air. If your rod has a recommendation of No. 7 line, that means it will work nicely when you are switching 30ft of line in the air.

Short casting

If the kind of fishing you do involves mainly short casting, and you will seldom have more than 24ft or so in the air, you will do better with the heavier No. 8 line. If, on the other hand, you often put 35ft or more into the air, then you should use a lighter line.

For dry fly and nymph fishing, floating lines are used; the sinking lines are mainly for

Wet fly lines

In the days when the only fly lines available to the game fisherman were of dressed silk, considerable time and trouble had to be expended to maintain or renew the oils and soft substances used in the dressing to ensure that the line remained waterproof and would continue to float on every outing.

This was particularly important for the correct presentation of the floating fly—the order of the day on very many fisheries, particularly the Southern chalk streams. In other parts of the country, fishing a sunken fly was perfectly acceptable, and many anglers discovered that they could work their sunken flies more effectively if the line dressing wore off, resulting in a waterlogging of the line and so, slow sinking.

Plastic-coated fly lines

In recent years the development of plastic-coated fly lines has proceeded apace, offering the angler a very wide choice of line profiles at varying densities. These have enabled him to fish efficiently in any water, no matter at what depth the trout (or salmon) might be feeding. The selection of the correct line profile is dictated by necessity. Where casting range is short, and delicacy and accuracy essential, the correct choice will be the double taper profile or the single taper lines offered by some manufacturers. After all, if one is talking about casting a maximum distance of some 15 yards, there seems little point in loading with a line twice that length.

The use of half a double taper line, attached to a backing of nylon monofilament or braided Terylene, reduces the size of reel needed, which, in turn, reduces the weight at the butt end of the rod, leading to more efficient and comfortable casting. It should not be overlooked that half a fly line costs proportionately less than a full one, whether one purchases from a cooperative dealer, or simply buys a full line and shares it with a friend.

Where longer casting is required, or the water is very deep or fast moving, the forward taper line is preferable. This has the casting weight at the forward end—hence the name—while the rest of the length is made up of fine 'running line'. Forward taper lines vary in length, ranging from the 30 yard standard up to 40 yards or more.

The shooting head

The shooting head is simply a variation upon the forward taper theme, whereby the actual fly line is restricted in length to that needed to give the rod the correct action— usually 7-12 yards. This short section is spliced to the backing line, generally of nylon monofilament, which can have a circular or oval cross-section. The latter section is far more resistant to tangling, which is possibly the only disadvantage of monofilament as a backing material. This particular set-up of shooting head and monofilament backing is ideally suited to such long-distance casting techniques as the 'double haul', enabling experienced practitioners to cast 50 yards or more with ease.

A further benefit is conferred upon the angler hooking a fish at long range, or in very deep water, namely that the fly line is, by its very nature, relatively thick, offering considerable resistance to the water. Thus, there is a risk when using a full line and playing a fish at long range that the pressure exerted by the water against the line can pull the hook clean out or even cause the leader to break. This risk is greatly minimized by the use of a short line and fine backing.

'Torpedo' and 'long belly'

Just as the shooting head is merely a variation upon the forward taper profile, so are there other variations, such as the 'torpedo' taper and the 'long belly', although the principle remains virtually the same in every case. That section of the line which carries the weight necessary to action the rod correctly and enable efficient casting is found towards one end of the line, so that the line is no longer reversible, unlike the double taper.

Manufacturers have developed their own specific descriptions for the line densities now produced, and in order not to confuse the issue for newcomers to fly fishing, it is probably as well to discuss individually the densities in common use, offering brief comments on the function of each.

Floating lines

Floating lines are ideal for the presentation of sunken flies which require little 'working' through the water, or require to be worked very close to the surface, either in stillwater or gently flowing rivers. The depth at which a sunken fly can be fished in stillwater is restricted by the length of the leader—on average some 3-4 yards. It takes quite a long time for an unweighted nymph to sink to that depth, and when trout are feeding close to the bed of a lake, it is common practice to use a dressing containing lead to speed the sink.

On the other hand, where the fish are feeding off the bottom, application of floatant to the leader will ensure that the nymph does not sink too deep. Sometimes, when the fish are feeding and sporting at the surface—and this is particularly common in reservoirs—a lure is fished on a floating line, stripped back so quickly that it skips across the surface, creating a definite wake.

Neutral density lines

Neutral density lines are the modern equivalent of the old silk line, requiring the application of a floatant if they are to be used as a floating line, or used untreated as a slow sinking line. The main advantage of this line was that a suitable length of the tip could be left ungreased, allowing it to sink, and enabling a sunk fly to be fished at greater depth than would be possible with a standard floater. This has now been superseded by the sink tip line.

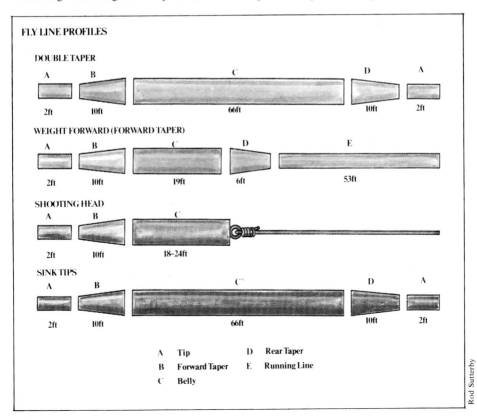

FLY LINE PROFILES

DOUBLE TAPER

| A | B | C | D | A |
| 2ft | 10ft | 66ft | 10ft | 2ft |

WEIGHT FORWARD (FORWARD TAPER)

| A | B | C | D | E |
| 2ft | 10ft | 19ft | 6ft | 53ft |

SHOOTING HEAD

| A | B | C |
| 2ft | 10ft | 18–24ft |

SINK TIPS

| A | B | C | D | A |
| 2ft | 10ft | 66ft | 10ft | 2ft |

A   Tip   D   Rear Taper
B   Forward Taper   E   Running Line
C   Belly

Rod Sutterby

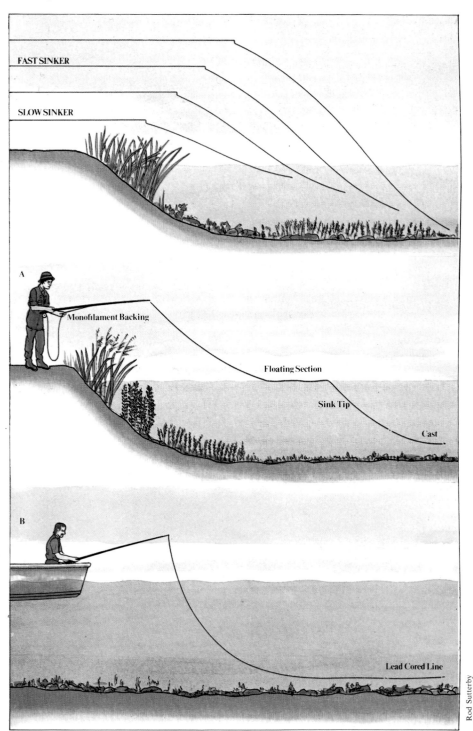

FAST SINKER

SLOW SINKER

A

Monofilament Backing

Floating Section

Sink Tip

Cast

B

Lead Cored Line

Rod Sutterby

Sink tip line

This is carefully manufactured so that the tip, which sinks at medium rate, is adequately supported by the floating body of the line. When fishing a nymph in deepish water, the 'take' is readily signalled by a movement of the floating section. It is equally efficient at indicating a take 'on the drop' (as the fly sinks), and with its use a faster retrieve of the nymph, fly or lure is possible than with the full floating line, because the pattern in use will not rise to the surface as readily as with the floater. This type of line can be very effective in deeper, or medium-flowing rivers, where it is important that depth is achieved quickly and maintained, or in stillwaters where the margins are full of snags which would tend to foul a full sinker. Some anglers claim to find difficulty in casting a sink tip line because of the imbalance between the dense tip and the less dense body, but this can usually be overcome by practice.

Slow sinking lines

With slow sinking lines, the term 'slow' can vary in meaning from manufacturer to manufacturer, because there has never been standardization of terms in this context, but matters seem to be improving, with many firms now offering a full range of densities, so that if a slow sinker is purchased from a range which includes medium and fast sinkers the angler is on safe ground.

The use of a slow sinker does not greatly differ from that of a sink tip, in that it can be used to take fish 'on the drop', or at slow to medium speed retrieve in stillwaters, and in the medium-running or deeper rivers. Nymphs can be fished on slow sinkers, but more commonly the larger wet flies and lures are used. The take of a fish is signalled, as with all sinking lines, by that familiar tug transmitted to the retrieving hand.

Medium sinking lines

Medium sinkers, as may be expected, sink faster than the slow sinkers, and are therefore more suited to deeper or faster-flowing water, and to faster than medium speed retrieves. However, with maximum speed lure stripping, the lure itself will rise very close to the surface, which can be an advantage when the fish are working in the upper levels but demand a fast moving lure which does not break the surface.

Fast sinking lines

Fast sinkers enable fast working of a fly in deep water and ensure that no matter how fast the retrieve, the lure will be unlikely to rise above midwater. Obviously they are well suited to the fast-flowing rivers where the trout or salmon are taking fairly deep.

Very fast sinking lines

Very fast sinkers are fairly specialized lines, often carrying lead in the core. By their nature they are ideal for the very deepest reservoirs, lakes and lochs where the quarry is feeding deep, and where it is important that a lure stripped quickly does not rise much above the bottom. Similarly, they are ideal for the biggest, fastest-flowing rivers, enabling the angler to remain in close touch with his fly throughout every cast. In a big stillwater where the bed snags the fly regularly on slower retrieves, it is a useful dodge to shorten the leader, and attach a dressing incorporating buoyancy material, such as Ethafoam, so that the fly floats up off the bottom clear of the snags, allowing retrieval to be slowed right down.

Lead-cored lines

There is one other type of line coming into use for fishing the deepest reservoirs and lakes—the level lead-cored line, without doubt the fastest sinker of all. This is not used for normal sunken fly fishing, but for trolling behind a boat which may be drifting, or propelled by oars or even a motor, depending upon local rules and regulations.

The purpose of the exercise is to drag the largest size of lure at a steady speed across the bottom, in the hope of attracting those very large trout which have adopted a bottom-feeding existence. It could be argued that this is not true fly fishing, being merely a minor variation on spinning tactics, but the fact is that a form of fly is being used, and so it really is a branch of fly fishing, although unorthodox.

Leaders

A fly is not attached direct to the fly line as the line's bulk would frighten off fish, and so a thinner line, the leader, joins the fly to the reel line. The *leader* is where the action is. The *point*, at the end of the leader, is where the action starts. Too thick a point and fish shy off or take short. Too fine, and the action is dead in seconds when leader and point part company. With a fish on, the leader and point must withstand every surge of its muscle-packed body, fins and tail; every slash of a leaping fish jerking its head to throw the hook. It must survive the hook twisting and wrenching in its nylon-knot socket, stretching and recoiling to absorb shocks before they hit the rod tip, and certainly before the angler reacts.

All this is expected of a piece of nylon some 0.15mm in diameter if you are using a 3lb b.s. point. At 4lb the point is still only 0.18mm, and even a 7lb point has a diameter of only 0.225mm.

Penny a point

A hundred yards of good quality nylon costs about £1.50. A point costs about a penny, and if you tie your own leaders, they cost between 60p and 70p. What is the purpose of £100-worth of carbon fibre rod and magnesium reel if a pennyworth of nylon fails? There is no sense in using last year's nylon or leftover leaders.

Above all it is important to change a point or leader whenever there is reason to doubt it. If it kinks, twists, necks or gathers a wind knot, take no chances—get rid of it.

Most leaders are between 9 and 15ft long from butt to point. A tapered leader is usually composed of many pieces of nylon, each with a progressively smaller diameter and joined together with knots. One or several droppers (flies set above the terminal or point fly) may be attached to this by more knots. With so many knots, you must be utterly confident of your knotsmanship. Alternatively, you can rely on someone else's

and buy made-up leaders. Most competent fishermen prefer to tie their own.

Use knots in which you have faith. The ordinary dropper knot will not let you down, but it is a bit tricky to tie, especially at the waterside. If you have trouble with it, use the water knot, which is easy to make. Many people tie this latter knot with as many as a dozen turns, but four are adequate.

Knotless tapers

An expensive alternative is to use manufactured knotless tapers, either for the whole leader or just for the tail end. These tapers turn over sweetly, reduce the risk of tangles during casting in gusty weather, and are available in a variety of sizes. Altogether they are excellent—but you cannot buy them cheaply.

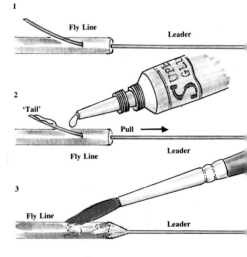

ALTERNATIVE TO NEEDLE KNOT

1

Fly Line

Leader

2

'Tail'

Pull →

Fly Line   Leader

3

Fly Line   Leader

RESERVOIR LEADER FOR SINGLE FLY OR LURE

Fly Line   Level Nylon (approx 0.022in)

'Super Glue' splice   12in   3-Turn Blood Knot

If you make your own leaders, a half-dozen 100-yard spools of different breaking strains are all you need for a season. Breaking strains of 12, 10, 8, 6 and 4lb should be an adequate range. Store the spools in a light-proof box to prevent deterioration and make up a couple of dozen leaders at a sitting. These can then be stored in marked envelopes in your tackle bag for selection at the waterside.

Spare line for points

Points have to be renewed occasionally on the bank, however. Carry a 50-yard spool of 3–7lb b.s. line (whatever you use) in your tackle bag for this purpose.

Opinions differ widely both about whether a leader should be tapered or not, and, if tapered, on how to taper it. Many successful reservoir anglers regularly fish simple 10–14ft level (untapered) lengths of 6lb or 7lb nylon. Others go to great trouble to taper their casts with six or seven lengths of nylon

(Left) How to make a Super Glue splice.
(Below) The efficient plastic cast connector.
(At foot) Dimensions of a reservoir leader.

1. Having perforated fly line (left) thread leader butt through.

2. Apply small amount of 'Super Glue 3' to tail. Without delay pull cast so as to draw 'tail' back into fly line.
   Roll between two flat surfaces to straighten join.

3. Apply 2-3 coats of liquid PVC to finish.

USING A CAST CONNECTOR

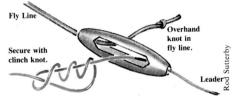

Fly Line

Secure with clinch knot.

Overhand knot in fly line.

Leader

Rod Sutterby

of differing diameters. In the early days of reservoir trouting, a double-tapered (tapered at both ends) leader, with a heavy belly to assist turnover, was very popular. This had as many as a dozen knots in it, but in the right hands it was very successful. Nevertheless, these complex tapers are now rare, although some anglers do use a simpler form of double taper.

The level leader is quite suitable for fishing heavy flies and lures, but less effective for lighter flies and small nymphs. Generally, the leader should be tapered to suit the point size. On many small streams, a 4lb point would be rather coarse, but few anglers go below 3lb except on special occasions. On most reservoirs you can expect to hook fish up to 3lb, or even 6–8lb if you are fortunate. In such circumstances, a point of 6–8lb b.s. is not too heavy.

Importance of fly size

The size of the fly is also important. A small nymph or fly never sits well on a heavy point and often the size of the hook eye precludes the use of large diameter nylon anyway. For small flies, a 3–5lb point is suitable, according to conditions. Conversely, a large fly or a heavy lure, especially a two or three-hook lure, sits awkwardly on too fine a point. A heavy lure imposes severe strains on light points during casting, and it is also prone to flick back and tangle with the point. In such cases, 6–8lb b.s. should be considered, especially if big fish are expected.

Sometimes your fishing style or local water conditions demand the use of a long leader, even though these are difficult to handle in boisterous weather. A long leader fished deep is often very effective. Much depends on how well you cast, and it is worth

Vary length of this section according to total leader length required.	3-Turn Blood Knot	Knotless Taper 0.020-0.011in (approx)	If finer point preferred add 18in 0.009in nylon.
0-72in		72in	

387

Leaders

G. L. Carlisle

A good leader proves itself by the way the fly line acts in the forward cast. With a long leader your fly casting must be good.

practising to get the rhythm right. In stormy weather or high wind, when the surface is rough and the fish are taking on top, you may require a *shorter* 'storm' leader.

Many anglers like to tie an 18in nylon 'leg' directly to the reel line and attach their leaders to this. It gets shortened inch by inch as the season wears on, and you may have to renew it at intervals. Attach it to the reel line with a needle knot or a nylon whipping. Whip over the knot and varnish it so that it slides easily through the top rings of the rod. Nothing is worse than having it stick in the tip ring when you are about to net a fish.

Check the connector knots

If you do not feel competent about attaching a leg smoothly, use plastic leader connectors. These sometimes have a rough finish, so rub them over with fine sand paper before use. It is also worth colouring them to suit your line. A green or brown felt-tip pen does the job admirably. Make sure the connector knots, both in the reel line and the nylon leg, are well made and do not slip through the connector under strain.

Some anglers advocate a loop at the end of the leg, with a similar loop to attach the leader. Two loops, however, often cause an undesirable 'wake' in the water, as well as being prone to catch up with the hook in flight during casting. The author prefers a water knot for leader attachment, although it means the legs need replacing frequently.

When not to use a dropper

Many anglers who consistently take good fish never use a dropper. Others regularly fish one or even two or three. When shortlining from bank or boat, a team of three flies can be very useful to indicate the taking fly, and sometimes the taking depth. But with long casting, things are different. Even a single dropper can drive you to distraction on a blustery day, although if you can manage it the fish often take the dropper rather than the tail fly. Perhaps it is the fly, perhaps the way it fishes on the dropper, perhaps it is the depth.

Many anglers forego the dropper after dusk, chiefly because of the hazard of fouling, but if you are shortlining with a team of buzzers, with care they are perfectly manageable even then. You can always easily cut them off.

Spacing the droppers

On professionally manufactured casts, the common practice is to fix droppers at 3ft intervals, which is fine if you fish that way. Many anglers using only one dropper, however, prefer it to be set halfway along the cast. This makes it more effective as a bobber during the last stages of the retrieve, and prevents the tail fly coming up too far at the same time. The length of the leader is probably the most important factor in deciding on how many and where to place droppers.

Colour is considered important by some. Nylon can be bought in various shades, or you can dye it instead. If a leader is coiled first, you can immerse half in dye, dry it out, and then immerse the other half in a different colour. This produces a splendid camouflage, and if it gives you confidence it is worth trying.

There are no rules when it comes to leaders. Experiment with likely patterns; then make up your own to suit your style.

Dry flies

Dry fly fishing has always been regarded as the supreme art in fly fishing circles. This is particularly so on rivers and chalk-streams where matching the hatch is only the beginning of the problem and where presentation has to be considered as well. But dry flies also play an important part in reservoir and lake fishing where trout are attracted by insects on the surface.

Favourite season

Of all the periods during the season when trout rise to a dry fly, the favourite is the time that the mayfly hatch. The huge flies emerge from the water in such large numbers that the trout literally gorge themselves to capacity, and the better fish rise freely. On these occasions almost any artificial pattern representing a mayfly will take fish. Unfortunately the mayfly only hatches in running water and in a few privileged lakes, so does not affect fishing everywhere.

Early in the season the hawthorn fly hatches in large numbers and very good catches can be made with the aid of a Black Gnat. Again this mostly applies to running waters, but vast numbers of hawthorn flies were noticed at Rutland Water. Although the fish were not rising to them at that time,

they will most probably do so in the future.

In late summer, one of the most popular flies that hatches on every wafer is the sedge. These medium-sized flies start to hatch in July and August and are present throughout the day, and in vast numbers at nightfall. If weather conditions are good and flies are hatching, a pattern representing a sedge can be very effective, for the 'spent' sedge falling back upon the water is the fly most likely to attract the attention of the trout. But they are by no means the only ones. Throughout the year there are hatches of buzzers, the dreaded caenis, which is too small to be imitated, and a number of Ephemerids such as the olives.

Land-borne insects

These insects all hatch from the water and return there to lay their eggs, and this is when the trout rise to them. In addition to these insects, there are also the land-borne kind which live and breed on dry land but are often carried onto the water by winds. Naturally these flies are more important to the reservoir angler because the large expanses of water are too much for the insects to fly across while maintaining a battle with the wind to stay in the air. They

G. L. Carlisle

390

(Left) These mayfly duns, newly hatched, will rest until they become spinners which swarm near the water to mate. Afterwards the females will return to the water to deposit their eggs. During a hatch the mayfly will cluster thickly on waterside vegetation even on anglers' clothing.

(Above) Silicone mucilage is applied to an artificial mayfly to ensure that it floats temptingly on the surface of the water.

(Right) After the flotant has been applied—as in the photograph above—the artificial mayfly sits on the surface film in imitation of the natural insect.

P. H. Ward/Natural Science Photos

391

Dry flies

then make a meal for any lurking trout.

Of the insects that hatch on land, the daddy long legs is the one which, year after year, adds to the larder of the trout.

In the late summer the daddies hatch in vast number in the bankside vegetation, and being fairly weak fliers, are easily carried onto the water when the wind rises. The trout then cruise the margins and wind lanes taking the daddy long legs with a great swirl or splash, and fantastic sport can be had with a natural or imitation fly.

Difficult match

The drone-fly also features on the trout's menu for a short period when it is present in sufficient numbers, and also another land-borne insect, the ladybird. Both of these are rather difficult to match, and it is often a question of sorting through the box; but once a pattern is found, sport becomes brisk.

The other land insect that really interests the trout is the flying ant. On rare occasions a swarm of these insects is blown onto the water and the trout feed heavily on them, so it is wise to have an imitation in the box, just

in case. The same also applies to bees and grasshoppers, but there are few recorded patterns of these insects. When trout are seen taking them the angler must be ready to tie an acceptable imitation.

Patterns of dry fly

In almost all instances where trout feed on land-borne insects, the rule is not to move the fly. It is not possible to simulate the vibrating motion of their legs and in any case they are soon dead or exhausted and then lay still. An imitation is far more likely to succeed if it is cast out and then left. Regarding the patterns of dry fly that are needed, every angler should include in his collection the following: Tupp's Indispensible, Mayfly, Sedge, Black Gnat, Grey Duster, Iron Blue, Daddy Long Legs, Sherry Spinner, Pond Olive, Lunn's Particular, Flying Ant and Drone Fly. These are by no means all the patterns available, but equipped with them in varying sizes the angler should be able to deal with almost every circumstance he is likely to meet in rivers, lakes and streams.

(Left) Harvey Torbett carefully selecting a suitable artificial fly while trout fishing on a West Country reservoir.
(Top, right) Some dry fly artificials which can be matched to the natural insect: 1 Iron Blue Dun; 2 Black Gnat; 3 Olive Dun; 4 Daddy Long Legs; 5 Brown Sedge; 6 Grey Duster.
(Right) In the chart, the black lines show times of the year when certain kinds of insect may be expected to be found. The angler is advised to have the tied artificials with him at these periods. From 1 to 6, the natural fly is in bold type; the artificial is in italics.

Bill Howes

Tourist Photo Library

MATCHING THE HATCH

Natural *Artificial*	May	June	July	August	September	October	
1 Caenis *Grey Duster*			———	———			1
2 Daddy Long Legs *Daddy Long Legs*					———		2
3 Flying Ant – during heat waves *Black Ant*			———				3
4 Hawthorn Fly *Hawthorn Fly*	———						4
5 Mayfly *Mayfly*	2nd week ——— 2nd week						5
6 Sedge Fly *Wickhams Fancy*		last 2 weeks ——— first 2 weeks					6

Lyn Cawley

Wet flies

In contrast to the dry fly, intended to imitate or simulate an insect floating or alighting on the water's surface, the wet fly is used to imitate a small insect or creature living and actively moving *below* the surface.

This fundamental difference of function is reflected in the manner of tying the fly and in the materials used. Although some fly patterns can be tied either for dry or wet fly fishing, each is distinctive to its purpose. Stiff cock hackles are necessary for a floating fly, but softer, easily wetted hackles help the wet fly to sink, as well as providing a semblance of limb movement when the fly is working by the action of the stream, or during retrieval.

Wet flies may be winged or wingless, fully hackled or with 'spider' type hackles, or even with reduced and lighter 'throat' hackles, according to type. In some cases there are permutations of these variables.

Winged wet flies
The winged wet flies are probably the best known, and several important wet flies such as the Mallard and Claret and the Teal and Red may be tied in numerous variations of colour, providing a whole series of alternatives on the main theme. Good examples are Mallard and Claret, Mallard and Black, and Mallard and Mixed. Other popular winged flies are the Golden Olive, March Brown, and the Connemara Black. These are usually tied with reduced or thin hackles at the throat.

Palmer tied flies
Other winged flies are built up with full hackles wound along the whole length of the hook shank, and even with small additional 'throat' hackles as well. These are exemplified by the famous Invicta and Wickham's Fancy. Sometimes the hackle is replaced with teased-out hair or wool, as in the case of the Gold Ribbed Hare's Ear.

Flies tied with the hackle extending along the length of the body are said to be Palmer tied, after the Palmer, which may be black,

(*Right*) *Nymphs, left to right: Orange Buzzer, Tiger Nymph, Coryxa, Pheasant Tail, Shrimp, Partridge and Orange, Amber Nymph.*

(*Below*) *Wet flies, left to right: Invicta, Greenwell's Glory, Mallard and Claret, Royal Coachman, Woodcock and Green, Black and Peacock Spider.*

red, or ginger. This is the prototype wet fly, tied wingless but with a full body hackle. A further excellent and killing example of this type is the Zulu.

Spider hackled flies
A further group of important wingless flies is typified by the Black Pennel. This is made up with a slim body, a short tail whisk, and a full shoulder hackle tied in at the head only. Another example is the Black and Peacock Spider, an excellent fly when fish are feeding on snail. The Snipe and Purple, and the Partridge and Orange are also of this type.

Nymphs
Nymphs are quite different in make-up, appearance and function. They are intended to imitate or simulate the larval forms of many underwater insects. The best known are probably the Pheasant Tail and the buzzer series of nymphs. There are also green nymphs, brown nymphs and black nymphs, all excellent in the right place at the right time.

Nymphs are often tied with an imitation thorax and wing cases, as well as a banded or

Wet flies

ringed appearance to represent the segmented abdomen common in many natural nymph forms. These may also have tiny hackles or hairs built in to give that important suggestion of moving limbs. Others may represent small adult beetles common in many waters. The Corixa, tied with imitation hard wing cases, is a good example.

Within each of the groups broadly described there are some examples intended to be accurate imitations of the natural insect, and others are intended to caricature or simulate a whole group of similar looking creatures. Examples of winged artificial flies are the Invicta and the Greenwell's Glory.

Important artificials

Other important artificial flies are the distinctive flies made up with gold or silver tinsel or with brilliant fluorescent colours, which owe their success to their capacity for triggering off the predatory instincts of fish in much the same way that is achieved by a small spinner.

The Jersey Herd is a nymph of this kind, and is very effective when fished fairly fast in deep water. The Bloody Butcher, Alexandra, and Dunkeld are examples of winged attractors. There are also many small fish imitations such as the Polystickle, which introduces one final grouping generally known as Lures, most of which are intended to imitate small fish.

Lures

Lures are usually tied on long-shanked hooks, or on two or three small hooks tied in twos. They can be between 1in and 3in in length, with flashy or coloured bodies and large wings over the shank, made of whole

Black Lure and Muddler Minnow. The Red Terror is an exotic salmon lure.

Wet fly action

Whatever the type, the wet fly often depends far more on its action in the water when fished, than upon its resemblance to a particular insect. When trout are feeding freely the actual pattern is not important, but when the fish are preoccupied or need tempting the angler must use his ingenuity to discover what the fish are feeding upon, and imitate it as best he can. Often, his speed and depth of fishing are also very important.

Unlike his dry fly counterpart, the wet fly angler may fish two or three flies on the same cast, the extra flies being attached to droppers off the cast at intervals of 4 or 5ft. The patterns are selected so that the tail fly can be fished deep, with the bottom dropper in midwater, and the top dropper near to the surface. He can even arrange for his top dropper (fly on a short cast) to dibble above the surface, while fishing the other flies below it. These tactics have the advantage of providing several opportunities to discover the appropriate or 'taking' fly and the required depth. A disadvantage is that a bad back-cast with a team of flies often produces a tangle which takes a long time to clear.

Of all kinds of wet fly, the lures are mostly intended to represent small fish. One of the most well known, the famous Polystickle, might be thought to imitate the stickleback. Some lures are tied on two or three hooks. From left to right: Baby Doll, Missionary, Church Fry, Black Chenille, Whisky Fry, Appetizer, and the Muddler Minnow.

Tourist Photo Library

Salmon flies

A salmon angler with a fine range of flies kept in an orderly state. Few working fly boxes look like this!

imitation of a natural insect. Indeed, the gaudy fly will always win over a drab one.

Such names as 'Jock Scott', 'Black Doctor', 'Blue Doctor', 'Blue Charm', 'Chalmers', 'Dunkeld', 'Thunder and Lightning', 'Durham Ranger' and 'Dusty Miller', 'Green Highlander' and 'Green King', the 'Logie', and many others, have become well-known to salmon fishermen.

Art form

An object as colourful as the traditional salmon fly lends itself as an art form, and probably for this reason alone its survival is assured, even though it has lost much of its practical popularity on the angling scene.

Modern flies with hair wings still retain the original brightness of the traditional ones, particularly regarding bodies, tails and hackles. In most instances these are retained in their entirety, only the wings being different. The hairs used for these wings are usually dyed the same bright shades of red,

Evolving from the early trout flies, the contemporary salmon fly shows little evidence to associate it with the imitation of natural insects. It is generally considered that early salmon flies were tied in ignorance of what the salmon actually thought they were, and only recently has it been realized that salmon do not feed while travelling to their spawning grounds in freshwater.

Shape, style and character

Colour has always been considered important of course, but as the ideas of one fly dresser are not necessarily those of his contemporaries, almost every known combination became available. In spite of this variety of colour, a great similarity among the patterns as to shape, style and character emerged. Type, size and presentation were considered less important than they are today: the reason being, perhaps, the greater abundance of salmon earlier this century.

The gaudy fly is still produced for fishing, but more as a fly-tying exercise than anything else. The more durable and easily produced hair-winged fly is brightly coloured, however, because it provides a better

The materials from which salmon flies are tied are very colourful. A gaudy fly will catch fish when drab ones fail.

Hardy's

A range of moose-hair salmon flies. The large flies at the foot are a 'Dusty Miller' and a 'Green Highlander', with a 'Hairy Mary' and a 'Thunder and Lightning' above. Small salmon flies should be fished between 3 and 5in below the surface.

blue, yellow, green and orange, but in some instances they are left in their natural state. The 'Blue Charm' is a good illustration of this, as the teal and mallard flank feathers of the original patterns are replaced by either brown bucktail fibres or brown squirrel tail fibres, according to the size of hook. To distinguish between the two dressings, the hair-winged version of the 'Blue Charm' was called 'Hairy Mary'.

Size of fly

Having decided on the kind of fly, you then have to choose how it shall be fished. The size of a salmon fly is most important; colour only secondary. The size used will depend largely on the height, temperature and colour of the water, and on weather conditions. If a salmon follows your fly or rises short this usually means that the fly is too big or your leader is too thick. The best way to start is to use a small fly—you can always increase the size later. As a general rule: the bigger the river, the larger the fly. A larger fly would also be used in coloured water, in very rough or broken water, or in deep holes that have a dark bottom. In conditions where wind, light and temperature are constant, a medium-sized fly is recommended. Low, clear water, usually referred to as 'summer' conditions, favours a much smaller fly, and usually one of a more sombre hue. One would also use this kind over a light-coloured shallow bottom. Another rule therefore is always to try to use a fly in colour contrast to its surroundings.

General and specific patterns

Flies tied on what are called 'Ordinary' or 'Rational' hooks are referred to as 'Standard' patterns, whereas those used for summer conditions are called 'Low Water' patterns. These latter patterns are often merely scaled down versions of Standard patterns, tied on hooks of a lighter gauge wire, and the dressings taken well forward of the hook bend.

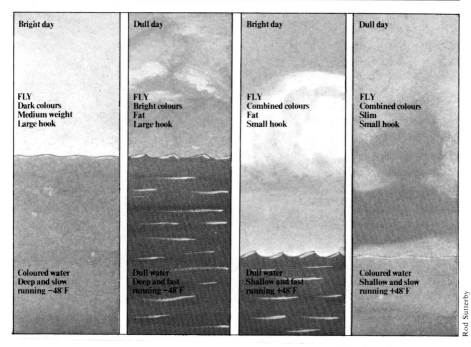

Bright day	Dull day	Bright day	Dull day
FLY Dark colours Medium weight Large hook	FLY Bright colours Fat Large hook	FLY Combined colours Fat Small hook	FLY Combined colours Slim Small hook
Coloured water Deep and slow running −48°F	Dull water Deep and fast running −48°F	Dull water Shallow and fast running +48°F	Coloured water Shallow and slow running +48°F

Rod Sutterby

The chart provides some general hints on the selection of large and small salmon flies according to the types of water and existing weather conditions.

In addition to these general patterns there are others which are designed for specific rivers. Two of the best known are the 'Spey' and the 'Dee' patterns (named after the rivers), made with rather sombre materials.

These flies are used in the early part of the season when the temperature can be at almost freezing point. They are dressed lightly on very large hooks, 3in being quite common, and this combination of lightness of dressing and heaviness of hook means that the flies sink deeper. They are therefore more likely to come within the field of view of the fish which lies close to the bottom when the temperature of the water is very low. In addition to the suitability of these large flies for the particular circumstances in which they are used, one of their best features is the extreme mobility of their hackles and wings, giving them a very lifelike appearance when they are worked in the water. In contrast to the gaudy flies described earlier, 'Spey' and 'Dee' flies are a very practical kind of pattern.

Satisfactory alternative

'Prawn' or 'Shrimp' fly as the name implies, is a fly version of the crustacean which forms part of the staple diet of the growing salmon during its life in the sea. These can be very successful during the early part of the season, and one theory is that they are attacked by the fish through force of habit rather than from a desire to feed. They also make a satisfactory alternative for dedicated fly fishermen who do not wish to 'spin the natural prawn'—a very popular method of salmon fishing on some waters.

The fly specifically produced for Irish waters is usually more heavily dressed than standard patterns, and is designed with harmonious body colour schemes. Its impression of warmth and rich colour is ideally suited to the peaty waters of Ireland.

Fly dressing is a very advanced craft and there are many books of instruction available. Your local tackle dealer should be able to tell you which are the most informative.

Fly tying

Anglers have used artificial as well as natural flies for centuries. Perhaps the idea of making artificial lures occurred when supplies of natural flies dried up and the angler decided to attempt a copy by binding fur and hair to a hook. The pattern of fly used depends on the conditions prevailing in the fishing water and on the kind of flies which occur naturally.

The basic fly

To create even a rough impression of a fly some knowledge of its anatomy is needed. The head, which is not simulated on many tied flies, is set on a body which is divided into two sections—the upper, larger thorax and the abdomen. The wings vary in size but can be represented by different hackles, usually made from pieces of feather.

Because dry flies, as their name suggests, are intended to float on the surface, lightness and buoyancy in their construction are most important. The tying must be tight and even to prevent waterlogging. Where heavy or porous materials would add to the attractiveness, these are given a last-minute coating of a suitable oil to help keep the fly afloat.

For tying your own flies a small fly-tying vice is essential. Select a model that has a firm base, covers most of the hook by gripping the sharp end, and can be tilted upwards to allow ample access to the fly. Hackle pliers are needed to hold the hackle firm and to prevent it from unwinding when released. Scissors with short, pointed blades are required for trimming. A scalpel can be used instead, but great care must be taken as this instrument can cause nasty wounds. A cake of cobbler's wax will also be needed before you can begin to produce your own artificial flies. A good selection of materials, including pieces of fur, tinsel, hair, feathers on the skin, wool, and silk thread, should be to hand as, after basic methods have been mastered, experimental and unusual varieties can be created.

(Above) Donald Downes, well-known fly tier. (Overleaf) Fly tying equipment including vice hackles, hackle pliers, silks, scissors, feathers and whip finishing tool.

There are other useful, though not essential, accessories. Among these are tweezers, bobbin-holders, and a whip-finish tool which completes the tying with a neat knot. The angler is now ready to tie a basic fly along the following lines.

A trout hook (size 14-11) is held in the vice with the shank and eye protruding horizontally and the barb clamped out of sight. The basic body is constructed out of about 10in of tying silk or a silk floss (which is fluffy and covers more easily). To make this first layer adhere, either coat the shank with vinyl glue or run the silk through fingertips that have been rubbed with cobbler's wax. Beginning 3-4in behind the eye, wind the silk neatly

along the shank, binding down the loose end with the first few turns and finish where the bend of the hook begins. If using tying silk, about 100 turns to the inch will be necessary, while the silk floss will cover the same length in far fewer turns. At this stage the tail is added, and for this the end of the thread is left hanging down, gripped by the pliers.

A tail can be made from the hairs of such animals as the badger and squirrel, or from the fronds of a stiff feather. These should be bunched and tied securely—so that the fly does not gradually moult—before being positioned at the bend of the hook and bound to the shank with the remaining tying silk or floss. A few passes under the bunched hairs as well as over them will cock the tail up jauntily.

Binding in the tail

When securing the tail, bind in the material for the body. A stripped poultry quill, softened in water, is good for building on top of the silk because its overlapping turns round the shaft will resemble abdominal segments. Wind on the quill towards the eye and fasten it down with tying silk. Tinsel or steel wool strands to add glitter can be bound in during the body's construction, and a thorax furnished out of materials with interesting textures, such as chenille or angora wool.

The bodies of the less streamlined flies are dressed or 'dubbed' with animal fur—mole skin for example—which is bound to the hook shaft with silk or wire. A foundation of cobbler's wax is needed, and the modern substitute, 'Vycoat', makes it possible to 'sculpt' a shapely foundation before dubbing on fur for a plump, succulent appearance. 'Vycoat' can be moulded into a glossy black head, which cleverly conceals any loose ends. Generally, the loose ends of thread left after every process can be held in and concealed by the next stage. The final thread, unless a moulded head is constructed, should be secured with a neat whip finish near the eye.

Hackles are feathers from the collar plumage of birds, and hackling is the reproduction of bristles at the shoulder of an

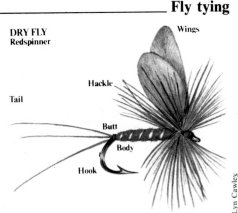

DRY FLY Redspinner
Labels: Wings, Hackle, Tail, Butt, Body, Hook

Lyn Cawley

artificial fly. In dry fly tying the feathers of aquatic birds are best for buoyancy, although poultry cock hackles are equally good as they are stiff, glossy and water repellent. Natural colours are varied, but dyeing can make the variety infinite.

To prepare a feather for hackling hold it by the tip and run moistened fingers down the fibres so that they stand out at right angles and separate. Then, having stripped the base of the quill, lay the feather at right angles to the hook-eye and lash the bared quill to the shank with tying silk. The fronded remainder is then held at the tip with hackle pliers and three or four turns made towards the tail. The weight of the pliers hanging down from the tip will prevent your work from springing undone while freeing your hands to fasten it with a couple of turns of silk. Next, cut off the tip of the feather. One basic hackle fly, the 'Palmer', is hackled along the whole length of its body, so more than one feather is needed.

Binding the hackle

Binding a hackle needs a steady hand since the binding (gilt wire in a 'Palmer') is pulled between each separate fibre of the feather: to keep these fibres from being crushed the wire needs to be kept taut throughout and drawn clockwise, then anti-clockwise, and so on, alternating between each fibre. The finished hackle should be fluffed out with a sharp needle. Wire binding in the 'Palmer' makes not only for durability but also for an attractive effect.

Fly tying

TYING A DRY FLY

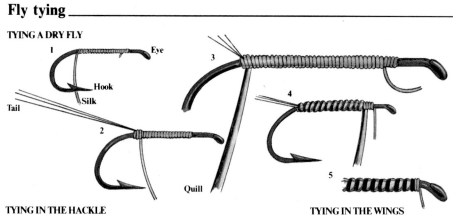

TYING IN THE HACKLE

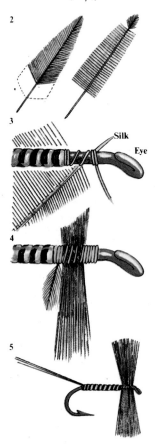

Tying a dry fly *(above)*.
*Begin by winding the silk to
the position (1); the quill is
tied-in at the tail(2) then
the silk wound back to the
front after the tail of stiff
hackle fibres is attached.
Give the tail an upwards tilt
by running one turn under
it. The ribbed body is
formed by winding a
stripped quill down to the
and tie-off using the silk.*
Tying-in the hackle *(left)*.
*Select a hackle whose fibres
match the distance between
the point and the eye (1).
Trim the hackle as in (2)
and pass it through the
fingers to make the fibres
stand out. The bared stem
can now be tied on (3). A
few turns of the hackle from
the eye leave you at position
(4). Bed it down with the
silk still hanging down on
hackle pliers and tie-off
finally with a whip-finish.*
Tying-in the wings *(right)*.
*These must be matched
pairs (1) either side of a
feather. Hold them securely,
following the turns in Nos.
2 to 6.*

TYING IN THE WINGS

Paired Wings

Rod Sutterby

ARTIFICIAL BAIT
DRY FLY
NYMPH
WET FLY
LURE

NATURAL FOOD
MAYFLY NYMPH
THREE SPINED STICKLEBACK (Breeding Colours)
CATERPILLAR (Chalk Blue)
SUMMER MAYFLY

Lyn Cawley

The simplest of dry flies—the 'Snipe' and 'Black Spider'—are simply hook, hackle and silk, but with natural colours or by dyeing this combination affords many possibilities. The addition of wings, however, can improve the balance of a dry (floating) fly and of course makes for more spectacular creations. They can be tied in at the same stage as the tail and the fastening shanks concealed when the body is built up. Alternatively, a space can be left between thorax and hook-eye, and the wings added when the body is complete, although there needs to be some silk round the shank before wings can be attached successfully.

Double wings

Dry flies often sport double wings which also makes them more buoyant. Two feathers are needed from symmetrically identical positions on either side of a bird's wing or tail fan. Symmetrically matched sections are cut from the centre of these feathers. These diamond-shaped sections have to be torn in half (for the double-wing effect) and eased into rectangles between finger and thumb (without the fibres separating). The 'wings' are rounded off with scissors and the four butt ends pinched firmly between finger and thumb and introduced at the shoulder, two on either side of the body.

Only practice, patience and steady hands

Many artificial flies are tied to match the natural counterpart. The wet lure apes the caterpillar or grub, the dry fly has all the appearance of a Mayfly. Nymphs resemble the real insect larva on weed-stems, while the polystickle imitates a stickleback.

make for successful wing tying. A loop of silk has to be squeezed between finger and feather, over the body, and down between feather and thumb. It requires concentration, but three turns of silk must be firmly drawn down without the wings splitting. To finish off, wind the thread in front of and behind the wings, passing it between them to keep them separate. The knots will be concealed by any hackle added afterwards—and often winged flies run to two hackles behind the wings and another pair in front. What perplexes the beginner is finding the space along a normal hook shaft for all these ornamentations.

Flies for coarse fish

The varieties of dry fly patterns have occupied many volumes, and the possibilities are not yet exhausted. Moreover, their use is no longer, as was traditionally the case, restricted to fishing for trout and salmon, for such coarse fish as rudd, roach, chub, dace, grayling, perch and pike are all taken on artificial flies.

403

New trout patterns

The last ten years has been unique in the history of fly-tying for two reasons. First, more new trout fly patterns have been produced than possibly during any other period of the same length. Second, from this explosion of new patterns there has emerged an unusually large number of dressings that dramatically break with tradition. Their impact has been immediate. Almost overnight the art of fly-tying in this country was turned on its head.

Revolutionary methods

These new patterns introduced revolutionary methods of dressing a fly and precipitated experimentation with new materials. This in turn lead to a re-examination of what it was that induced a trout to take a fly, with the suggestion that a close representation of a natural fly was not necessary. Trout, it is claimed, will take any brightly coloured attractive fly. Such a change was no accident, for it directly

coincided with a meteoric rise in the popularity of trout fishing that accompanied the stocking of large public reservoirs and disused lakes and ponds with trout in the mid-Sixties.

With more anglers able to afford quality trout fishing, more time and effort began to be devoted to finding more effective ways of catching them. This meant developing new techniques and, more importantly, new flies to meet the demands of specific problems. Because of this, artificial flies became less a subject of interest to the angler with nothing better to do on the long winter nights of the close season, but the result of thoughtful, practical design. In this search for new ideas, British fly fishermen were quite willing to look to fly fishermen in other countries— France, Sweden, but most notably America—and exchange views. It was in America that the best known, most successful and probably the most innovative of the

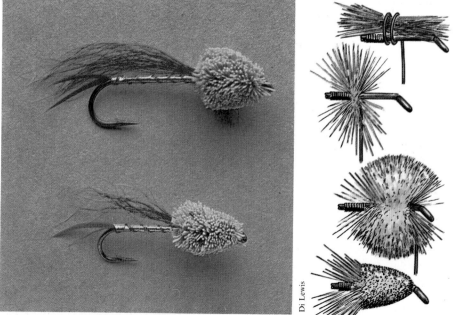

Di Lewis

Rod Sutterby

new patterns of this period had its origins—the Muddler Minnow.

Many people believe that the Muddler Minnow got its name because of the way it moved in the water. They say it confuses the trout into taking it. This is not true. The Muddler Minnow was a direct attempt by its creator, Don Gapen, to tie an exact imitation of the flatheaded Cockotush minnow found in the Nipigon River in northern Ontario, nicknamed 'muddlers' by the locals.

Muddler Minnow

Whereas the majority of flies before the Muddler relied on feather fibres in their construction, the Muddler Minnow is largely made of hair fibres. The part that makes most people tying the Muddler for the first time wish they had never started is the head and shoulders made of deer hair. This material is believed to have been used by North American Indians to make trout lures. However, the method used to tie the head is quite original and certainly not as difficult a task as is often made out.

The space at the head of the hook where the deer hair is to be tied should be left bare.

A small bunch of stiff fibres is cut from a deer skin and held horizontally over the hook where the silk has been wound off, having tied in the body and wing. Two loose turns of silk are wound round the fibres and hook shank with enough tension to hold the fibres on the hook so that they need no longer be held in position with your fingers. The silk is then pulled tight and the fur spins like a hackle round the hook shank.

Having done this, the silk should be behind the fibres. Wind the silk through the fibres and make a half-hitch knot. This knot is then pressed close up to the fibres. This operation is repeated 4-5 times depending on the size of the head. Press each 'spinning' close up to the last one until the hook shank has been sufficiently covered. When this is completed, the head of the Muddler should look something like an electrocuted sheep-dog. Clip the fibres so that the head is bullet-shaped, leaving some fibres nearest the body to act as a hair hackle.

The Muddler Minnow has been used as the basis for several variations and tied in many different colours using dyed buckskin

Muddler Minnow
Hook: 6-12 D/E long shanked hook.
Tying silk: Black.
Tail: A section of oak turkey wing quill that slightly extends the length of the hook.
Body: Flat gold tinsel.
Wing: A bunch of grey squirrel tail hair sandwiched between two sections of oak turkey wing feather. This extends the end of the tail and is tied pointing slightly upwards from the hook.
Shoulders: Deer hair—tied as explained in detail in text.

Chomper
Hook: 10-14 D/E.
Tying silk: Black.
Body: Ostrich herl.
Overbody: Raffine. A strip of polythene is tied behind the hook eye and wound backwards and forwards over hook shank to build up a body.
Head: Tying silk built up to form bold head.

Di Lewis

New trout patterns

fibres and impala hair, instead of grey squirrel, in the wing. Further additions to the fly have appeared recently in a search for an even more life-like resemblance. A pattern has been developed, for example, with pectoral fins made of pheasant tail fibres.

The Chomper family

The Chomper Family of flies were developed for quite different purposes from the Muddler Minnow. Their creator, the British angler Richard Walker, set out to develop a fly that was simple in design but did not necessarily imitate any one food in particular, but could resemble trout food in general. This idea has earned Chompers the title of 'Impressionistic Flies' rather than precise imitations. They are possibly the easiest of all flies to tie. Simply wind ostrich herl on to the hook shank until it is covered. When a body is formed, lay a back—or shell—of damp raffine over the herl.

Using various different combinations of colours, a variety of trout foods can be loosely imitated using the same tying method. For example, white ostrich herl with a brown or green back looks like Corixa. ostrich herl dyed amber or green with a light brown back looks like a sedge pupa or a shrimp. Because of its simple design, the Chomper can be weighted with thin strips of wine bottle lead under the dressing to make it sink faster without the shape of the fly being dramatically affected. Its adaptability also enables it to be fished in the water at any possible speed.

The Polystickle

Richard Walker is also the originator of the range of flies known as Polystickles, an ingenious imation of sticklebacks, roach and perch fry that trout often feed on in the shallows of the larger lakes. The effectiveness of the Polystickle is without a doubt achieved by the translucent effect of polythene covering the body of the fly. Its success can also be accounted for by its imitating the red and silver 'guts' of the natural by the use of silver hooks and the addition of a layer of crimson floss two-thirds of the way up the hook shank towards the eye that shines through the clear PVC

Di Lewis

406

used to build up the shape of the body.

The Polystickle's design enables it to sink quickly to the depth of the trout, and being made of almost totally trout-tooth-proof materials has proved itself to be extremely durable. Lastly, the Polystickle can very easily be adapted to deep water and muddy conditions, or when the light is dull—trout moving into the shallow to feed on fry at dusk. To cope with these conditions, a body of white raffine—instead of clear raffine— can be used. Alternatively, white day-light fluorescent wool covered with polythene can be used with a back of orange raffine.

The Grey Wulff

Because the recent interest in trout fishing has been largely centred on stillwaters, it is there that we find the majority of new patterns. However, one fly-tying innovation designed more specifically for river and stream fishing should be mentioned here— the Grey Wulff.

This is a dry fly pattern developed by Lee Wulff of America. The peculiarity of this fly is the way the wings are positioned—sloping

forwards over the head of the fly. Instead of feather quill, the wings are tied with a bunch of deer or other hair fibres. This makes the fly a remarkable floater—something few dry flies can claim to be. When tied in various colours and sizes, the Grey Wulff successfully imitates every species of up-winged fly likely to be found on rivers and lakes.

The Grey Wulff has also proven itself a remarkable imitation of the up-winged fly emerging from its nymphal, or larval, form if fished in the surface film instead of dry on top of the surface.

The four patterns discussed here have all displayed their value to thousands of fly fishermen all over the country. They have earned their spurs in terms of number of trout caught and for that reason have also earned a position in the fly-boxes of every fly fisherman. Not many new patterns win this kind of respect.

When considering buying or tying up a new pattern for the first time, remember that innovation alone will not improve your catches.

Polystickle
Hook: 6-12 D/E long shanked hook.
Tying silk: Black.
Tail and back: A strip of dampened raffine.
Body: Open spirals of black tying silk wound two-thirds of the way up the hook.
Throat: Crimson floss silk.
Overbody: A strip of polythene is tied behind the hook eye and wound backwards and forwards over hook shank to build up a body.
Throat hackle: Red or orange hackle fibres tied under hook shank.
Head: Tying silk built up to form bold head.
Grey Wulff
Hook: 10-16 D/E.
Tying silk: Black or olive.
Whisks: Blue dun hackle fibres, or brown barred squirrel fibres.
Body: Grey squirrel fur.
Hackle: Medium blue dun cock hackle.
Wing: Deer hair or small brown barred squirrel hair.

Di Lewis

407

Tube flies

Although the tube fly is not a modern innovation, its worldwide popularity is only recent. And although it will probably never oust the standard and low-water flies tied on a normal single and double hooks, there is no doubt that it is here to stay. The tube fly, as its name denotes, consists of a length of polythene or metal tubing, round which are whipped hair fibres from the tails of different animals. Orthodox salmon fly bodies are generally added to the tubes, and long-fibred hackles may be used in conjunction with the hair fibres, or even in place of them.

Tube Fly's history

The history of the tube fly is vague, and in fact there was at one time a great deal of discussion as to who was its originator. The history of the salmon fly itself has been dealt with in an earlier section, so it is sufficient to say that the tube fly is an extension of the traditional salmon fly, taking an evolutionary place in that history.

One of the first to reach the attention of salmon anglers was the Parker tube fly, since when all tube flies have followed a very similar style and method of construction. One of the earliest to earn a name was the Stoat Tail which, in its original form, consisted merely of fibres from the tail of a stoat, whipped round one end of a piece of tubing. As with all patterns which achieve a measure of popularity, variations soon began to appear, and these usually either took the form of additions to the tube body itself, using silk and tinsel as coverings, or by additions of different coloured hairs to those used on the original Stoat Tail.

Heron breast and guinea fowl body feathers are good examples of the feathers which are now used for tying tube flies, as

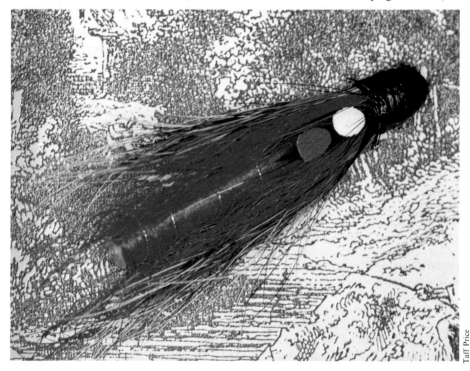

Taff Price

(*Above* A *Stoat-Tail tube fly still lodged in the vee of the salmon's jaws.*
(*Right*) *The basic tube fly.*
(*Left*) *Squirrel and Orange tube fly with eye spots painted on the head.*

they have long, flowing fibres which work well in the water when the fly is fished. Some tubes are made of brass in which a polythene tube has been inserted, thus giving weight for deep water fishing without creating too much wear and tear on the leader.

A double advantage

The tubes are used in conjunction with a treble hook which is tied to the end of the leader. The tube is then slid down the leader tail-end first, until it is stopped by the eye of the treble hook. From this you will see that the tube is running free on the leader, a factor which has a double advantage. When the fly is being fished, the pressure of water holds it tight to the treble hook, whereas when the hook is taken by a fish the reverse applies, and the drag caused by the fish's run drives the tube up the leader towards the line. This prevents damage to tube and dressing.

For colour variations or for increased size, two made-up tubes may be used together and two appropriate methods are illustrated.

Conventional fly tying equipment can be used to make tube flies, plus one or two sizes of tapered, eyeless salmon hooks on which the tubes can be slid to facilitate tying. Hook sizes 4, 2, 2/0 and 4/0 should cope with most tube diameters. There is also a device, designed by Anne Douglas, which fits into a normal vice clamp and which has several sizes of spike set onto an axle at the top. The size needed is turned to the right of the stem intended to take the tube while the other sizes are turned left out of the way.

To prevent the treble from hanging at an angle to the tube during casting, a small piece of cycle valve rubber, or another short piece of polythene tubing, can be fixed over the hook end of each tube when it is completed. The eye of the treble can then be drawn into it before you start to fish. Unless you take this precaution, the hook can snag itself on the leader in front of the tube, resulting in a large number of useless casts.

The Hairy Mary tube fly, chosen here for step-by-step demonstration of tying, is a very well-known tube adaptation, being a hair-

Tube flies

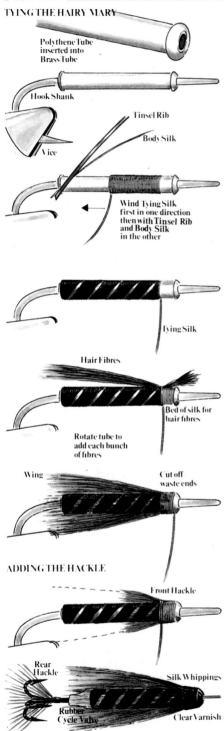

TYING THE HAIRY MARY

Polythene Tube
inserted into
Brass Tube

Hook Shank

Tinsel Rib

Body Silk

Vice

Wind Tying Silk
first in one direction
then with Tinsel Rib
and Body Silk
in the other

Tying Silk

Hair Fibres

Bed of silk for
hair fibres

Rotate tube to
add each bunch
of fibres

Wing

Cut off
waste ends

ADDING THE HACKLE

Front Hackle

Rear
Hackle

Silk Whippings

Rubber
Cycle Valve

Clear Varnish

winged salmon fly in its original form, which in its turn was an adaptation of the Blue Charm—one of the best known and most popular flies in the salmon angler's fly box. It varied only in that the original feather wing of the Blue Charm was replaced by brown bucktail (deer) fibres. The original tail tag, body and hackle ingredients were left intact.

Tying a Hairy Mary

To tie a Hairy Mary, first press the tube onto the tapered hook shank, firmly enough to hold it well but taking care not to split or damage the end of it. The bend of the hook is then held in the vice and tying silk run down the tube. Body silk and tinsel rib are tied in where the tail end of the fly would usually be. Wind the tying silk back the other way and follow it with the body silk and tinsel rib, in that order. Now put a layer of the tying silk on the remaining piece of tubing to form a bed for the ends of the hair fibres which are to be added.

The wing of the Hairy Mary is made from brown bucktail or, in the smaller patterns,

Rod Sutterby

squirrel tail. The best fibres for small tube flies, whichever kind of tail is used, will be found at the base, and for larger flies the fibres should be taken from whatever part of the tail suits them best, so that for very large flies the fibres would be from the tip. This makes best possible use of any variegated colour in the tail.

The hairs are cut off by twisting a small bunch of them together, and trimming them close to the root. Any fluffy fur—found at the base of most hair fibres—should be pricked out with the point of a dubbing needle: this fur has no use in the wing and only makes the finished head thicker than it need be. The size of the head should be kept to a minimum to prevent a bow-wave and speed entry into the water.

Do not try to put on too many hairs at a time: a good measure of quantity is their thickness when they are twisted together. The maximum, even for large flies, is a thickness of about $\frac{1}{16}$ in. The bunch of fibres is now tied in on top of the tube, making the

loop of tying silk over the fingers as you might for tying-in normal wings.

The waste ends should be cut off now and after each bunch of fibres is tied in. This makes for precision in each ensuing stage of the tying-in, whereas a large bunch of splayed-out waste fibres would obscure the head of the tube.

The tube is now rolled round the hook shank, bringing to the top the next portion which is to be covered by hairs. Another bunch of fibres is now tied in, the turns of silk being to the immediate right of those turns securing the first bunch. Continue in this way until the whole tube has been covered.

Keep the head small

Placing the silk turns to the right as each bunch is tied in will keep down the size of the head. If all the turns were in one place it would be quite bulky. Try to fix the 'steps' of tying silk so that the last bunch of fibres is completed just as the end of the tube is reached. A single layer of silk is wound round all the fibres where they are tied in. This forms a neat head and gives a uniform slope to the fibres. All the waste ends of the fibres were cut off as the body progressed, so that all that is now needed is a whip finish and one or two coats of thin clear varnish—Cellire is ideal—to the head. The silk whippings should be soaked well in the varnish for strength, and when dry, a final coat of black or red, as desired, completes the fly—apart from the addition of the hook.

If the tube fly requires a hackle in front, this is wound at the point where the first bunch of fibres was tied in. Using the fingers of your left hand, all the hackle fibres are drawn to the rear. Wind a few turns of silk over their base so that they contain the hair as closely as possible. Body hackles can be added as with a normal fly.

If heron hackles are used in the place of hair, one hackle is wound at the front and all its fibres pulled to the rear. On a larger pattern, it can be wound 'Palmer'-style.

Two kinds of body hackle (in blue) used on the Hairy Mary tube fly.

Taff Price

Sea trout flies

The life cycle of the sea trout is almost the same as that of the salmon, with the important difference that whereas salmon do not feed in freshwater, sea trout perhaps occasionally do. Consequently, when tying flies to tempt the sea trout, try to offer them something appetizing as well as attractive.

The first flies to concentrate on are those that represent the sea trout's main diet while at sea—small fish. These are still uppermost in its mind when it enters freshwater. Sea trout also feed on prawns, shrimps, sandeels, and small crabs, but small fish ranging from ½in–3in constitute its main diet.

There are several established patterns that are always worth a place in the fly box. Teal Blue and Silver is one of the most successful the author has come across, and it should be tied in sizes of 10 or 12 through to long-shanked flies or tandem lures of up to 3in.

Other successful flies are Peter Ross, Silver Wilkinson, Teal and Red, Mallard and Silver, Mallard and Gold, and other bright patterns, all tied in the styles described to imitate small fish.

'Medicines'
One of the greatest authorities on sea trout fishing is Hugh Falkus. In his book *Sea Trout Fishing* he gives details of seven types of sea trout fly to suit different conditions. The first kind, which he calls 'Medicines', are effective all night but are best fished before midnight. They are big silver/blue patterns such as the Silver Blue or the Mallard and Silver, and are tied very lightly on low water salmon hooks. These are longer-shanked and lighter in the wire than normal hooks.

The second group, 'Sunk Lures', are good late night flies. They consist of two size 8 or 10 short-shanked hooks tied in tandem. The

(Left) A big sunk lure, a small sea trout fly with flying treble, and a small sea trout fly.
(Below) Sea trout versions of the Silver Wilkinson and the March Brown. There are various patterns of these well-known artificials.

MARCH BROWN

Lyn Cawley

Arthur Oglesby

SILVER WILKINSON

ZULU

CONNEMARA

Lyn Cawley

(Above) The Zulu and the Connemara, two flies known to attract sea trout.
(Right) The 'Medicine', created and named by a great fisherman, Brigadier G H N Wilson. It is tied on low-water salmon hooks, sizes 3, 4 or 5.

overall length of the lure should be about 2½in. The wings are constructed of blue hackle feathers, strands of peacock herl, or blue-dyed fur. No hackles are wound in front of these lures, nor do they have tails. In fact, Falkus states that tails are unnecessary on most sea trout flies.

The third group, 'Maggot Flies', is a well-established method of sea trout fishing, and the pattern recommended by Falkus is: hook, short-shanked and snecked; body, white thread or silk; hackle, brown hen. Use these flies in conjunction with two or three maggots fixed to the bend of the hook.

Fourth is Falkus's specially constructed pattern—the 'Secret Weapon'. These flies are designed to overcome the frustration caused by fish that are 'taking short', nibbling at the end of the bait without getting near the hook. Their secret is a flying treble extending beyond the bend (and parallel to the wings) of a normally baited maggot fly.

Falkus lists two other flies. The 'Small Double', consists of a size 12 double-iron hook, silver body, teal or mallard wing, and a black hen hackle. It is recommended when the fish are in a finicky mood in low water. The other lure, the 'Worm Fly', consists of a peacock herl body, about 1¼in–1½in long, with brown or black hen hackles. It is very good in low water, fished in tandem.

'Surface Lure'

Falkus's final lure, the 'Surface Lure', merits special attention. It is a dark-night lure which is quickly dragged across the surface. It can be made of almost anything that floats as it is not the fly itself but the wake that attracts the trout, although it is normally constructed from a piece of trimmed cork about 1½in long. This is whipped to a tandem mount of a leading single and a rear treble hook. The fly is then adorned with two wings of small, dark feathers.

Sea trout continue to feed after entering freshwater. As the season progresses other types of flies, representing freshwater food, can be used with success. Such patterns as 'March Brown', 'March Brown Silver',

'SECRET WEAPON' MOUNT

Wind on a few turns of silk (red) as a seating. Loop 12lb nylon round a No 16 treble and pass the ends out through the eye.

Whip nylon to shank and whip nylon together above eye.

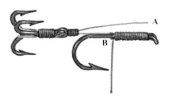

Hold size 8 Hardy Perfect in vice and take a few turns of silk from opposite hook point to eye. Cut off end A just behind eye. Bring end B through eye and back along underside of shank. Whip back towards point tying in strand B.

Wind silk back towards eye, this time trapping end A. Whip finish. Ensure eye of the treble is level with bend of hook.

Add sparse wing of mallard and a black cock or hen hackle for dressing.

'Invicta', 'Mallard and Claret', 'Butcher', and 'Zulu' all catch fish. Double hooks are useful when the fish are in a fussy mood.

The size of a fly is more important than its shape, and a great deal depends on the weather and water conditions. Standard patterns should be about size 8–10 under normal conditions, with 6–8 being used on windy days. Colour is also important. Dark flies are best in waters with dark, rocky bottoms, such as Irish lakes and rivers, and suggested patterns for these conditions are 'Black Pennell', 'Connemara Black', 'Butcher', and 'Black Zulu'. If you fish a team of three flies, the 'Black Pennell' seems to be the most successful as the tail fly on any water, although the body should be varied in colour from time to time. Use claret or yellow for example, but always with plenty of bright silver or gold ribbing.

Whether to use a large fish imitation or a smaller freshwater fly depends largely on the season. In the early season you may well

Rod Sutterby

414

adopt the maxim that a big fly will catch more fish than a small fly used at the same time in the same water. But the longer a fish stays in a river on its return from the sea, the more is it likely to return to the food available in its new environment. As its instinct for sea food fades, it will turn to the nymphs and flies found in freshwater.

Learn the feeding habits

Having learnt the feeding habits of sea trout, the angler who ties his own flies has all the advantages. He can make lures resembling small fish, as he knows them to be and which are not the creation of someone else's imagination (very often that someone has never fished for sea trout in his life), and flies that represent the insect life in the particular water he fishes. With his own individually designed flies he is far more likely to succeed. One of the author's friends had six sea trout on one outing, the largest 11lb. All were taken on a 'Teal Blue and Silver' of his own design, tied on very long shanked hooks, very sparsely and with no tails, the wing being of widgeon feather, not the usual teal.

Taff Price.

(Above) A selection of sea trout flies including Teal and Blue, Mallard and Claret, Alexandra, Peter Ross, Woodcock and Yellow, and Silver March Brown.
(Right) A surface fly in the muddler minnow style.
(Below) The best standard sea trout lure, the worm fly.
(Far left) How to tie the famous 'Secret Weapon' sea trout fly. The lure was designed in 1962.

WORM FLY

Lyn Cawley.

Taff Price

Fly boxes

The only criterion by which to judge a good fly box is whether it caters for your needs, whether it holds all the flies that your particular brand of fishing demands. In my case this adds up to several thousand, and although this may sound unnecessary, I would hate to leave any of them behind. But each angler asks something different of a fly box, and this article can aim only to introduce the various categories of box along with a few specific models.

The firm of Richard Wheatley has been making fly boxes of all types for a considerable time, and have satisfied the needs of many fishermen. The No. 1601 model from the Wheatley range is fitted with small metal clips on both sides and will hold 119 flies. On one side of the box there are large clips for the bigger flies and on the other, small clips for your nymphs and smaller patterns. The whole box is neat, will fit into most pockets, and is light, being made from aluminium.

Held by the hooks

There are other boxes in this range, some with an extra flap inside to hold even more hooks, as well as boxes that will take salmon flies, gripping them by the hooks. This method of securing the flies may be considered unsatisfactory because it spoils the hackles—which in these days are hard to come by. So Wheatleys have produced a different design in model No 1607F which incorporates a neat, hinged, sprung lid to each compartment. By simply flicking the catch on each lid, it springs open revealing the flies soundly protected inside. The box has 16 compartments with sprung lids and should hold 80 to 100 dry flies. In size it is only slightly thicker then the previous box. Another model has compartments on both sides and, while quite expensive, it is a first-class box for the really keen dry fly man.

Without a doubt, for the man who likes to travel light, the best value for money is John Goddard's box marketed by Efgeeco. This box will answer all your needs if you are content to carry only a small selection of flies to the waterside safe and in good condition and leave the larger boxes behind. The box is made from a very durable plastic lined with polythene foam which acts to stop hooks rusting. It will hold about 140 flies and is very light to carry as you walk your favourite chalk-stream. The designer recommends the box—by using it himself.

To get away from shop-bought boxes, you can make all manner of containers if you are

The Wheatley box (below left) holds flies under spring clips; Efgeeco's box (left) keeps the flies firmly in rows; (above) this box, again by Wheatley, has eight compartments.

at all 'DIY' minded. A wooden cigar box is often put to good use in this way. The first step is to take any paper off the outside and give the whole thing—including the inside—a good rub down with a medium sandpaper. Put two or three coats of varnish on the outside to make the box waterproof. Next, get some polythene foam from your tackle shop.

If you line the box with white Fablon before you stick the foam in, it seems to help make the flies stand out more clearly, especially when you are searching for one particular pattern at night. You can either put a complete layer of foam in the top and bottom or cut the foam into strips and stick them into the box, depending on whether you want to keep just lures in the box or hackle flies as well.

Protecting hackles

A box which answers this description is available commercially from Benwoods of London. Handmade by a skilled tool-maker, it is made from wood and lined with Fablon. Polythene foam is stuck into it in narrow strips so that the hackles of flies do not get damaged. (This can happen when the whole inside of a box has been lined with foam.) It is a model which the author recommends.

A recent box to come onto the market is the Gripstrip fly box. Normark manufacture and sell the box along with a free Adapta-

417

leader. (This 16ft knotless tapered cast should fill a long-felt want in the leader market.) The method of holding flies is quite revolutionary; it consists of hundreds of tiny nylon fibres gripped at one end in a metal strip. Two of these strips face each other, the loose ends of the fibres facing. A fly is secured simply by pushing it in between the nylon fibre-tips.

They seem to grip the flies very well; they do not fall out even when the box is banged forcibly. It is most important that flies should not shake loose from the device holding them because otherwise you will regularly open the box to find your flies in a tangled heap.

This is the great disadvantage of the magnetic styles of fly box. When dropped, the flies shake loose from the magnetic strips or the sheet of rubber-coated magnetized metal which lines this kind of box. In addition, the sheet-magnet design tends to bend fly hackles drastically out of shape. For these reasons, the magnetic box cannot be strongly recommended.

The next box can be worth every penny of its small cost. The box consists of six separate compartments, three on each side, with a sprung lid. It is manufactured in clear,

strong plastic and holds a good quantity of flies. It is particularly useful for river fishing when, if you know your river well, you can select the most 'likely' flies for the conditions, and leave the bigger stock of flies behind in their cumbersome boxes. An additional asset is a small ring on one end so that it can be attached to a waistcoat. These cheap, imported boxes are definitely value for money, and your local tackle dealer will probably have such a product in stock.

Selection of fly boxes

When buying fly boxes, decide in advance exactly what you require; whether you want all your flies stored together or whether you want to keep the various kinds separate. Several small boxes can help if you are trying to develop ranges of the same type of fly, e.g. wool-bodied, seal's fur or floss-bodied buzzer nymphs. A collection of flies in a good assortment of sizes will need plenty of room if they are to stay neat.

If you buy a box that has a lot of metal inside, keep the box as dry as possible when fishing—otherwise you will find that all your carefully tied flies have rusted. You should also check the box to make sure that it is as waterproof as possible and would float if dropped into water at any time.

(Left) Flies can quickly become tangled. (Below left) Nymph and wet fly collection. (Below) The standing box is made so that nylon fibres grip the hooks securely.

Mike Prichard

Irish Tourist Board

D. Laffin/Benwoods

Gaffs and tailers

The task of lifting a fish from the water and landing it safely on the bank can, in the vast majority of cases, be accomplished with a net. But a net large enough to lift a heavy fish from the water makes quite an encumbrance if it is to be carried across the shoulder or trailed from place to place by the lone angler. There are two alternatives to using the net: one is the gaff, the other a tailer. Both are lightweight, sure and convenient; each possesses disadvantages that need careful consideration before purchase.

For many anglers, especially pike fishermen, a gaff has become a status symbol which shows that the owner means business and intends to land big fish. Unfortunately, they use the gaff on every fish that is caught, regardless of size, and have no qualms about returning such fish, despite any wound that has been inflicted. Worse still, many of the gaffs that are used would be quite inadequate to deal with a very big fish.

Collapsible or telescopic gaffs seem to be most popular. They range from lightweight

419

Gaffs and tailers

alloy to heavy models. Those made from alloy cost less but tend to corrode over the years, often resulting in their joints sticking when extended. Light oiling helps smooth running, but will not cure minor dents and distortions that so easily occur when using handles made of soft alloy.

Protecting gaff heads

Good quality gaffs have steel or heavy gauge brass sections with a firm rubber or cork handle, and the added safety precaution of a leather thong that can be looped over the wrist. Even if this is not fitted to the gaff when purchased, it can be easily added. Gaff heads are invariably made from steel, and should be kept oiled.

(Previous page) Pity the gaff has to be used here but perhaps a tailer was not to hand. The salmon is an autumn fish, taken on the Yorkshire Esk near Whitby.
(Below) Tackling up, with the effective tailer standing ready for action.

Much is written about sharpening the point of a gaff at regular intervals, but if the point is adequately protected, this should not be necessary other than at the beginning of the season. Protection should be in the form of a brass safety cup into which the point will fit, and not a loose piece of cork haphazardly pushed onto the point.

The gape, or distance between the point of the gaff and its shank, is vitally important. Too little and it will be impossible to draw the point home; too much will effect balance and cause the handle to turn in use.

Fixed gaffs consist of a wooden pole to which a head is firmly screwed and then close-whipped with copper wire. It can be carried bandolier-style across the shoulders by a cord, clipping just below the waist with a spring clip that allows immediate release. Many anglers construct their own with a large sea hook and a broom handle—a practical approach provided that a large-enough hook is used. A tope hook is only just big enough and conger hooks are worse than useless. Every trace of the barb must be removed and any sneck, or offset angle, at the bend should be straightened.

Correct use of the gaff

To gaff a fish once it is played out needs a steady hand and a lot of common sense. Movement made by the gaff as it approaches the fish will often cause the creature to lunge away, and all temptation to strike at the fish should be resisted at that critical moment. Only when the fish is lying prone on the surface should the point be introduced, and then at the point of the jaw, where there is likely to be less movement than along the stomach or shoulder.

Once the point is well home, the fish should be lifted straight onto the bank in a single movement, taking care to lift with the handle and shift held vertically. A horizontal lift will throw an enormous strain on the handle and is the prime cause of gaffs bending and distorting. Several steps should be taken away from the water's edge before any move to release the fish—many premature struggles result in a fish's escape.

Bill Howes

420

Bill Howes

Used properly, with a sharp rap, the priest kills cleanly and quickly.

While the gaff relies on penetration in order to land the fish, the tailer uses a grip around the 'wrist,' just before the caudal fin, to hold and lift a fish onto the bank. Its business end consists of a heavy length of stiff, cabled steel, bent and held open by a thin, flexible wire that connects to the handle. When the fish is played out, the open wire loop is slid over the tail and back onto the 'wrist' immediately before the caudal fin.

How to use the tailer

Once in place the handle of the tailer is raised sharply; the wire noose will immediately clamp tightly into the flesh, rather like a snare around a rabbit's neck. The fish can be lifted clear of the water by the same vertical lift that would be used with a gaff.

The advantage of a tailer is that, with sensible use, an undersized or out-of-season fish can be released with little or no damage—something that is impossible when a gaff has been used. But there is one annoying disadvantage in the tailer, and that

is the tendency of the trip wire that holds the loop open to slip off its support every time it is knocked, closing the noose. The device needs constantly to be reset.

Killing a fish should be carried out as quickly and humanely as possible. Most anglers realize that the easiest way is to strike the head with a heavy object, but often this simple action is carried to extremes and anglers are seen using large pieces of wood, bottles, and even kicks from an angler's heavy boot to despatch the fish. Incidents like this are fuel for the anti-blood sport lobby, and as likely to bring discredit to the sport as leaving a fish to die on the bank.

The humane priest

For a very small price it is possible to purchase a priest—a short length of weighted wood, metal or horn, that can apply the final stroke neatly and humanely—hence the angling expression 'visited by the priest'. Two or three firm blows across the top of the head, behind the eyes, and the dead fish is ready for wrapping in the damp leaves or rushes that will keep it fresh until it is time for cooking or storing in a deep freeze.

421

Clothing

The fisherman should not select clothes in order to look attractive. He wants hard wear, warmth, and water-proofing. He needs clothes that can stand up to barbed wire, thorny foliage, and the worst the weather can throw at him. Colours should be subdued, even camouflaged.

Even so it is difficult to resist the romance and sheer snob appeal of clothes specially designed for golfers, campers, mountaineers and yachtsmen which are displayed in the sportswear shops. A glance at the garish colours and fancy buttons, however, usually stops the angler being caught, and the thought of flying drawstrings and toggles tangled with fishing line should drive him out of the shop in a near panic.

Perhaps it is time anglers stopped using old clothes for fishing as they are a pretty scruffy-looking lot. Maybe they should change their image, and if you feel that way there is plenty of high-quality clothing specially designed by anglers for anglers. It is not available in the sportswear shops, but local tackle dealers have a wide range.

A good jacket
The priority is a good jacket, and this must be comfortable and warm. It should be a size larger than the best tailor would recommend, so that it has space for an extra sweater underneath without making the arms uncomfortable.

At its best, and if you can afford it, it should be waterproof with a strong zip-fastener which can unzip from the top and from the bottom. This should be covered with a press-fastened flap. Ideally it should have storm pockets and elastic wrist fittings under roomy sleeves and cuffs, with well-designed ventilation holes under the arms. A wide turn-up collar is preferable, and valuable optional extras are a clip-on hood, and a stud-fastened inner lining, both of which can be fitted or discarded at will. Several well-known manufacturers produce this kind of garment, and they are made in both lightweight and heavyweight fabrics. Some offer an optional lining.

Other jackets are designed only to be shower-proof. These are cheaper, and if that is all you need then they are excellent. In heavy rain a lightweight over-mac can be worn, and if it fits in the pocket when not in use it makes a good alternative kit.

There are two basic waterproof materials available. The old-established oiled silk or cotton has stood the test of time. It retains its water resistance for years, but usually needs cleaning and re-proofing at intervals of up to five years. It has only two minor faults. In very cold weather it goes stiff as a board and may cut into your neck unless a scarf is worn, and when wet fly fishing the oil may soak on to the cast, preventing it from sinking properly. The more recently manufactured

heavy-duty kapok-lined nylon jacket or anorak is snug and warm in a boat in mid-winter and with its detachable lining it can be light and windproof on milder days.

Match fishermen tend to favour the shower-proof jacket with an ultra-light plastic or nylon portable overjacket which rolls up and fits easily in a pocket. They rely chiefly on their umbrellas for protection from the rain, but they also use waterproof over-trousers, which take the suffering out of sitting on a wet seat and protect the legs and thighs from the rain that cascades off plastic macs. Anyone who fishes from a boat regularly would also find these valuable.

Matching 'accessories'

For 'matching accessories' most anglers still rely on the old fashioned string-vest under a heavy twill or cotton shirt to retain inner warmth. The ex-serviceman's long woollen underpants might raise a laugh from friends in the hotel in the evening, but they are well worth it for the warmth they provide. Gloves are essential but not always effective—cold

(Above) Jack Lucas, the well-dressed game fisherman with three brace of good trout. (Below) Fly casting on the Dee from a rock, but well prepared to wade waist-deep.

Irish Tourist Board

fingers are something to which the angler must steel himself against, or stay at home when it's frosty. Mittens are an excellent compromise which enable tackle to be managed easily and at the same time reduce the cold.

The angler's waistcoat is popular with most people. It is invaluable for carrying disgorgers and forceps, scissors and shots and a host of other small equipment for which you would otherwise have to rummage in the tackle bag.

One universally popular garment is the angler's hat. Fashions keep changing, but what really matters is the protection it offers in a sport where hooks are thrown about willy-nilly. Polaroid sun glasses are an extra protection from other people's flying hooks and from the glare off the water.

Footwear

Finally, footwear is important. Anyone who has walked long distances in wellingtons or waders without proper understockings hardly needs to be told that thick sea-boot stockings or something similar are essential. So your footwear must be a size larger than usual to accommodate them. This also allows some ventilation space and helps keep feet warm. Most waders have press-stud and strap fittings at the knee which enable them

The sun may be shining, but lough fishing in Ireland demands that the angler be ready for any emergency the weather can bring.

to be folded down and worn 'Buccaneer' fashion. This is useful when walking between swims, and especially when sitting on a boat where the creases under the knees are uncomfortable.

Whatever footwear you choose the soles must be suitable for your kind of fishing. If you fish off concrete, or scramble over or wade in rocky hard-bottomed waters you must have metal-studded leather soles. Rubber is slippery and almost suicidal. For reservoirs and grassy banks and generally soft-bottomed waters composition plastic soles are excellent provided they have a deep tread. Once the tread has gone they become extremely dangerous and should be thrown out immediately.

Clothing is still very much a matter of personal choice and preference according to the kind of fishing you do, but warmth and comfort certainly provide the confidence and concentration which enable you to fish successfully. Attractive appearance might help in the local pub at lunch time, but on the bank only the fish can benefit, and if they see you first then you are wasting your time.

Basic flycasting

Rod tip at eye level

Reach

Stripped line

1

Pull

2

Lift

3

Stop

4

Forward cast

5   6   7   8

The technique of fly casting was described by Izaak Walton like this: 'In casting your line, do it always before you, so that your fly may, first, fall upon the water and as little of your line with it, as is possible'. This advice, in *The Compleat Angler*, is as true today as it was in 1653. The aim is to present the artificial fly to the fish in as natural a way as possible. This means that it must alight on the water in imitation of the natural insect, creating that small spreading ripple which induces the fish to take. But fly casting is a practical skill, very difficult to illustrate as a single, flowing motion. It is not a difficult skill to learn once the basic requirements are understood.

The basic problem

It is important to understand that there is only one basic problem and therefore only one real mistake to be made in fly casting.

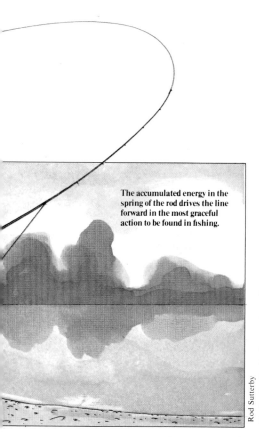

The accumulated energy in the spring of the rod drives the line forward in the most graceful action to be found in fishing.

The problem is that you must make the fly rod do the work, and not your arm. The rod must be made to act as a spring in order to propel a virtually weightless object, the fly, through the air. The function of the spring is to store up energy, and then release it when required. This can be understood in terms of two simple arm movements, which are equivalent to the loading and unloading of the spring.

The back cast

The action of fly casting, simply described, is that the line is lifted from the water by the rod and briskly thrown back behind the caster. This is called the 'back cast'. There is a pause while the line streams out and straightens behind the caster, who prevents the rod from straying back beyond the vertical by thumb pressure on the top of the handle. In that essential pause, the line, while streaming out behind the caster, is also pulling back the rod tip, making the whole rod flex. The rod and line are then driven forward again on the 'forward cast'. This flexing of the rod is the equivalent of a spring being wound up.

The base of the spring, in this case, is the butt of the rod. As with all springs, the base has to be locked firmly, or its energy will leak away. The locking action is achieved by the

Try to achieve a smooth motion, first of the back cast then the forward cast. (1) The angler strips about six yards of line from the reel and works it through the rod rings. (2) The back cast begins as the rod is held with the tip roughly at eye level and then lifted sharply upwards (3), with the left hand ensuring that the line is not pulled through the rings by the surface tension of the water. (4) The back cast continues to (5), where the position of the thumb should ensure that the rod does not go too far back beyond the vertical. As it stops, the spring of the rod will act to store energy for the forward cast. With the rod at full tension (6) the forward cast can begin (7), energy stored in the spring of the rod being released (8).

Rod Sutterby

Fly casting

'stopping' of the wrist at the point when the rod butt is roughly level with the ear during the back cast. The wrist is locked and as it is dragged back by the power applied to the back cast and the weight of the pulling line, the rod is forced to flex.

Wrist movement

The role of the wrist is actually far more complex than this necessarily simplified description of a cast. Experienced fly casters use wrist movement and virtually nothing else to control the rod and line, both in basic overhead casting and in other kinds of cast, to be described in later issues. Beginners should concentrate on stopping the wrist from following the rod backwards, as it would naturally do. If this is allowed to happen energy will not be stored in the base of the rod. This means that the angler will have to compensate for the lack of energy in the rod by applying extra muscular power to the forward cast. This in turn will lead to a weak or lazy back cast, simply because it becomes unnecessary to have a strong one.

Maximum results

Correctly done, fly casting will seem to require little effort or have little power behind it but will have maximum results, that is, the angler will be able to cast a long way without feeling tired. It is correct to say

that if the casting arm is tired after half an hour, then there is something wrong with the angler's casting technique.

Use the spring—not force

Really good fly-line casters are extremely rare, and the gap between the standard of their performance and that of the average fly fisherman is enormous. Many fly fishermen with years of experience do not use their fly-rod as a spring. They use force instead, but nevertheless believe that they are casting correctly because they can send the line some distance. In Britain there seems to be very little interest in casting as a separate, important part of fly fishing. There are fly-tying clubs but casting clubs usually fail for lack of support. Most anglers seem reluctant to learn from an expert and seem quite happy to go on casting in a haphazard fashion.

Importance of lessons

It is important to have several lessons with a professional instructor as this allows the student to gain a natural technique based on direct observation.

The technique of fly casting has been shown many times as a series of frozen poses, each one illustrating where the angler's arm, wrist, or the line, should be at a given moment. But it must be stressed that the action of the fly rod and line is a fluid motion

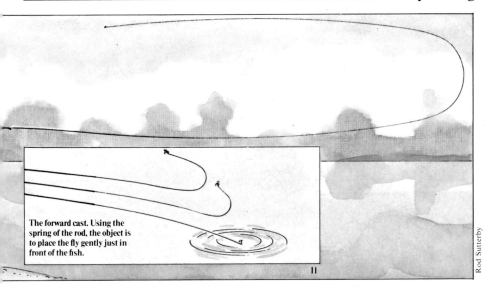

The forward cast. Using the spring of the rod, the object is to place the fly gently just in front of the fish.

II

Rod Sutterby

which should comprise one graceful arm movement. Any errors picked up and not corrected immediately by a teacher could easily become a habit. If you practise the wrong technique several times and become used to it, it will be very hard to correct later. Rather than focusing on the errors and trying to correct them one at a time, you would probably have to start from the beginning again, because the process must be learnt as a whole rather than broken up into stages. It is a mistaken approach to teach or learn such a technique on the basis of correcting errors, since concentrating on only one small part of the casting routine will cause it to lose its fluidity and be broken up.

The object: to catch fish

In spite of its importance as a technique to be mastered, casting is a means to catch fish, and not an end in itself. Where the fly lands on the water is an essential part of the skill: for example, successful reservoir fishing often depends on the ability to throw a very long line. But wherever you fish, accuracy of casting is vital. Right from the beginning of your tuition in fly casting, aim to reach the fish. Accuracy will enable you to do that.

Like life in general, bad habits are hard to correct. So start as you mean to go on—with good habits.

(Above) The forward cast continues (from previous page). When the pull through the rod rings is felt by the left hand, the line is released to shoot through, allowing the line to unfurl. As the line straightens out the angler lowers the rod horizontally, allowing the line to meet the water gently. (Inset) Properly cast, the fly touches the water exactly like a natural fly alighting. (Below) A fly casting demonstration. The forward cast is nearly completed.

Bill Howes

429

Arthur Ogelsley

Roll and spey casts

Despite what some people say and what is written about fly casting, it is a comparatively easy operation. Nevertheless, it is one that makes all the difference between enjoying fishing and not becoming fatigued at the end of the day, or becoming frustrated or tired, possibly losing many flies and fish.

The first essential is to understand what happens when a rod loaded with the correct weight of line is turned through an arc from a horizontal position to the vertical, held for a slight pause and then returned to the horizontal. This is the basic casting action and can be adjusted to give various types of cast, but each must have the same pendulum action from the rod handle.

As the rod is turned through its arc, it acts as a spring being wound up and then, as the spring unwinds, it transmits power to the piece of line at its end. This section of line then starts travelling forward and as it does so gradually turns over until it has completely unfolded and straightened out the rest of the length of line. This is only possible because a tapered line decreases in weight per unit length and each reduced weight portion is able to be moved by a decreased amount of energy. The energy is, of course, decreasing all the time from the moment the rod has imparted its energy to the line.

Three simple steps

To go a step farther, and smooth out the line, consider the movement to be in three parts. To do this, visualize a clock between nine and twelve. For the back cast, start with the rod in the nine o'clock position. Raise the rod slowly to eleven o'clock—this movement will lift most of the line from the water. The wrist then comes into action, accelerating the sweep of the rod and propelling the line backwards. During the wrist action the forearm still continues its stroke. This power stage must never carry on past the twelve o'clock position. The rod, however, may be allowed to travel beyond the vertical position, provided that it is merely drifting and that all the power has been cut off completely. At this point the rod must be held stationary for a brief pause in order to allow the line time to fully extend behind. The length of pause depends upon the length of line being cast and the wind conditions.

The forward cast is a repeat of the lift or back cast, but in the opposite direction. From the vertical the rod is moved slowly at first, then, when it reaches the eleven o'clock position, the wrist again accelerates the movement until ten o'clock, when the power is cut off and the rod is followed through (i.e. drifted) to nine o'clock.

Roll cast

By the time you have progressed with the basic mechanics of casting and can cast a line into the air behind you, allow it to straighten out and then reverse the procedure, casting a quiet, straight line onto the water where you want it, you should then be able to make the roll cast.

In some cases it is necessary to fish with some obstruction such as trees or perhaps a very high bank behind you, which rules out a normal overhead back cast. But it need not prevent you fishing in this particular stretch of water, and it is in such places that one can very often catch more fish as the inexpert caster will avoid this part of the river and always fish where he can make a conventional back cast. To cast under such conditions calls for the slightly different technique of the roll cast.

In this cast the line never goes behind the caster's body and never leaves the water. In order to create the weight (i.e. the pull of line against the rod) required to bend the rod into its loaded form, the friction of the line on the water in front of the caster is used. To perform this cast, the rod point is raised very slowly right up to one o'clock and held there until the line bellies to such a position that the extreme point of its curve is roughly in line with the caster's back. When the line reaches this position, a normal forward cast is made with a little more effort than usual, and the rod point is carried on down almost onto the water—in other words, instead of the power being cut off at approximately ten o'clock, it is carried on right through past nine o'clock, and in this particular cast there is no follow-through. This may sound difficult, but in fact is very easy indeed when it is tried out and these simple points are remembered.

The power stroke

One such point is that when making a roll cast the line must always be clear of itself and the cast must never be attempted in such a way that the line which rolls out will go over the line which is already on the water at the beginning of the power stroke. The following

simple rule explains this more clearly: when you intend to roll your line to a point to the right of where it already lies on the water, it must be brought up during the backwards slow lift to a position at the *left* side of the rod. When the line is to be cast to a position to the left of where it already lies then the line must be brought up slowly to a point to the *right* of the rod. If this rule is followed the line is always going away from itself and never tangles.

In some cases a strong side wind may be blowing against the caster, which could blow the line into a position in which it might foul. Under these conditions, the rod must be laid over more to the side during the backward slow-lifting stroke, but it must be remembered before the normal power stroke is carried out that the rod must be raised to the

vertical position and cast forward in a vertical plane.

Spey cast

Where the roll cast is useful in trout fishing with a single-handed rod, the Spey cast comes into its own in salmon fishing with a double-handed rod for fishing down tree-lined river banks.

The basic difference between the roll and Spey casts is that in the simple roll cast the line never leaves the water, while in the Spey, the line is completely lifted from the water and dropped back again in a new position from where a roll cast can be made. The cast is made in the same way as the simple roll

A demonstration of the roll cast by a past expert. The late Tommy Edwards, on the Spey, showing how the cast should be made.

Arthur Oglesby

cast. It is the pre-positioning of the line which creates a difference.

The timing of the Spey cast is extremely critical (more so than in any other type of cast) and this makes it the most difficult cast of all to do properly.

Consider making a Spey cast from the left bank of a river: it is desirable to have the right hand at the top of the rod handle and the left hand at the bottom. At the same time, the right foot should be pointing forward.

Using the current

Having fished the fly around and into your own bank (i.e. in this instance the left bank) and having let it 'hang' in the current for a while immediately downstream in order to fully straighten the line out below you, the rod is first of all lowered to ensure a good clean lift.

Now, raise the rod straight up to the eleven o'clock position. The body and feet are not moved during this movement of the rod. This movement gets the line on to the surface of the water and in a position in readiness for the next part of the cast.

Placing line upstream

The next movement is fairly complex and involves the swivelling of the body and the transference of the line to a position upstream and to the right of the angler. He is now facing the new direction in which the cast is to be made.

Move the rod in a 'half-moon' curve from the eleven o'clock position to a one o'clock position upstream. During this movement it moves through 180° and at the same time goes from eleven o'clock to a horizontal position at 90° (i.e. half way) and back up again to the one o'clock position.

Acceleration

Because the rod is moved in a semi-circle it follows that the line comes round from in front of the caster to a position upstream. The movement of the rod is accelerated during the second half of the curve and as the rod is raised (from a horizontal position back up to one o'clock) the line is completely lifted off the water.

Now, the rod is arrested briefly, allowing

Roll and Spey casts

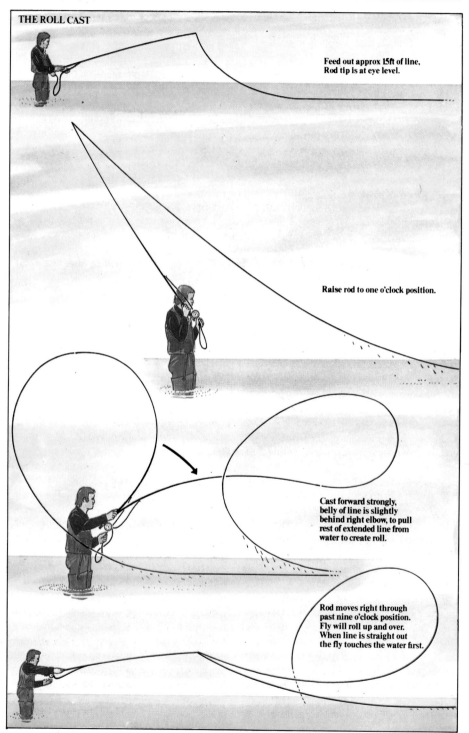

THE ROLL CAST

Feed out approx 15ft of line,
Rod tip is at eye level.

Raise rod to one o'clock position.

Cast forward strongly,
belly of line is slightly
behind right elbow, to pull
rest of extended line from
water to create roll.

Rod moves right through
past nine o'clock position.
Fly will roll up and over.
When line is straight out
the fly touches the water first.

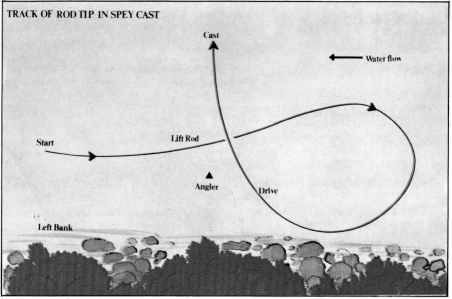

TRACK OF ROD TIP IN SPEY CAST

Cast

Water flow

Lift Rod

Start

Angler

Drive

Left Bank

Rod Sutterby

the line to drop on to the water. As soon as the line touches the water, the power is applied from the one o'clock position all the way through to about eight o'clock without any follow through. This motion is exactly that which is used in a simple roll cast.

While the 'half-moon' movement is being made the body must swivel from facing directly downstream to facing in a direction across the river in which the final delivery of the cast will be made.

After the lift of the rod from downstream and as the 'half-moon' curve is made, the body is swivelled by pivoting on the right heel and left toe to face the new direction. From this position the final execution of the cast can be made.

Critical timing of the Spey cast
The most critical part of the timing of the Spey cast is the pause while the line drops on to the water. If this is too long and as a consequence too much line lands on the water, the drag becomes too much and the line cannot be rolled out fully. If, on the other hand, insufficient line is on the water (because the pause has not been long enough) then the point of the line will flick into the air with a 'crack' and again the line

will not be rolled out as it should be.

The pause and the resulting length of line on the water can only be measured in parts of a second, so practice is essential in order to make a good Spey cast.

To make a Spey cast from the right bank, exactly the same movement is employed but the hands and feet are reversed.

Double Spey cast
If there is a very strong downstream wind blowing and this results in the line being blown under the rod, making the Spey cast difficult, the double Spey cast can be made. This cast (from the left bank of the river) is made with the hands and feet reversed; i.e. left hand up the handle and left foot forward.

In the first part of this cast the rod is taken upstream in an identical movement to the Spey cast. The line, however, is not dropped onto the water but is led back downstream with a 'half-moon' curve of the rod (without returning the body to face downstream). The line is dropped on to the water and the final delivery is made. Because the line is downstream the wind blows it away from the rod, allowing a cast to be made where otherwise it would be impossible.

Wet fly fishing

Wet fly fishing is, quite simply, the art of fishing an artificial fly beneath the surface of the water, either in imitation of a natural food item, or as an 'attractor'—a pattern which seems to bear no resemblance to any living creature but which induces a fish to strike at it in curiosity, anger or defence. Patterns referred to as 'nymphs' and 'bugs' usually attempt to imitate specific life forms, although there are more than a few patterns which bear a general resemblance to a number of different creatures and therefore are imitative of a range of natural forms, rather than one specific form.

Traditional wet flies

Traditional wet flies tend, very often, to fall into the 'attractor' category, bearing no close resemblance to anything in nature. There are others that do, nevertheless, imitate, either in colour or shape, living creatures such as small fry, or the pupal or larval forms of insects. Of the vast range of lures now available, some are designed to resemble small fry of all manner of species, while others merely suggest small fish by their outline and the way that they move in the water when retrieved correctly. It is probable, however, that the majority are neither shaped nor coloured like any small fish, and succeed in catching trout by the attractor principle.

'Point' and 'dropper' flies

The traditional version of wet fly fishing involves the use of a team of three flies, although, in times past, there are records of anglers using a dozen or more patterns at the same time. A modern wet fly leader has one fly attached to the end of the leader: this is the 'point' fly, and more often than not is a dressing tied to simulate a nymph or bug. Perhaps a yard above the point fly there is a 'dropper', a loose length of nylon projecting from the leader to which the second fly, also called a dropper, is attached. This often tends to be an attractor pattern, like a

Bloody Butcher, which some anglers believe to be recognized by the trout as a tiny minnow, or stickleback. A yard or so above the dropper, is another dropper, to which the 'bob' fly is tied. This usually tends to be a biggish, bushy dressing, such as a Zulu, or a Palmer, which bounces and bobs across the surface of the water during the retrieve.

Standard tactics when river fishing are to commence at the upstream end of the beat, casting upstream at an angle of 45°, allowing the line to sweep around with the current, and lifting off again when the line forms an angle of 45° downstream. After each retrieve, the angler moves a yard or so downstream and repeats the process. This is virtually the opposite of the dry fly fisherman's tactics, since he will normally prefer to work upstream, so it is easy to understand why there is conflict between the two schools of thought.

Modern practice

Of course, there is no reason why the wet fly exponent cannot adopt the tactic of working upstream, and modern practice is very often to use just one fly on the leader— the point fly, in fact—and follow exactly the same tactics as the dry fly purist—working upstream and casting only to an observed fish. In such cases, the selected fly will almost always be a sound copy of a natural life form, preferably one which exists in good numbers in the particular fishery. Specific nymph copies can be excellent, as can shrimp patterns. In stillwater fishing, with no current to work the flies, the angler has to learn to

HOW TO MAKE YOUR OWN 'TEAM OF THREE' LEADER

Fly Line   Knotless Taper   48in

Needle Knot   0.020 in to 0.012 in approx.

Hill's Patent Cast Carrier, a neat and handy way of carrying made-up casts and teams of flies without tangling.

Eric Birch

manipulate the flies manually. When fishing from the bank, the choice of a floating line, or one or other of the sinking lines is the same as it is on the river. Whereas line selection on the river, however, may be dictated more by current speed than any other factor, on stillwaters the final selection may well be dictated by the depth of water in front of the angler, the depth at which the trout are feeding, and the speed of the retrieve required to induce a take.

What line to use?

If the trout are taking food close to the surface on slow moving food items, then a floating line and slow retrieve—or no retrieve at all—is indicated, and the take of an interested trout is signalled by a movement of the end of the line. Where the trout are deeper, and only willing to accept a fast moving object, it will be necessary to use a sinking line. Whether one uses a slow, medium or fast sinker is governed by the particular circumstances.

On the larger waters, lure fishing has come into prominence in recent years. Normal practice, almost invariably, is to attach one lure at the point of the leader and cast this out as far as possible by means of the double haul cast. Distances of 50 yards can be achieved with practice using this technique. A sinking line is usually employed, and retrieval tends to be very fast indeed, so fast that it is known as 'stripping'. Occasionally trout are willing to accept a lure stripped across the surface using a floating line, which

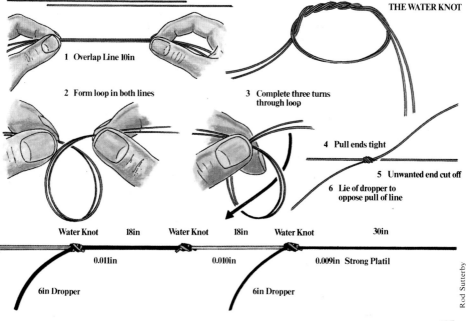

THE WATER KNOT

1 Overlap Line 10in

2 Form loop in both lines

3 Complete three turns through loop

4 Pull ends tight

5 Unwanted end cut off

6 Lie of dropper to oppose pull of line

| Water Knot | 18in | Water Knot | 18in | Water Knot | 30in |

0.011in   0.010in   0.009in Strong Platil

6in Dropper   6in Dropper

Rod Sutterby

Wet fly fishing

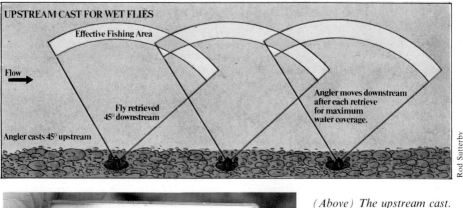

UPSTREAM CAST FOR WET FLIES

Effective Fishing Area

Flow

Angler moves downstream
after each retrieve
for maximum
water coverage.

Fly retrieved
45° downstream

Angler casts 45° upstream

Rod Sutterby

(Above) The upstream cast.
(Left) A box of lures ideal
for nymph fishing.
(Below right) When the
trout are not feeding on
surface insects, the nymph
can be fished sink-and-draw.
Trout feeding on hatching
flies might be tempted by
one using the style shown in
the lower illustration.

P. H. Ward/Natural Science Photos

creates a pronounced wake behind the lure.

It seems to be less well known that a lure on a sinking line, fished so slowly that it bounces along the bottom, can be very productive, and often leads to the capture of larger trout. Where it is permitted, the static sunken fly can also prove very killing. This involves casting out a fairly heavily dressed lure on a medium sinking line, letting it sink to the bottom, and just waiting for a trout to snap it up. Sometimes the lure will be taken as it sinks, or is picked up off the bottom shortly after it has settled, but on other occasions one has to resort to an occasional short retrieve before allowing it to settle again. The bed of the lake has to be clear of weed and obstructions for this to be successful, and the water should preferably be at least 6ft deep.

Fishing the traditional 'team of three' from a boat can be very exciting. The method is to let the boat drift, casting before you, and retrieving line just fast enough that you keep in touch with your flies as the boat drifts

towards them. Sometimes it pays to retrieve a little faster, so that the bob fly dibbles nicely along the tops of the waves. Sometimes a trout will take the bob fly so close to the boat that the angler can be completely taken by surprise.

Drift problems

Lures can be fished very efficiently from a boat, and so can a single fly or nymph, usually on a sinking line. If the boat drifts too quickly, this can create difficulties, so the normal practice is to slow down the rate of drift by using a drogue or 'sea anchor'—a cone of heavy canvas attached securely to a spreader ring, and allowed to trail over the side—acting as a brake. Alternatively, anchor the boat in a chosen position and fish in exactly the same way as one would fish from the bank.

Catching the biggest trout from reservoirs and very large lakes can be difficult because of the vast expanse of water that has to be covered. Fortunately, a great many small stillwater fisheries have opened up across the

438

country, and many of these have the twin attributes of possessing clear water and quite large trout. Usually it is more expensive to buy a day ticket on these small fisheries than it is on the reservoirs, but usually value for money is obtained because the average size of the fish is larger and the density of stock very much higher. The average angler catches one reservoir trout of about a pound in weight on each visit. On small fisheries the average is usually three trout weighing more than twice the reservoir average.

Many of the small fisheries have rules banning lure fishing, or the use of more than one fly on the leader. This makes sense because long casting on a small water is hardly ever necessary, and would interfere with the enjoyment of other anglers. Also, it is easier to persuade a good-sized trout to take an imitation of a natural insect than it is to get it to take a gaudy lure. The most successful anglers study the water very carefully, first of all to locate a trout, and secondly to try to see what it is likely to be eating. The more visits an angler makes to a particular water, the easier he finds it to locate his trout, and guess what the trout is feeding on—or likely to feed on. Once the trout has been seen, and the decision made

which fly to tie on, the angler casts his nymph or bug to that trout, just as the dry fly anglers does with surface-feeding trout.

This type of wet fly fishing is, however, a little more difficult than dry fly fishing because the trout might be feeding 6ft down from the surface and the angler has to be very accurate with his cast, not only to get the distance right, but also to know that his fly will sink fast enough to reach a trout before it moves on to feed elsewhere. If the water is very deep, it may be necessary to use a sink tip line, but usually it is sufficient to use a floating line with a long leader, and perhaps some lead wire added to the artificial fly when it is being dressed.

Salmon and the wet fly

Wet fly fishing for salmon can be grand sport, although usually very expensive. The usual practice is to make long casts across the river, let your fly drift downstream over likely holding areas, and then retrieve slowly. The flies are often very large—larger even than reservoir lures—and mostly look like nothing on earth. When the water is low, much smaller flies are used, with fairly sparse dressing, and indeed, it is probable that some of the more effective reservoir lures have been developed from low water salmon flies.

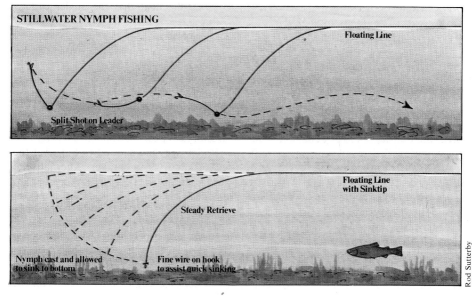

STILLWATER NYMPH FISHING

Floating Line

Split Shot on Leader

Floating Line with Sinktip

Steady Retrieve

Nymph cast and allowed to sink to bottom

Fine wire on hook to assist quick sinking

Rod Sutterby

439

Chalk stream fishing

During the middle of the 19th century the great traditions of dry fly fishing developed on the chalk streams of England, particularly on such world famous rivers as the Test, Itchen and Kennet, in the Southern Counties. Fortunately for the modern angler the purism associated with the use of the dry-fly-only rule to a large extent disappeared when nymph fishing was introduced in the early 1900s. Today, on many of our chalk streams, nymph fishing is only allowed after 1 July. This is a sensible rule, as hatches of surface fly during the height of summer are often minimal, and so the use of a nymph during this period at least provides the angler with some interesting and demanding fishing.

During the past 20 years fly fishing has developed enormously. Today, there are many thousands of anglers, proficient at casting a fly, who regularly fish on lakes and reservoirs. Many would undoubtedly love to fish a chalk stream but probably feel they are not sufficiently experienced. This is nonsense. If you can cast a fly delicately onto the water, the art of dry fly or nymph fishing on chalk streams can be quickly acquired.

Slow, stealthy approach

The angler must appreciate that he will be fishing in very clear water, which means the trout can see him from a considerable distance, so that the fly fisherman tramping along the bank looking for trout will scare more trout than he catches. A slow, stealthy approach to the water is essential and at times it may even be necessary to crawl and cast from a kneeling position to fish successfully from an open section of bank.

Of equal importance is the actual presentation of the dry fly or nymph. Use as

RED-RIBBED OLIVE

RED SEDGE

LEADED SHRIMP

Lyn Cawley

(Above) Three typical flies for use in chalk stream fly fishing.
(Left) The Lambourne, a chalk stream tributary of the River Thames.

G. L. Carlisle.

440

FLY PRESENTATION

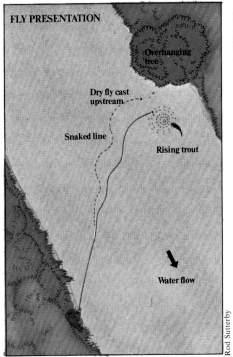

- Overhanging tree
- Dry fly cast upstream
- Snaked line
- Rising trout
- Water flow

Rod Sutterby

(Above) Trout, like many species of fish, are attracted by overhanging vegetation. So watch for rises and cover them by 'snake' casting beyond the rise. As the line straightens the fly will drift down to where the fish lies.

light a line as you can handle proficiently, plus a fine leader. Nothing will scare trout more than to have the fly line landing on the water within its field of view, or even the fly or nymph itself if it lands heavily.

When you have the choice of using either a dry fly or a nymph, it is best to decide beforehand which method you are going to employ on any given stretch of water. When fishing with a dry fly you should concentrate on looking for rise forms on the surface, but when using a nymph you should be looking into the water for feeding fish. It is not possible to combine the two successfully. Try to cast the fly so that it lands delicately, to one side of the fish or rise, or better still well upstream (although this will depend on your position relative to the trout).

A good general pattern

Many fly fishermen think that it is essential to have considerable knowledge of the natural flies that the trout may be rising to, so that a matching artificial may be used to deceive them. This is not strictly true; while it may be necessary for a particularly wary or difficult trout, a large proportion of fish will succumb to a good general pattern of dry fly. These include such names as 'Kites Imperial', 'Rough Olive', or 'Black Gnat' during the day, or as dusk approaches, a 'Lunns Particular' or a small 'Red Sedge'.

TROUT'S CONE OF VISION

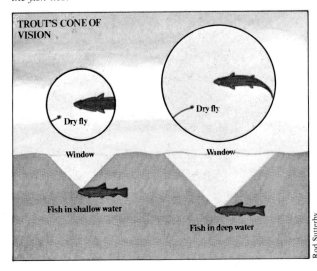

- Dry fly
- Dry fly
- Window
- Window
- Fish in shallow water
- Fish in deep water

Rod Sutterby

(Left) Fish have a cone of vision which is related to the depth at which they are swimming. The smaller cone allows the trout less time to react to any unnatural movement of the fly or line. Here, the fly must drift across the trout's nose. With a deep-lying fish the fly should drift to one side of the trout. For objects above the surface, due to refraction, the deeper-lying fish will see the angler before the shallow-swimming trout does.

441

Chalk stream fishing

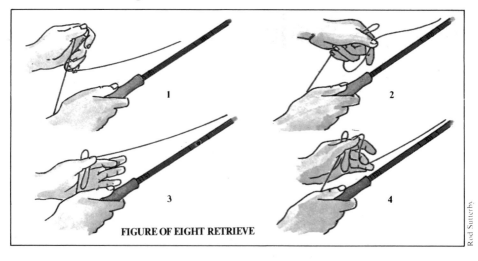

FIGURE OF EIGHT RETRIEVE

Rod Sutterby

During the latter half of the season, when hatches of surface fly are sparse and few trout are rising, it is necessary to use a nymph. This is because trout are feeding below the surface. In chalk streams the main underwater diet of trout is various species of olive nymph, although some trout may be observed searching the bottom or probing weed for shrimps. It is only necessary, therefore, to have an unweighted nymph to offer to fish feeding just below the surface, or a weighted 'Pheasant Tail' or 'PVC Nymph' to offer to deeper feeding trout. Where trout feed on shrimps in deep water a heavy-leaded shrimp pattern may be used. Weighted nymphs should be cast well upstream of a feeding trout and allowed to drift downstream.

Watch for the flash
It is often difficult to see the nymph underwater so it is important to watch for the flash of the fish as it turns to take the bait, or the wink of white as he opens his mouth, and strike immediately.

Should the trout consistently refuse your offering, try the 'induced take' technique. Correctly applied this technique can be a very efficient method, but it does require some expertise. When you think the nymph has appeared within the visual field of the trout, slowly raise the rod tip. This will make the nymph rise towards the surface—which most trout find irresistible.

(Above) The 'Figure of Eight' method of line recovery while fly fishing.
(Below) Fly fishing on chalk streams can be practised in the most attractive surroundings. Because of the nature of the gin-clear water the angler must always make a cautious approach.

S. L. Ward Natural Science Photos

Reservoir fishing

The reservoirs of Britain are all large expanses of water, averaging around 800-1,000 acres, with Grafham Water at 1,600 acres and the giant Rutland Water 3,200 acres.

With such large areas, the first problem is finding the fish. Not only might they be concentrated in a fairly small area, they could also be feeding at the surface, the bottom, or somewhere inbetween.

Weather conditions

When starting to fish any reservoir, the first consideration is the weather. If the wind has been blowing in a particular direction for several days previously, it is safe to assume that there will be fish around the windward bank. If the day is cloudy and overcast fish are more likely to be at the surface than if the

This angler took two fine rainbows from the 1,600-acre expanse of Grafham Water.

day is bright. Choose the method and place to fish accordingly.

When boat fishing, you can use a rudder or drift-controller if the reservoir rules allow. The method then would be to set the rudder so that the boat drifts along the bank, and to cast at right-angles to the boat. Allow the line to sink, and when it has gone through an arc and is straight behind the boat, retrieve your fly. Takes very often occur just as the fly is passing through the bend of the arc, because at this point it suddenly speeds up, and any fish following will often be fooled into taking it rather than let it escape.

If rudders are not allowed by the reservoir

443

Bill Howes

rules, one can control the rate of drift with a drogue—an attachment similar to a parachute in appearance—suspended in the water behind the boat to slow down the rate of drift. Similar tactics may be used with the drogue as with the rudder.

With both of these methods it is possible to cover a great deal of water, and if fish are not contacted within a reasonable space of time, it is advisable to change and fish a different depth. This is achieved by using either a slower or faster sinking line or allowing more or less time for the fly to sink.

Floating line tactics

If fish are seen to be rising or feeding just under the surface, it is obviously sound tactics to use a floating line and a team of nymphs or wet flies. These are fished very slowly, across the wind, with no movement whatsoever, except the movement given by the drift of the boat. Fish moving up wind are very susceptible to this method, and if none are caught quickly when you know you have covered them, change the fly, or grease or de-grease the leader in case you are not fishing at their depth.

If the boat is drifting fast, it is advisable to anchor in an area where fish are, and fish across the wind, again not retrieving.

Recommended flies are the Tiger Nymph, Buzzer Nymph, Black and Peacock Spider, Amber Nymph, Sedge Pupa, Greenwell's Glory, March Brown, Butcher, Dunkeld and Invicta. Of course there are others, but these flies usually score well anywhere and in most conditions.

If you do not often fish at anchor, it is a good idea to do so if the fish are obviously on the bottom or concentrated in a small area. On these occasions you will find that a small lure worked slowly through the water works well. Flies such as the Appetizer, Black Chenille, Church Fry, Baby Doll, Whisky Fly, Jack Frost, Matuka, and Sweeney Todd are very effective.

These methods work very well from a boat but can still be adopted if you are restricted to bank fishing. Make for the windward

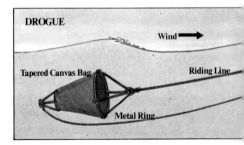

DROGUE

Wind ➡

Tapered Canvas Bag

Riding Line

Metal Ring

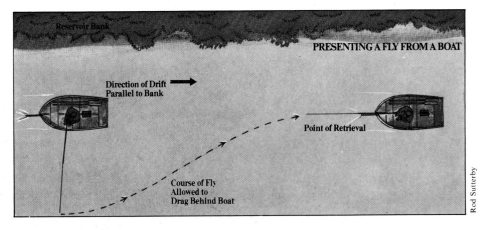

PRESENTING A FLY FROM A BOAT

Direction of Drift
Parallel to Bank

Reservoir Bank

Point of Retrieval

Course of Fly
Allowed to
Drag Behind Boat

Rod Sutterby

(Left) Early season trout fishing at a popular Midlands reservoir, Draycote. (Above) On the drift, a fly is cast at right angles, to finish up astern.

bank, and if there are bays there, so much the better. Standing on the point of a bay it is possible to cast across the wind with a team of nymphs or wet flies swinging round, as described previously.

If the water is deep from the bank, use a sinking line which will enable you to retrieve slowly without snagging, or a floating line with a long leader. That is, of course, if you need to fish deep. Use the same flies as you would when boat fishing.

Roving pays off
One spot from the bank might be fished very thoroughly, so if nothing is contacted, it often pays to move along. When the wind is blowing onto the bank, the wave action varies according to the depth of the water. In shallow water, more of the bottom is stirred up, which might attract feeding fish. This is something always worth considering, so try all depths of water possible from the bank until you start catching.

As you will never know all about every reservoir you fish, consult local anglers when fishing a new water—it can save time.

Rutland Water
Of the many reservoirs in England, Rutland Water is certainly to be recommended. The fish there are fast-growing and hard-fighting, with a high average weight, and will come to all methods. After Rutland, Grafham must still rate highly in everyone's estimation because there is always the chance of a record-breaker, while Pitsford is very scenic and produces some beautiful brownies to nymph fishing tactics.

Chew is a large water with great potential, and neighbouring Blagdon is well established, and picturesque, with some very good fish. Both Chew and Blagdon can prove to be very difficult indeed, but are superb when going well.

Ravensthorpe is small but pretty, and some big fish have been caught there in the past, although good fish are rare now. Other reservoirs to recommend are Ardleigh and Hanningfield. These reservoirs tend to be favourites but it is also a good idea to visit others each season.

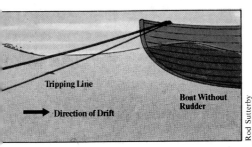

Tripping Line

Direction of Drift

Boat Without Rudder

Rod Sutterby

Rudders are sometimes not allowed, so the drogue acts to stream behind the boat and slow the rate of drift.

Salmon fishing

For most experienced salmon anglers the epitome of skill in their sport comes, perhaps, in the months of May and June when the salmon are in a playful mood and will condescend to take very small flies fished on a floating line. This style of fishing is not as complex as it may appear and by far the most challenging aspect of the exercise is to be on the right river at the right time and place. This injects a degree of chance into the success or failure of salmon fishing and there are few short cuts to assist the novice.

Small flies, floating lines

Fly fishing with small flies and floating lines is one of the easiest and most successful forms of salmon fishing providing that the water temperatures have been sustained over the 10°C (50°F) mark for a few days; the water lacks an excess acidity and is clear and not excessively deep. The Aberdeenshire Dee is a classic example of a fly river, but there are many others where similar conditions are found.

Basically the fly is cast across the current and slightly downstream. The angler may

have to wade to successfully cover known lies, but the object is to make the fly pass over the lies slightly submerged as slow as possible to make it move. The take from a fish may appear as nothing more than a slow but solid draw. In any event it is a grave mistake to strike and it is quite normal for the salmon to merely hook itself as it pulls the fly. A hooked salmon has a few ideas of its own and the angler may expect to struggle with a fish for roughly one minute for each pound it weighs.

It cannot be stressed too strongly that the primary requirement is to know the salmon lies, what to do and when. Casting or placing the fly may be quickly learned, but it may take years to acquire knowledge of an area.

Spinning technique

Undoubtedly, the form of salmon fishing that requires the most practice is spinning with a double-handed rod and a fixed-spool or multiplying reel. This technique must account for the lion's share of all salmon

(Below) An angler enjoying autumn salmon fishing on the Tweed at Innerleithen.

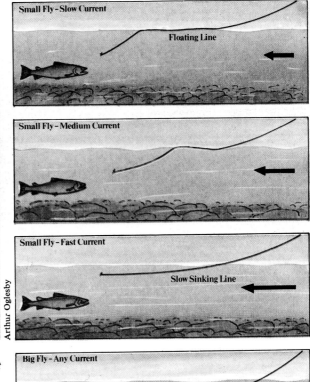

Small Fly - Slow Current
Floating Line

Small Fly - Medium Current

Small Fly - Fast Current
Slow Sinking Line

Arthur Oglesby

(Right) To be on the river at the right time is one of the essentials of salmon fishing. But then the fly, the line, the current, and the angler's skill must all combine to land the taking fish.

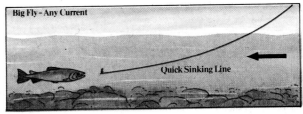

Big Fly - Any Current
Quick Sinking Line

Rod Sutterby

Steve Bicknell

Selection of the lure for salmon fishing depends upon weight of the lure and the strength of the current.

caught, but it is often over-used and abused and there are some rivers where its continued use may do more harm than good. It is a useful technique to apply in the early spring when the water is cold and deep and when the fish are reluctant to move far from their lies. At such times it is barely possible to make the bait move too slow and deep. Of course, it is not much fun to be continually hung up on the bottom, but if the right weight of bait has been chosen it should be possible to cast it across the current and have it swing round (just like our fly) without winding the reel handle. The current is generally strong enough to make the bait revolve. Any form of reel handle winding before the bait is out of the

447

current and dangling immediately down-stream will make the bait move to fast and too high in the water.

Choosing the weight in the bait is therefore one of paramount consideration. The angler must assess current strength and depth and then choose a bait which, when cast across the current, will swing round at good depth without fouling the bottom and, in all but semi-stagnant water, without winding the handle of the reel. Good salmon baits are to be found in the wide range of Devon minnows, and the myriad of spoon baits on offer are available in a wide choice of colours. During the colder months there is rarely a call for baits smaller than 2in long.

Other methods

Although spinning and fly fishing form the basis of most salmon fishing technique there are several other legitimate methods which the angler may resort to when the going gets tough. It is possible to limit all

salmon fishing to small flies and floating lines in late spring and summer and big flies and sinking lines for early spring or late autumn. However, many times the worm, prawn or shrimp has saved an otherwise blank day or week. At certain times and seasons the use of these natural baits can be very effective, but there are still too many anglers who will resort to them without trying other more sporting methods.

It should not be implied that fishing with any of these natural baits is easy. There is a

This sequence illustrates the correct way of presenting a worm across salmon lies. Start upstream (1) to cover any possible fish. Move to 2, then down to position 3. If no salmon takes, move up to 4, then to 5, where a fish may be lying in front of the stone. Lastly try lie 6 on the far bank by casting out and letting line out to drift the worm down behind the obstruction.

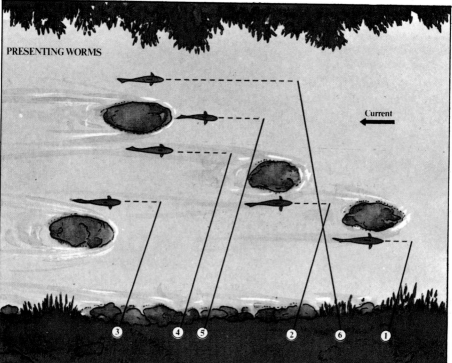

PRESENTING WORMS

Current

Rod Sutterby

sense in which successful fishing with a worm or prawn is more difficult than fly fishing, but there are times, conditions and situations when they might prove too effective and spoil the sport for others.

The same basic requirement for good weight assessment is necessary for successful worm fishing. The worm has to trundle over the bottom of the river and if the weight is too heavy there will be frequent hang-ups. If it is too light the worm may not get to the bottom.

Worm fishing

The best time for worm fishing is, perhaps, after a recent flood when the water is still coloured and higher than normal. The salmon may be laid quite close to the bank and there is again no substitute for knowing the waters. Whatever happens the angler must be at great pains not to strike at the first bite he detects. A salmon will frequently play with the worm for several minutes before taking or rejecting the bait.

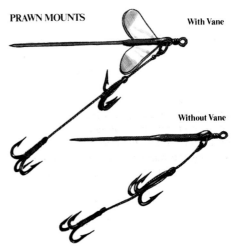

PRAWN MOUNTS

With Vane

Without Vane

(Above) Prawn mounts can be obtained with and without spinning vanes. (Below) Shrimp and prawn can be used with spinning tackle and (bottom) with a float. Drift-lining without a float gives exciting and surprising fishing.

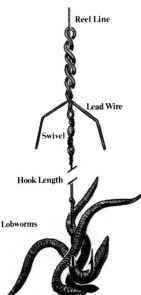

(Below) A spiral of lead wire above the swivel often helps to prevent snagging hooks on the bottom.

Reel Line

Lead Wire

Swivel

Hook Length

Lobworms

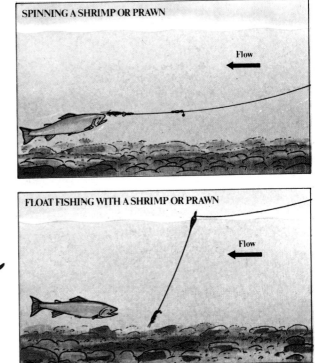

SPINNING A SHRIMP OR PRAWN

Flow

FLOAT FISHING WITH A SHRIMP OR PRAWN

Flow

Rod Sutterby

Sea trout fishing

A good motto for the angler seeking sea trout today would be, 'First find a sea trout river!' The sea trout's environment, like that of the salmon, is slowly being eroded; and where it abounds its runs and migrations tend to be more fickle and unpredictable than previously. So the angler must do some intensive homework: to find an adequate sea trout river and then, miraculously, contrive to be on the river when the ephemeral sea trout is in the pools of his own beat.

Many dedicated sea trout anglers feel that fly fishing for sea trout with a floating line presents the ultimate angling challenge in Britain today. This must be a matter of opinion and opportunity, but undoubtedly the sea trout is one of the shyest fish to inhabit our waters. For this reason, most sea trout fishing, in normal to low water, is done under cover of dusk or darkness.

The ideal sea-trout rod is single-handed and about 10ft long. It should be rigged with a No 7 double or forward taper line, attached to a 9ft monofilament leader of not less than

Fishing the tail of Polchrain, a pool on the River Spey noted for the excellence of its sea trout fishing.

Arthur Oglesby

6lb b.s. To this tie on a No 10 single or double-hooked fly. Add waders and net and the sea trout angler is ready for the fray.

Patterns of sea trout fly are as legion as the colours on Joseph's coat. Most anglers have their favourites, but there is little doubt that the angler is much more fussy in this respect than the fish. In the dark it sees the fly as only a vague silhouette, so it is size and not colour which is more important.

Wait for the signal

There is a magic about the eerie dusk of a summer evening. The best nights often come after a sharp but warm shower of rain, when it is cloudy rather than clear and a myriad of insects are dancing over the water. But do not be in a hurry to begin fishing, however; it is a mistake to start too early. While it is still light, and with a discreet reconnaissance, establish where the sea trout are lying—but do not assume that they will stay put as darkness descends. Initial activity from the fish often takes the form of splashing or surface rises. This is the signal to start. Concentrate at first on the streamier sections of the river and leave the quiet glides and tails until full darkness.

Make your first cast out to a point slightly downstream and across the current. Further casts will have to be made in the dark, so it pays to stick a small piece of cotton wool onto the line to indicate the correct amount

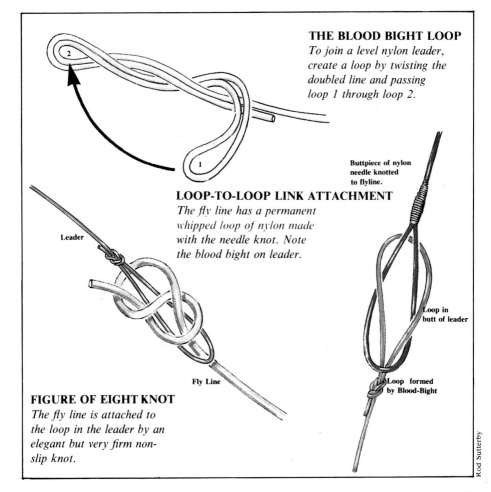

THE BLOOD BIGHT LOOP
To join a level nylon leader, create a loop by twisting the doubled line and passing loop 1 through loop 2.

Buttpiece of nylon needle knotted to flyline.

LOOP-TO-LOOP LINK ATTACHMENT
The fly line has a permanent whipped loop of nylon made with the needle knot. Note the blood bight on leader.

Leader

Loop in butt of leader

Fly Line

Loop formed by Blood-Bight

FIGURE OF EIGHT KNOT
The fly line is attached to the loop in the leader by an elegant but very firm non-slip knot.

Rod Sutterby

Sea trout fishing

FALKUS' SUNK LURE

1. Put a few turns of silk (red) as seating on a short-shanked sneck bend hook.

2. Loop nylon round hook and pass both ends through eye. Nylon should be stiff enough to support hook without drooping.

3. Whip nylon to hook shank and varnish.

4. Wind a seating on a second hook, from about halfway on shank, forward to eye. Take Strand B through eye and whip silk back towards the point, tying in Strand B. Cut off B. Trim Strand A level with eye. Whip forward to eye, tying in Strand A along top of shank. Ensure hooks are in alignment.

(Above) A 2lb sea trout caught from the Lune on a small fly and floating line.
(Left) The stages in tying Hugh Falkus's Sunk Lure, a night-fishing sea trout lure.

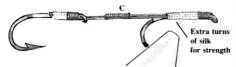

5. Whip nylon mount at C. Varnish mount. Paint hook shanks silver. Allow 2 days to dry.

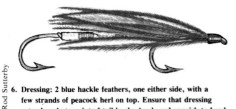

6. Dressing: 2 blue hackle feathers, one either side, with a few strands of peacock herl on top. Ensure that dressing extends only to point of tail hook. Apply red varnish to head.

Rod Sutterby

to use. With a little practice, the angler can sense when everything is going right, but even the experts experience the most diabolical tangles. When tangles happen, the best remedy is to retire well away from the water and, with the aid of a torch, exchange the leader and fly for another cast ready made up. Care must be taken not to let the torch beams show anywhere near the water. This can put sea trout down quickly.

Playing a spirited sea trout

On a good night, it is not long before the angler feels a determined tug. If the fish is properly hooked, there may then follow a hair-raising display when the fish seems to be more out of the water than in it. The rod suddenly arches into a taut bow, the fish pulling with frenzied runs and leaps. Fresh-run sea trout, however, have very tender

Arthur Oglesby

for the angler to take a brief rest, have a dram of whisky, and change his line for one that sinks. For the rest of the night a subsurface fly is generally the most productive lure.

Try a big tandem lure

After 0200hrs it is also worth while to try a big tandem lure fished deep. This lure represents a small fish and will often bring a response from some of the biggest fish in the water. The takes may be more gentle and delicate than to the subsurface fly, so all suggestions of an offer should be treated with a firm strike.

Not all sea trout fishing is practised at night. Following a good flood, when the water is falling and clearing, it is frequently possible to make good catches in daytime with the type of fly used for brown trout. This, however, is opportunist fishing in which it is essential to have quick access to good water and to be able to down-tools at a moment's notice and get to the river as soon as the keeper or gillie 'phones to say conditions are right. It is not usually long before the water is too clear for the shy daytime sea trout, but some good fish can be taken while murky conditions last.

Deadly baits

Other tactics involve spinners and worms. A small Mepps spoon is particularly good, spun in much the same way as for salmon. The $1\frac{1}{2}$in Devon minnow is a known killer in the Eden (Cumbria) and Border Esk. A worm is perhaps even more productive. Both can be deadly in slightly coloured water in daytime, but local knowledge of where to fish is essential, and this is not quickly learned by the casual visitor.

The fly, therefore, is not only the most aesthetically pleasing bait to most sportsmen, it is also the most effective sea trout method over a season. But the season is all too short. In many years it is possible to number on one hand those few nights when conditions are ideal. Such rarity prompted the anonymous comment that 'When conditions are right, there is nothing that will get the dedicated sea trout angler to bed—not even a new wife!'

mouths, and not all fish which pull at the fly are successfully hooked. Even many of those that are escape when the hook comes free during a twisting leap. The thrill of hooking and playing a spirited sea trout in the inky darkness never loses its excitement. The catch might be anything from $\frac{1}{2}$lb to a specimen topping 10lb, providing not only excellent sport but also gourmet fare.

Divide the night into three

The undisputed authority on sea trout fishing today is Hugh Falkus. In his book *Sea Trout Fishing* he divides the night into three distinct sections, which he calls 'first-half' (before midnight), 'half-time' (up to about 1 am), and 'second-half' (from 1 am until dawn). These periods reflect the changing habits of the sea trout during the night. The fish are active at the surface during the early night, retiring to deeper water after midnight. During the 'first-half', therefore, the angler should use a surface fly on a floating line. Then follows 'half-time' when the fish are uncooperative. This is the time

Fly fishing afloat

Most lake and reservoir trout fisheries provide boat fishing for those who prefer it. Many anglers would argue that the boat fisherman consistently catches more than his bank-fishing counterpart. Others heartily oppose this view. The majority choose according to prevailing conditions and what suits their pocket.

With half a gale blowing, the boat angler may find it impossible to fish either because the drift is too fast, or because the anchor will not hold bottom. It may then be wiser to stay on the bank, where some shelter may be found. Another day, he may find the bank lined with anglers, with hardly room to fish. If the water looks good he may decide to use a boat and take advantage of the greater freedom of movement this provides.

Some anglers travel light, prepared to walk the bank with only rod, reel and fly box—an excellent day's fishing if you are in the mood. Others carry a lot of gear to cover all the possible variations required. Then, a boat is very useful indeed.

Whatever your motives for fishing from a boat, there are a few essentials which will improve your chances. The most obvious is a good anchor. A length of regular or nylon rope about 30-50 yards long is indispensable, and a heavy lump of concrete attached by a ringbolt will suffice either to anchor, or to trail behind the boat in a high wind to slow the drift. A proper anchor is preferable, however, especially of the folding variety, which makes for easy stowage and portage when not in use.

Irish Tourist Board

The anchor rope should never be fastened to the rowlocks but must be taken twice around the thwart (the oarsman's bench) and fastened with a tucked half-blood knot. It can then be passed through a crutch or over the side direct, according to fancy. The anchor will always sit and hold better if it has about 6ft of light chain attached at the business end. This prevents the line being pulled upwards, and stops the anchor from dragging, except in a very high wind.

Usefulness of the drogue

A drogue is also very valuable for slowing down the rate of drift (see Small Boats feature). Anchor and drogue lines must be coiled neatly under their respective thwarts in readiness for use, and the drogue should be fitted with a trip-rope to help pull it in when no longer needed.

If you have ever lifted an oar to get it inboard and found that the crutch is inadvertently caught on the oar, lifted from its socket, and neatly dropped over the side into 20ft of water, you will not need to be reminded that a couple of split pins made of fence-wire slipped through the holes provided, can be valuable to secure crutches in their sockets. These are easy to remove at the end of the day, but be sure to stow them in your bag when setting off.

Finally, you should carry a lifejacket or support of some kind, against emergencies.

On many waters it is mandatory to carry the boat cushions provided, and these are designed to double as life-savers. Many anglers feel it worthwhile to have their own, for they provide the comfort needed on a hard thwart, and in emergencies they may save a life.

The cost of a boat normally demands that you should share it with a friend. Such friends must be chosen for their tact, and their capacity to sit silently in a boat, for nothing is worse than having to share a boat with a noisy idiot.

Occasionally, you meet a partner who is left-handed and provided you are right-handed the two of you can have the best of both worlds, neither having to cast across the boat. Otherwise, you should change seats at intervals so that you both get a share of the best position. Unless you are both experienced at changing seats while afloat, take the boat ashore to do so.

Do not stand up

It is surprisingly common to see anglers fishing from a standing position in a boat. This can be dangerous (and ill-mannered if you are sharing the boat). Those who are most accustomed to boats rarely, if ever, do it. Unless the boat is large (unlike those on most reservoirs), avoid standing up.

Depending on conditions, there is a choice for basic methods of fly fishing from a boat.

(Left) The enjoyment of fly fishing from a boat. Here, on White Lake, Co Westmeath, Ireland, the angler is properly seated, his boat not cluttered with too many items of unnecessary equipment. With the soft breeze on his back and the fish rising, the day is perfect.
(Right) Short-lining, when fishing the drift, gives one the chance to use the dropper well, skittering it on the surface.

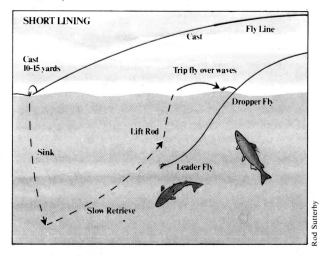

Fly fishing afloat _____

(Left) A quiet corner on a Midlands reservoir. While the angler fishes the drift, parallel wind lanes could be the clue to feeding fish. (Right) How two anglers can cover the maximum area in front of a drifting boat. (Below right) A happy angler with five stock trout from Sundridge Lake, one of the many prolific Kent waters.

The commonest and best-known is simply to fish the drift. This is most suitable when the wind is not too strong, and when fish are known, or believed, to be feeding on or near the surface. When fish are sought on or near the bottom it is better to fish at anchor, which enables you to pause for the fly to sink properly before retrieving it. In strong wind conditions, dapping is a useful alternative, and when the water is still, with a mirror-like surface, it may be expedient to use the dry fly.

Assess the wind direction first

When fishing the drift, it is usual to assess the wind direction and row to a starting position estimated to allow the boat to drift in a course which avoids bank anglers, but at the same time covers the major headlands, or waters where known weedbeds or alternate shallows and deeps hold fish. If a long, uninterrupted drift can be established, it is often very effective, but it is frequently necessary to take short drifts, rowing upwind to resume a parallel of similar drift.

When the wind is fairly brisk boat anglers usually look about for wind lanes caused by headlands, woods, or shoreline contours which affect the wind. Wind lanes can generally be seen quite clearly as areas where the wind creates long strips less broken than the surrounding water. This effect is usually due to relatively less wind turbulence on the surface, and since it often causes large numbers of wind-borne creatures to be deposited there, fish soon learn to feed along

these areas, and can indeed often be seen moving among them. To fish such a lane on the drift entails placing the boat at the head of the lane, drifting with the drogue out, and occasionally giving the oars a tweak in one direction or the other to keep in the lane.

Sooner or later, the drifting boat arrives on the shore at the end of the drift and it is necessary to row upwind again to resume. In high winds this can be a daunting business, requiring a sustained and lengthy pull at the oars. There is usually one bank at least slightly sheltered from the wind, and the tactic is to set the boat across wind at an angle, rowing gently enough to hold your position and allowing the the wind to 'sail' you into the sheltered bank. Once in the lee of the bank, you can usually row up with little effort, taking advantage of bays and inlets and only venturing into the wind when you have to pass headlands. When the boat is sufficiently upwind, you can take up position for the next drift.

Fishing the drift usually entails what is called 'short lining', which means making casts of 10-15 yards only, then giving the fly time to submerge before retrieving it slowly. As the fly reaches a midway position, the rod is raised slowly, bringing the dropper fly up to break surface. This is then tripped across the surface by further raising the rod and retrieving line as required. The fly is thus made to trip from wave to wave in a very effective manner. Often fish will slash at the

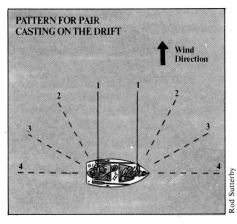

PATTERN FOR PAIR CASTING ON THE DRIFT

Wind Direction

Rod Sutterby

If the wind dies off altogether, fish will often refuse the fly that accurately covers them, especially when it is towed across them with a great wake which, in the clear undisturbed water, makes the cast look like a wire hawser. In these conditions it is often profitable to switch to the dry fly, fishing a line greased to within an inch of the fly, which is positioned and left to simulate the natural insect. Takes are often sudden and powerful, and if your rod is inadvertently pointed towards the fly, you risk being smashed on the take.

When the boat fisherman really needs to fish the bottom, he must almost invariably anchor. Then fishing a sinker and making fairly lengthy casts may pay off, a method similar to that adopted by bank anglers fishing the bottom. Perhaps the greatest danger for the boat angler is his tendency to create powerful rocking movements of the boat which send out shock waves and put down fish. If you cannot make lengthy casts without this, you would do better to fish a medium or shortish line.

dropper, and then the rod top must be lowered slightly to allow the fish to turn before striking. Fishing the surface in this manner can be very successful, and if two anglers each fish a team of three flies, at least to begin with, it often enables them to establish the taking fly or flies.

The rate of retrieve can, of course, be varied at intervals, and an occasional longer cast serves to clear any twists imparted to the line by short lining. Anglers must cast alternately to avoid tangles during the back cast, and each should keep his fly in his own sector and avoid poaching. Casts should be fanned out to cover the whole of the sector to ensure that the water over which you drift is thoroughly explored.

Dapping rests the arm
Short lining demands almost continuous casting and can eventually be very tiring. For a change it is useful to change over to dapping for a spell. This is best carried out with a long dapping rod fitted with a nylon or floss silk dapping line, but it can be done with light fly lines if the wind is brisk. The technique is to get the fly hovering a few inches above the surface, at intervals dropping it on the top to float or simply touch. Fish can often be seen following the fly before it alights, and they frequently take with a thump the moment it touches down. It requires considerable control not to strike such a fish too soon and the golden rule is to *see* it turn first.

Bill Howes

The evening rise

The evening rise is that special time towards evening, usually just before or after dusk when, attracted by failing light and a profusion of food, the trout begin to feed in earnest on or near the surface. Their behaviour is advertised by their continual rising, sloshing, topping and tailing, or cruising with backs awash. The evening rise conjures a picture of solid thumps, dancing rod tips, screeching reels, and anglers scooping up fish in all directions.

Yet, the sober fact is that the evening rise is an angler's fondly cherished myth—a delusion originating in the days when a few lucky anglers fished the famous chalk streams in a semi-pastoral England that no longer exists.

Most trout anglers today fish large lakes and reservoirs stocked with farm-bred, pellet-fed trout which prefer, ignoring the rules, to feed on the bottom, rather than on the surface in traditional style. They often fail to rise in the evening or at any other time. So on lakes and reservoirs you cannot depend on such a rise, even when wind, temperature, humidity and millions of floating insects seem to demand it.

Magic of the evening rise

Perhaps this accounts for the sheer magic of an evening rise when it *does* happen. There are few more awesome sights and sounds for the angler than the plop, sip, or splosh of rising fish all about him, especially when the sun is just disappearing behind distant trees, the atmosphere is tinted with red, and great widening ripples spread across a blood-coloured surface.

It is idyllic and might last ten minutes or an hour, but the magic may be tinted with sheer frustration and fury. To many anglers

Irish Tourist Board

it also means a chance of a face-saver after a daunting day with no sign of a fish moving, and with nothing but a weary arm and an aching back that is miraculously cured for the duration of the rise. Despite the evening rise, many will still finish the day empty handed, while others will take the limit.

The anticipation

Up to a point, you can sometimes anticipate the evening rise. When you see and hear buzzers hatching and flying freely during the afternoon, you can often expect at least a localised buzzer rise coinciding with dusk, or shortly after it. Now is the time to fish a buzzer team of red, white and blue nymphs (or any other colour for that matter) for you may with patience, skill, and a bit of luck coax a couple of fish to the net. Alternatively, when sedge flies appear in great clouds and start out towards the ripple line, you can expect the trout to start slaughtering them at any moment. You must then try longhorns, silverhorns, black sedges, red sedges or greys, although sometimes you do better with the larvae or their imitations. Whether to fish wet or dry adds to the dilemma.

If your clothing is covered with tiny white-winged flies which also carpet the water, you can expect a maddening rise of fish to take the *Caenis*—the well-named 'Angler's curse'.

(Above) Before the evening rise there is a period of calm, quiet anticipation.
(Left) A still evening on Lough Corrib.
(Below) This evening the rise was not a myth. It occurred, and a trout is netted.

P. H. Ward Natural Science Photos

Irish Tourist Board

The evening rise

Often on such occasions the trout splash and leap at the insects on the water but you need more than skill and luck to take fish then whatever you try to catch them on.

Sometimes it is just possible, if your eyesight is excellent and your entomology better, to discern which fly the fish are actually taking. But whether they will accept your imitation is quite another matter. By the time you've tried all the possibilities in terms of fly and tactics, you may have pricked several fish without netting one, although, alternatively, your skill and finesse may have brought you several to the net. Soon the rise is over either way, or perhaps the fish decide to eat something else which you failed to recognize earlier.

At other times, it is quite impossible to tell which is the taking insect on the water. At the same time it is usually too dark to see what comes out on the marrow spoon, so you cannot find out what the fish are eating that way either.

Don't panic!

Unfortunately, as your vision deteriorates in the half light, the fish see better. The problem of changing a fly in these conditions calls for nimble fingers, great care and good sight. It is easy to get into a panic deciding whether to fish wet or dry, and once flustered you are likely to ruin your cast to the only rise within reach. It takes nerve not to strike too soon when a take does occur—and more than a touch of luck not to hook the only bush within 50 yards on your back cast!

Before the light disappears completely you should examine your rig, especially if you are bold enough to fish more than one fly. It would not be unusual to discover that you have been fishing a ball of nylon with your artificial flies apparently mating in the middle of it.

Despite the disappointments, however, there are evening rises which make it all worth while. On these too rare occasions the fish bite unfussily and profusely. A fish may be hooked by an angler on your right, followed by another on your left. You enquire to discover that one took a Bloody

John Wilson

(Above) This superb brown trout came as a direct result of choosing the right artificial. (Right) Eric Horsfall Turner fishing the Lune on a spring evening. (Below) Scott's Fancy, not an artificial Caenis but another 'Angler's Curse'.

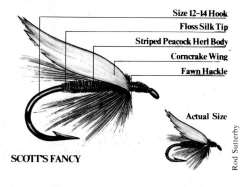

Size 12-14 Hook
Floss Silk Tip
Striped Peacock Herl Body
Corncrake Wing
Fawn Hackle

Actual Size

SCOTT'S FANCY

Rod Sutterby

Butcher and the other a Coachman. Should you change to one of these? As you hesitate, you get a great thump on your Mallard and Claret and you land the trout and fish on as before. Should you fish dry? Would a nymph be better? You catch another fish and suddenly the rise is over.

Over or not, all along the bank dozens of anglers are patiently fishing the water with every fibre of their being. Anglers are optimistic people, and rarely stop before it is simply too dark to fish on. But the memory of the evening rise persists all the way home.

Arthur Oglesby

Trout autopsies

A most important aspect of trout fishing which many anglers are inclined to overlook is the performing of autopsies on trout. To the uninitiated this may seem an unnecessary chore, and many fly fishermen tend to think that the examination of the stomach contents of a trout is a particularly scientific operation best left to the trained angler-entomologist. In fact, nothing could be further from the truth, for with the right tool and a basic knowledge of the more common insects, this is a comparatively simple task.

History of autopsies

The history of autopsies in trout fishing can be traced back several centuries. The method, then, was to slit open the belly of the dead trout exposing the stomach contents. As this was rather a messy business, it was eventually realized, as trout fishing progressed, that a slim spoon could be utilized. The spoon was inserted into the mouth of the fish and pushed into the stomach cavity, thereby removing its contents for examination. The present-day method is basically the same, except that the simple spoon has evolved over the years into an effieient piece of equipment generally referred to as the Marrow Scoop.

Various designs of scoop

Various shapes and designs are now obtainable, including a recent innovation made of clear plastic and fitted with a rubber bulb to suck the contents out of the stomach. Whichever tool is used, a small shallow glass dish is needed in which to transfer the contents. This should be filled with water as it helps separate the partly digested contents and makes identification easier. The object of the operation is to discover on what particular species of insect the trout may be feeding so that an appropriate pattern of artificial fly may be mounted.

It may take a little time for the average angler to become reasonably proficient at recognizing the many species of insects on

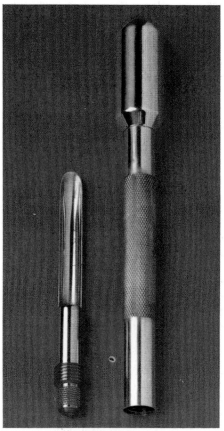

Kim Sayer/Tackle by Farlows, London. Eric Birch

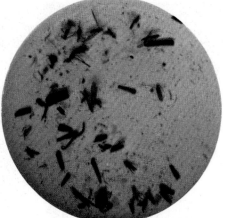

which trout feed, but many books are available on the subject. To start with, it is a good plan to familiarize oneself with some of the more common fauna such as shrimps, louse, snails, midge larvae, daphnia, demersal nymphs or olive nymphs—and so on. Precise identification of the various species of upwinged flies, sedge flies, sedge pupae or midge pupae can follow at a later stage when the angler becomes more proficient.

Autopsies are not always positive. In some cases the stomach cavity may be empty because trout often regurgitate while they are being played; or perhaps they may not have fed for a long period. But the stomach is usually packed with food, and the angler can quickly establish their diet during the last 24 hours. To ascertain on which species the fish has been feeding immediately prior to capture, the angler must look for the specimen that appears the more intact.

While autopsies may be performed on fish other than trout, it is generally accepted to be of more value to the trout fisherman. It also follows that it is more important to fly fishers on stillwaters than to those on rivers. The

(Left) Objects needed for an autopsy: priest to dispatch the trout and marrow scoop to extract stomach contents. (Below-left to right) Results: a stomach pump used on a brown trout, and no need for a spoon as shrimps are found in the mouth.

majority of rivers capable of supporting a good head of trout are relatively clear, and it is usually possible to see on what they are feeding. On other occasions when trout are taking surface fly, specimens can be quickly captured to establish identity. On fast rocky rivers in hilly country, where the wet fly is used extensively, and it is difficult to see below the surface, autopsies can be of considerable assistance.

Selective food habits

On reservoirs and large lakes it is physically impossible, except on rare occasions, to see on what the trout are feeding, so when the angler arrives at the waterside he often has a problem in deciding which pattern of artificial fly to use. He can make a sensible guess, according to the time of the year, or if the water is familiar to him, can known from past seasons' experience roughly what to expect. Even so, there can be no certainty that the angler has made the correct choice. Trout tend to be selective and during any month there will be a wide variety of species from which they can choose. The only certain way to know which species the trout is choosing is to perform an autopsy.

First you have to catch your trout. A good plan, particularly if you are unfamiliar with the water, is to use a general attractor pattern such as a Mallard and Claret, Dunkeld or Invicta, to mention but three of the many popular general artificials available.

Robin Fletcher

John Goddard

Arthur Ogelsley

INDEX

Bold page numbers refer to illustrations

A
Adipose fin **341**
Aerator 251
AFTM line coding **378**
Air-Sea Rescue 315
Alevin **327**
Anchoring **278**, 284, **314**, 455
'Annatto' 101
Antenna float 75
Anti-kink devices 90, **93**, 228
Arlesey bomb 69, 71, 132, **223**
Artificials 254ff, 300
Automatic reel **375–6**
Autopsies **336**, 462ff
Avon balsa 125, **148–9**
Avon rod 48, 53, **148**

B
Back cast 427–8
Backing line 62, 375, 381, **384**
Bacon rind 114
Bait dropper 140
Baited feather rig **306**
Baited pirks 266–7
Ball leads 222ff
Ballan wrasse 178ff
Balsa float 73–4, 125
Barbel 74, 79, 110, 119
Barbule 162, 172
Barleycorn lead **70**
Barrel leads 222
Barspoon 89–**92**, 154
Bass 253, 258, **270**, 300
Bathypelagic eggs 196
Batting 53–**4**
Beachcasting 167, 202ff, 222ff, **223**, 290ff
Beachcasting rods 202ff
Billy Lane stop knot **77**, 153
Binocular vision 39
Bite indication 48, 82ff, 133
Bivalves 260
Blood 115
Blood bight loop **451**

Blow lug 236
Blue shark 193, **298**
Boat fishing (f/w) 443–5
Boat fishing (sea) 206ff, 225, 231–2, 312ff, 316ff
Boat rods 206ff
Bobbin-type indicators 82ff
Booms 227ff
Bottom-feeding 21
Brackish water 275
Braided line 61–**2**, 214ff
Bread 110ff
Breakaway leads 223ff
Bream 18ff, 102, 110, 134, 139
Bream (sea) 284–**6**, 289
Breeding maggots 98–101
British Hook Scale 220
Bronze bream **24**
Brood fish 352
Brook char **340**
Brook rods 369ff
Brown trout 330ff, **340**, 355
Butt pad **287**
Buzzers (electronic) 84–5
Buzzers (insects) 344, 459

C
Caenis 459
Camouflage **188**, 370
Camouflaged lines 61
Capta lead 70–1, **130**–2
Carbon-fibre 203, 207–8, 362, **363**–7, **371**
Carp 26ff, 71, 79, 83, 110, 114, 144
Cast carrier **437**
Cast connector **387**
Casters 102ff
Casting 205
Castings **51**, **152**–4, 290ff
Casts 386ff, 437
Caterpillars 105ff
Centrepin reel (f/w) 53ff
Centrepin (sea) 210ff
Cereal baits 8, 115
Chalk stream fishing 372–3, 440ff
Char **340**–1
Chub 10ff, 74, 96, 102, 110,

119, 120, 134, 150
'Chub Trotter' 148–**9**
Clement's boom 188, 231, **232**
Closed face reel **59–60**
Clothing 233ff, 422ff
Cloudbait 140–1
Coalfish 170–2, 265, 284
Coarse baits 95–123
Coarse tackle 42–94
Cockles 262
Cocktail bait 104
Cod 162ff, 236, **246**, 266, 269, 280
Codling **164**, 304–5
Coffin lead 69–**70**, 131
Coloured water 21
Colouring maggots 101
Common bream *See* Bream
Conger 196ff, 211, **246**, 248, **284**
Conger rig 270
Conservation 79, 158ff
Continental-type shots 66–7
Cooking fish 189
Corkwing 181
Courge 251–3
Crab **181**, 257ff
Crowquill 128
Cruisers **316**
Crust 110
Cuckoo wrasse 182
Cuttlefish 248ff
Cymag 118

D
Dace **12**, 102, 111, 120
Daddy-long-legs 392–3
Dapping 105–6, 369, 457
Deadbaiting 145
Deal yellow-tail **237**–8
Decca Navigator **283**
Deep diver **96**, **153**
Devon minnow 51, **89**
Digestion in fish 4
Disease 326, 361ff
Disgorger 65, 86ff
Diving vanes 95–**7**
Dogfish **278**
Double-grinner knot **381**